THE EMERGENCE OF MAN
INTO THE 21ST CENTURY

THE EMERGENCE OF MAN INTO THE 21ST CENTURY

Patricia L. Munhall
Ed.D., ARNP, NCPsyA, FAAN

Ed Madden
Ph.D.

Virginia M. Fitzsimons
Ed.D., RN, C., FAAN

JONES AND BARTLETT PUBLISHERS
Sudbury, Massachusetts
BOSTON   TORONTO   LONDON   SINGAPORE

World Headquarters
Jones and Bartlett Publishers
40 Tall Pine Drive
Sudbury, MA 01776
978-443-5000
www.jbpub.com
info@jbpub.com

Jones and Bartlett Publishers Canada
2406 Nikanna Road
Mississauga, ON L5C 2W6
CANADA

Jones and Bartlett Publishers International
Barb House, Barb Mews
London W6 7PA
UK

Library of Congress Cataloging-in-Publication Data
The emergence of man into the 21st century / [edited by] Patricia Munhall, Ed Madden, Virginia Fitzsimons.
 p. cm.
 Includes bibliographical references.
 ISBN 0-7637-1172-1 (pbk.)
 1. Men. 2. Masculinity. I. Munhall, Patricia L. II. Madden, Ed. III. Fitzsimons,
 Virginia Macken, 1943–
HQ1090 .E45 2001
305.31--dc21   2001038039

Production Credits
Acquisitions Editor: Penny M. Glynn
Associate Editor: Christine Tridente
Production Editor: Anne Spencer
Editorial Assistant: Thomas Prindle
Manufacturing Buyer: Amy Duddridge
Cover Design: Philip Regan
Marketing Manager: Taryn Wahlquist

Design and Composition: Carlisle Communications, Ltd.
Printing and Binding: Malloy Lithographing

Printed in the United States of America
05 04 03 02 01   10 9 8 7 6 5 4 3 2 1

Contents

VOICES TWO: Not Yet Men 55

VOICES THREE: Man as Father 85

PREFACE

Of the three books thus far in the Emergence series, this volume on men has been the most challenging to bring to fruition. Clearly, the processes of coming to understand these three groups—women, the family, and now, men—offered interesting contrasts. We were able to identify actual differences in the production of each volume, both in content and process. Sometimes, writing books has been likened to giving birth, and in this instance all three "deliveries" were so interestingly different. Since we did not anticipate such starkly different dynamics in these deliveries, we have encountered a bonus in our endeavor to seek understanding and meaning, a bonus addressed in this preface. And like so many interesting research findings, this bonus was serendipitous.

Each of these three volumes in its individual development actually yielded in a very phenomenological way* understanding of how these groups, as individuals and as groups, allowed themselves to be revealed. In what they have said, what they would not say, and how they participated in the project, each group tells a story of its own.

What then becomes fascinating about each of these volumes is that each one was born with different characteristics, emphases, personalities, and priorities. The differences were often very much in line with some of our stereotypical understandings of women, family, and in this volume, men. Stereotypes do not evolve from fiction, but from observation. They certainly are not fair because not all members of any group fit that group's socially constructed stereotypes. But in the instance of this book, in order to complete it, the search had to be aggressively taken to find many men who did not fit some attributes that comprise the stereotypical male.

One moment in desperation, I thought that since a postmodern perspective also undergirds this series, we would have a cover for the book, much like the last two, with the title *The Emergence of Man into the 21st Century*. Then the reader would open the book and find just blank pages! There would also be a list of the men who agreed to be an editor or contributor of this book, and

---

*Phenomenology, in a simple manner of speaking, is a way to understand the meaning of being human in specific experiences.

then at the very last minute with all contriteness, calmly let me know that they could not meet their commitment. One of these men, whom I still love, let me know this 3 weeks before the book was due! With that, he said he would still ask the men he had asked to contribute to send on their narratives. None ever arrived.

Yes, blank pages would have told the story. But I get ahead of myself here.

Let us return to the first book, which illuminates understanding of women, not only within the book itself but also in the analysis of how women contributed to the volume. In that moment, I did not take notice of "how" women contribute to such a project, until I began to understand the appearance of diversity that went beyond the narratives, to the process of the production itself.

A new understanding emerged with the second volume on family, as to how our contributors participated in the writing project. The men's participation bore out another understanding. And these understandings are important to contemplate for their implications in our lives and in our living with one another.

Because these understandings do support many of our beliefs about these groups, it is necessary to elucidate and be specific about these dynamics. Briefly, I will describe the books on women and families. The reader can have a better understanding of these groups by returning to the specific volumes, where descriptions are more fully articulated.

In the volume on women, most of the contributors were women, as it should have been. What can now be said about the contributors for the women's book is that each one wanted to tell a story of her own or some other woman's experiences. They were glad to have the opportunity to write about being a woman in many different voices and in many different experiences. This desire to speak out has been noted by others, and may be attributed to all the years when women's voices were silenced.

Each contributor to that book seemed to be cooperative and introspective in her narrative. Each allowed her vulnerability to show itself. The women wrote about relationships and children, topics often thought to be important to women. However, of all the three volumes thus far in print, the women's volume also contains many more chapters on social and political problems. Markedly so, to the extent that a stereotype is dispelled, at least in that volume. In comparison to the family and the men's volumes, a reader might think that it is women who really care about the world at large. It is women who care about the suffering of others, the homeless, the poor, and the chronically ill. It is women who care enough to write about the political and social realms of these problems.

And the women accepted an invitation or volunteered to give voice to an experience with enthusiasm. Not only did women want to write, they did. Women met their commitment and did so in a timely way. They were cooperative. Surprisingly, not one woman withdrew from the project once she had made the commitment.

The dynamics in the family volume seemed very different and it was hypothesized that those dynamics reflected the dynamics of family life itself. It is noted in the introduction of that book that, when writing from the context of family life, few writers were willing to take on sensitive issues. Ironically, the ones who did were criticized after publication, as if they had been disloyal. Loyalty to family perhaps does exert an inhibition to giving voice to what we know exists, which would give voice to the physical and psychological traumas of many family experiences. Perhaps the reexperiencing of family conflicts and cruelties through the process of reflective writing is just too painful. This absence in itself helps us to understand family dynamics.

In the family book, as in phenomenological philosophy, it is not only what is said, but also what is not said that leads to greater in-depth understanding. In that volume the possibility of the family reflecting the flux of our times gave rise to the hypothesis that, in addition, writers were reluctant to cooperate in the same way as in the women's book because the subject or experience of family created flux, conflict, and ambivalence, which became deterrents to writing. These may be characteristics of today's families.

The family in the 21st century is not confined to one image, and breaking down or shattering the myths of "family" might have been too jarring. When confronted with the writing of the family experience, the writer may have chosen silence rather than stirring up inward conflict.

This was the first experience of realizing that not all writers were going to be as cooperative as the women were in writing about women or larger issues. I knew that the family volume was incomplete, in a way that had greater implications than the incompleteness of any one volume with specific groups. Many experiences of families went untold, though they were solicited. (A short interpretation of all of the foregoing may be found in the introduction to the family book.)

However, nothing prepared me for the dynamics of this book on men! An e-mail I sent out, in response to the *fourth male editor* saying he could not do this project on men, *three weeks before it was due*, because he was overwhelmed, probably says it all. What I was feeling was calamity all around me. Once again the process of writing about a specific group, in this instance men, was producing another behind-the-scenes scenario. Anyway, my SOS to colleagues:

To: All
From: P. Munhall
Re: Call for Help

Hi! I am writing to you all with a great sense of urgency.

As many of you know, the 21st century male book is due in 4 weeks. The latest male editor, who had assured me of 20 narratives, has just e-mailed me to say that he is so overwhelmed that he cannot meet this deadline. He asked to have the deadline extended another 4 months.

Since I have already asked for an extension, requested by more than half the contributors, and have been given to April 1, I know I can not do that. Besides to make matters worse the writers that I had solicited are dropping like flies in spite of the extension.

Each day of this past week, the week that the chapters were due, I opened the e-mail most gingerly and with great trepidation, to find the newest reason why someone who had promised to write cannot meet this expectation right now.

This never occurred in the other two books. What is going on? Are men really the way they are stereotyped? Do they really make commitments and then withdraw? Are they really not expressive? Is it truly difficult for them to express meaning, feelings, or emotions about experiences? Is it true that they cannot write experientially, or just sit and write about the personal?

The theoretical first third of the book is complete. Men can write theoretically, that is apparent. The problem is the experiential and existential sections. The sections where we want to come to understand their experiences. The reluctance is no longer an isolated case.

I am not faulting them. So many men when they agreed to write about an experience had been more than enthusiastic. Some even kept me up with their progress, which turned out often to be a way of not saying no in that moment or perhaps still believing that they would complete the narrative.

All were apologetic and hoped this would not cause problems. Individually not perhaps, but with the numbers at present, I am writing this SOS for your assistance.

If you know of any men who would be willing to write, in a very short time, about an experience they had or what it is like to be in some particular male role (father, son, husband, brother), or an experience from a male perspective, would you please let me know. I will send them the conceptual framework for the series and suggestions for authors. Also, please assure them that I will work closely with them if they need.

Thank you so very much for your assistance with this and I surely will return the favor . . . the reality of this is that it should just be left this way. That we come to understand that this is part of the way men live and go through life. However, the publisher will not be pleased with this interpretation, but it is a very important one.

So the book will become about men who are willing to commit to write and then fulfill the commitment. Once again I thank you for helping me find such men. I can be reached at this e-mail.

I hope this finds you all well. With warm regards, Tricia

From this e-mail eight new contributors were found. To place this in context, this e-mail went to 30 people who had participated in similar projects and had wide networks. I was still in difficulty. Plus, I still did not have a new male editor, which I considered vital to the inevitable question of identity politics concerning this book. But it was more than just that. A male editor was essential to the validity and perspective of this book. However, I was beginning to wonder if such a man could be found!

Serendipitously, I attended a St. Valentine's poetry reading (on a personal note, what makes this all the more serendipitous is that the last poetry reading I had been to was over 15 years ago). This wonderful event, which made me wonder why I do not go to more of them, had been organized by an English professor at the University of South Carolina, Ed Madden, whom I did know. During the poetry reading many of the men and women gave wonderful readings and I approached Ed about their contributing, and also asked if he would be interested in this new vacancy, coeditor of the male book!

Thus far in the series, there had not been a coeditor from an English department. I did know of Ed's extraordinary creativity and writing skills and came to realize his in-depth understanding of postmodernism and phenomenology. This volume is greatly enriched by his talents.

An added bonus was that Ed was *enthusiastic* about the project, and with ease understood the conceptual framework, including the most challenging framework: the urgent time dimensions we had to work within.

What have I learned? Not surprisingly, English professors know a whole lot of people who want to write, who are introspective, and who are able to write emotively. Men who want to write and are grateful for the opportunity. Wow! Not exactly how people had been previously asked to join the project, but now a blessing. And another finding for the differences among the groups being written about.

So out went another e-mail, this time from Ed Madden. A call for papers on the experience of being a male in today's world. Ed had a listserve to envy. Now I admit to having listserve envy!

We stretched the 3 weeks to 7 or so, and Ed was able to procure and edit about 40 pieces of chapters, anecdotes, and poems. Because they were all motivated writers, who love the act of writing and expressing themselves through language, the stereotypes about men had to be placed in an analysis of a social construction of roles.

Good writers are expressive. Good writers are able to move us, to stir within us some emotion, some feeling, some new awareness toward understanding. This needs to be noted for the legitimacy of the series. Many of the men who have written herein are writers, whereas in the other series, the contributing authors were not "writers" per se, but individuals whose professions or occupations may, or may not, have required academic writing.

The book became alive! We were able to group various "voices," as is indicated in the table of contents. The book took on a different tone from the others. We have included some more "artsy" pieces (even experimental), and though they may be unusual for this series, these pieces often speak to us in a frank, poignant, and raw way about the male experience.

These diverse pieces contributed to a new richness and enabled a volume in which we heard and read the voices of men who did come through with their promise to write, and in addition the voices of men who were writers waiting for someone to ask them to write. Actually, it was quite postmodern!

So now when I look at the voices and what men write about, there are a few comments that I would like to share with the reader. Some comments can be thought of as interpretive but need to be thought of as only my interpretations. In the e-mail included in this preface, I questioned some male stereotypes. Many men will perhaps recognize themselves, and others will deny those characteristics and perhaps find them "old hat!" However, that is the experience as I lived through it, in all its panic moments.

Ed Madden will do a fuller interpretation of this volume in the introduction. And, of course, the reader will read through his or her own interpretative lens and the contributing authors or poets will often offer their own interpretations. Who the text belongs to, as to the question of interpretation, has become a source of postmodern debate, where the assertion is that the text belongs to all of us.

However, in addition to this postmodern lens, the series places great emphasis on and indeed states explicitly the phenomenological philosophical purpose of increasing understanding of others. So within this series, *the most critical interpretation is the one made by the writer of the piece*, if that should be present. Through an author's own interpretation, we gain access to the meaning of the experience for that particular individual. We *come to understand how it is for that person*. It becomes a way of being for us to consider and attempt to understand.

This is even more important when a viewpoint does not gel with our own worldview. This increase in awareness of difference, we wish for the reader. To be surprised that someone thinks and feels so differently than we might awakens us to move beyond the scientific quest of generalizability and, on a more important and influential scale, beyond our own egoism.

We become aware of how we do not know how others derive meaning and are reminded that a state of "unknowing" is a better place to be, in order to understand another person. We are reminded that "knowing" closes off new possibilities. "Knowing" closes off hearing, leads to blurred vision, and validates our prejudices and biases. We read and see from a state of already "knowing."

Here is an example of my own "knowing" being off base. Outside of the initial problem of promised pieces not being completed, there was also a realization that what I thought men were most interested in, generally, were not the subjects they chose to write about.

For instance, I thought ("knowing" men) that men would want to write about sports, competition, food, sex, power, women, politics, cars, and their relationships with their mothers. As a mother of two adult sons I could not fathom otherwise. My own "knowing" or wishful thinking was that men would write about how wonderful their mothers were/are and the great influence they had on their lives. I certainly had my own awareness increased!

There are references to some of these experiences in some of the narratives, but not overwhelming references. And perhaps this is a good time to mention that there are many experiences and contingencies within the specific experience a writer may be writing about yet in a more subdued manner. It is also important for readers to reflect upon these contingencies and contexts. What has contributed to this experience? What else appears in this poem, in this narrative? What is in the background, as well as the foreground?

I was most surprised, as a mother, about my "new" awareness of the significance of the father-son relationship for men. Reading the narratives and poems about the importance, reverence, and sometimes disappointments of this relationship, I grew to understand that this critical relationship questions our assumptions about the importance of the mother-son relationship. It is predictable to find this relationship to be a plot line in myths, history, literature, and films. The mother-son relationship has long been the one focused on most in psychology.

One interpretation of this focus on the father-son relationship is that it may be the most important relationship in a man's life. Even women, other than mothers, received passing attention in this volume. Another interpretation of this focus and others in the volume itself is that men wrote often about relationships and experiences that held the greatest conflict for them. And we do see sons and fathers writing in ways that indicate some underlying conflict, some very painful.*

Freud certainly had interpreted these conflicts as a source of neurosis but did not limit it to father and son. Are these writers telling us something different? Since the experiences written about are not prescribed, but are chosen by the writers, we need to hear their voices. Are these voices deconstructing some commonly held myths?

In gender and sexuality, as well as race, we see more writing that indicates meaning coming from a place of conflict. This is not uncommon, as we know that writing often helps sort out conflict. Writing often illuminates conflict for both writer and reader to contemplate. Conflict is, of course, an inescapable part of life. In the last of the voices in this volume, where we hear voices in search of meaning, one becomes aware of attempts at reconciliation or resolution of conflict. Like so many pieces in this volume, these last voices are very powerful in their humanness.

This volume, like the others, is offered to the reader for sense making and meaning making. We can hypothesize as to what is "behind" the writing, what is "not shown," but for purposes here, these men and a few women who wrote for the book are sharing with you their meanings and their interpretations of men emerging into the 21st century.

---

*Another dynamic quite different from the family book, where conflict seemed to be avoided.

This sharing needs to be revered and appreciated for the way in which an individual lives in his or her own world, not ours. We all live in our own realities, influenced by all that has preceded this moment and the moment just passed and the ones we wish to come. We all might appear to live somewhat similar lives, but we live those similarities differently.

This "awareness" is where respect of others' perspectives begins. This is where understanding and compassion begin. The writers in this volume assist us in embracing our differences, questioning our presuppositions, and understanding the diverse meanings of our experiences.

The postmodern book about men, which I once contemplated holding blank pages, is now filled with poignant meaning because of the writers within, who have demonstrated generosity and courage. It *is to these individuals* who have shared their experiences, through their theoretical writings, experiential narratives, and poems, *that this volume is dedicated, with utmost respect and gratitude.*

Patricia L. Munhall

June 2001

PROLOGUE

In what has become a series of volumes addressing the emergence of various groups into the 21st century, we are pleased to present the third of the series: *The Emergence of Man into the 21st Century*. *The Emergence of Women* was the first volume and the second was *The Emergence of Family*. We are aiming to expand the series to provide for the inclusiveness of other groups within our diverse population. Our primary aim is at once simple and complex, and that is to increase our understanding of the human condition.

Regardless of the group we are seeking to understand better, the underlying philosophical and conceptual underpinnings remain the same, as we believe they should, to maintain continuity of our goals and aims.

The immediate times around a change of century and more dramatically, a millennium, create an occasion to reflect on the meaning of being human in this socially constructed time and place, where "being in the world" is lived through multifaceted experiences.

The *Emergence* books, whether on the experience of woman, family, man, child, the aging, or another group, are an attempt to provide a snapshot, a slice-of-life series of theoretical, existential, and experiential narratives to assist us in understanding the contingencies and contexts in which we find our lives embedded today. In this particular volume, the experience of man is described and narrated, so that we may come to understand some contingencies, issues, and experiences that men today are engaged in within the larger backdrop of their own history, culture, race, and class, among other contexts.

AN OVERWHELMING CONCERN

This particular book of the series is guided by an overwhelming concern for the human condition of men. If we are concerned about the human condition and in particular if we are to understand one another with all our similarities and differences, we first need to understand the meaning individuals make out of their experiences. We need to envision an individual or group as part of a larger context, where the influence of individual and context is ever present in an existential rhythmic exchange. The experiential human voices narrate for us the story of experience, the interpretation, and the context in which it occurs. The narrative is further enhanced as we attune ourselves to the nuances and contingencies of the lives of the narrator. This is how it is for this particular man in his everyday world.

The interior of a man's experience and the meaning he attaches to the experience should be of first concern to the human and health science researcher's agenda when studying man within his situated context. Individuals interested in health, social, and public policy need not be guided so much by their own expertise, their own theories, and their own statistics, but rather, as suggested within this series, by what constitutes experience as it is lived by those who live it. For example, research on relationships has been more concentrated on the experience of the woman than on the man in the particular experience. The attempt within this series is to provide voice to the different perspectives of those involved in the same experience. A picture of the whole, with everyone's perspective. How can problems be solved otherwise?

QUESTIONING THE CULTURE OF EXPERTISE

However obvious this may be, this focus on particularity of experience and the voices of those living that particularity is not how policy is developed. Instead we have a culture of expertise—the ones who know best and the ones who prescribe the solutions. This series attempts to enlarge the lens to include the greatest "knower" of all, the individual who interprets and gives meaning to his or her experience. "Being in the world" is far too complex to be understood solely by examination of variables and statistics. Embedded in their own individual contexts, human beings try to make sense of their world, and in sharing that with the reader, they can assist us in understanding particular experience in all its messiness, not in a clearly defined landscape, such as a laboratory, but within the life-world of temporality, the time we live in and through. The male voices in this volume generously provide us with their perspectives. There are some female voices as well, and they are also necessary to allow male readers to hear a few different voices. (However, for the male reader to understand the worldview of the woman or family, referring to those specific volumes in this series would be more helpful.)

In this series, voices become the discourse, the platform for understanding. As we are beginning this new century and millennium, many problems, some ancient and some new, challenge us to think in different ways. They challenge us to read and hear the experiences of those we think might be just like us and those we see as different than us.

This volume is on the experience of men within the situated contexts of their life-worlds of time, space, relations, and embodiment of mind, body, and spirit.

An Agenda

This is not a "Hallmark" series. There is an agenda. The agenda is one of healing and moving toward a more compassionate way of being with one another. We enter this century with various forms of discrimination still present in our culture: racism, sexism, homophobia, ageism, self-righteousness, and other forms of intolerance and oppression. We enter this century with violence in the home and on the streets, people suffering with terminal illnesses (AIDS among them), homelessness, poverty, tortured souls left alone without assistance, and the list seems endless. Each volume attempts to "get inside the experience" through the voices of those who live inside such experiences.

The agenda is not a pre-established plan, or a "new" program, but the agenda is to come to "understand." Perhaps that is the most difficult agenda of all. Many social programs have failed to solve the suffering of individuals because this first action, to understand through the perception of the individual who is within the experience, is seldom taken. The perception of the expert, outside of the experience, is the one that usually drives policy.

This volume, like the others, then becomes a call to action from individuals who tell of experiences where change in social and political policies is urgently needed. These voices tell us how it is, how it feels, what it means, and what is needed. These are the voices to guide problem solving and policy. The call is to understand experience from the perception of the individual, the one who really knows.

Guiding the Series

Phenomenological and postmodern philosophical perspectives guide the series. The different editors of each volume use these lenses for constructing each book and to make critical sense of the contents.

From the phenomenological perspective, we attempt to demonstrate concern for the meaning of individual experience as the person experiencing the phenomenon interprets it. Readers need not be concerned with generalizability. Each experience is unique to the individual, yet often we find, among the differences, some similarities as well. When the editors ask individuals to contribute to a volume, we simply ask them to tell a story which has significance to them and to stay as close to the experience as it unfolded for them or may still be. In their own voices, from their own contexts.

Tell Us Your Story: The Phenomenological Framework

"What is this experience like for you? Tell us your story, the meaning of the experience, and how you have interpreted the experience. Are there any other aspects of the experience you would like to share?" These questions are the fundamental beginning of a person's narrative. Contributors usually come to this work, in two different ways. One of the editors of a particular volume, in this instance the male one, listens to the conversations of men and if the experience being discussed seems to demonstrate the existential human condition, the individuals are asked if they would be interested in telling about this experience.

Another way of obtaining narratives is to let a subgroup of the population know of this book and to invite individuals who would have had an experience, significant to them, to write to the experience with the above questions to guide the writer.

The volumes do not discuss samples. That is a term used in quantitative studies. Our contributors are by necessity a select group. One of the most important characteristics of our contributors is their willingness to write their stories or narrate to someone who will write for them. So our volumes have specific limitations. They attempt to be beginning narratives—to place some human experiences within this time of our being, to be open, and to be understood by others.

Researchers who work from a phenomenological perspective believe this is the essential foundation for theory or action of any kind. If it is to be effective, the gleaning of understanding from the authentic sources of the experience, the individual or group, needs to be the underpinnings of theory toward action.

Knowing "meaning" and knowing "behavior" is where phenomenologists and behaviorists often part. Phenomenologists believe that all experience has meaning and it is the "meaning" that calls for our attention, not the behavior. The behavior is secondary. If we want to change or prevent some of the above mentioned problems, we need to intervene or create solutions at the level of "meaning."

ALSO GUIDING OUR THINKING: POSTMODERN PERSPECTIVES

The second philosophical underpinning for this series comes from a postmodern perspective. Within this perspective, we acknowledge the world as it appears to be in this moment of time. What are some of the characteristics of this time we live in, in our Western world, if not globally? There appear to be multiple realities, multiplicity of lives, multimind, flux, disorder, ambiguity, chaos, tension, and confusion. Perhaps these conditions existed at other times. What makes this time different is awareness that we cannot harness all this energy into order. Science with a capital S, like religion, is not going to create order out of this disorder. The human laboratory with all the varied contexts defies "control" and that, we might agree, is ultimately good.

So from a postmodern perspective we acknowledge and celebrate the complexities of this world. Where there is pain and suffering, we acknowledge the need for action emerging from the narrator's voice. No longer are we trying to force homogeneity, or one policy or program that "fits all," but we are desiring the diversity of different ways of being and attempting to respond to these differences with sensitivity and reverence.

The wish of the editors of these volumes is to allow readers to come to understand some differences they may not have otherwise, and to join in the feeling of awe which often comes from new awakenings of understanding.

The editors understand that there are contingencies and contexts in each author's life that have political, economic, social, cultural, educational, and environment implications, as well as implications tied to age, gender, class, race, and other forms of difference—implications we need to reflect upon and integrate into our understanding. Readers also come to each piece from a context and a world of contingencies, where reading the piece may become a source of revelation, of recognizing that perhaps they did not understand some thing or "way of being" as the same as their own. If that should happen, then the editors and contributors have realized their hope to increase human understanding and all the good that may flow from new streams of understanding.

READING THIS BOOK ON MEN

The first third of this book is philosophical and theoretical to provide a foundation or perspective through which to read the narratives. In this section the situated context of history, the prevalent sociological interpretations of this time, various psychological perspectives of men, and other theoretical concerns on men are discussed and opened to different viewpoints. These writers represent their own historical, psychological, and sociological perspectives.

The reader is encouraged to read this section critically, as this section could be viewed as "expert" driven. The chapters in this section then are perspectival, and there is no claim to truth, other than the author's representation of reality.

The remaining two thirds of the book are placed together in "voices" of similar experiences, or clusters. We have voices or narratives from individuals who are so generous as to share their life experiences.

In this volume, we have men who tell us narratives about the challenges of growing up as boys to men, the experiences of father-son relationships, relationships with others, and experiences of gender, sexuality, and race. The clusters of experiential narratives also include those describing experiences of violence and abuse, loss and pain, men's journeys to work, and health experiences in social contexts (including disruptions in health). The volume concludes with narratives addressing man's search for meaning. However, all stories told in this volume have that element embedded in the narrative—sense making or meaning making.

With restraint, the editors in the preface, prologue, and introduction make interpretations of the experiences and the volumes as a whole. Following the phenomenological and postmodern framework of this series, we respect that the first interpretation belongs to the author. The editors can attempt to make sense of the material from their own perspectives and situated contexts, but the opportunity to grow to understand has to come from the reader, who reads from his or her own situated context where, we hope, the mind is open and receptive.

IN CLOSING

Every writer, I believe, would like to make a small difference. This series is dedicated to removing the veils that often prevent us from seeing and thus understanding. At the turn of this century, we are coming to a place where we are beginning to recognize that the "expert" driven model of social, health, and political problem solving for social and health issues does not always work. In these volumes an attempt is made to provide a space for the voices and narratives of specific groups to be heard, embedded in the complexities of their contexts. The diverse meanings of experience are articulated, so that our own social and health programs can be derived from the greatest "knowers," the ones who have lived within the experience. In this volume, the experience of men, as they emerge into the 21st century, echoes through the voices. Those voices beckon us to understand.

Patricia L. Munhall

June 2001

INTRODUCTION:
THE EMERGENCE OF MAN
INTO THE 21ST CENTURY

When I was young, I longed for scars
like my father's. They were the best
scars on the block, startling, varied,
pink as a tongue against his whiskey skin.
　　　　　　　　—Peter Meinke

BECOMING A MAN

When I was in junior high in the mid-1970s, two of my friends, Dudley and Charles, pulled me aside in Coach Simmons's history class and told me to stop carrying my books "like a girl." I was in the seventh grade. I played the clarinet. I had zits and glasses and braces. I had spontaneous erections during English class and big clumsy feet I tripped on in gym. I had a body that seemed determined to embarrass me. And I carried my books in my arms as if I were holding a baby, carried them, that is, "like a girl."

I carried a lot of books—I was a rather nerdy kid—and since I carried so many, it seemed natural to hold my books the way I did. But the guys at my school carried their books in one hand, slung loosely against a hip (if they carried books at all). Although it didn't make sense to me to carry my many books that way, and though it wasn't at all comfortable, as I stumbled toward the school bus, my glasses sliding down my nose, I did learn to carry my books "like a guy." Though I would never excel in sports or take shop or agriculture classes or brag about my heterosexual exploits—things I saw my male friends doing—I learned to perform, at least in part, my masculinity.

Becoming a man isn't the result, necessarily, of genitals, chromosomes, or hormones—though testosterone and chromosomes play their part. We learn to become men through the conscious and unconscious expectations of those around us, as well as through the social and cultural gender norms inculcated in us from childhood. We like to think that sexual and gender identity come to us naturally. Indeed, more often than not we assume that biological sex and socialized gender—as well as the complicated mix of nature and nurture we call sexuality—are normally and naturally connected. However, becoming "a man," whatever that may mean in a particular social context, may be anything but natural. Sometimes becoming a man means learning how to *act like a man*. Becoming a man, like becoming a woman, is an odd process of socialization, education, and performance organized around biological, sexual differences.

That embarrassing moment in history class with two friends marks a moment when I began to understand something of the performativity of masculinity. I was reminded of this incident as I was reading back through this collection, because some of the essays included here suggest that the moments by which men define themselves aren't always the obvious ones. And if these defining moments do involve the obvious events and rituals of male development (sports and sex, for example), they may be fixed in a man's mind for less than obvious reasons—for the ways he failed to measure up to cultural or family expectations, or the ways such events remain more complex than any stereotypical rendering of manhood can suggest. The power of a collection like this lies in the rich and various representations of how men understand themselves as men—whether through the expected rites of passage and versions of becoming a man, or through the failures of cultural expectations and social norms, yet always through the particularities of their own experiences.

THE PROJECT: EMPHASES AND ELISIONS

When Patricia Munhall asked me to collaborate on this book, she made clear the challenge: I had to solicit and edit enough pieces to constitute at least a third of the collection. These pieces would fill out the experiential and narrative sections of the book, but they also had to fit within the philosophical and editorial frameworks that have guided the series thus far. I set to work, e-mailing writers, friends, and colleagues. I posted calls for essays on everything from an academic gender studies listserve to the alumni listserve for my college fraternity. I also read through the work already collected by Patricia and her collaborator, Virginia Fitzsimons, looking for ways I might fill out the collection.

As the work came in, I was thrilled by the diversity of voices. There was a young father describing his fears and another suggesting his ambivalences about coaching. There was a poet from Pennsylvania who described his father's terminal illness in a series of poignant poems. There was an African-American preacher who works with troubled youth, who submitted several reflections on black masculinity. A poet from Texas sent poems about being a man in a network of male relationships—son, brother, lover—in the locker room and the emergency room. A priest and doctor who teaches medical ethics considered his own fatherhood at the impasse of science and religion. A professional journalist, one of the few women contributing to this collection, wrote about raising her son as a single mom—and about the obsession with absent or distant fathers she saw in the men around her.

A number of emphases and omissions quickly became apparent, with the obsession with fathers being one of the most striking and consistent themes we noticed. As Kwame Dawes suggests, fatherhood offers for many of these men an imaginative focus for the web of male roles and relationships—whether those roles are celebrated or disavowed, whether those relationships are supportive or dysfunctional. Strangely, though many men were writing about their fathers, no men were writing about their mothers. Was that because the mother-child relationship is so overanalyzed in our culture, because of cultural fears of "momism" and "mama's boys?" Or was it because the mother-son relationship seems unproblematic to adult men, or at least not as problematic and conflicted as their relationships with their fathers? Could it be, too, that the father is not only a parent but a figure for manhood—for the structures, roles, and norms of being a man?

Mothers weren't the only subjects missing. In fact, many of the topics we expected to see—sports, adolescent heterosexuality (the sexual and social rites of passage), male bonding (as well as hazing and initiation rituals), courtship and marriage, that is, the normative narratives of manhood—either weren't showing up in the work, or were showing up in conflicted and complicated ways. A man who grew up in rural Mississippi would write about hunting, for example, but more precisely of how his refusal to kill a deer could be seen as a failure to attain manhood. Instead of the thrill of male bonding under fire in the military, we got an indictment of military men in their sexual exploitation of others. Instead of the joys of marriage, we got a painful diary from a recent divorce.[1]

I posted further pleas on my fraternity listserve, hoping for narratives about mothers and sons, adolescent heterosexuality, sports, marriage, and male bonding (on a fraternity listserve, this should be a given). I wanted home runs and touchdowns, baptisms and bar mitzvahs, body building and bachelor parties. But nothing. I began to wonder if those most willing to write—or those most driven to tell their stories—were those who felt some sense of marginality, inadequacy, or difference. There seemed to be so many men questioning the expectations of the past in the context of their present lives—in the process of changing jobs or recovering from a past of alcoholism or abuse, in the act of recalling a father's terminal illness or abandoning a father's religious

---

[1]We had also hoped to see or solicit essays suggesting the influence of popular culture on male development, as well as an essay on body image among men—not just in terms of bodybuilding and physical culture, but also in terms of the body image disorders more and more common among young men (such as the Adonis Complex, a body image obsession which may result in eating disorders, compulsive exercise, and the abuse of steroids). We hope to include work on these topics in a forthcoming volume on adolescents in the 21st century.

tradition. It seems that for many of these men, as Patricia Munhall has suggested, "meaning comes from a place of conflict."

I don't mean to suggest, of course, that the traditional roles and rituals don't have power. Clearly, there are certain events and experiences that continue to hold symbolic and psychological power in our cultural imaginings of what it means to be a man. In the traditional stories of manhood, there are inevitable formative moments: first date, first sex, first fight, first hunt, first kill. Similarly, sports and military experience (a fundamental experience for many men of the previous century) retain particularly powerful associations with masculinity. Clearly, too, there are certain psychological ideas that we've come to expect when we talk about boys becoming men, ideas about identification and desire (separation from and yet desire for the mother, identification with and yet fear of the father).[2] We expect to see a man's anxious recollection of his first disavowal of his father, or his nostalgic reconstruction of male bonding—whether in the locker room or the boardroom, the college fraternity or the fraternal lodge. In a book about male experience, we have certain expectations.

CONTEXTS: PROFESSIONAL AND PERSONAL

It is those expectations that lend Patricia Munhall's statements about the phenomenological context a special force for me. As editor of this series, Munhall has described in previous volumes and in the front matter of this book the phenomenological and postmodern perspectives that provide the framework for this book. The postmodern moment is one in which universalizing theories have lost their power, challenged by the voices of the margins and the marginalized, the dispossessed and the disenfranchised. As ideas about what is generally true (and generalizable) lose their value, we must pay attention to the contingent and the particular. We must notice the limitations of perspective (including our own) and the power dynamics of any story. That is, as Munhall argues, we must be aware of the contingencies of truth as it is constructed in particular contexts and particular lives.

Phenomenology, she suggests, provides a framework by which to value the particular. It teaches us to enter into the experiences of others, to listen to their particularities, to pay attention to their contexts (social, cultural, and historical), and to learn from the meanings constructed by those present in the experience. Phenomenology emphasizes the essentially relative and subjective nature of reality, concentrating on the ways people understand the world through their own perceptions. The phenomenological and postmodern frameworks compel us to pay attention to the experiential, the contingent, and the contextualized. Though we have expectations about what it means to become a man, we will find—as she argues and as this book suggests—our ex-

---

[2]In one of the most interesting essays of this collection, Howard Covitz reflects on the inadequacies of these psychological narratives.

pectations reexamined through the stories of men living in the present moment.

This moment is a particularly charged one, of course, historically. As Lynne Dunphy and David Bossman suggest in their essays, American men are working toward new understandings of who they are and what it means to be male in a culture transformed by war, sexual revolution, and—most recently—the feminist movement and the resulting transformations of workplace and social spheres, women achieving greater (if not yet equal) financial and social power. As feminism redefined gender as a social and ideological construct distinct from biological sex, a growing men's studies movement emerged in the late 1980s, and with it a developing awareness of the historical and social contexts of contemporary masculinity.[3]

Over the past 40 years, ideas about gender have undergone both radical and reactionary reformations—from the sexual revolution of the 1960s to a sexual culture transformed by AIDS, from the failed campaign for an Equal Rights Amendment to the steady codification of Title 9 access issues and sexual harassment law, from the gay liberation movement to "don't ask, don't tell," from the "sensitive male" models of Alan Alda and Phil Donahue to the masculinist backlash of the 1980s (*Lethal Weapon* and *Rambo*, the cowboy politics of Ronald Reagan, and "real men don't eat quiche"), from the glam rock androgyny of the 1970s to the "Iron John" movement of the late 1980s. As Richard Shweder (1994) jokes in his survey of "male identity crisis literature," which he characterizes as "a long-delayed response to 20 years of feminist critique" (of men, patriarchy, and sexism): "In a post-modern world lacking clear-cut borders and distinctions, it has become hard to know what it means to be a man and even harder to feel good about being one." At the end of the millennium, even as there is more and more scholarship about masculinity, there are many confusing messages about what it means to be man.[4]

In such contexts, this book offers a number of useful perspectives—personal, experiential, theoretical, reflective—for thinking about masculinity and manhood. It inevitably draws on and addresses scholars in the fields of cultural studies and gender studies, even though primarily intended for an

---

[3]Among the many studies of men and masculinity, I would recommend E. Anthony Rotundo's *American Manhood: Transformations in Masculinity From the Revolution to the Modern Era* (1993), R. W. Connell's *Masculinities* (1995), George Mosse's *The Image of Man: The Creation of Modern Masculinity* (1996) and his *Nationalism and Sexuality* (1985), and Lynne Luciano's *Looking Good: Male Body Image in Modern America* (2001).

[4]The Promise Keepers, for example, suggest that men can be racially sensitive and openly emotional in their all-male gatherings, while echoing the masculinist posturings of muscular Christianity and insisting on traditional patriarchal power in family and social structures. In a review of the top movies of 2000, including *Gladiator* and *The Patriot*, women insisted on their desire for seemingly incoherent male images of sensitivity and violence—"the tough guy and the nurturing male all rolled up into one irresistible package" (Zoroya, 2000). At my local newsstand, the clerk jokes that the fitness magazines with their hypermasculinity are just a "stepping stone" to the gay porn, displayed conveniently nearby.

audience of health care and therapeutic professionals. As a book for health care practitioners, it also falls in the context of a growing medical humanities movement. In the medical humanities, there is an emphasis on the human story—on patients as human beings with stories, not diagnoses with case histories. In this field, there is also an emphasis on literary works as complex and poignant representations of human experience, representations often neglected in medical education.

More importantly, throughout scholarship in the medical humanities, there is an emphasis on human engagement and empathy, on the ability of medical practitioners to enter into and empathetically experience the lives of others. Such terms echo the work of this series, framed within Munhall's emphasis on phenomenological engagement and an "overwhelming concern for the human condition" in its diversity. It was these echoes, in fact, that drew me to this project—as a creative writing teacher and a scholar in both literature and the medical humanities. Although there is an element of qualitative research throughout, this project presents not simply case studies, but an extraordinary range of writings, from poignant and sometimes complex literary pieces by published writers, to nonliterary and sometimes therapeutic texts with compelling human stories and rhetorical force.

Even as I consider these professional contexts, however, I can't help but recall the personal contexts we bring to reading these pieces. That embarrassing and formative moment in history class, when I was told to stop carrying my books "like a girl," brings to mind further struggles with gender and sexual identity. About the same time, I was also trying out for the junior high basketball team, mostly to please my father. I wasn't interested in basketball, but I was interested in trying out, since my father had been a basketball star in high school. I wanted to be in his shoes—literally—I even played in his old Chuck Taylor's. But my father's shoes were a little too tight, too confining. I was also beginning to realize during those junior high years something of my sexuality, the desires I would do my best to repress and deny and misunderstand for several years. So when two friends told me to stop carrying my books "like a girl," it was a moment charged with possible meanings about not only what kind of boy I was, but also what kind of man I might become.

As I consider the cultural and social contexts of our indoctrination into gender norms, I think of the specific culture in which I grew up: a small town in the rural South during the 1970s, a world of evangelical religion and economic depression. I never had sex in high school, but I learned a lot about sex in high school—though not, I should point out, in sex education. If I recall correctly, there was no systematic sex education in my small town in rural Arkansas. I remember a few days on the mechanics of reproduction during 10th-grade biology class, after which all the fundamentalist boys sat in the back of the room and discussed whether or not they were still virgins if they only had oral sex. (The consensus was yes.) No, it wasn't in sex ed that I learned about sex. It was from the stories that circulated through the halls—stories of sports and sex, the kinds of stories I expected to see submitted for this collection. Stories about initiation and adolescent male bonding. The stories of Memphis and New Orleans.

Anyone in rural Arkansas knows the importance of the high school football team to the local community. My hometown was no different. A winning team can get all kinds of perks from the local booster club, including team trips to bowl games. One year the team went to Memphis for the Liberty Bowl. During that trip, a rich boy (a benchwarmer courting approval) hired a prostitute for the team to share. They took turns with her in a hotel room. I'm not sure how common such heterosexual male bonding is, though inevitably one hears of similar stories among fraternities.[5] A couple of the good Christian boys on the team—one of them told me this story—only had her perform oral sex on them, to stay virgins, since that's not real sex. He explained that they also chose to have oral sex in order to protect themselves from disease (this misinformation was another result of our sporadic sex ed curriculum).

Another team trip was to the Sugar Bowl in New Orleans. While there, the boys quickly hit the local porn theaters. One boy—the hero of the story as it was told and retold in the halls of my high school—was accosted at a theater by another man. Outraged, the boy started a fight, and as the story went, he picked up the "faggot" and threw him through a window at the back of the theater. His teammates told this story of homosexual panic with approval and awe.[6]

If I didn't have formal sex education in high school, I did in college, a small religious school where I took a class entitled "Christian Home." The course foisted onto college sophomores some of the most appalling stereotypes under the guise of sociological studies and Christian counseling. The textbook noted that guys like to get dirty working on cars, and women like to stay clean and shop, and maybe we should learn to accept those differences in each other. While we were learning to accept those differences, my group of friends were practicing the simultaneously homophobic and homoerotic rituals of male bonding. I think, for example, of my many turns as a groomsman in weddings of my fraternity brothers. Being good Christian boys, we didn't go out to stripper clubs. Instead we had parties where we pulled the most bizarre of pranks—stripping a groom of his clothes and leaving him somewhere public, naked. Not only naked, but sometimes written all over with permanent markers—"I was here" across a chest, or "This way to paradise!" and an arrow pointing down to his crotch.

What was I thinking, a closeted gay man, scrawling my name in colored marker across the stomach of a male friend? What were they thinking, my straight friends, rubbing their markers across his bare flesh? We have never spoken of this since.

---

[5] One of my students in Austin once told me how he and his fraternity brothers would arrange to watch each other having sex through the slats in a closet door.

[6] A longer version of this material appears in my memoir essay, "Most Likely to Succeed."

BOYS DON'T CRY: SILENCE AND DIFFERENCE

When I think of contexts, though, I also think of the education we receive through our popular culture, especially movies, which offer us stock figures of masculinity—the cowboy, the soldier, the athlete, the capitalist, the good father—images that are compelling if not always compatible.[7] I think of the paradigmatic Western *Shane*, in which a young boy, Joey, must choose between his strong but clearly settled father and Shane, the virile wandering gunslinger, whose power is marked in his sexual attraction (the boy's own mother is drawn to him), his freedom, and his gun. Which of these men should Joey become—the settled father planting seed, or the wandering hero slinging a gun?

Or I think of the cinematic perennial *It's a Wonderful Life*, in which George Bailey—denied the manly initiation of war because of a deaf ear, and denied the freedom to travel the world that he craves—must choose between a bad capitalist father, Mr. Potter, and the good capitalist father, his own father, who runs a small savings and loan. Despite Potter's financial power, his deficiency as a man is denoted by the fact that he is paralyzed from the waist down and does not, probably cannot, have children. Though George, like his father, repeatedly faces financial ruin, he still has children. Even when there is a run on his bank, he describes his last two bucks as "ma and pa dollar," ready to procreate. In the American dream of this movie, we learn that sexual and economic virility are two primary forms of our national manhood.[8]

Films also teach us the importance of denial and silence. We are taught stoicism, the disavowal of emotion and pain. Even though we are expected to cry at certain kinds of movies (the "male weepie" genre[9]—those that feature dead fathers and dying athletes or both), in general we are taught not to cry, not to express emotion. The hero—strong, independent, brave—never shows pain. Shane, as Joey insists, would never let you know he had been hurt. George may cry on the bridge as he considers suicide, but he can't bring himself to tell his own wife about the financial ruin that threatens them. Such silences seem symptomatic of American masculinity.

Though it might seem odd to say about a book divided into "voices," this is a book full of silences, telling silences, men unable to speak or hear. The lit-

---

[7]Is the athlete, for example, an image of discipline, teamwork, and healthy competition, or a violent aggressor and sexual predator? As Bernard Lefkowitz has suggested in his analysis of the Glen Ridge rape of 1989—in which white middle-class high school athletes raped and sexually brutalized a young woman—the dark side of the American cult of the athlete is a hypermasculine, hyperaggressive, sexual predator, unable to empathize with his female counterparts.

[8]On the contradictory forms of masculinity that structure Hollywood film (including *Shane* and *It's a Wonderful Life*), see Robin Wood's "Ideology, Genre, Auteur."

[9]See Bruce Handy's "treatise on the male weepie," "Big Boys Do Cry" (1999).

eral deafness of Carl Jenkinson's father and the stoic silence of Pete Mackey's father in the face of terminal illness have their figurative equivalents throughout the book, from the stammering adolescents of Joe Goeke's Missouri amusement park, to a pseudonymous essay about the constraining silences of living in the closet, to the father and son unable to talk to each other in Andrew Collins's essay about the death of his brother. Silence seems almost pathological in Anna Moore's description of her dysfunctional family, and in Mark Nugent's story, it is clear that the breaking of silence—getting past the symptomatic male inability to share feelings and admit weakness—is central to his recovery from alcoholism.

Such an emphasis on silence might be expected, given the insistent instruction in our culture on stoicism, repression, and denial. Boys don't cry. Or as men's studies scholar Sam Femiano says, "Real men don't complain and don't react to pain." The repression of emotion—and the corollary inability to deal with emotion—are part of the social construction of masculinity. "The way men are socialized," says Femiano, "makes it hard for them to be emotionally available, whether to themselves, their partners, their children, or even their friends" (Bloch, 1998). However, we are expected to express anger, encouraged to be competitive and aggressive, and taught to measure our achievements in the language of sexual and material competitiveness. We are also taught to fear difference.

I think of a poem I regularly teach: Gary Gildner's "First Practice" (1969). In it a coach, "the man with the short cigar," takes a bunch of young boys into the storm shelter beneath the school, preparing to badger them into manliness. He tells the boys that he is a man who believes it's a dog eat dog world and that he once killed for his country, adding, "If there were any girls present/for them to leave now." (No throwing like a girl—or carrying your books like a girl—allowed here.) He then lines the boys up facing each other, telling them "across the way. . . is the man you hate most/in the world." This short anecdote of athletic and military experience captures so much of the aggression, fear of difference, competition, and violence we are taught as young men. Gildner ends the poem with one final admonition from the coach: "I don't want to see/any marks when you're dressed." No matter how violent the practice, he doesn't want the bruises to show. The violence young men are taught to direct against others—even against their own friends and their own bodies—is also a violence directed against ourselves, the effects of which must be hidden, invisible, silent.

May this book give voice not only to those silences, but also to new and beneficial visions of what it means to be a man in the century to come.

Ed Madden

July 2001

REFERENCES

Bloch, E. (1998, Fall). On men and psychotherapy: An interview with Sam Femiano. *Men's Studies News: Newsletter of the American Men's Studies Association,* 7(1), 3–5.

Connell, R. W. (1995). *Masculinites.* Berkeley: University of California Press.

Gildner, G. (1969).*First practice.* Pittsburgh, PA: University of Pittsburgh Press.

Handy, B. (1999, March). Big boys do cry. *Time,* March 1, 1999, 74.

Lefkowitz, B. (1997). *Our guys: The Glen Ridge rape and the secret life of the perfect suburb.* Berkeley: University of California Press.

Luciano, L. (2001). *Looking good: Male body image in modern America.* New York: Hill and Wang.

Madden, E. (2001, June). Most likely to succeed, most likely to be remembered. *The Point* (Columbia SC) 11(102), 10, 22.

Meinke, P. (1992, May). Scars [Poem]. *The Atlantic Monthly,* 104.

Mosse, G. L. (1985). *Nationalism and sexuality: Respectability and abnormal sexuality in modern Europe.* New York: H. Fertig.

Mosse, G. L. (1996). *The image of man: The creation of modern masculinity.* New York: Oxford University Press.

Rotundo, E. A. (1993). *American manhood: Transformations in masculinity from the revolution to the modern era.* New York: Basic Books.

Shweder, R. (1994, January). What do men want? A reading list for the male identity crisis. *New York Times Book Review,* Jan. 9, 1994: 3, 24.

Wood, R. (1995). Ideology, genre, auteur. In B. K. Grant (Ed.), *Film genre reader* II (pp. 59–73). Austin: University of Texas Press.

Zoroya, G. (2000, July 11). The men of our dreams: Women swoon over Hollywood's strong-but-selfless ideal male. *USA Today,* p. D1.

ACKNOWLEDGMENTS

There are many individuals who make such a book possible, even though as was described in the preface of this book, there were moments when we wondered if this book was even going to be possible to complete! *Under those circumstances, then, the acknowledgments take on a more profound meaning.*

In particular, we gratefully acknowledge our contributing authors and poets who did make this volume more than just conventionally possible but ironically surpassing our page limitations! We are thankful for the writings from the scholars that provide the philosophical and theoretical components of this book. Some have written before for this series, and we are fortunate to have them back to share their wisdom in this volume. For the returning and new writers of these papers, we express our deepest appreciation for your thoughtful, interpretive, and insightful chapters.

To the contributing authors and poets who provided us with the experiential and existential writings, we are delighted to have this wonderful opportunity to share your personal understandings and the meanings of your experiences with others. We praise your writing skills, but even more so admire your courage and generosity in sharing your personal narratives and verse, which illuminate the male experience. Your writings have made us laugh. Your writings have made us weep. Your writings have contributed to our compassion. They have given us new meanings and understandings. How generous you are, and how very grateful we are for your openness.

Each one of our writers has contributed to a mosaic of multistoried, polyvocal, and diverse realities. Each is unique and each has our appreciation. It is to them that this book is dedicated with our awe and reverence.

Meanwhile, behind the scenes is another group of individuals who make such volumes possible. The talent and vision of this group are gifts to us. Expressing gratitude in order of the process, we first thank Penny Glynn, acquisition editor, for "acquiring" the *Emergence* series and us. We thank her for her support and creativity. Christine Tridente, associate editor, always deserves our applause, this time for organizing three editors and over 60 pieces in this volume. She is truly amazing! Also at Jones and Bartlett are other members of the team who contribute to the fruition of a volume and to whom we also want to express our gratitude for the distance they traveled to effectively assist us.

Many thanks to Thomas Prindle, editorial assistant; Anne Spencer, production editor; Taryn Wahlquist, marketing manager; and Eileen Ward, special markets manager.

One more person deserves acknowledgment for her many talents and characteristics, especially her characteristic patience, and that is Janet Kiefer, project editor at Carlisle Communications. Her efficient work is of large consequence to the completion of each volume.

We thank each person involved for providing a platform once again, for understanding a specific group of individuals, herein the 21st-century man in all his multiplicity, contingencies, and new ways of emergence.

Lastly, and within the context of our own emergence, we want to thank our significant others, adult children, and friends whom we love and appreciate. The support and patience they have given so generously as we traveled through this unusual human experience demonstrate the gifts that come from understanding.

Patricia L. Munhall
Ed Madden
Virginia M. Fitzsimons

June 2001

CONTRIBUTORS AND EDITORS

EDITORS

Patricia L. Munhall
Professor and Psychoanalyst
Women's Studies Program
and Institute for Families in Society
University of South Carolina
Columbia, South Carolina

Ed Madden
Associate Professor of English
University of South Carolina
Columbia, South Carolina

Virginia Fitzsimons
Professor
Department of Nursing
Kean University
Union, New Jersey

CONTRIBUTORS

Ronald Applbaum
President
Kean University
Union, New Jersey

Amittai Aviram
Associate Professor of English and
Comparative Literature;
Computer Programmer
University of South Carolina
Columbia, South Carolina

Richard Barber
Businessman
Somerset, New Jersey

Ronald Baughman
Professor and Division Chair, Media
Arts
University of South Carolina
Columbia, South Carolina

Jeffrey P. Bishop
Assistant Professor of Medicine and
Ethics
University of Texas Southwestern
Medical School
Priest Associate
Episcopal Church of the Incarnation
Dallas, Texas

Richard Blanco
Professional Civil Engineer
Poet in Residence at
Central Connecticut State University
Hartford, Connecticut, and Miami,
Florida

Joshua E. Borgmann
Graduate Student in Creative
Writing
University of South Carolina
Columbia, South Carolina

David Bossman
Professor and Director
Institute of Jewish-Christian Studies
Seton Hall University
South Orange, New Jersey

Brad Bostian
English Instructor
Central Piedmont Community
College
Charlotte, North Carolina

Jack Brannon
Poet, Writer
Austin, Texas

Claudia Smith Brinson
Writer, Newspaper Columnist,
Writing Coach
Columbia, South Carolina

Carolyn Brown
Writer
Boca Raton, Florida

Jared Delaney Chesson
Student
University of South Carolina
Columbia, South Carolina

Andrew Collins
Middle School English Teacher
Chapin Middle School
Columbia, South Carolina

Daniel Collins
Writer
Media, Pennsylvania

Howard H. Covitz
Psychoanalyst and Director
Institute of Psychoanalytic
Psychotherapies
Philadelphia, Pennsylvania

Christopher Davis
Associate Professor of Creative
Writing
University of North Carolina at
Charlotte
Charlotte, North Carolina

Kwame Dawes
Poet, Musician, Associate Professor
of English
University of South Carolina
Columbia, South Carolina

Lynn E. Dunphy
Associate Professor and Coordinator
of Graduate Programs in Nursing
College of Nursing
Florida Atlantic University
Boca Raton, Florida

Bert Easter
Computer Support Tech
National Resource Center for the
First Year Experience
University of South Carolina
Columbia, South Carolina

Julie Evertz
Writer and Doctoral Student
Centralia, Illinois

Dennis Finger
Associate Professor
Department of Psychology
Kean University
Union, New Jersey

Neil Fitzsimons
Businessman
Spring Lake Heights, New Jersey

Elizabeth Forbes
Professor Emerita
College of Nursing
Thomas Jefferson University
Philadelphia, Pennsylvania

Fred Gibbs
Attorney
Barnegat Light, New Jersey

Joe Goeke
Graduate Student, English Instructor
University of South Carolina
Columbia, South Carolina

Gordon Grant
Assistant Professor of English
Baylor University
Waco, Texas

Gerald Greaves
Priest and Pastor
Guardian Angel Roman Catholic
Church
Allendale, New Jersey

Hayes Hampton
Assistant Professor of English
University of South Carolina at
Sumter
Sumter, South Carolina

Carl Jenkinson
Graduate Student in Creative
Writing
University of South Carolina
Columbia, South Carolina [orig.
Bedford, England]

Brian Johnson
Graduate Student in English
University of South Carolina
Columbia, South Carolina

Preston Jones
Contributing Editor, Books and
Culture
Professor of History
Logos Academy
Dallas, Texas

"Sam Kennedy" [pseudonym]
Middle School Social Sciences
Teacher
South Carolina

"Ted Kramer" [pseudonym]
Professor
South Carolina

Kevin Lewis
Associate Professor of Religious
Studies
University of South Carolina
Columbia, South Carolina

Pete Mackey
Writer
Galway, Ireland

Ed Madden
Associate Professor of English
University of South Carolina
Columbia, South Carolina

Stephen R. Marrone
Vice President of Nursing
Mount Sinai Medical Center
New York, New York

Dee McFarland
Retired Physician and Artist
Columbia, South Carolina

Ray McManus
Poetry Teacher, Graduate Student in
English
University of South Carolina
Columbia, South Carolina

Anna Blackmon Moore
Writer, English Instructor
California State University at Chico
Chico, California

Patricia L. Munhall
Professor and Psychoanalyst
Women's Studies Program and
Institute for Families in Society
University of South Carolina
Columbia, South Carolina

Mark Nugent
Teacher
Dellwyn, Virginia

Kenneth D. Phillips
Associate Professor
College of Nursing
University of South Carolina
Columbia, South Carolina

Patrick Pinnell
Student
University of South Carolina
Columbia, South Carolina

Joey Poole
Graduate Student in Creative
Writing
University of South Carolina
Grocery Stocker
Pelion, South Carolina

Mark Powell
Writer
Mountain Rest, South Carolina

Larry Purnell
Professor and Chair of
Administration
College of Health and Nursing
Sciences
University of Delaware
Newark, Delaware

Timothy Reigle
Associate Professor
Department of Design
Kean University
Union, New Jersey

Florence Sitelman
Writer
Riverdale, New York

Robert Sitelman
Professor
Department of Philosophy
Kean University
Union, New Jersey

John R. Spann
Director of Litigation Activities
Mortgage Loan Division
South Carolina Housing Finance and
Development Authority
Columbia, South Carolina

M. Shawn Stinson
Physician and Associate Professor of
Medicine
School of Medicine
University of South Carolina
Columbia, South Carolina

"Robert Therrer" [pseudonym]
Professor of English
University of South Carolina
Columbia, South Carolina

Deaver Traywick
Farmer, Graduate Student in English
University of South Carolina
Columbia, South Carolina

Ben Triana
Editorial Assistant
Pawley's Island, South Carolina

Bryan Waterman
Assistant Professor of English
New York University
New York, New York

Charles C. Weathers, Sr.
Consultant and Minister
Development Director, Children
Unlimited
Executive Director, New Slate
Ministries
Columbia, South Carolina

Ted Wojtasik
Assistant Professor of Creative
Writing
St. Andrew's College
Laurinburg, North Carolina

Ivan Young
Senior Production Editor
The Haworth Press
Hazleton, Pennsylvania

VOICES ONE

SITUATING MAN IN THE 21ST CENTURY

CHAPTER 1

IMPOSSIBLE FLYING, XLV

Kwame Dawes

This poem is part of a book-length memoir in verse which charts the complex mesh of relationships between my brother, my father, my son, and me. Caught at the end of one crisis and in the heart of another, the poems reveal why poetry can heal in its own painful way.

For Neville, my father; Kojovi, my brother; and Kekeli, my son

> *No sharp screams, although after they lifted him,*
> *his brown body covered in the soft white clay*
> *of his birth waters, he thumped the air and made sounds—*
> *alive now—plucked out from the ribbons of her flesh,*
> *the neat line in her skin stretched; him with the umbilicus*
> *taut around his neck. And it is only in that*
> *instant of limbs, navel string, slick hair*
> *and the glare of the OR's blue lights, the crowd*
> *in their green uniforms floating around us*
> *as if a fog suspended everything in soft motion,*
> *and my Lorna, too far gone now under the drugs—*
> *only then did I understand that the fear in my chest*
> *and stomach was not for the drama, the rush, the sprint*
> *through the halls to open her and extract him intact,*
> *not the fear of his death, no, but the shock of his penis,*
> *the fresh knowledge of his maleness (so well had we*
> *protected the surprise); the sound of the word "son",*
> *its alienness, and the rush of every image, every fear,*
> *every awkward silence, every tension, every hunger*
> *for my meaning in my father's flesh, in his memory,*
> *in his history, in his face—these things clutched*
> *my gut—it tasted of fear. And a word can make language*

3

bloom in us a rash of memory—"oh world I have lost!"—
the narrative of father and son. And in that moment,
I thought of you, saw you sitting in the dark talking
to our father, enacting the ancient rituals of how
legacy is passed down. You were there when I was not
and you received the secrets of a father's memory.
At last, I was a father, it seemed. This thing
was not other, not like my daughter—it was me,
seed, penis, blood, the replication of me;
and maybe now I understood Neville's silences,
his calculation of how not to remake us in him;
and how, when night came during those last days,
he found you in the dark, and in those deep tones
you confabbed, made something of the mystery
of this blood passing from flesh to flesh. At last,
I knew what I feared most was that I did not know
how to love myself, and for the first time it mattered.

CHAPTER 2

MANHOOD: FROM THE 20TH
TO THE 21ST CENTURY

Lynne Dunphy

A young man is so strong, so mad, so certain, and so lost.
He has everything and he is able to use nothing.
— Thomas Wolfe, Of Time and the River

When we think of manhood, it is often best understood as a journey or a quest, beset with trials and tribulations. The hero wears a thousand faces (Campbell, 1968). He is Odysseus journeying toward Troy; he is Prometheus, endlessly pushing the rock uphill; he is Christ agonizing toward Calvary; he is Napoleon conquering the European continent; he is Pip in pursuit of great expectations; he is Huck Finn setting out on the Mississippi. Achieving a mission is often not the point. Rather, the point is progress. The trajectory of the progress is masculinity—and in classic Freudian terms, that trajectory is up, out, and away (from the MOTHER; from the OTHER). The literary record suggests a discouraging conclusion that few have cared to dwell on: men do not live happily ever after (Hawley, 1993, p. 28).

The story of man in the 20th century may be likened to one of a lost young man. Man began the century filled with strength and certainty, yet consumed with enough anger to fill two monumental world wars, as well as numerous smaller yet no less horrific skirmishes. The 20th century witnessed a young man mad enough to design an atom bomb, unleashing an unparalleled potential for self-immolation. Man in the 20th century truly had everything—but in other ways, had been able to use nothing. The hope for the next century is in sprouts of maturation, a possibility of learning from the past, and a profound rearrangement of social and power relations, at least in the West, which hold a promise of resynthesized notions of manhood.

Where does the beginning of the 21st century situate notions of manhood? What is his trajectory? What is the 21st-century quest? To understand this, an examination of 20th-century manhood is warranted. Traditional scholarship, until recently, had no reason to examine masculinity. As the reigning, dominant paradigm of all humanness, it was self-evident. The "discourse of gender" in literary, cultural, and historical studies, begun in the latter part of the 20th century, was essentially a discourse about women. But we now understand that masculinity is as much a social and historical construct as femininity, and its manifestations are equally worthy of close examination (Izenberg, 2000, p. 5).

In reality, constructs of femininity and masculinity have always been closely aligned. Each highlights and reflects the other. During medieval times, notions of chivalry prevailed, personified by the medieval knight. The ideal man possessed physical strength, courage, and loyalty. The Christian ideal integrated earlier and more brutal manifestations of manhood to a transcendent level, that of duty through service to God. The essence of manhood involved both idealizing and protecting women, often mingling the seeds of respect and contempt into thorns of ambivalence. The Renaissance saw the emergence of a model of masculinity built on this early ideal but melded with the attributes of the courtier: good manners, cultivation, and liberality of spirit (Mosse, 1996, p. 3).

A bourgeois reworking of these earlier ideas occurred by the middle of the 18th century as aristocratic qualities were transmuted into values of productivity, self-discipline, moderation, and balance (Mosse, 1985). "The authentically manly man," writes Peter Gay in The Education of the Senses (1984), "was at once self-assertive and self-controlled" (p. 103). Victorian masculinity was explicitly defined as the opposite of femininity. Work and home became "separate spheres"; men were pillars of rationality, women of emotionality. Some suggest that this polarization led to a "crisis of masculine identity" at the end of the 19th century. Economic changes were occurring. The independent entrepreneur, for example, evolved into the salaried manager of the large corporation, producing anxiety and loss of self-identity (Hobsbawm, 1989). Others point to the rise of mass political power on the left and the right and its attack on bourgeois liberalism as another factor shaking the edifice of traditional manhood (Schorske, 1986). Others dispute the idea of a crisis of masculinity at the turn of the century, pointing to the resurgence of the warrior ideal of manliness that gripped European nations after the unification of Germany and Italy and the resultant rise in nationalism (Mosse, 1985).

It is the male reactions to the emergence of the vivid "New Woman" around the 1870s and 1880s that speak most profoundly to the case of an underlying threat to manhood at the turn of the century (Gay, 1984; Dykstra, 1986). The vast majority of men opposed the women's emancipation movements that arose in the late 19th century. "Men could be 'men' only if women remained 'women' " (Izenberg, 2000, p. 11). Much of Europe embraced Otto Weininger's Sex and Character, published in 1906. An open denunciation of the women's rights movements, Weininger characterized maleness as "being" itself, the totality of human qualities, and femininity correspondingly as nothingness. Demonized images of the "femme fatale" arose at the end of the century depicted in the works of Wilde, Beardley, Strindberg, and Klimt. Revealed were man's "psychic vulnerability" and the inexorable collapse of masculinity this portended. This was the birth of the Modern World. It was against this backdrop that the final century of the millennium began.

"Good-bye to All That": World War I

Nonetheless, the beginning of the 20th century may be characterized as a time of optimism, unbridled growth, and technological progress. Hope reigned serene despite seeds of discontent and anxiety. The first ostensible and massive blow to a serene and continuous view of manhood (read: SELF) was World War I (1914–1918). We have yet to recover from its blows. The peace and prosperity of the Victorian era was abruptly ended with the eruption of a conflict of unprecedented ferocity, unleashing such demons of the 20th century as mechanized warfare and mass death (Izenberg, 2000). By the end of the war, three great empires had collapsed—the Austro-Hungarian, the Russian, and the Ottoman. The experience of World War I, and its bitter aftermath, shattered the faith in rationality and liberalism that had prevailed in Europe since the Enlightenment and ushered in what is referred to as the Modern Age. The years between 1914–1918 were ones of blood, battle, stalemate, and disillusionment. In a wartime essay, "Thoughts for the Times on War and Death," Sigmund Freud wrote, "If we are to be judged by the wishes of our unconscious, we are, the primitive man, simply a gang of murderers. . . . War . . . strips us of the later accretions of civilization and lays bare the primal man in each of us" (Freud, quoted in Ferguson, 1999, p. 357). It is the job of civilization, after all, to educate man to the distinction between being strong and being destructive. But "civilization" as we had known and understood it no longer existed.

A stripped-down vision of the reality of war emerged, deromanticized, deconstructed so to speak. Take Robert Graves's poem, "Dead Boche":

> To you who read my songs of war
> And only hear the blood and fame
> I'll say (you've heard it said before)
> "War's Hell!" and if you doubt the same
> Today I found in Mametz Wood
> A certain cure for lust for blood:
>
> Where, propped against a shattered trunk
> In a great mess of things unclean,
> Sat a dead Boche; he scowled and stunk
> With clothes and face a sodden green,
> Big-bellied, spectacled, crop-haired,
> Dribbling black blood from nose and beard.

Never would things be the same. As Graves's famous wartime memoir, first published in 1929, was named, it was "Good-bye to All That." The Modern Age had arrived.

FAST, FREE, AND EASY: THE 1920S

Relief and economic recovery followed for the victorious nations; Germany, in defeat, and Russia, in the tatters and chaos of the Russian Revolution, had less to celebrate. In the United States, the stock market soared. But the relentless liberation of women persisted. New art forms emerged—in paintings, in novels, in music. This was the Jazz Age. Sexual mores loosened. Margaret Sanger agitated for birth control for women. Hair was bobbed; skirts were shortened; and an Age of Reaction ushered in Prohibition in America. Medicine began a new dominance and objective science was emerging supreme. Darwinism was winning the day. New mechanisms of control were within men's grasp; yet psychic peace remained elusive. Power structures between the sexes in place since the very beginnings of recorded time were becoming unmoored. Women worked outside the home. Man's role as defender and provider was over. Although the independent woman was characterized as perverse— a lesbian—traditional notions of masculinity were quaking (Dunphy, 2000, p. 7). This emerging change was hammered home during the 1930s, years of the Great Depression.

DOWN AND OUT IN THE 1930S

New assaults on manhood came with the economic crisis of the 1930s. Jobs were scarce; homes and families fell apart. The diaphragm was invented. Birth control was a reality. Restless, rootless men—"hobos"—rode the rails of the United States. Men could no longer provide. Governments began to usurp this traditional role with the beginning of the welfare state. Industrial progress had also proved a sham, another betrayal. Labor proved powerless. The cowboy was dead and there was no "Home on the Range." Going westward had a limit: California without the Gold Rush. Even dreaming was dead. The journey was difficult. The journey seemed downward and inward. The struggles were profound. There was no relief in sight.

Although the slogan "Get the man back to work" was everywhere, keeping the notion of women in the home firmly fixed, in reality many women worked. Approximately 85 million Americans went to the movies every week, many of them women. And in the movies, career women abounded. The carefree, dance-mad flapper was still alive; but she had to go to work (Dunphy, 2000, p. 9). Rarely were women portrayed solely as wives and mothers; more often, in the movies, they were detectives, heroines. And they sparred with men.

MOBILIZATION AND TRIUMPH FOR THE WEST: WORLD WAR II

Change was generated from external sources. Political forces on the right and left mounted a gigantic clash. Led by a madman, Germany plunged Europe into a new circle of hell in the form of the second World War of the 20th century. Threat from the outside focused energies outward. Male heroism reemerged (if only briefly and only in the movies). A new quest was begun— for the good. There was a resurgence (albeit brief) of the role of man as defender and protector of woman. Traditional role boundaries were reasserted. Although women were freed up on the homefront, to work, to organize, to MANAGE, it was all in support of the men. It was the men, after all, who did the fighting; women tended the home fires. And the good triumphed. There were enough goods to spare, at the end, that help was extended worldwide to the defeated.

LOVE, LIFE, AND CHANGE IN THE POSTWAR ERA

The years immediately after the war were initially confused. France and England, devastated from wartime losses and damages, turned to the welfare state. In the United States, prosperity was fueled by the Cold War defensive buildups and a resurgence of war in Korea. The men were home again and it was up to the women to adjust. After all, the men had won the war. It was the men who needed to work, to manage, to reassert control. In the United States, opportunities were everywhere. The GI Bill subsidized education. Affordable, assembly-line family homes were built and the family structure was reinforced, albeit in a surburban enclave. Wives were young and fertile; men were working and providing. All appeared right with the world. It was the calm before the storm.

THE 1960S: MALE POWER CHALLENGED

Brown vs. the Board of Education brought widespread changes into the realm of civil rights. A resurgence of interest in the rights of women was not far behind. The torpor of the 1950s was thrown off. Jessica Mitford exposed the funeral industry; Elisabeth Kubler-Ross placed headlights on the process of dying; Rachel Carson decried the poisoning of the environment; Marjory Stoneham Douglas fought to keep alive the Florida Everglades; and Betty Friedan decried the "feminine mystique." The pill was placed on the market and a true sexual revolution was begun. Playboy bunnies reigned supreme and woman as sex symbol appeared secure. But emerging notions of equality created waves. Affluent World War II "baby boomers" stormed the campuses of elite universities, protesting government policies, defying all authority. Communal life followed "on the road." Rock music, pot, and LSD spread an aura of "love." The phrase "make love, not war" became a rallying cry for a generation of protesters against the U.S. policy in Vietnam.

But a large number of young men, especially those from the working class, continued to go to war. There was a draft after all. Not all felt it was "manly" to elude military duty and responsibility. Notions of chivalry, loyalty, courage, and physical prowess died hard. Despite a culture of news reporting that made it difficult to deny the brutal realities involved, many young men went to war. Opposing views shattered a nation. Yet the decade ended with man conquering space; man walked on the moon.

THE NEW AGE MAN AS "CORRECTED MAN"

Despite the extension of traditional boundaries beyond those of the earth (and perhaps because of this extension), notions of manhood, as well as ideas of God, were essentially dead. Men were skewered by feminist critiques of manhood as a summation of dangerous aggression, insensitivity, and sexual domination. Some men accommodated, attempting to get in touch with their "feminine" selves, taking on traditional female tasks of child-rearing and household duties. The New Age man accepted axiomatically the feminist assertions of his nature, realizing that he is dangerous. Some men even admitted that they didn't really "like" football! According to Robert Bly, author of *Iron John* (1990), this "New Man"—named the "soft man" by Bly—was not "liberated"; rather, he was depressed. The soft man had fallen out of touch with his deep maleness: "a phallic, precivilized energy sometimes projected in symbolic form as a monster or giant" (Hawley, 1993, p. 10). Bly's prescription was regressive—a return to a forceful and strong masculine birthright. The features of the "Iron John" model espoused by Bly are associated with a primitive male sexuality—hairiness, wetness, redness. They are not easily acceptable, not "nice." And rapprochement with energized and liberated women would not come easily.

REFLECTIONS ON THE END OF THE CENTURY AND THE MILLENNIUM

Human nature presupposes elements of action and reaction—two steps forward followed by the inevitable step back. Jane Fonda has apologized to Vietnam era veterans for her 1969 trip to Hanoi. And noted feminist Susan Faludi, in her book *Stiffed* (1999), has recently popularized the idea that men are being "stiffed" by American culture, victimized by distant fathers and insecure jobs, aggrieved by feminist demands for equality. Faludi "feels their pain," validating their desire for older forms of masculinity (Gardiner, 2001, p. 28).

Sally Robinson, in *Marked Men: White Masculinity in Crisis* (2000), views such discussions of masculine crisis as overstated. The social and cultural revolutions of the 1960s and 1970s did not overthrow white male power, although they did provoke significant anxieties. According to Robinson, instead of generating questions about the nature of our social organization, dominant males reacted by claiming that they were "victims" too. Masculinist men's movements, such as Richard Bly's *Iron John*, dwell on the "wounds" and hazards of contemporary manhood to obscure the continuing benefits. These "therapeutic" models of masculinity call for men to be healed rather than society to be transformed (Gardiner, 2001, p. 27). If it is civilization's job to educate men to the distinction between being strong and being destructive, it is also civilization's job to learn that the solution to civic and domestic violence is not to weaken men to the point that they cannot commit it (Hawley, 1993, p. 11).

Gardiner (2001), in her review of Robinson's book, reminds us of the recent, widely popular TV show, *Survivor* (first season). The last "survivor" was not a grizzled and reconfigured male hero àla Tom Hanks's recent role in the movie *Castaway*, but rather a "newly-minted male millionaire who out-manipulates a rival woman" (p. 27). She notes that the woman who played the *Survivor* game most like her male counterparts, with collusion and betrayal, was called a vicious "snake," who should be left in the road, dying. In contrast, Richard, the epitome of the "corporate male," appeared as a master strategist. He had suffered, struggled, put his male body on the line, and "deserved" to win. Robinson's thesis is that American white men have responded to feminism by highlighting their physical vulnerabilities, by cleverly recasting themselves as individual victims, not social oppressors.* Like dogs, they have slunk off in a corner to lick their collective "wounds." And to demand recompense for their pain. Men, according to Robinson, are reacting to being "marked" by race and gender.

NOT THROWING OUT "THE BABY" WITH "THE BATHWATER"

"What a piece of work is a man! How noble in reason!
How infinite in faculty! in form and moving how express
and admirable! In action how like an angel!
In apprehension how like a god! The beauty of the world!
The paragon of animals! And yet, to me, what is the
quintessence of dust?
　　　　　—Hamlet, II, ii.

---

*Editor's note: To perhaps further complicate this argument, we should add that the survivor, Richard Hatch, was an openly gay man, and during the filming, a nudist as well. Another contestant noted the humor of giving America a "fat naked fag" as its ultimate image of survival.

Freudian notions are now internalized. We understand, for example, that the male trajectory, the "quest," on a psychological level is a journey away from the mother, from the *other*, from Woman. Psychoanalytic feminists see the boy's dread of his mother as infinitely exceeding his dread of his father, because his very life emerges from and, for a time, depends on her. She is his foremost nurturer as well as the agent of all his fears and dissatisfactions. He has issued from her very flesh, he needs her, but he increasingly realizes that he is *not* like her; the very source of his well-being is alien (Hawley, 1993, p. 6). Horney (1973) maintains that of necessity mothers, and by extension, all females, become objects of masculine "dread." The developing male gains psychological control by distorting the value and reality of the female. He either idolizes and adores all women or debases and abuses them. Adoration elevates the mother figure into beneficent harmlessness; debasement devalues her into contemptible harmfulness. As the child identifies himself as "male," he exaggerates his tendency to adore or to debase the female and to deny the feminine in himself, as well as elevating his own aggressive and "masculine" tendencies. "The machismo, the will to power, and all manner of other exaggerated tendencies may be the only maleness there is; masculinity may be all compensation" (Hawley, 1993, p. 8).

However, this is a distinctly feminist interpretation. Are we not all, male and female alike, grappling with issues of separation, individuation, meaning, and change? Does either gender have a distinct market on existential choices? Are not both men and women encouraged to be economically changeable parts? Does either gender really have a "reliable" record of defining "the other"? Are we not all really struggling with *human* issues, superceding categories of gender, race, and culture? Are we not all ". . . this quintessence of dust"? And does "the dust" negate the obverse, the varying constructions of civilization?

BREAKING NEW GROUND IN TIMES OF ASTONISHING CHANGE

The recognition of human issues *beyond* gendered interpretations does not negate the facts of that matter: that a world of patriarchy *did* indeed exist. In a world governed by power relations, this would only be natural. Might *did* make right. To deny the obvious would be absurd. However, we are in times of radical and unchartered change. All the stunning events that have occurred since the fall of the Berlin Wall in 1989, however unthinkable a decade ago, are merely the installments of a broader upheaval in human affairs. The 1990s marked the climax of a major phase in world history that began in the decades when Columbus sailed for America and an ethos of chivalry truly prevailed. The industrial economy based on a manipulation of raw resources at a large scale is giving way to an information economy based upon manipulation of data on a small scale. A shift in the technology of power brought about by the microchip may profoundly alter the organization of life (Davidson & Rees-Mogg, 1993, pp. 24–27). "Might" in the traditional sense is what is dead. If that is all we equate notions of manhood to, then one could support an argument that manhood is in "decline." I would argue, however, that that is merely a narrow interpretation of the concept.

Megapolitical analysis is built on the assumption that the organization of societies is largely determined by the physical limits on the exercise of power. Raw power has a more sweeping impact than people in generally peaceful societies tend to imagine. As technology and other factors change the limits within which force can be exercised, they change society. What is the power today may not be the power of tomorrow. At the dawn of the Information Age, what this portends for notions of manhood and masculinity one can only imagine. But it is something with which men must come to grips. Current surges of violence can be seen as the last gasps of a dying order, presaged on the waning of traditional male power structures.

MANHOOD REFASHIONED

According to Richard Hawley (1993), "Disturbing as the notion may be, manhood may be an illusion"(p. 165). What Hawley refers to is the idea of ". . . a settled masculine maturity." According to Hawley, manhood has no happy ending because the masculine quest knows no end. The quest is merely being reconceptualized in the terms and language of new realities. Paradoxically, part of that journey means giving up traditional notions of masculinity. Dan Kindlon (1999), coauthor of *Raising Cain: Protecting the Emotional Lives of Boys*, and therapist to numerous disturbed young men, says, "Many of the boys I see are so straitjacketed by their sense of manhood that they can't enjoy being boys" (p. xvii). Kindlon and coauthor Michael Thompson see boys suffering from a too-narrow definition of masculinity and strike the call for change, essential for a humanistic society. Boys, they say, must be given permission to experience the full range of human emotions, vulnerabilities, fears. Mark Twain wrote the following description of courage: "Courage is resistance to fear, mastery of fear—not absence of fear." Men, like women, have fears, vulnerabilities, and inner feelings. These need to be acknowledged, not denied.

Men, like women, also have dreams, hopes, and desires for their futures. Of the Modern Age and 20th-century consciousness Paul Fussell states in *The Great War and Modern Memory* ". . . there seems to be one dominating form of modern understanding; that it is essentially *ironic*. . . ." The essence of irony is detachment. What is needed is permission for a passionate attachment, for belief in ideals, for courage rooted in morality, not in mere physical strength. Thompson and Kindlon (1999) see strong and healthy boys as a product of acceptance and affirmation of their humanity. They urge us to communicate every day, every time we are in the presence of boys: "I recognize you. You are a boy   full of life, full of dreams, full of feeling" (p. 258). Boys love heroes; they all have dreams of greatness. They are open to inspiration. What models do we offer them? Are they the old and outdated images of masculinity that have existed for centuries, rooted in different realities? Or do we provide models that are flexible enough to weather the changes of the future? And varied enough to account for different proclivities? And rooted in a humanistic understanding of the fullness of manhood? There's got to be something for everybody. Thompson and Kindlon (1999) conclude as follows:

> We have to teach boys that there are many ways to become a Man; that there are many ways to be brave, to be a good father, to be loving and strong and successful. We need to celebrate the natural risk-taking of boys, their energy, their boldness. We need to praise the artist and the entertainer, the missionary, and the athlete, the soldier and the male nurse, the store owner and the round-the-world sailor, the teacher and the CEO. There are many ways for a boy to make a contribution to this life. (p. 257)

REFERENCES

Bly, R. (1990). *Iron John: A book about men*. Reading, MA & Menlo Park, CA: Addison-Wesley Pub. Co., Inc.

Campbell, J. (1968). *The hero with a thousand faces*. Princeton, NJ: Princeton University Press.

Davidson, J. D., & Rees-Mogg, W. (1993). *The Great Reckoning*. NY: Simon & Schuster.

Dunphy, L. M. (2000). "Families on the brink, on the edge." In Munhall, P. L. & Fitzsimmons, V. M. (Eds), *The emergence of the family into the 21st century* (pp. 3–15). Boston, MA: NLN Press, Jones & Bartlett Pubs.

Dykstra, B. (1986). *Idols of perversity: Fantasies of feminine evil in fin-de-siècle culture*. NY & Oxford: Oxford University Press, cited in Izenberg, G. N. (2000). *Modernism & masculinity: Mann, Wedekind, Kandinsky through WWI* (p. 12). Chicago, IL: University of Chicago Press.

Faludi, S. (1999). *Stiffed* cited in Gardiner, J. K. (2001). "Anxiety Attacks." *The Women's Review of Books*, Vol. XVIII, No. 5 (February, 2001) (pp. 27–28). Wellesley, MA: The Women's Review, Inc.

Ferguson, N. (1999). *The pity of war*. NY: Penguin Books.

Fussell, P. (1975). *The great war and modern memory*. Oxford: Oxford University Press. Cited in Hawley, R. A. (1993). *Boys will be men: Masculinity in troubled times* (p. xv). Forest Dale, VT: Paul S. Eriksson, Publisher.

Gardiner, J. K. (2001). Anxiety Attacks. *The Women's Review of Books*, Vol. XVIII, No. 5 (February, 2001). Wellesley, MA: The Women's Review, Inc., 27–28.

Gay, P. (1984). *The education of the senses, vol. 1, The bourgeois experience: Visotria to Freud*. NY: Simon & Schuster, Inc.

Graves, R. (1981). *Goodbye to all that* (Revised Edition). London, UK: The Folio Society (originally published by Jonathan Cape, 1929).

Hawley, R. A. (1993). *Boys will be men: Masculinity in troubled times.* Forest Dale, VT: Paul S. Eriksson, Publisher.

Hobsbawm, E. J. (1989). *The age of empire, 1875–1914,* cited in Izenberg, G. N. (2000). *Modernism & masculinity: Mann, Wedekind, Kandinsky through WWI* (p. 6). Chicago, IL: University of Chicago Press.

Horney, K. (1973). *Feminine Psychology.* NY: Norton.

Izenberg, G. N. (2000). *Modernism & masculinity: Mann, Wedekind, Kandinsky through WWI.* Chicago, IL: University of Chicago Press.

Keegan, J. (1999). *The first world war.* NY: Alfred A. Knopf.

Kindlon, D., & Thompson, M. (1999). *Raising Cain: Protecting the emotional lives of boys.* NY: Ballantine Books.

Mosse, G. L. (1996). *The image of man: The creation of modern masculinity.* NY & Oxford: Oxford University Press.

Mosse, G. L. (1985). *Nationalism and sexuality: Respectability and normal sexuality in modern Europe.* NY: Basic Books.

Robinson, S. (2000). *Marked men: White masculinity in crisis.* NY: Columbia University Press.

Schorske, C. (1981). *Fin-de-siècle Vienna: Politics and Culture.* NY: Vintage Books.

CHAPTER 3

WHAT MAKES A REAL MAN: A SOCIETAL INQUIRY

David M. Bossman

Looking back at the changing roles of men in the second millennium, we sense a wide range of values associated with masculinity. What strikes the observer as strange is that even though biologically the male function has remained constant, albeit shrouded in prescientific myth, the *social* meanings that constitute the roles of father, son, husband, brother, male friend, and partner, vary from culture to culture. A survey of male social roles and values over time and in social contexts presages notably different social expectations and values for the third millennium.

It is worth noting at the beginning that in the matter of biology, awareness of the role of males changed during the scientific revolution of the 17th and 18th centuries. Previous to advances in the natural sciences, the male typically was believed to plant the seed while the female provided the "soil" in which the father's child grew. This perception of the father's dominant biological role helped shape the female's subordinate social role. Such notable medievals as Thomas Aquinas believed that when a female child was born, something or someone had interfered with the formation of a full, ideal human, a male child. Such was the state of the natural sciences that supported the social perception of men into the second millennium.

Diverse societal perceptions of men produce perceptibly different gender values that even endure today. We shall see that differences exist not only over time, but between social worlds. It is necessary, before characterizing men for the 21st century, that we recognize the varieties of ways that societies view men over time and within cultures. A good starting point is a review of *Manhood in the Making: Cultural Concepts of Masculinity* by social anthropologist David D. Gilmore. This study examines the social functions of men in diverse settings around the world.

THE CIRCUM-MEDITERRANEAN MALE AND THE BIBLICAL CANON

The fact that a biblical view of men often passes as the most normative prompts us to reflect on the cultural matrix of the circum-Mediterranean social world whose cultural context produced these traditional male values. The spread of a biblical view of men is particularly significant when examining how people in the Judeo-Christian-Muslim worlds tend to characterize men and their social roles. The reach of the circum-Mediterranean model of manhood even today extends from the Eastern Mediterranean societies of the Semitic world to the Western Mediterranean societies of the Hispanic world, ranging as well into Latin American societies. While these societies manifest notable differences among themselves, overarching similarities in their socioreligious values of manhood are identifiable and deeply rooted.

Gilmore begins his study of the circum-Mediterranean world by explaining that many anthropologists have successfully examined this region in terms of their common view of manhood:

> Although not representing a unity in the sense of cultural homogeneity (Herzfeld 1980), many Mediterranean societies place importance on 'certain institutions' (Pitt-Rivers 1977:ix) that invite comparison. Aside from obvious resemblances in ecology, settlement patterns, and economic adaptations, what seems to provide a basis of comparison more than anything else is, in fact a shared image of manhood. . . . 'I also have a mustache' is an emblematic way to denote not only manliness, which is so common a concern around the Mediterranean, but also a style of anthropological argument calling for respect. (p. 31)

Manliness in this world is an essential requisite for honor. It brings both respect to the individual and "security to his family, lineage, or village, as these groups, sharing a collective identity, reflect the man's reputation and are protected by it" (p. 31). Forceful sexuality is typically associated with such manliness, as Gilmore explains: "This assertive courting . . . is an important, even essential requirement of manhood. . . . It is a recurrent aspect of the male image in many parts of southern Europe, whereas it seems less critical in the northern countries" (p. 40). He concludes:

> Most of what we know about Mediterranean ideas of manhood, in fact, concerns their more expressive components—more precisely, their sexual assertiveness (Pitt-Rivers 1977): the *machismo* of Spain and the *maschio* of Sicily (Giovannini 1987) are examples. There is also the *rajula* (virility) complex of Morocco (Geertz 1979:364), which has been likened specifically to Hispanic *machismo* by a female anthropologist (Mernissi 1975:4–5). There are parallels in the Balkans, which anthropological observers Simic (1969, 1983) and Denich (1974), male and female scholars

respectively, independently identify with the *machismo* of Hispanic culture. A real man in these countries is forceful in courtship as well as a fearless man of action. (pp. 40–41)

Accordingly, Gilmore observes how masculinity supports *honor*, the public recognition of status, the core Mediterranean value:

> [M]asculine honor is always bound up with aggression and potency. A real man in Sicily is 'a man with big testicles' (Blok 1981:432–33); his potency is firmly established. Among the Sarakatsani of Greece, also, an adult male must be 'well endowed with testicles' (J. K. Campbell 1964:269), quick to arousal, insatiable in the act. Such beliefs also hold true for much of Spain, especially the south (Pitt-Rivers 1965: 1977; Brandes 1980, 1981; Mitchell 1988), where a real man is said to have much cohones, or balls. Such big-balled men, naturally, tower over and dominate their less well-endowed and more phlegmatic fellows. (p. 41)

The ultimate test of a man's virility is procreating offspring, preferably boys to carry on his name and occupation. A large and vigorous family is a man's best sign of virility and honor, and a man's ability to provide for his family is similarly a confirmation of honor. Responsibility for family life is foundational in Mediterranean societies. It is a man's duty, which, when shirked, brings shame. A man's well-disciplined family confirms his honor and brings honor to all in the household. Duty to household and kin is ultimately central to Mediterranean notions of honor: "Honor is about being good at being a man, which means building up and buttressing the family or kindred" (p. 43).

Bravery accompanies the ability to procreate and maintain family discipline as a sign of virility. Self-control and courage (*hombría*) may take many forms to show off manliness and willingness to defend family against any threat (p. 45). Cunning to protect and advance family fortunes demonstrates male potency (see Pilch, 1992) (p. 48).

Biblical scholar Bruce Malina, in two articles published in *Biblical Theology Bulletin* (Malina, 1989, 1992), finds prescribed gender roles in the Bible similar to these anthropological findings. The importance of Malina's studies, and those by biblical scholars who use social scientific resources to aid in interpreting the Bible, is the recognition that the Bible mirrors many of the cultural characteristics of circum-Mediterranean sexual stereotypes. Thus, biblical values reflect the Mediterranean cultural context in which they had their primary application. Malina observes that men in the Bible characteristically are social role-players more than introspective individuals as assumed in our own more psychological culture. Thus, Malina observes: "The extreme Mediterranean emphasis on the human genitals (e.g., circumcision, phallus as evil-eye apotropaic, castration concerns), on sexual transgression, and on the male uncertainty of his maleness are part of the same scenario . . ." (1989, p. 133). These are factors that require due attention when citing biblical texts as somehow a statement of the way things "ought" to be, or as "God intended them."

Is there another way of exercising masculinity than this honor-bound, family-dependent, physical mode of public demonstration? A survey of other social worlds can help answer the question, what makes a real man.

MALE VALUES IN AN EMERGING PLURALISTIC SOCIETY

Pluralism exists as a sociopolitical system when society recognizes individuals as having personal identity rights that society acknowledges and respects. Lacking such civil liberties, the prerogatives of collectivities take over and the dominant group assumes control and defines behavior of both persons and groups. While many societies have experienced diverse groups in their midst, lacking personal civil liberties rendered them a conglomerate rather than a pluralistic society, since individuals are tightly bound to their groups and defined by them.

In pluralistic societies, where operative civil rights allow people to be independent individuals with guarantees of nondiscrimination, people can break loose of stereotyped sexual roles and be freed of predetermined cultural and group-enforced scripts. It should not be assumed that such a pluralistic society now fully exists so much as that it has become progressively more realized as civil rights are more liberally interpreted in favor of individuals and their independent identities.

In his book *Manhood in America: A Cultural History* (1996), Michael Kimmel traces the development of the independent man, or self-made man, as a core factor in defining the male that now faces the 21st century: "Part of this start, the American Revolution, brought a revolt of the sons against the father—in this case, the Sons of Liberty against Father England" (1996, p. 18). Already the break from duty to father and family, so foundational in Mediterranean cultures, became a characteristic of American life, and this, in favor of personal liberty. It should be noted that in the Gospels, the sin of the prodigal son was precisely this, that he left his father; evil consequences could only follow upon such a decision. Now, in revolutionary America, it becomes the norm. What follows upon this is the redefinition of manhood: "Many Genteel Patriarchs looked to England not just for political and economic props but also for cultural prescriptions for behavior." Accordingly, "The real problem was that as long as the colonies remained in British hands, it seemed to all that manly autonomy and self-control were impossible. Being a man meant being in charge of one's own life, liberty, and property." Thus, "The American Revolution resolved this tension because, in the terms of the reigning metaphor of the day, it freed the sons from the tyranny of a despotic father. The Declaration of Independence was a declaration of manly adulthood, a manhood that was counterposed to the British version against which American men were revolting" (pp. 18–19). But, before we get ahead of ourselves, Kimmel sagely observes,

"Of course, the rebellion of the sons did not eliminate the need for patriarchal authority. George Washington was immediately hailed as the Father of our Country, and many wished he would become king" (p. 19). The tendency seems to be that once one's liberty is achieved, it is soon compromised by a call for a return to some version of the previous conformity.

The next form of subordination came to men as artisan-producers. Kimmel describes this return to subordination in these terms:

> The sons of the Sons of Liberty were fast becoming, as they put it in a letter of protest to President John Tyler, 'mere machines of labor.' Ironically, the same experiences that cemented their solidarity and underscored their autonomy now left them isolated and defensive. While, politically, democracy had 'hastened the destruction of onerous forms of personal subordination to masters, landlords, and creditors that American working people had historically faced,' writes the labor historian David Montgomery, it also left them unprotected from unscrupulous masters and conniving employers and disconnected from others who shared a similar fate. (p. 31)

Voluntary political groups, distinct from family or clan power structures, formed to help defend the individual's rights: the Mechanics Union of Trade Associations (1827), the Workingmen's Party (1828), and the Equal Rights Party (1833). Kimmel notes, "These organizations' rhetoric was saturated with equations of autonomy and manhood. Loss of autonomy was equated with emasculation, economic dependence on wages paid by an employer was equivalent to social and sexual dependency" (p. 31). Andrew Jackson emerged as a charismatic male whose passion for independence helped define an emerging masculine ideal, characterized by historian Frederick Jackson Turner as a "tall, lank, uncouth-looking personage, with long locks of hair hanging over his face and a cue down his back tied in an eel skin; his dress singular, his manners those of a rough backwoodsman" (p. 33). Kimmel comments: "It is difficult not to see Jackson and the men he stood for in starkly Freudian terms. Here was the fatherless son, struggling without guidance to separate from the mother and, again, for adult mastery over his environment. Terrified of infantilization, of infantile dependency, his rage propelled the furious effort to prove his manhood against those who threatened it . . ." (p. 33).

The doctrine of self-control emerged in the 19th century, according to Kimmel's study, as a means by which men defined their otherwise shaky identity, set adrift from family and subordinating corporate structures.

> For a young man seeking his fortune in such a free and mobile society, identity was no longer fixed, and there was no firm patriarchal lineage to ground a secure sense of himself as a man. For the first time in American history, young men experienced 'identity crises.' 'Sons had to compete for elusive manhood in the market rather than grow into secure manhood by replicating fathers. Where many could never attain

the self-made manhood of success, middle class masculinity pushed egotism to extremes of aggression, calculation, self-control and un-remitting effort.' The Self-Made Man was a control freak. (p. 45)

However, what was seen as needing control were men's sexual expression and drinking habits. Self-control became the focus for numerous self-im-provement manuals; abstention from sex and liquor, and dedication to the se-vere life were at the heart of their message. Curtailed sexual intercourse and the elimination of masturbation became prime objectives for self-control. Ear-lier heavy drinking habits were shunned in the name of self-discipline. Kim-mel adds: "Other social reformers promoted temperance as part of larger reforms. Abolitionists William Lloyd Garrison and Theodore Weld, for exam-ple, linked intemperance and slavery; each, they argued, was economically wasteful as well as immoral" (p. 50). A curious confusion concerning women emerged in this repressive environment: that women were seductive temptresses or pious, asexual angels, "who, at the merest mention of the body and its desires, would faint straight away. These projections led to what was perhaps the most significant development in the relations between the sexes prior to the birth of feminism" (p. 50).

This development was the separation of male from female spheres by which "men ceded both responsibility and authority over household man-agement" so "the home would be a balm to soothe men from the roughness of the working day. The workplace was masculinized, the home feminized" (p. 53). Accordingly, "women were not to be excluded from participation in the public sphere as much as exempted from participation in such a competitive and ugly world" (p. 54). The Cult of True Womanhood was invented and in the succeeding social manuals the woman was characterized as " a moral, a sex-ual, a germiferous, gestative, and parturient creature 'whose head is almost too small for intellect but just big enough for love' " (p. 54). In addition, the woman's job was "to act as moral restraint, since men, alone, were not capa-ble of restraining their baser emotions, their violence, their aggressive, com-petitive, acquisitive edge."

Abolitionists and supporters of women's rights played an ambiguous role within this complex of emerging issues of sexual identity. The morality they preached was of a feminine cast of compassion for the enslaved or subordi-nated. Male abolitionists had to prove their masculinity against this associa-tion with the feminine. Kimmel explains: "Such a debate illustrates a theme we encounter again and again throughout American history. Support for femi-nism or civil rights has been seen as an indication that a man is less than manly—as if support for inequality somehow made one more of a man" (p. 72). On the other hand, for the slaves, fighting for freedom was regarded as a manly endeavor: "The Civil War also represented a claim for manhood on the part of black men" (p. 73). Thus, Frederick Douglass, a freed slave, claims that he "'was a changed being.' He had been 'nothing before; I was A MAN NOW,' he writes in *My Bondage and My Freedom*" (p. 74). On the other hand, "for southern men, defeat meant a kind of gendered humiliation—the southern gentleman was discredited as a 'real man'" (p. 77). Amid all this dislodging of values, "the combined impact of these processes led many men to feel frightened, cut loose from the traditional moorings of their identities, adrift in some anomic sea. By the last decades of the century, manhood was widely perceived to be in crisis" (p. 78).

THE 20TH-CENTURY IMPACT ON MALE VALUES

At the turn of the century, masculinity was in crisis. The time-honored ways of exercising masculinity were threatened in the North by the dizzying growth of cities, where men were caught in a web of rapid change, crowded conditions, and bitter competition for economic security amid the rising tide of immigrants and the migration of Blacks to the North. Waves of resentment washed over various groups that threatened male security—immigrants, Blacks, women, homosexuals. Thus, nativism, racism, antifeminism, and homophobia became fixtures in the threatened male domain. In the South, "The Ku Klux Klan and other fraternal orders, the founding of and expansion of military schools designed to produce 'officers and gentlemen,' and a revival of dueling to preserve personal honor all temporarily gave southern white men a respite from this perceived assault on their manhood" (p. 95). The rhetoric used by Klan members was "saturated with images of heroic and chivalrous Southern manhood" and "members were required to demonstrate 'manly' character and courage."

At the same time that defensive efforts were under way to push women out of the workplace, by the end of the 19th and the beginning of the 20th century the growth of a visible gay subculture began to emerge in the nation's cities. Kimmel argues that at the turn of the century "masculinity was increasingly an act, a form of public display; that men felt themselves on display at virtually all times; and that the intensity of the need for such display was increasing. To be considered a real man, one had better make sure to always be walking around and acting 'real masculine'" (p. 100). Considerable energy was expended to distance this demonstrative masculinity from gays, who, perhaps because of styles of the day, came to be caricatured in a feminine mode and as such became targets for men attempting to "prove" their masculinity.

The war against women in the workplace took a political turn when women's liberation came to be associated with the emergence of socialist ideals. Some men, including those of the Men's League for Woman Suffrage, founded by Max Eastman in 1910, supported women's liberation. "Many of these men saw the social revolution offered by feminist demands for personal autonomy as the personal complement to the socialist revolution," writes Kimmel, and thereby "linked socialist economic critiques of American capitalism with a feminist critique of sexual repression" (p. 115).

The teaching profession became the emerging occupation open to women at this time. According to Kimmel, in 1910 four of every five elementary-school teachers were women, an increase from three fourths in 1900 and two thirds in 1870 (p. 121). This created anxiety that women were thereby "feminizing" boys. Others believed that "over-civilization" had made men "over-sophisticated and effete." To counter this, gyms and sports playing fields took on a new importance as men sought to exercise their muscles in pursuit of a strong, competitive male physique. Men like Theodore Roosevelt touted the benefits of the rugged outdoors to restore the "flagging manhood of modern civilized men" (p. 135). War served to flaunt American male prowess over flaccid Europeans. Cowboys became a "mythic creation" as "fierce and brave, willing to venture into unknown territory . . . and tame it for women, children, and emasculated civilized men" (p. 149). Edgar Rice Burrough's novel *Tarzan of the Apes* (1912) emerged as an icon representing the contrast between modern civilization and the virile man's ability to control nature.

Wars have provided proving grounds for male virtues. Twentieth-century wars offered an ample antidote to the cultural crises of the late 19th and early 20th centuries. Early in the century, boys were expected to "stand up and fight" to assure themselves of respect by their peers. Stiff discipline assured boys of a proper education in manly ways, to which hazing was a valued means for "toughening up" new students. College sports emerged as battlegrounds. The Boy Scouts of America's founders imagined that they were re-creating virile backwoodsmen and Indian fighters, resourceful men of action noted for their patriotism. Religionists turned to a "muscular Christianity," which, in the imagery of the Reverend Billy Sunday, a former professional baseball player who became an itinerant evangelical preacher, produced fighting saints. "Moral warfare makes a man hard. Superficial peace makes a man mushy," he proclaimed, "The Prophets all carried the Big Stick" (p. 180).

So it was that Big Stick diplomacy came to rule in the 20th century. But while warfare enabled many men to distinguish themselves as heroes, a variety of factors arose in 20th-century warfare that disturbed the received view of masculinity, both in the United States and around the globe. First, the war efforts brought women back into the workforce and demonstrated that women are fully able to meet a variety of job demands previously deemed suited only for men—management, teamwork, technical skills, deferred child-care responsibilities, financial independence. Second, war challenged the caricature of men as robust warriors, easily aggressive and violent on demand. Many who came back from war could only attest to their fear, inability to fight, despair in the face of enemy fire, injuries that left them totally dependent—realities that flew in the face of jingoistic fantasy about manhood and warriors. Third, upon reentry following the wars, men had to face new challenges that war had not resolved, only postponed. The Depression of the 1930s reduced many war heroes to poverty. The prosperity of the 1950s brought men back into a society that demanded conformity as much as vigor. And, as the century ended, the fallout of the Cold War quickly demonstrated that the Big Stick simply wasn't adequate to right every wrong or meet every challenge.

Kimmel identifies several of these as factors in defining male values in the 20th century in the light of changes brought about because of war and depression: efforts to remasculinize the workplace through bonding and to exclude others from it (p. 197); turning toward the future in terms of providing sons with more advantages than Depression-era fathers had (p. 201); clearly delineating male and female characteristics so that parents could affirm gender-appropriate qualities in their children, eschewing homosexual identity factors (pp. 204–210). Freudian assumptions about the male sex role—static, a historical container of attitudes, behaviors, and values that are appropriate to men and define masculine behavior—became reified in an array of male-specific interests and activities in American life, producing what became known in literature as the Hemingway hero. Cult film figures like Clark Gable, Montgomery Clift, Rock Hudson, Tom Selleck, and Sean Connery exemplified this male icon. In fact, they were often roles rather than actual sexual identities as was later learned when several such icons' sexual orientation became known, as did Rock Hudson's, through the contraction of AIDS, which spread widely through the gay community. Soon, "coming out" as a gay man carried much less societal impact than it did at the time of Oscar Wilde, whose homosexuality won him a prison term, as it had gained abuse and contempt for many others throughout the 20th century.

The vacuousness of attempts to "remasculinize" society became progressively more clear as women in fact did not leave the workforce, their positions made secure by legislative and judicial guarantees of nondiscrimination based on gender. Discrimination against homosexuals has recently begun to subside as issues of civil rights have been taken up by legislatures and courts, exemplified by nondiscrimination laws as well as fledgling efforts at securing equal treatment legislation in the matter of civil unions. The century that began with men in identity crisis ended on the edge of a sexual revolution that returned to the foundational questions of individual freedom, personal identity, and the right to make independent choices. Men's liberation began to be seen as the right of men to be individual persons, free to live their lives in ways that best suits their abilities and personalities.

THE 21ST CENTURY RISING

Competition in the workforce, responsibilities at home, and mutuality in marriage are all on the rise as the 21st-century man emerges from the crises of the 20th century. In a workforce characterized by few remaining men-only limitations, the workplace progressively is oriented toward gender equality, although that goal is not fully realized, as the term "glass ceiling" for women suggests. Efforts to enact an equal-rights constitutional amendment (ERA) having failed, it becomes the responsibility of individual states to enact nondiscrimination legislation and to oversee the manner in which it is enforced. At the dawning of the 21st century, virtually every state has such legislation—the same cannot be said for discrimination based on sexual orientation. Movement is afoot in this direction, notably within Democratic legislatures. Conservatives, especially in the Republican party, tend to see any such legislation as troubling or abhorrent. But many Republican legislators have voted for nondiscrimination based on gender, and even, in some cases, on sexual orientation. Gay children or siblings of legislators have tended to exert some influence on the legislators, regardless of party affiliation, but this is not a guarantee of legislative concern. Today's Vice President Cheney and his wife, Lynn, remain largely in denial about their daughter being a lesbian. Newt Gingrich's sister, who is also a lesbian, has had small impact on the attitudes of her brother in the matter of supporting antidiscrimination legislation for sexual orientation.

Similarly, conservatives have largely opposed legislation supporting affirmative action, by which women and minorities having equal qualifications for a position should be given priority based upon past manifest discrimination. In the 2000 presidential debates, Al Gore, the Democratic candidate, supported affirmative action without quotas, while George W. Bush refused to give his support for anything more than "affirmative access," a term he refused to define or specify in terms of concrete steps for implementation. Nonetheless, the path has been laid for women to gain protection from discrimination in the workplace. Court cases have increasingly awarded damages when women have suffered discrimination, been harassed, or otherwise missed opportunities for equal treatment in the workforce. Men in the 21st century are largely more sensitive to diversity, more willing to accept women coworkers and bosses, and in general engage in less sexist language and activities. Television sitcoms, such as *All in the Family*, as well as documentaries, such as *One Woman One Vote*, have underscored the societal change in attitudes that emerged during the 20th century and have largely taken root in mainstream American life at the dawning of the 21st century.

Mutuality in marriage partnerships and household management has become commonplace, in which the husband and wife act by mutual agreement rather than by gender-specific roles. Parenting is less a matter of "father knows best" than of shared time and commitment to family. In the home, parents are partners, not complements, making joint decisions, sharing tasks, and contributing to the common table with growing equality. Employers now routinely supply parenting leaves (formerly maternity leaves) for both men and women at the birth of a child. Personal days are afforded both men and women for childcare. Single-parent custody of children can be either father or mother, depending on individual circumstances. Adoptions by single parents are becoming more common.

Civil unions may increasingly become the wave of the 21st century as traditional marriages begin to occur well into a live-in arrangement within heterosexual as well as homosexual relationships. Even traditional families now tend to accept this change in social mores, allowing for living arrangements that in the past might have been deemed scandalous. In place of the more formal traditional religious wedding ceremony, there may well be a civil union for both forms of sexual orientation, with a civil ceremony confirming a relationship that has effect in law without raising the question of religious affirmation unless and until the couple choose to pursue a religious ceremony. This civil union would provide spouses with the legal rights without defining the union "marriage" in the religious sense. Long-term sexual partnerships have gained a legal footing for both sexual orientations, and legislatures may be inclined to regularize the implicit reality by setting up procedures to clarify such unions. This would allow the actual partner to participate in health-care plans, participate as the responsible party and primary caregiver in the case of medical necessity, and share in spousal rights in case of separation.

While these developments are "in the works," in many instances they remain trends rather than full realities. There remains the question of how masculinity is to be defined amid such changes in community customs and laws. What seems to be on the downslide is the earlier strong need to prove masculinity in a world in which being a man carried notable benefits and demands. Lessening the benefits and demands makes it less incumbent on men to assert or prove masculinity by living a stereotype or exaggerating a sex-specific role. This does not mean that sexual attraction has been displaced. In the case of courtship and partnering, there will continue to be a clear exploitation of sexual characteristics that attract interest and support partnering. Even in same-sex partnerships, there is increasing comfort in maintaining social friendships regardless of one's own sexual orientation. Living amid diversity seems to be the norm rather than the exception, with friends supporting friends in whatever their choices in partners may be. Similarly, family ties, which in the past were gravely at risk for gays choosing same-sex partners, are largely left intact as simply "a fact of life" to be accepted, along with other forms of diversity that impact families within a pluralistic society.

Finally, it should be noted that the continuing impact of AIDS within society should not be underestimated. A recent op-ed column in the New York Times (Herbert, 2001) points to the devastation that has occurred among African-Americans and can be expected to rage largely unchecked unless dramatic steps are taken. No longer "the gay scourge," which extreme religionists and moralistic scolds once proclaimed as God's punishment on homosexuals, AIDS has become a disease for one in 60 black men and one in 225 black women in the United States today, to say nothing of its frequency in other countries and regions of the world. The raised frequency in black *men* seems to stem from a longstanding economic and social demoralization of black men, who turn in despair to drugs, sharing contaminated needles that spread the bloodborne virus. Women addicts as well as sex partners share equally in the spread of the virus. What seems most important in this correlative evidence of male economic and social dysfunction is that those men whose sexual identity and psychological well-being has been undermined within society must be understood for the social and economic reality that they represent. Education, job placement programs, and minimum wage laws are vitally important in redressing the reality of the plight of minorities of both sexes. Funds deferred in providing these government programs will otherwise be spent in medical and penal system costs. The cost to taxpayers is the same, but the human devastation is inestimable.

CONCLUSIONS

With respect to comparisons and contrasts, men in American culture continue over time to seek personal means by which to express their individuality, find and fulfill their potential, and provide meaningful service and support to loved ones and society. The great difference that might be underscored is between men in traditional collectivist societies that define relatively stable gender-specific roles, compared against men in evolving individualistic societies in which persons have more freedom to define themselves and seek their place in society. This distinction is necessary to make when viewing sacred texts as somehow normative for people of all ages and places. The religious traditions that have the greatest influence within American culture today emanate from a collectivist social world, that of the circum-Mediterranean matrix, which assumes a radically different basis for personal identity. Men in the collectivist social context learn how to be men in largely predefined and scripted roles. Men in an individualistic social context must learn how to create their own sexual identities in a changing set of societal circumstances. In the end, we witness two diverse kinds of men—those who are men according to a set formula, and those who are men through personal choices.

Given this distinction, the norm by which men internalize their gender identity is much broader and more nuanced for the individualist male as he works through the particularities of his own personality and the opportunities and needs of the world around him. Thus, the individualist male becomes what the U.S. Army recruitment slogan says, "a one-person army," in the sense that he must make choices, take responsibility, and be effective. It should be noted, however, that now this one-person army can be either male or female. What was once the charge to men has become shared with women in a universe that no longer defines a person by his or her sex. On the contrary, any partnership that today's man enters into is based on equality and mutuality with other persons, regardless of their sexuality. Biology has its place but is not the singular controlling factor in personal identity.

The 21st-century man has the legacy of a pluralistic society that more and more values respect for individuals over subordination to roles. This allows the ongoing displacement of role expectations with the creation of responsible individuality, a promising feature for a society that values diversity and builds creatively upon it. Values associated with individualistic pluralism move to valuing integrity as an internal disposition of honesty rather than gender-based honor; assessing personal worth based on achievement rather than family status; preferring strength in personal control over domination of others; and celebrating a father as one who nurtures rather than one who claims authority, a son as one who sets goals and works toward them rather than one who stays home to inherit his father's estate, and a partner as one who is a team player rather than master of the house.

REFERENCES

Gilmore, D. D. (1990). *Manhood in the making: Cultural concepts of masculinity.* New Haven, CT: Yale University Press.

Herbert, B. (2001, January 11). The quiet scourge. *New York Times,* Op-Ed page.

Kimmel, M. (1996). *Manhood in America: A cultural history.* New York: The Free Press.

Malina, B. J. (1989). Dealing with biblical (Mediterranean) characters: A guide for U.S. consumers. *Biblical Theology Bulletin,* 19, 127–141.

Malina, B. J. (1992). Is there a circum-Mediterranean person? Looking for stereotypes. *Biblical Theology Bulletin,* 22, 66–87.

Pilch, J. (1992). Lying and deceit in the letters to the seven churches. *Biblical Theology Bulletin,* 22, 126–135.

Tiger, L. (1984). *Men in groups.* New York: Marion Boyars.

CHAPTER 4

REFLECTIONS OF A MIDDLE-AGED MALE PSYCHOTHERAPIST ON THE SENSE OF OTHERNESS IN MALES[1]

Howard Covitz

> *He thought he saw an Argument*
> *That proved he was the Pope;*
> *He looked again, and found it was*
> *A Bar of Mottled Soap.*
> *'A fact so dread,' he faintly said,*
> *'Extinguishes all hope.'*
> —Refrain from the Gardener's Song in Lewis Carroll's *Sylvie and Bruno*, 1889

I sometimes imagine an array of mirrors. Some of these surfaces are fine reflectors while others are foggy or cracked or only partially reflective due to some aging process in the surface's material. Some face each other and others face away. Diagonal, orthogonal, pairwise skewed—a congeries of mirrors set in a never-to-be-replicated pattern.

I imagine choosing a spot in a singular mirror upon which to focus my gaze. I shall have arrived at this moment and this place and this choice of spot after years of trekking through many other such *mirror mazes*. Still, I shall now marvel and fascinate at the array of sequential visions that are visible through this chosen spot in this mirror. The images will stare back at me at that moment. Not simple images, but compound ones that, if I look with care, may include

---

[1]While these thoughts borrow freely from ideas set forth in this author's Œdipal Paradigms in Collision: A Centennial Emendation of a Piece of Freudian Canon (1897–1997), a volume which proffered a gender-free object relational model for Œdipal development, they owe their origins with all due thanks to Marsha, with whom I have been involved for some 35 years in matrimonial experiments surrounding matters of similarities and differences, of male and female, of mother and father. The author would like to extend thanks, as well, to the editors of this volume for affording a quite rare opportunity to speak about and to be heard articulating the life and private theories of a singular therapist.

me, the intrusive observer who has inadvertently been cast as a shadowy figure in his own observations. And after all is done and looked at, what shall I know of what I see? What is? What is smoke and mirrors? And what may be contingent on the choice of the chosen spot arrived at here at this random point in the midst of travels? And what shall be known of the identity of others who fortuitously may be looking in on this maze of mirrors just as I do?

Still and all, we participant-observers draw conclusions about the observed and write up these conclusions following consensually acceptable professional-literary guidelines in well-parsed sentences. Some of these conclusions are communicated to others. Some are maintained in silence. Many such conclusions that arise from such observations are responsive to queries relating to who I am in the diverse roles that I come to play in life. Who am I as child to parents? Sibling to brothers and sisters? Friend to friend? Lover to lover? Parent to child? Among them are those relating to who I am as a gendered other to my others. Male to Female and other Male? Female to Male and other Female?

Walzer (1987), while attempting to define criticality in social thought, opined that:

> Criticism requires critical distance. But what does that mean? . . . critical distance divides the self; when we step back (mentally), we create a double. Self one is still involved, committed, parochial, angry; self two is detached, dispassionate, impartial, quietly watching self one. . . . Self three would be better still . . . We form a certain picture of ourselves and the picture is painful. But this is most often a picture of ourselves as we are seen or think we are seen . . . by people we value. We do not look at ourselves from nowhere in particular but through the eyes of particular other people. . . . We apply standards that we share with the others to the others. (pp. 49–52)

Walzer has, in some sense perhaps, captured my dilemma. I feel a compelling need for attachment to a multiplicity of constituent parts of me that meet the World. These allow for the possibility of experience and feeling that are birthed, in part, by some repeated internal feedback mechanism from the others who populate my World and who appear peering back at me in and from my maze of mirrors.

Like Carroll's befuddled and befuddling Gardener (in the opening vignette), I may come to imagine that the organization of my visions about myself and about who I am represent a structured *argument* about the observed. These may be thought to have the *infallible* force of the Mathematics that Carroll, the eccentric teacher of this subject, presented as Tutor to Christ College. Like the Gardener, however, who mouths these words with tears rolling down his cheeks, I must be prepared to consider that, in fact, I typically find aught but a cursorily assembled handful of miscolored fats that may well melt away under the pressures of a lone trickle of water. A voice calls out to me from an inhospitable and poorly landmarked wilderness: Change your focus in the mirrors and change your reality! Maybe so.

In any case, I shall take this opportunity to reflect on a number of matters that relate to the interweaving of my senses of myself as a person and as a male person. Particularly, I find myself drawn to matters connected to my perception of myself as another to another. I shall be hard-pressed to separate out what others perceive in me from what I imagine they see in me. Therefore, I shall be unable to unambiguously separate between the two that I continue to consider the standard equipment that I bring to any and all considerations of this kind. I shall be satisfied to have shared the views of a singular male who *qua* child, sibling, lover/husband, father, and male therapist has arrived . . . somehow and somewhere or other into the 21st century.[2]

IDENTIFICATIONS: AM I BUT MY FATHER'S SON?

Let me be more direct and personal about my intentions in this brief communication which seeks to place nagging questions in the path of growing theoretical certainties surrounding matters of *gendered identifications*. To begin! I am a male therapist originally trained in the Freudian *genre* who has come to an idiosyncratic object relations perspective in his practice. The visitors who occasion my office are either female or male and typically consider themselves either homosexual or heterosexual, as the case may be. My image of myself *qua* therapist is of a carefully attentive but blind beach-walker accompanying a sighted companion. My fellow traveler chooses, from time to time, to share with me his or her visions from the nearby surf to which we both—in our own ways—attend and from which, in some odd fashion, our forebears first crawled up upon dry land.

My blindness is, alas, a part of my ideal image of myself as therapist and not fully realizable. This is to be expected and a flaw for which, due to its ubiquity, I need not apologize. We all arrive at the *maze of mirrors* (alluded to at the beginning of this discussion) situated at some locus from which we view our world. I *am*, as just noted, *a male*. But what can this possibly mean? Does it denote the fact that I was androgenized *in utero*? Does it refer to the fact that I belong to a group that—statistically speaking—wields more power than the group that remained true to its Universal female origins by eschewing fetal androgenization? Perhaps, the statement that I *am male* specifies a pathway by which choices were made to identify more strongly with my father than with my mother? I think not!

The first two alternatives sound too pat and the third appears to circumnavigate the complexity of the matter. True, it is, that I was androgenized by some miracle of my mother's endocrine system. Truth, too, it may well have

---

[2]As an aside, I find it a daunting experience to have entered this new century and, yet, to be aware that I shall always be thought of as a 20th-century thinker. It is only recently that I have been able to experience the violence that my own generation perpetrated against those who came before us and whose works straddled two centuries. These subdivisions and their ilk, be they like century markers cutting up time or gender classes separating people, are among the most curious and, perhaps, gratuitously destructive creations of clan *anthropos*.

been preferable during the half-plus century of my life to don the attire and behaviors of other males. And it is even so that in a variety of ways I am identified with my father and (maternal) grandfather; I recognize, for instance, a delight in the visceral that I adopted from my father and an equal pleasure in the ethereal that I borrowed from my ecclesiastical *grandpa*. But how, pray tell, do I separate out my father or, for that matter, my grandfather from the *fathers* I visioned or fantasied in my mother's eyes? Or carrying it a bit closer to my own *maze of mirrors*, how may I separate either of the above identifications from the one that obtains from looking at my father's view of my mother's images of her husband and father? And so on—throughout a never-ending sequence of mirrored images which includes *inter alia* a multiplicity of identifications with my mother.

Statistical discoveries about gender identifications are statements about a group and are, in this manner, pertinent only to the study of social psychology and to probabilistic guessing about a given individual's psyche. Clinically speaking, matters are never so forthright. While Freud's views on the child's identification with the similar-sex parent are well known, his doubts about whether children in the post-Œdipal phase identified predominantly with the same-sex parent or rather with both parents are less often cited. He notes, for instance (Freud, 1923, pp. 33–34): "In my opinion it is advisable in general, and quite especially where neurotics are concerned, to assume the existence of the complete Œdipus complex . . . the four trends of which it consists will group themselves in such a way as to produce a father-identification and a mother-identification." I would add that, beyond these first-order identifications with mother and father, we must attend to the mirrored second-order ones—father-in-mother and mother-in-father—and others beyond. No template is, alas, available for the *gendered maze of mirrors*, thus generated! And the experimental literature is no more helpful in extricating this therapist from his *perplexities* in treating either a nominally female or nominally male patient (see appendix which reviews a number of studies) or in coming to understand his own *maleness*. I am left, then, with myself and with my singular images of myself as a male and all remarks that follow must be examined in this narrow context—the phenomenology of me.

BEING ANOTHER: CONFESSIONS OF AN ENVIOUS MALE[3]

Maleness and femaleness elude the boundaried world of measurable biological and psychological gifts passed down from father to son and mother to daughter. Without denying the impact that endocrine/hormonal messengers

---

[3]There is always some danger in providing personal anecdotes. This study is, after all, an attempt to offer a contribution to the sense of maleness at the turn of the century. Many in the world of science equate objectivity with rigor—and subjectivity with either sloppiness or polemics. And one who openly demonstrates his personal interest in the subject matter of his work is, at times, not looked upon favorably. I have, however, so frequently exposed this penchant of mine that one more occurrence can hardly change the world's view of this author or his work.

may have on behavior, nearly as much of our taste for the world seems to be inherited from our other-sexed parent as from the same-sex parent (again, see appendix), and variation within each gender class may well be equally far-ranging as comparable variation between these classes. Still and all, my experience of the world as a male—as well as my perception of how this world perceives me—may well possess qualities that are unique to my gender class.

As I write these words and repeat them to myself, I fear gagging on them. Did I not spend the past 22 years of my life talking-up, promoting, and writing ponderously (Covitz, 1997) about a revised Œdipus? This model was a gender-free developmental paradigm whose maturational goal in both sexes was the development of a capacity for cherishing the inner stirrings and relationships of others—an ongoing battle that was to be, in each instance, first tested out on the parents. Was I not the same person who often spoke light-heartedly about the many similarities between the most fundamental wishes of men and women?[4] Hadn't my wife and I tried to raise our three children in an unambiguously egalitarian style? Perhaps I was the same person. Perhaps not. These thoughts bring me to adult memories. In each such instance, the sense of otherness was manifest and may well—in some manner or another—have related to my sense of maleness. They represent my confessions as an envious male and a sense of the potential healthfulness that may precipitate from the role of *the other.*

I Want Mommy

Bettelheim (1954) studied the envious male in African and Australian tribes and with children in his Orthogenic School. He went so far as to claim that all creative endeavors relate to mimicry and envy of the fecund mother. This information was certainly never a necessary condition, however, in order for me to envy my wife and her ability to birth and her further abilities, thereafter, to remain *as one* with each child; I came to these, myself.[5] Everywhere I looked, the power of the mother and her relationship to her child were heralded and praised. I recall when my wife and I were dating and joined throngs of souls, cued up from morning till night at the New York World's Fair to pass by and steal a brief glimpse at Michelangelo's *Pieta.* All gathered to view Mary with the crucified Jesus draped over her lap. And when we traveled, everywhere were statues of *Maria mit kind* and everywhere, too, were youngsters tagging along after mothers, holding on, like devotees clinging with sacred reverence to Goddesses.

We thought *we* would be different. My wife and I would rear our young with attachments—more or less equal—to both of us! Ah! But as the youngsters of a later generation might say: *Right!*

---

[4]When asked to address an audience in 1995 about Gray's popular Mars-Venus model, I agreed providing only that the talk was titled: Women Are from Mars and Men Have a Penis.

[5]I use the word *envy* generically, separating out in my own mind between *malignant envy,* in which one seeks harm for the possessor of the envied object, and *benevolent envy,* where good wishes may be directed at the other, in spite of their good fortune!

No. I suspect Abelin (1971,1975,1980) was closer to the truth. He argued (based on observational studies) that among the father's most important roles is to permit the child to initiate detachment from the primary symbiotic relationship to mother. This phase of dual-unity with mother is essential to the development and solidification of the all-important ability to love. Important, too, is the child's capacity to increase the orbit of applicability of this love and to reach out to others. Father appears as a first such *other*. His presence allows for triangulation out of the maternal dyad, would foster a sort of emotional parallax, and would promote a depth of field in relationships by being *background* to mother's *foreground*. *Mater semper certus*, the Roman law said, and while it meant to refer to the relative certainty of maternal identity over the relative uncertainty of paternal identity (*pater semper incertus*), it may well hide a more profound truth. Namely, the relationship to mom is in some fundamental way more substantive and less shadowy than that with dad.

In this world, a saying goes, you have to take your medicine but you don't have to lick the spoon. Try as I might to be warm and available, I was not *the Mommy* and throughout the early years of our children's lives—at least from time to time—was relegated to the role of some Virgil who might guide a despairing and frightened Dante toward safety but could never be the source of that security. I *want Mommy*, they would say. At best, perhaps, I could see myself as the *other or surrogate mommy*. At worst, I might become the envious outsider not to be permitted, except as an observer, into that sacred meeting.

Why Can't You Be Like Other Fathers?

I came to appreciate my role as *other* and helper, as my children and I developed relationships different from the one they had with my wife but quite intimate and close, nonetheless. If I may paraphrase *Ethics of the Fathers*: Who is healthy? He who comes to rejoice in his life's roles. I was better at play than my wife (though, *qua* fan of such contests, they tended to watch televised professional athletics with her), more comfortable with intellectual frolics (Bettelheim's comments recalled), and was, perhaps, better at listening without advising. I had gifts to offer, that is, and enjoyed sharing them. And then came adolescence! One of my kids struck the blow that began, as memory would have it, the demolition of my fantasies for an uninterrupted life of shared moments with my kids:

> Dad, I can't invite people over to the house on Sunday. I just can't. Fathers are supposed to be chilling out, leaning back with a beer can in one hand and the remote in the other, transfixed on the tube. That's the way dads are. *Why can't you be like other fathers*? You sit there reading and doing stupid stuff.

And so, beginning precipitously—and lasting for some five years—I, again, became the other—this time to our older children. It was not, let me add, that my wife was not distanced from the children, as well, during and after a life's moment that we came to call *pubic shock*; she was. In our discussions, however, there has been some considerable agreement that her sense of alienation with the children was never quite so complete. Additionally, in some sense or other, the cooling off between our children and myself had a certain resonance with the past, a curious sense of *deja vu*, as if I'd been there before and would revisit this space, again and again. And while this period of life has long since come to a close, I still vividly recall a sense of dejection, as if I'd been prematurely taken away from something wondrous, plucked from a source of nurture . . . and alone.

How Do You Dare Presume?

By the mid-1980s, I found myself leading seminars at an institute that trained psychoanalytically oriented clinicians. The teaching of a two-semester course on Freud fell to me after a senior and much loved colleague died suddenly. I had long since questioned the precise form of many psychoanalytic constructs and found myself, in this seminar, steering a course between extremes, feeling neither compulsion to deify nor to crucify Freud, and felt a characteristic ease in freely fascinating about this or that in his writings. I was speaking one day of Freud's much criticized comment on the female conscience (Freud, 1925), wherein he notes that it is never quite so inexorably separated from a woman's feelings as it is in the male. I wondered out loud about how much better it might be if the male conscience were not similarly constructed. I conjectured that the combination of male leaders' sense of justice and their similarly androgenized foot-soldiers' propensities for tolerating what Freud referred to as the exigencies of life might well be responsible for the madness we call *war*. Was it not possible, I queried, that, as *anthropos* developed, our consciences, our superegos, might come to more closely resemble the female version described (or invented) by Freud?

I went on to criticize the good doctor from Vienna for his casting my own gender as lost in viewing the world through an erect ureter (something akin to the image of the serpent, Uroboros, swallowing and fixated on his own tail) and to further criticize him for the untenability (from empirical studies) of many of his constructions surrounding penis envy. I was immediately and soundly chastised and thrashed by one of the students for putting her through such an onerous task—having to listen to a male who not only presented this odious material but preemptively usurped her right to criticize it by criticizing it, himself. *How do you dare presume*, she queried, *to criticize this material before I do?* Classes sometimes behave like frenzied sharks and within moments I found myself cast as the designated prey.

I offer no claims for the reasonability of the feelings of vulnerability I experienced in this classroom situation on that particular day, any more than I would for similar vulnerable feelings I experienced as an outsider to the idyllic bliss of the mother-infant dyad or during my expulsion from the *Garden* during my children's adolescences. Feelings are not subject to such scrutiny and would rarely pass muster on any test of reasonability. I was surprised, though, by the degree to which I felt excluded and full of sadness. As a man, as a male teacher, perhaps, I had no place and was not permitted entry into this one particular student's view of the feminist dialogue. *And the Lord God cast him out of the Garden of Eden*—and I, perchance, had no place to go except *into* these feelings.

I Want Mommy (Again)

Without ever articulating the I *want* Mommy, from time to time, it is abundantly clear that in certain rites and rituals, there is little room for me *qua* father. When hurt, when pained, when anguished, when giving birth, *the Mommy*, as my wife is good-humoredly and affectionately called by her adult brood, rules! And after many years of scrutinizing my own feelings about this, I have become a good helper and more comfortable in being the arranger, in bringing the Mommy and her grown children together. Planning for our youngest child's wedding, I accepted the task of making certain that no one was offended in the planning process, that a comfortable blending of ideas would result. I do my tasks well and, still, I occasionally envy *the Mommy*. I envy her the right to enter into these sacred moments in which not only ideas but souls blend. I shall come back to this soon, but for now: *Enough said.*

How Do You Dare Presume (Once More)?

In 1995, I attended a meeting on multicultural counseling and presented some notes on some consonances of worldview that occurred in the treatment of a woman. She was approximately my age, a therapist with an interest in education as I was, and had grown up, though 100 miles removed, in a Philadelphia neighborhood similar to the Brooklyn of my childhood. I noted that interestingly the fact that our skin colors were different seemed to play almost no role in our work together, so much so that I had wondered aloud in one such session, how it was that this difference caused no untoward dissonance. Perhaps, I opined, we had colluded not to be disturbed by our differences and were denying the role that it played. The patient responded, apparently having considered this matter at an earlier time. She explained that in her estimation we *had* been colluding in keeping something silent, but it was not related to our skin color. Instead, she reasoned, her Baptist background and my Jewish background were difficult to reconcile. I had, she reasoned, difficulty in recognizing how hard it might be for her to articulate certain thoughts. Her Christian religion taught her that fantasies and words could buy her, maybe not a one-way ticket, but a ticket, nonetheless, to Hell. I might have a hard time understanding that; she was correct. I had, in fact, long been annoyed by the admonition in Matthew 5: *And I say whosoever shall have committed adultery in his heart, has committed adultery.* Every sinew in my Freudian body called out loudly: the nonthought is father to the deed, antithetical to the statement in Matthew.

And, yes, this would be something we both needed to understand in our therapeutic relationship, together.

In any case, I had chosen to present this vignette to the seminar that day from work that was very important to me with the hopes of shedding some light on the subtle differences in culture that might intrude on relationships in and out of therapy. Indeed. Light may not have shone, that morning, but of heat there was a sufficiency! *How do you dare presume*, a male participant raged, *to treat a woman and an African-American woman, at that? Where do you come off doing that?*

As in the case of my chastising student (mentioned earlier), I offer this up not to settle any matter surrounding the correctness of the espoused views. Perchance, it would have been better for this woman to have been treated by another African-American woman; she chose, after interviewing a number of therapists, to be treated by me. Rather, it is my own consistent reaction that continues to surprise me. I felt excluded, once again, disconnected from an acceptable lot of therapists, *persona non grata* in the seminar and with no right of inclusion. Sadness followed, as it had in the other situations to which I've alluded. Perhaps, after all, sadness in men and women represents a much undervalued sentiment. In any case, my own sadness seems to relate to this sense of exclusion, to this sense of *otherness*, as I've now frequently noted. Sometimes I fret that we were better off 50 million years ago before awareness entered our cognitive armamentarium, before we were able to reflect on the *sadnesses of everyday life*. Most of the time I revel in the joys of this awareness in spite of the feelings it may bring.

THE OTHERNESS OF BEING MALE: HOW *DO* I FIND MY MOTHER?[6]

One cannot help but be struck by the compelling nature of our human drive to unite, to join with another—sexually and otherwise. And while I see certain differences, the compulsions seem equally strong among both of these classes that are, in our minds, separated out as male and female. Furthermore, as a result of my own clinical work, it seems likely that both men and women, in their pursuit of lovers, are seeking to reinstate something akin to the dual-unity that exists between a mother and her infant. And similar to that earliest relationship in which all types of needs and sensations are provided for, healthy adult sexuality incorporates sensations and/or behaviors that are customarily thought of as oral, anal, *and* genital. The good enough lover/mother revels in, glorifies, and seeks to holistically satisfy—*body and soul*—the lover/infant. Perhaps, it is no mere linguistic coincidence that since Roman times,

---

[6]In the brief discussion that follows and in these thoughts, in general, I mean to suggest no substantive distinctions between homophilic and heterophilic relationships.

marriage is referred to as matrimony (*matrimonium*), a word that combines the root word for mother (*mater*) with a word signifying singularity (*monium*). Perhaps, the use of this word, itself, heralds some subliminal recognition of the pursuit of the mother in any such coupling.

Even now in the 21st century, there do appear to be—at least anecdotally speaking—certain notable differences that may well relate to the sense of the male *qua* outsider. I offer three perhaps related and maybe controversial thoughts.

- The female lover can hope to emulate and become (like) mother, while at the same time seeking unity with her; the male lover can only hope to recapture a lost dual-unity with his mother.[7]
- In humor and common cultural rites, as well as in the reports (anecdotal) of therapy patients, men are more commonly the seekers and women are the gatekeepers and welcomers.
- The fantasied[8]—and to some extent even the realistic—mechanics of the dances representing the varieties of human intercourse are reportedly experienced, by men and women, as following similar patterns—with men seeking and women welcoming.

One woman reported the fantasy of "repeatedly birthing and expelling, welcoming and exiling" during intercourse. Another noted rather matter of factly. "After penetration, I feel as if I am giving life and after orgasm I feel like I have given life." One man noted that, until penetration, he felt "removed and denied" by his lover and that it was only after intercourse that he felt "united and together." Another man reported his belief that after penetration "in losing a part of myself inside of her, I felt as if I was no longer separate from her, no longer alone." The man, it must be said, who has made no peace with and has no ownership over the fantasied nature of these mostly unconscious constructions may well come to believe that his denial by his lover is real and may come to act like a petulant child . . . a sulking and/or raging outsider denied entry to some sacred ground. And while my own reaction to being excluded (from the mother-infant dyad, from my children's adolescences, or from accepted membership in groups) may have centered on sadness, I cannot help but wonder whether or not there is some heightened sense of being an outsider that is intrinsic to maleness. I go on to fascinate about whether these feelings and the awareness of these feelings may not still be usable in pursuit of *the good life*.

---

[7]The male envy of the woman (Bettelheim, 1954) fits quite nicely with this inability to become mother, which in turn logically aligns with the substantially greater prevalence of men's violence toward women than *vice versa*.

[8]It would have been safer to omit reference to this discussion. Truth be told, writing a personal paper with anecdotal information is never as safe as writing a statistical paper or one which, in any case, avoids one's own experiences and what one personally imagines to have seen/heard. In the end, the varieties of human sexual/fantasied experience are so diverse that any such attempt at clarification will be incomplete and inconsistent with many people's experience.

HEALTH AND INTERSUBJECTIVITY

While uncertainty, for those who require certainty, may breed anxiety, Sextus Empiricus claimed that the suspension of judgment for those with a willingness to tolerate ambiguity and doubt (skepticism) gives birth to what he called *ataraxia* and that we might translate as *quietude*. The later part of the last century and the new one have witnessed a welcome-for-many blurring of gender boundaries. My wife and I work and make decisions and make love and spend and save, *sometimes together and betimes in parallel!* How blessed I feel to be untethered from the specific tasks that previous generations considered masculine. How favored I feel to share the burden of some of the less-blessed tasks of masculinity. And how good-fortuned do I feel to partake in some of those (previously) culturally designated feminine tasks. Thus, having suggested a sense of *otherness* that betimes washes over this one male person, I will briefly address the manner in which I see the acceptance of this otherness as consistent with one of the paths that may lead to the *good life*.

In a previous work (Covitz, 1997), I sought to introduce a specific line of psychological growth that, or so it was suggested, was the underbelly of the symbolic Œdipus Complex that Sigmund Freud first reported to his friend and collocutor, Willhelm Fliess, in 1897. This more general (than Freud's) developmental line claimed to chart the individual's growth from a paranoid-like state in which even the thoughts of another had to be recast in the language of the self to a mature stage in which the central necessity, perhaps, for membership in communities of mutual concern and interest would be developed. This most progressed endpoint of this developmental line included an ability, at least with specially selected others, to cherish the inner stirrings, thoughts, and relationships of these others. This capacity was there referred to as *intersubjectivity*, a name chosen to connote, in a sense akin to its grammatical one (object vis-a-vis subject), *the ability to perceive the other as a subject in their own right.* It was argued that there was a natural propensity to imagine that all God's creations somehow and in some way or another were created to satisfy one's own needs and that the manner in which the senses worked[9] also boded poorly for an ability to transcend this narcissistic mode of dealing with one's others and their *silly preoccupations*. It was further argued that Freud's Œdipus, a particular and very special case of these developments, underscored the need in each of us to first settle this self-referencing matter with our parents in learning to accept and even to cherish the relationship that they had with each other. Freud's primal scene was reinterpreted, then, as the child's struggle against accepting that everything the parents do has to do with ongoing efforts to best raise the child. Freud's superego, his uber-Ich, was reconceptualized in this new language, as well.

---

[9]The senses tell us, for instance, that all sounds come to our ears and that we are situated in the center of all visually perceivable activity.

The five stages that were suggested may be abbreviated, as follows:

Stage I.   The propensity to reject that another thinks, desires, or needs

Stage II.   The refusal to acquiesce to another's inner world unless it is self referenced back to the other

Stage III. The propensity to recoil from another's thinking about yet another

Stage IV.   The tendency to recoil from the recognition of another's relationships

Stage V.   Incipient forms of intersubjectivity and a *primus inter pares* view of the world as it relates to the other in a given relationship and the resulting ability to cherish the inner thoughts and stirrings and the actual relationships of another

In this particular conceptualization of health (i.e., the attainment of a degree of *intersubjectivity*) there are two significant benchmarks that must be reached and that must be in some degree of alignment if development is to succeed. The first of these is a capacity for the melding and fusing with another. This precipitates from a healthful period of bonding with a mother-figure who is capable of celebrating the joys of her infant while withstanding the particular threats of this kind of fusion *for her* that emanate from this lengthy period of attachment required by the human infant.[10]

The second benchmark to which I refer has to do with the capacity to stand outside and away from, while supporting, such a fused pairing. Here, too, there are celebratory aspects and dangerous ones. On the joyous side, there is a satisfaction that arises from meeting one's own expectations relating to how one ideally ought to behave[11]—becoming, so to speak, who one wants to be. In addition, such empathic attunement with a pair of others brings with it the fruits of the gratitude that these others betime experience. And while there appears to be preciously scant evidence that punishment functions as a deterrent, there seems considerable evidence that empathy breeds empathy (Covitz, 1997, chapters 7 and 8). Still and all, there remain liabilities that may accrue and feelings of exclusion and abandonment do appear quite regularly—and therefore may be assumed to be in some sense intrinsic—with those adopting this position. To have the ability to bond and to choose, instead and for a moment, to function as a

---

[10]My wife and I sit in awe, sometimes, watching our youngest child's ability to revel in each and every step forward taken by the *brilliant 2-year-old granddaughter she shares with us!* The mother-figure's life is on partial-hold, as her ability to tolerate daily regressions is tested.

[11]Psychoanalysts speak of the pressing urgency of aligning the Ego Ideal (how I feel I ideally ought to be) with who and what I am.

support for two others who are thus bonded together is, simultaneously, a developmental achievement and an opening for the vulnerabilities that may accompany the outsider.

Freud (in his theory of somatic compliance) and Adler (in his theory of organ inferiority), each in their own way, postulated that psychological defenses were frequently enlisted to compensate for an absence, for something that was weak or missing. I am, in these thoughts, suggesting, instead, a built-in pairing of naturally acquired and evolutionarily *required* skills or gifts that bring with them expectable liabilities against which we each must defend ourselves.[12] If the female (or the male taking her role) of our species is required by the needs of her infant for long periods of time to give up her sense of separateness, then it is quite expectable that she may defend against this requirement for fusion with another. And if the male (or the female taking his role) is similarly required by the needs of a next generation to become the supportive outsider to the mother-infant dyad, then it is equally expectable for him to defend against his assigned role and to recoil from it.

As an aside and without belaboring details in textual analysis, allow me a brief digression into biblical characterology—a detour that may demonstrate a comparable pairing of skill with conflict about that skill. In exegetical writings, the commentaries make no small fuss about Abraham's capacities as a host, as a welcomer of guests. And in a similar manner, both text and commentaries extol Moses' virtue as being *humbler than any other person who lived.* And yet, a fair reading of the texts exposes, if anything, men who struggled with these virtues and, perhaps, never prevailed in these inner battles. Abraham's singular attempt at being hospitable (opening lines of *Genesis* 18) sees a man instructing his wife to bake breads and his older son to roast a tender calf. True enough, Abraham makes the decision to provide for his three desert visitors. Still, I wonder how it has been for the generations of wives and children who have read these texts in which their ilk do the work, while pundits credit the virtuousness of the husband and father who, in high fashion, *entertains.* Similarly, throughout *Exodus, Numbers,* and *Deuteronomy,* as readers read the explicitly stated humility of the Man Moses, the text screams to be read differently and paints an all too clear picture of a leader who struggles with this very issue as he attempts to govern his obstreperous, petulant, and disobedient people, chides his God for burdening him with them, and suffers his lot.

And so I end my brief phenomenological journey into who I am as a man entering a new century and how the sense of being an outsider may interweave with a male identity, so constructed.

---

[12] It is fair, perhaps, to say that I am near, in these thoughts, to Jung's paired Anima/Animus model of forces and counterforces.

CLOSING THOUGHTS

Who among us fails to wish for some guiding star or for a mentor (saffron-robed or cigar-smoking and bearded—it makes little difference) who might light the path that best follows *that star*? Alas! There are preciously few compasses and no well-marked charts to follow in pursuit of understanding ourselves or others! In meeting another—or ourselves, for that matter—we have, in the end, no druthers but to follow the exquisitely intercalated structure of each person's *maze of mirrors* and to patiently wait until this other admits us to gaze inside from the unique position that they have come to occupy. Looking from within this labyrinth, reflecting on my own experiences as a man and inviting others to see what I believe to have witnessed, I chose to focus on a singular difference that I imagined or observed—who can tell—between men and women. This difference had to do with a relative dominance of either inclinations to meld and to defend against such fusing or else to function as an outside supporter with its defensive liabilities of envious onlooking and feelings of exclusion.

And yet I hold to my belief, the one which flies in the face of the experiences I have elaborated (above), that both men and women, in order to partake of the richness of life, must make some peace with both the subjectivity that arises in dyadic blending and with the lesser subjectivity that is a part of the legacy of those who must—from time to time and as outsiders to the dyad—be content with observing and supporting. The balancing of these is, alas, no mean task!

Perhaps, the emphasis nowadays on gender studies is best understood as another complex optical illusion, this one a reflection of certain societal movements that have dictated the paradigmatic divisions of the world that we are led to study by our philosophies. We may come to believe that we can abbreviate the job of learning about another by coming to understand group statements about a culture to which we imagine he or she belongs—racial, sexual, ethnic, or otherwise. There is, however, no way to avoid the complexity of the often messy task of being with another—sometimes fused and sometimes watching. As we men and women meet, we are unalterably an admixture of mother, father, and a host of others. Each of us is an oleo of all the caricatured dichotomies, including male and female; narcissist and object-related lover; war-mongerer and pacifist; white and black; fused lover and envious voyeur; and all the other *splits* that sentient beings bring—fortunately or otherwise— to order the madness of differences.

As a therapist and as a person, I cannot afford the luxury of these simplifications, of even the tentative application of statistical conclusions about the group to an individual—even the ones to which I've tentatively admitted in these pages. Interestingly for me, experience suggests that the visitors who occasion my office are frequently less inured to these dichotomies than are the clinicians and theoreticians whose volumes adorn my shelves. As healer,

I move throughout any given clinical day, becoming this person's father and another's mother or sister or brother. I become an older sibling to an octogenarian and either a John Birchist or loving kin to a member of some racial or ethnic minority group to which I do or do not belong. On some psychic-scape, perhaps, I *am* and *we are* all these beings that look into and peer back from the maze of mirrors. And still, I do wonder about some of these differences that seem to occasion my own trek as a man.

Appendix
Some Empirical Studies Relating to Gender Identifications

These appended notes are included as antidote to my suggested and tentative bifurcation of our species into predominantly fusing types and those who view themselves as outsiders to the sacred dyad. Any such split would require evidence for a predominant identification of son with father and daughter with mother which the following researches fail to rigorously support. And such an appendix may function as a reparation for the essentialist heresy that I have proposed and may permit a comfortable return to my origins as generic offspring of two parents!

A number of studies have attempted to demonstrate the dominance of same-sex identifications in the child; and while I have found no studies that directly tested the two-sided propensity for identification, as a group, it may be said, they support this view, as I shall attempt to demonstrate in this brief review of some empirical studies.[13]

Levy (1954) had 10- to 11-year-olds match male and female names to objects and found no preferential patterns. Acord (1962) discovered that third, sixth, and ninth graders failed to demonstrate such same-sex identifications, while Lessler (1964), using similar techniques, found that fourth and ninth graders' behaviors did follow this prescription of same-sex identification. Ward (1969) had children (K–2 in school) associate a variety of adjectives to self, mother, and father; he, thereafter, analyzed the frequency of consonance with each parent. Although no statistically significant difference was noted (i.e., the hypothesis that identifications were equally distributed was not rejectable), there was a nonsignificant trend for the boys in the group to be more identified with mother. Hartup (1962) attempted to investigate this matter with doll play, wherein, children (aged: 3.5–5.5) were asked to carry out a series of activities and then to carry them out as their mothers and fathers might. Here, the group as a whole behaved in a manner consistent with the

---

[13]The reader is referred to Covitz (1997, chapters 7–9) for further discussion of the misapplication of grouped data conclusions to gender differences rooted in identification with the same-sex parent.

hypothesis of *same-sex identification*—but only in a *statistically* significant sense with the actual proportions being quite close. The conventional prediction collapsed, however, when the groups were split into older and younger sub-groups, where it might be anticipated that the older children would identify more strenuously with the same-sex parent than the younger group. Here, too, it should be noted that the difference, while *statistically significant*, was not *quantitatively significant*. Like the aforementioned Hartup, Kohlberg and Zigler (1966) utilized doll play to examine consonant styles of behavior in children and their parents. Their results generally supported the hypothesis of same-sex identification. However, while in the case of females, there was a greater identification with mothers than with fathers during the explored ages (4–6 years), there was increased identification with father during this same period of time. So far, one sees no overwhelming evidence to support one-sided or predominant identifications.

Brown and Tolor (1957) reviewed more than 16 studies that claimed to ex-amine preferential identification patterns manifest by the gender of the first figure drawn in Draw-A-Person techniques. While confirming the conventional view that normal college men (91%) and women (63%) draw a picture of their own sex first, they conclude their study noting (p. 210): "At the present time, the only valid conclusion is that the basis or significance of drawing a person of the opposite sex first is not known."

Cameron (1967) took a different attack on the question of identification, choosing to highlight developmental movements in the identification process. A sample of 2,336 children were asked to choose between 12 pairs of pictures (originally utilized by McElroy, 1954) with each pair containing a phallic-shaped object and another with a rounded, *containing*, and, presum-ably, more female shape. He predicted that until the age of 4, no preference would be manifest in the data; from 4–6 years of age, children would prefer the shapes associated with the opposite sex; from 7–11 preference would be for objects associated with the same sex; and from age 12 onward, preference would return to the opposite sex. Cameron's hypotheses were, he suggests, confirmed (sign: .10). While one may argue for or against the clinical utility of such group preference tests in evaluating such complex responses, even the question of their support remains unanswered.

Cameron's data (p. 36) for latency aged children (ages 7–12, N = 965), those who (theoretically) should demonstrate a strongly skewed same-sex identifi-cation, are as follows (I list only the totals for the 12 modified McElroy Cards):

Boys' Choices		Girls' Choices	
Male Symbol	Female Symbol	Male Symbol	Female Symbol
3668	2281	3530	2364

Cameron appears to argue (pp. 34–35) that these results support a view of same-sex identification during the post-Œdipal period if we control for factors in a "U.S. . . . male-oriented culture." In spite of his arguments, however, I leave

Cameron's study struck by the similarity of values in these two subgroups. While one may accept Cameron's statistics and not be notably concerned with the choice of significance levels for his tests (sign: .10), I remain unconvinced of their relevance to an hypothesis of preferential identifications.

Fisher and Greenberg (1977), in reviewing this literature (while citing works by Gray and Klaus, 1956; Beier and Ratzenburg, 1953; Sopchak, 1952; Pishkin, 1960; Ryle and Lunghi, 1972; and Byrne, 1965) suggest that the hypothesis of same-sex identification seems to be generally supported. They go on to note (p. 186):

> It is true that a number of studies have not found evidence for identification with the same-sex parent. . . . But it is still fair to say that the majority of evidence indicates that same-sex identification is the prevalent pattern.

I should like to suggest, to the contrary, that the conjoin of these studies seems to suggest that whatever method one chooses, there are notable identifications with both parents *qua* individuals, and, perhaps, identifications with culturally masculine and culturally feminine stereotypes—as, for instance, in Cameron's study. Kohlberg (1966) and Lynn (1969) have each, interestingly, argued that what may be thought of as identifications with the same-sex parent may well relate to both parties' *coincidental* membership in the same gender class—an early articulation, one might say, of theories of the socially constructed nature of gender.

A number of studies sought to investigate an association between identification or its absence and psychological disturbances. Cava and Raush (1952), in a study with 37 twelfth-grade high school boys, sought to demonstrate that (p. 855) "those individuals who show greater conflict in areas . . . related to identification . . . will indirectly perceive themselves as less-similar to their like-sex parent than will those who show less conflict in these areas." The Strong Interest Inventory was administered twice, first as they would answer it themselves and, then 3 days later, as they imagined their father might. A Blacky Test (Blum, 1949) was administered 5 days later. Students were rated as weak or strong in Œdipality on five dimensions of the Blacky Test. Differences between the two groups were significant only on the Castration Anxiety Dimension and for the Total Identification Score—and, once again, showed no overwhelming differences that might permit generalization to any given individual in clinical treatment.[14]

In a similarly designed study of a possible connection between identification and conflict or disturbance, Sopchak (1952, p. 159) examined "the relation between the tendency toward identification with parents and tendencies towards specific types of abnormalities as measured by the Minnesota

---

[14]The Blacky Test was a popular test for such studies; it showed pictures of various members of a dog family doing such things as cutting off a puppy's tail, a sight which might make many two-legged puppies and even some upright middle-aged curs shudder.

Multiphasic Personality Inventory (MMPI)." He sought to test two psychoanalytic hypotheses: one suggesting that normal development requires identification and the second that certain psychopathological conditions arise due to identifications. The MMPI was given four times to 78 men and 30 women. It was to be taken as Self, as father, as mother, and as *most people*. A straightforward count of similar responses was used as a measure of identification.

Sopchak was able to confirm the following hypotheses, among others. He confirmed that—once again, as a group—normal men tend to identify with fathers *somewhat more* often than with mothers. Men in the group with tendencies toward abnormality showed a greater lack of identification with father than with mother, but showed less identification with both than normals. Men who failed to identify with their father tended toward the MMPI's *psychotic triad* (paranoia, schizophrenia, and hypomania) more than toward the neurotic dimensions; this held true for women, as well. Women with abnormal scores on the MMPI showed a similar tendency to be less identified with their fathers. Positive identification with mother—among women—was correlated with some types of abnormality. Johnson's (1987) study of delinquents confirmed some of these differences, as well.

I leave these studies, then, *unmoved* and without a compass to guide the way in understanding my own responses to life's surprises and without unambiguous means of interpreting within the gender maze of mirrors with which I began. Life is, after all is said and done, *complex and messy*.

REFERENCES

Abelin, E. (1971). The Role of the father in the Separation-Individuation process. In *Separation-Individuation*, J.B. McDevitt and C. Settlage (Eds.), 229–252. New York: International Universities Press.

——— (1975). Some further observations and comments on the earliest role of the father. *International Journal of Psychoanalysis*, 56, 293–302.

——— (1980). Triangulation: The role of the father and the origins of core gender identity during the Rapprochement subphase. In Rapprochement: *The Critical Subphase of Separation Individuation*, Lax et al. (Eds). New York: Aronson.

Acord, L. (1962). Sexual symbolism as a correlate of age. *Journal of Consulting Psychology*, 26, 279–281.

Bettelheim, B. (1954, 1968). *Symbolic Wounds: Puberty Rites and the Envious Male*. New York: Collier Books.

Blum, G. (1949). A study of the psychoanalytic theory of psychosexual development. *Genetic Psychology Monographs*, 39, 3–99.

Brown, D., & Tolor, A. (1957). Human figure drawings as indicators of sexual identification and inversion. *Perceptual and Motor Skills*, 7, 199–211.

Cameron, P. (1967). Confirmation of the Freudian psychosexual stages utilizing sexual symbolism. *Psychological Reports*, 21, 33–39.

Cava, E., & Raush, H. (1952). Identification and the adolescent boy's perception of his father. *Journal of Abnormal and Social Psychology*, 47, 855–856.

Covitz, H. (1997). Œ*dipal paradigms in collision: A centennial emendation of a piece of Freudian canon* (1897–1997). New York/Bern: Peter Lang Publishers.

Fisher, S., & Greenberg, R. (1977). *The scientific credibility of Freud's theories and therapy.* New York: Basic Books.

Freud, S. (1923). The ego and the id. *Standard Edition,* 19, 12.

Freud, S. (1925). Some psychical consequences of the anatomical distinctions between the sexes. *Standard Edition,* 19, 243.

Hartup, W. (1962). Some correlates of parental imitation in young children. *Child Development,* 33, 85–96.

Johnson, R. (1987). Mother's versus father's role in causing delinquency. *Adolescence,* 22(86), 305–315.

Kohlberg, L. (1966). Moral and religious education in the public schools. In T. Sizer, *Religion and public education.* Boston: Houghton-Mifflin.

Kohlberg, L., & Zigler, E. (1966). The impact of cognitive maturity on the development of sex-role attitudes in the years 4–8. *Genetic Psychology Monographs,* 75, 89–165.

Lessler, K. (1964). Cultural and Freudian dimensions of sexual symbols. *Journal of Consulting Psychology,* 28(1), 46–53.

Levy, L. (1954). Sexual symbolism: A validity study. *Journal of Consulting Psychology,* 7, 881–918.

Lynn, D. (1969). *Parental and sex-role identification.* Berkeley, CA: McCutchan.

McElroy, W.A. (1950). Methods of testing the oedipus complex hypothesis. *Quarterly Bulletin of the British Psychological Association,* 1, 364–365.

Sarnoff, I. (1971). *Testing Freudian concepts: An experimental social approach.* New York: Springer.

Sopchak, A. (1952). Parental identification and tendency toward disorder as measured by the Minnesota Multiphasic Personality Inventory. *Journal of Abnormal and Social Psychology,* 47, 159–165.

Walzer, M. (1987). *Interpretation and social criticism.* Cambridge, MA: Harvard University Press.

Ward, W. (1969). Process of sex-role development. *Developmental Psychology,* 1, 163–168.

CHAPTER 5

MEN IN MODERNITY: REFLECTIONS OF A PHYSICIAN, FATHER, AND PRIEST

Jeffrey P. Bishop

As a medical student, I delivered several babies at the county hospital where I trained—25 to be exact—so I was familiar with the flurry of activity that occurred as Cyndy, my wife, went into labor with our first child. The nurses strapped the monitor to Cyndy's abdomen, and as the monitor kept track of the baby's beating heart, I began to keep the beat with my head. Gradually the beat moved through my whole body, and soon I was all but dancing. I do not remember the beating hearts of the other babies being so rhythmic and infectious. Perhaps I was too focused on technical proficiency to notice those rhythms. As I kept beat, the members of the delivery team threw a few castigating looks my way. They seemed to be saying, "How could you be dancing as your wife lies here in pain?" I must admit, Cyndy found my rhythmic movements quite annoying at first, especially before the epidural. But I couldn't stop; the rhythm of nature filled my whole being.

This story has become Madeleine's story. Over the past years, the story has changed a bit. The castigating looks are left out of it and Cyndy's annoyance with me has been forgotten. Whenever Madeleine is sad that I am away at work or on-call at the hospital, Cyndy tells her how I danced around the delivery room to the rhythm of her beating heart. It has become our story.

After her delivery and as I held her for the first time, I was in awe of Madeleine. Wonder filled my soul as I stood there. As a new father, I was already proud that, within a few minutes of birth, she was looking around the room, not crying, just taking it all in. What a smart one I had! I pondered her little hands and her tiny little toes. I saw in her face some of her mother's features and some of my own. Like most fathers, I did not want my little girl to look like me. I wanted her to be beautiful, like her mother, and to avoid the coarse features of her father.

This desire led me to reflect and to ask, "What of this child is me?" At this question the angst of modernity reared its ugly head. My first reflection on that frightful question rendered the answer, "Half this child is me." Well, not really because half of her genome came from me. But on second thought, that should mean that half of her DNA is my DNA. After further reflection, I concluded that I was wrong. In fact her DNA—all the adenines (A's), cytosines (C's), guanines (G's), and thymines (T's)—came from what her mother ate. All of the "stuff," all of her DNA came from her mother. So what of this child was of me? What was left of her that was of me? I was in horror as I searched for some connection. Nothing of any tangible significance, or at least nothing that I could get my hands around, was from me. The only thing that came from me is half her genetic sequence. Half of the sequence of her DNA was similar to mine. What, in God's name, is a sequence?

Fathers are only sequence donors. Mothers have the real bodily connection, the tangible connection with the child. The child takes in the nutrients that the mother has eaten. The very stuff of the mother becomes the stuff of the child—both *in utero* and while the child breast-feeds. The matter of the body of the child is of the matter of the body of the mother. Fathers, on the other hand, are just donors. Indeed, because of our technological advances we need not be present for the act of conception at all. Fathers merely donate gene sequences. We are little more than conduits for information—for genetic sequences. How disillusioning this revelation was to me. After all, what is a genetic sequence? At the center of modern biology is the gene sequence, a big nothing.

With modernity, our lives have become separated into various categories—social, biological, economic, and so on—usually divided along the boundaries of various academic disciplines. And the deeper we look into human existence by means of these various fields, the further away we get from the notion of human flourishing. The Enlightenment tried to clear away the social setting and the human *telos* to attain objectivity. For most premodern societies, including those premodern societies that have not yet encountered modernity, to flourish as a human means to live in community and to play several communally oriented roles. Man, the individual, is a modern invention as Michel Foucault points out in *The Order of Things*. Of course, Foucault did not mean that the human animal comes into being in modernity. Rather, he means that the conceptual framework of modernity allows a concept like man to come into existence. The concept of man then allows for the examination of what is at the core of man. The episteme of modernity created the concept of man, and the more the subject-man looks at the object-man, the less he finds at his core. With modernity, things begin to be classified according to functions that cannot be identified easily with the eye. Thus, Foucault claims, the concept of life came into being and gives rise to another way for man to classify living things. What makes something alive is the function that lies deep down inside the thing, but when you actually look for it, you cannot really find it. No one has ever seen life as such deep down inside a thing. Cut open a body and you see organs; you do not see a *thing* you can identify as life. In fact, no matter how deep you go, you find nothing that you can get your hands around.

How do you get your hands around a sequence? What exactly is a genetic sequence? In fact, what is a gene? That seems like a good question. Aristotle said that a good question is the best place to start for good answers. For Aristotle the starting question was, "What is mankind?" Translated into less male-dominated language we might ask, "What is human?" Aristotle's answer: a body. Yes a body, but even the dead have bodies. Well then, it is a body plus something else. Body plus the animating principle—body plus that which makes something alive. Body plus *psuche*; better translated as body plus soul. In *On the Soul*, Aristotle reverts to his physics to get at what he means by body plus soul. In his physics, matter must have a form. All things are made of matter plus form—the material plus the immaterial. Take a bronze statue as an example. The matter of the statue is the bronze; the form, the nonmaterial part, of the statue is of a man. Melt the statue and you no longer have a statue. The matter is present with a different form. It is no longer a statue because it has lost its nonmaterial form.

So by analogy, the human is body plus *psuche*—the material plus the form. Without the soul you could not have a living human body, and likewise without the matter of the body, you could not know about soul. Bodies do not exist without souls and likewise souls do not live without bodies. The soul is the form of the body. On Aristotle's rendering, the soul is that which makes one alive. Plants have plant souls because they are alive and are plants. Animals have animal souls, because they are alive and are animals. Humans have human souls as shown by the fact that they are alive and are humans. For Aristotle, what things are is intricately related to their *telos*—that is to say, their end. The animating principle, that which makes alive, of the human manifests in the body those characteristics that are human. From the *telos* you can know the potency, the potential, the soul. By observing the human being, you can see the soul. There is a certain simplicity in this explanation. The form—the soul—is expressed in the body. By observing the body, you know the soul.

With the rise of scientific explanation, thinkers moved away from teleology. The *telos* of a thing could not be part of the explanation. Explaining something according to its end is not scientific. Moreover, science eschews a concept like soul, because it is nonmaterial and therefore not observable. Yet, the way we think about and talk about the genome today, to my reading, is just a weaker instance of the very same Aristotelian notion of the soul.

Several optimistic statements have come out of the genome project concerning the possibility of curing all disease once we know the genetic basis for all disease. The frenzy even prompted one authority to claim that we will even be able to end homelessness. In popular parlance, there is this thing called a gene. It directs and guides the various functions and characteristics of the

body. Genes make themselves known in the body. We see the genotype manifested in the phenotype. If you have the gene for breast cancer, you are prone
to breast cancer. If you have the gene for heart disease, you have a great risk
for heart disease. The same holds for schizophrenia or Huntington's disease.*
It is also true for various forms of deafness or blindness. The phenotype is reduced to the genotype. Thus the common notion of gene is a type of reductionism that, interestingly, does not escape an Aristotelian conception.

Even this highly technical and scientific conception of gene does not escape certain Aristotelian notions. The gene, like the more traditional notion
of soul, makes itself known in the body. Of course the scientific version of
the gene is more sophisticated. Scientists speak of penetration. The gene
may not penetrate; it may not make itself known in the body. The gene for
Huntington's disease penetrates in all instances. The gene for heart disease, in the face of different environmental circumstances, may or may not
penetrate into phenotypic expression. The gene for schizophrenia in all
likelihood must interact with other genes before the phenotype of schizophrenia is manifest. Thus it is more accurate for one to speak of the *genes* for
schizophrenia. The gene for breast cancer may interact with other genes as
well as environmental factors before it expresses itself. In this scientific version, there is a reductionistic attitude that prevails. Even those researchers
who argue that they are avoiding reductionism do so by appealing to unknown variables. They claim that with so many variables we cannot possibly reduce the genome to theories that can predict diseases. However,
the logical extension of the multivariate theory is that once we know the
variables—the sum-total of all genes and all environmental factors that
contribute to the trait—then we will be able to predict who will get the disease and who will not. To my reading this conception remains reductionistic. It claims that if we just know all the variables and we are smart enough
to do the statistics, we could really predict the manifestation of the gene.
All is reduced to the observable, which itself can be quantified. Even in this
reductionistic mindset, we still want to talk about a gene making itself
known, expressing itself, in the body.

This language brings us back to the Aristotelian conception of *psuche*—the
animating principle. What is a gene? A sequence of DNA. But you really cannot know a gene sequence without examining the string of A's, G's, C's, and T's
of DNA—that is, the matter of the DNA. We know what DNA is, but what is a
sequence? It is that part of a gene that cannot be known except through the
matter of the DNA. In this sense, it is the nonmaterial part of the gene. It is that

---

*Huntington's disease, formerly called Huntington's chorea, is a chronically progressive neu-
rodegenerative disorder. The patient will have choreoform movements (which are slow, constant, and uncontrollable) resulting in discoordination. The onset of symptoms is typically in
the mid-30s and death occurs by the mid-50s from dementia. Fifty percent of the offspring of
a parent with the gene will be affected.

which makes the DNA a gene. Scramble the DNA into a different sequence and you do not have a gene. Without the matter of the DNA, you really cannot know the sequence and you certainly do not have a gene. How is this really different than Aristotle's claims for the soul?

The concept of soul is no more ridiculous than the concept of a nonmaterial sequence of the genome. Aristotle would claim that the soul is not known except through the matter of the body, and the modern geneticist would claim that the sequence of the DNA is not known except through the matter of the DNA. Aristotle: the soul expresses itself in the body. Modern geneticist: the genotype is expressed in the phenotype. Aristotle claims that the soul is the immaterial part of the human that makes the body animate. What is it that I as a father contribute to my daughter? Well, it is not really DNA, but a sequence. What is a sequence? If the actual A's, T's, G's, and C's of the DNA that I contributed to my daughter are gone, then what is it that persists? The sequence. This sounds nonmaterial to me. Aristotle's notion of soul parallels the contemporary notion of the gene sequence. Fathers donate gene sequences, as do mothers, of course, but mothers get all the bodily connection. Fathers provide no material substrate to their progeny, thus our predicament as fathers.

Yet, there is a much broader dimension to the notion of the nonmaterial soul in Aristotle than there is to a nonmaterial genetic sequence. For Aristotle, to be human is to be human in a particular social context. A human is not the mere expression of physical characteristics. In fact, even the biological cannot escape the social. Take as an example the genes that might result in deafness. Very few hearing-impaired people think themselves to be defective; it is precisely because the human is social that they do not think so. They flourish because there is the social context of deaf culture. Human flourishing does not cease because the biological or genetic in some way misfired. To the contrary, humans move and shape the social contexts to accommodate the biological. For Aristotle, human flourishing cannot be separated into biological and social.

In fact for Aristotle, we humans are striving for *great-souledness*. Aristotle's concept of soul does not result in merely biological characteristics the way that modern genetics does. For Aristotle, we are in transition from a minimalist soul of biology to *great-souledness*. Humans strive to get from human-life-as-it-is, the bare minimum that qualifies as human, to human-life-as-it-could-be. For Aristotle, that means we must acknowledge that there are characteristic ways of human flourishing, which must occur in a social context. The human *telos* cannot be divorced from social and cultural contexts. For Aristotle, one arrives at *great-souledness* by practicing the virtues of prudence, temperance, generosity, justice, and wisdom. These virtues are learned through habituation. They are learned through observing those who are in the social circle. When a child encounters something new, she will look to her mother or father to see if she should be afraid. In other words, there can be no human without the context. Human flourishing is social as well as biological. Fathers have become so alienated and removed from their children precisely because parentage is understood in biological terms and not in human terms; that is to say, fatherhood, and motherhood for that matter, cannot be separated from the sociological dimension.

As a physician, I see the world through the lens provided to me by science. As a father and priest that scientific lens seems distorted. I really do not see Madeleine's genes as explained by science, nor do I see the metabolic functions that occur within her body. I see her mother and myself. I see a 4-year-old struggling to make sense of the world and struggling to understand a world that is not reduced to the vacuous explanations of modernity. I see a toddler struggling to appropriate a world full of meaning. The gene for Huntington's disease does not explain the courageous struggle of a father who tries to comfort his children as his disease progresses. The breast cancer gene does not tell me whether to recommend to a 20-year-old woman to have mastectomies. It does not tell me how her self-image or her social circumstances will change should she choose this route. Only the lived and meaningful experience of a human being can aid in making these kinds of choices. And for these situations to make sense, to have meaning, there is necessarily a social context.

I am a father because I live in a human community with certain specified roles and relationships. One of those relationships resulted in the birth of two daughters. Fatherhood carries with it certain responsibilities and duties by virtue of those roles, which cannot be ascertained through an examination of the biological. My role is to assist in the flourishing of another human—a role for which donating of genetic sequences is merely the first step. My role as a father is to see that my children flourish. And through their habitual observation of me, they learn what it is to flourish. I am struggling to be just so that my girls will learn justice. I attempt prudence that they might learn to be prudential. I pray for wisdom that they might be wise.

A father's real connection gets distorted in modernity. That connection exists, not by virtue of the biological or genetic. The *telos* of a human life is not contained in the genome or the genetic sequence. I cannot look at a gene and know a single meaningful thing about human life. For science to believe that teleology only confuses the picture—as modern science, including medical science, has believed since its inception in the mid-17th century—is to further empty the human of meaning. After all, what good are genes unless they serve a meaningful *telos*? Genes tell us nothing about human flourishing. My role as a father is to point my children in the direction of human flourishing—from human-life-as-it-is to human-life-as-it-could-be. From time to time, I must discipline Madeleine to that end. She is now at the age when she can get mad at me after I put her in time-out or withdraw certain privileges. And whenever she is mad at me, I remember a certain beat in my body, in my soul—it still pulsates through my being to this day—and I pick her up and we dance to that beat until we laugh so hard that we cry.

REFERENCES

Aristotle. *De Anima: On the Soul.* Translated and Edited by W. David Ross. Oxford: Oxford University Press, 1956.

Aristotle. *The Nichmachean Ethics.* Translated with commentary and glossary by Hippocrates George Apostle. Grinnell, Iowa: The Peripatetic Press, 1984.

Foucault, M. *The Order of Things: An Archaeology of the Human Sciences.* New York: Vintage Books, 1970. Originally published under the title *Les Mots et les choses* by Editions Gallimard, 1966.

MacIntyre, A. *After Virtue: A Study in Moral Theory.* Second Edition. Notre Dame: University of Notre Dame Press, 1984.

VOICES TWO

NOT YET MEN

CHAPTER 6

THE PROVING GROUND

Ronald Baughman

Years ago I saw Van Gogh's charcoal drawing *The Potato Eaters*, and since Baughman is a German-Dutch name, I tried to incorporate the image into my poem.

> *Our first contest of size, how deep to plant potatoes.*
> *You said deeper, I shallower.*
> *In your red-faced anger, father,*
> *all light-heartedness withered.*
> *But I stood my ground, these rows yours,*
> *those mine.*
>
> *For you the garden was something to beat back*
> *the cost of living. But throughout the green summer*
> *I pushed the wobbly-wheeled plow until hardpan*
> *became as fine as flour.*
>
> *In August the divided garden stood*
> *showing for all to see*
> *which of us right. That winter we sat about the table,*
> *silent potato eaters in a dark Dutch portrait.*
> *You made your small loss my empty victory,*
> *and we grew apart, deeper and deeper,*
> *over such shallow contests, until the costs*
> *to each of us climbed almost out of reach.*

The poem first appeared in *Out of Unknown Hands*, ed. by Libby Bernardin and Linda Kirszenbaum (Columbia, SC: R.L. Bryant, 1991). Reprinted with permission.

CHAPTER 7

SHOE SHINE

Richard Blanco

Ritual is one of the most important things a child can share with a parent. For me, the weekly or biweekly ceremony of shining shoes for all the members of the family remains special and vivid. It was a chance to learn who my father was, even if we just sat in silence for an hour or so.

Every other Thursday night I'd collect
the family's shoes from the dark corners
of the closet floors where they waited
like injured birds, awkward and helpless,

or like dead fish hooked on my fingers,
two pairs in each hand, the proud catch
of oxfords and pumps spilled on the tile
floor of our Florida room for Papá sitting

with legs crossed, inspecting my catch,
sorting the pile by gender and color, until
I'd return with my pairs, take my place
beside him ready for our ritual cleaning:

first, a few brushstrokes to loosen the dust,
then a light soapy wash with a soft cloth,
and after drying, a second inspection with
his eyes approving pairs ready for polish

applied with the middle and index fingertips
in light taps saying—así, así, suavecito—
holding my hand by the wrist, guiding it
over the leather, teaching me his method.

And I learned, and even after I learned
I would out live him, I pretended not to
know, ignoring the sense I had even then
that Thursdays would be what little I'd be

able to remember of him: a horse hair brush
played like a violin bow across the vamp,
the wisp of those strokes, years after years
of saying and doing, of going and coming,

I return to the pleasure of returning a shine
to shoes, those nights spent with nothing
but the good feel of a brush in my hand,
with nowhere to be and nothing to build.

CHAPTER 8

FOOT-LONG CHILI DOGS
FOR EVERYBODY

Joe Goeke

This poem is, for the most part, autobiographical. As teenagers in St. Louis, Missouri, around the age of 13, my friends and I saved up our weekly wages from rolling newspapers for a delivery man, and with it we bought season passes for the local Six Flags amusement park. Purchasing your first season pass amounted to a rite of passage in my family, where both of my older sisters got theirs around the same age as I did. Once we had our passes, my small group of friends started going to the park at least once a week, usually catching rides with my oldest sister who worked there at the fried chicken stand. When we began this routine, we expected that something mysterious would happen and suddenly we'd find ourselves able to talk and laugh with girls— maybe even ask them out. The event recounted in this poem illustrates how desperately we wanted that moment to come—and, indeed, how pitifully desperate we were, for we always found reasons to delay the inevitable and convinced ourselves that, somehow, we were outsmarting the very girls we had failed to impress.

> At the exit from Thunder River,
> where the wet riders walked out with wet t-shirts,
> we used to play a game of skill.
>
> The object was to toss a hula hoop,
> clearing Spuds Mackenzie's head, to land flat
> like a ring around the box he sat on.
>
> What made the prize so valuable
> wasn't its size—though it was big,
> big as the dog in the old beer ads.

It was sex appeal that you won him for.
Whenever a guy had a dog,
he brought it with him everywhere he walked,

and it caught the girls' eyes—you could tell
they wanted it by the way they looked.
You remember that old Van Halen song,

"Everybody Wants Some"?
It played loud in my head whenever I leaned
and threw the hoop and watched it fall.

Spuds's eyes were plastic beads,
the trademark spot surrounded one.
He wore a bandana, brilliant blue,

and if you were cool, you tore it off
and tied it round your neck or leg.
Sometimes I tore off and tied mine too.

Then, one day, I won three dogs
and gave one each to Todd and Justin.
The three of us walked around proud,

in disguise, legs flashing neon blue.
We could feel the girls watching us,
and I wondered if they knew.

Then one of them with friends, like us,
stood in our way—about our age,
maybe older, but just by a year or two.

How did we win so many dogs?
She wanted to know, and I felt
my head get tight, my elbows stiff.

Blood rushed to my cheeks—I know—
I felt the heat when Justin looked at me
like I should be the one to speak.

I don't know—lucky throw, I guess.
I think that's what I said,
and the girlfriends giggled,

and the guys behind me froze.
Wouldja sell me one . . . for five bucks?
I can't seem to win—no matter what I do.

Sure, I said, five dollars is fine.
I mean—sure,
that's plenty.

As she dug into her pocket,
her hair fell in her eyes,
and she pushed it back again.

Then, she pulled out the bill
and put out her hand.

I wanted to give her the dog for free,
because she smiled, and she talked to me,
but instead I was dumb: I took the money.

And once she had the dog, they turned away.
They left us standing in the arbored tunnel—
three boys, two dogs, and a patch of shade.

It was a dim place to be,
and it stayed that way, indefinitely,
until Todd grabbed one of my shoulders and yelled,

Foot-long chili dogs for everybody!
Sell another one and we've got cheese fries!

Chapter 9

Confession: I Never Killed a Deer

Bert Easter

For many men, participation in sports or hunting is a rite of passage. Growing up in rural Mississippi, this author saw his failure to actually kill something as a failure to complete a necessary rite of passage into manhood.

It's true. I never killed a deer.

Where I come from, that is one of the rites of passage and signs of growing into manhood. It's right up there with walking down the aisle of the local Baptist church. Oh, don't get me wrong—I always looked forward to the hunting trips with Daddy and the guys of the local hunt club. But when it came to killing a deer, I just didn't see the point or the need, though I knew it was expected of me from when I was too young to shoot a gun.

And by the way, I owned guns even then. You see, they give guns to young boys in Mississippi, even before they are trusted to carry them. I received a gun for my birthday on the earliest birthday that I can remember, at 6 years old. It was presented and then taken away and placed in my grandfather's collection—for safe keeping. Oh that gun didn't stay there long till I was in the woods with it. It always seemed a burden to carry that gun along for the day-long trip, especially since I always knew I was never really going to shoot anything. So why even worry with keeping up with the heavy thing.

Confession: I did leave it once, propped against a tree, and then I spent most of a hot afternoon trying to retrace my steps to find that gift from my grandfather.

Getting up early in the cold of an early winter and getting out in the fields to hunt was sometimes rewarded with a great day of sightseeing and nature spotting. Most of the time you can see lots of animals in the woods when it's not hunting season. Early on I wondered if Nature had told the deer that it was their season and to lay low in the brush—to take this day off from the corn field that they had enjoyed earlier in the fall, and to visit the stream only in the late evening or on the too-cold-for-the-hunter mornings. But later I figured that it was the lost member of the herd that fell earlier in the season, when the shot that rang out in their too large ears really told them that this place was not safe. After they went into the brush to hide, they had to be flushed out to be found, and this would send them off like bullets, running from the dogs and the hunters and the buck shot that rang out behind them.

But not running away from me. "I didn't get a clear shot." "They were too fast." Fast and beautiful, leaping and flowing across the hillside and then out of sight.

It wasn't until some of the boys younger than me had "bagged a big one" that I began feeling the pressure to kill. Pictures were taken, and the other boys moved into manhood in the eyes of the older men.

Confession: I never understood how farmers who had stopped cleaning their own hogs and cows could enjoy stringing up a fresh shot deer.

Years earlier, my Uncle Ted had announced that the local meat market would be cleaning his farm animals. Most farmers followed suit, and the family hog kills that turned into family socials came to a close. But a proud hunter with a fresh kill taken back to the hunt club attracted more hunters than flies. They all wanted to take their own knives to the deer, to lay claim to the one cut down from the herd. Many posed with the proud victor—and the loser. Cameras were always loaded for this moment. It was part of the tradition, as was the picture later posted inside the club for all to see. I always wondered why no pictures of the fatted calf were taken—more work and time was spent getting it ready for the big day. All this bonding in the woods escaped me, and often I felt alone in the woods with the hunters all around.

I was a liar in the woods in search of the wildflower that I couldn't name. I just wanted to spot the animals and watch them.

Confession: One warm day after the trails in the woods led me to afternoon and a bluff to rest on, I heard movement beyond me in the fall leaves. I lowered my gun from its shoulder strap and crept to look over the rise into the woods. There on a sandy slope near a small stream stood the most beautiful buck, and moving in behind him to the water were a doe and a small buck. I lay silently and watched the deer as they with caution watched after each other. The small bluff had provided protection for their access to water. I watched as each took a turn at drinking and taking rest from the day's heat. It seemed as if they had been there for quite some time before I noticed that the buck became aware of something. I thought he had noticed me, my noise or scent. But then I heard the dogs and guessed that he had heard them too. I stood up and scared the deer, sent them all running off in the other direction—away from me and away from the oncoming dogs of the hunters. I fell into line with the hunters and chased the dogs. They later ran into a swamp and we couldn't follow them.

It was soon after that day that I gave up the hunting trips, and retired my grandfather's gift, which had only been used for target practice anyway—target practice at cans before hunting season and at trees during the race of the hunt. I had gotten pretty good at it. I've since moved to South Carolina, and I still don't hunt. The gun is still in Granddaddy's shotgun case at my father's house in Mississippi—as far as I know.

CHAPTER 10

I Can Look You in the Eye Without Shame: A Story of Recovery

Mark P. Nugent

When I was asked to write about my experiences as a man, I immediately had to laugh and was utterly amused. I am amused because the past 5 years of my life have changed my perspective on life and what manhood is.

I have recently run into a saying that has quickly become a favorite of mine and that can give a small idea of what you will hear from me:

"Those who are weak have to act strong; those who are strong are able to act weak."

What I am trying to tell during my story is that fitting a role doesn't work very well and that you need certain things as a human being that will allow you to be genuinely happy without material possessions or mind-altering substances.

I simply believe that we humans, especially men, are losing out on the good life. We get stuck in a role that keeps us hiding all our insecurities, fears, and secrets in order not to look weak.

Ideas on Becoming a Man

For each person there are different extremes. I have been working with at-risk boys for 5 years and it has completely changed my life, as well as taught me a lot of the negative impacts on having a male image. I know for me it has been something I needed to throw away to create a new concept of what a man should be. I needed to get rid of my old ideas and be willing to come up with new ones.

The idea of what a man is and what a man should be gets thrown at you from an early age. I do not know why this is or how it came about. I just know it's true. A man is someone who should be self-reliant, be strong, and not show any emotion. He should be tough and no matter what is thrown at him, he should be able to handle it on his own.

A man doesn't need any help and to show any sign of weakness is not allowed because you will then be taken advantage of. You have these very prevalent ideas growing up. You have the movies of tough men who overcome incredible odds. You see it on the playground, growing up where those who are not athletic or weak are made fun of and rejected. You have your cliques in school of cool guys, jocks, nerds, druggies, and more. There is a lot of pressure to fit in and find your role as a man and create your own identity.

The sad part is most of us do not know who we really are and do not know how to connect with people on an emotional and personal level. That is why male bonding is always talked about.

It is a bunch of guys sitting around playing football, getting drunk, talking about women, or any other male activity that allows men to feel a closeness to each other without getting paranoid about looking weak.

Now this is the idea of what being a man is and how to fit in, or at least it is the way I see it, and I could be wrong.

GROWING UP

When I was a child, my parents gave me everything I needed and a lot of what I wanted. My parents are great ones. They have been married over 30 years now and have always given me, my brother, and my sister all the love they could and all the support they could. I really do have a great family. Unfortunately, I have always felt a little different from others and a little weaker than others.

I don't know where it came from and I don't know why it's there. I have almost always had problems connecting with people, and I will explain what that means a little later on. But growing up, I moved around some and ended up settling in New Jersey in third grade.

Growing up, I was athletic. I played a lot of sports and was pretty good at it. I had no real problem fitting into the male crowd and feeling all right. I'm not real sure where the idea of being a man and the image that goes with it started to be a problem, but I'm sure it was somewhere in the 14-to 16-year-old range. I am now 27, so my memory of those early years is not very good. My high school years were filled with good times and bad, just like everyone else's.

The thing I remember most about high school is that I saw a lot of people who seemed relaxed and on top of things and I knew I wasn't. I was insecure and not really sure how to talk to people in large crowds. One-on-one I wouldn't have a problem, but put me in a crowd and I got scared.

Now, how do you tell that to anyone growing up? Being a man, or at least my perception of being a man, was that I was weak and different. No one else seemed to have this problem and some people were always the center of attention. Me, I always wanted to be the center of attention but hated being in the spotlight. I doubt I could have put all of this into words back then, but I can express it now.

I did have friends and I still am friends with them today. I was a good athlete so I played on some teams and there were times I was happy. But I always knew something was a little different. Women intimidated me and that is not a manly thing, especially in high school.

I always heard stories about sex and saw couples walking around and having fun. Me, I was scared to death to go and talk to women because I didn't think I was good enough. So I felt different and weak, and that is not manly either.

So what do you do when all of this is going on inside you and you're not supposed to look weak? I hid it and put on the image that everything was OK and I could handle my problems.

PROBLEMS AND NEEDS

I have always had the idea that I don't need help from anyone and that I can fix my own problems. I'm a man, damn it. If I have a problem I will work it out on my own, and if I can't do it on my own then the problem can't be fixed. This way of thinking got me into a lot of trouble, and every now and then still does. But this was the way I thought a man was supposed to be growing up.

Another important part of my life that I haven't mentioned yet is that I'm an alcoholic (I've been in recovery for over 2 years now). And a lot of what I think deals with alcoholism because we are such defiant people. But growing up with all these anxieties, fears, and lack of self-worth—and with no one to talk to—left me getting somewhat depressed. Then I learned what alcohol did for me.

The first time I drank I blacked out, which should have told me something about myself, but it didn't. All I remember about the early days of drinking was that after a couple of drinks I relaxed. All the feelings of difference and weakness went away. I was able to talk to people without being worried how they looked at me.

I was able to go and talk to women, and if they didn't like me I considered it their loss. I was funny and able to entertain a crowd and feel at ease while doing it. I finally felt like I fit in and I was enough as a person. Unfortunately, I did have to sober up and then all of those feelings would come back.

Now don't get me wrong, I was not miserable in those days. Some days were good and some days were bad. Overall, growing up was fun. It's just that I had some struggles along the way that I didn't know how to handle and no one to talk to and therefore kept it all to myself. But life was pretty good.

In high school, I didn't drink all that much. I drank when I could and smoked a little dope and just went through life. I did get into several problems with my parents over all of this. I got caught several times for it and it made life a little more tense.

FREEDOM AND REBELLION

My parents are good parents. They didn't want me to be drinking and getting into trouble. Today I don't blame them, but when I was a teenager I figured they had too many rules, didn't want me to have any fun, and therefore I would have to lie to them in order to do the things I wanted to do.

I was just a teenager being defiant, thinking I had all the answers and could handle myself. Luckily, nothing too severe happened, at least in my opinion, and I made it through high school and went to college.

I don't know why I went to college. It was just something that everyone in my town and school did. I didn't know what I wanted to do when I grew up, but I did know that it meant me getting out of my house, having no more rules to follow, and being able to do what I want.

So I went to college. College was quite an experience. I wasn't real worried about grades and finding out what I wanted to do with my life. It was a time to party. In my first year I found people who drank like I drank. We all drank to excess and did whatever we could get our hands on. I am not going to go through 4 years of drinking and partying because it really is not all that important to me. Needless to say, I rebelled against all those rules I always had. I had the freedom to do what I wanted.

I grew my hair long and my alcoholism went into full bloom during those 4 years. I had fake IDs, connections for whatever else I wanted, and people who partied like me. I caused a lot of tension in my family with bad grades, getting arrested and calling my mom from jail, going into debt, not calling home a lot, and many other things. This was not the way I wanted my life to be and I knew it. I would sober up the next day, try to figure out what I had done the night before, and the guilt and remorse would come.

KNOWING AND NOT KNOWING

I would feel lonely and different from the others. Even though I knew the same guys for 4 years, I never really knew them. We drank together, talked trash together, and had many crazy times together, but that doesn't mean I knew them. I didn't have any close friends who I could talk to.

During those 4 years things went up and down. I could be happy, on top of the world, and then I could be absolutely depressed and feeling like I had nowhere to turn.

Being a man, I knew no one else felt this way and I wasn't about to tell anyone. So what do you do? Me, I drank and partied all the more.

I could always drink and feel better or at least go and black out and then not think or feel anymore. But there were times I got scared because I knew I was drinking too much.

It got out of hand sometimes. I would try to quit or control my drinking habits but it would never last very long. After a day or two, I would get bored and all these feelings would come back and the memories of the trouble I got into last time would wear off and off I would go again.

I was lucky that I never got caught or hurt anyone during these days, and for that I thank God for watching out for me. But I graduated college and moved back home.

CAREER TIME

Now after 4 years of college I was not ready for a job and decided to keep working at my summer jobs.

I did landscaping and put in fences during the summer. I loved the manual labor, and the guys I worked with liked ending the day with a couple of beers. I was content. But drinking the way I did and living at home doesn't work very well, so I started looking for a real job and ended up moving to Virginia, which started turning my life around.

I worked at a wilderness school that deals with at-risk youth ages 11–18. They come from all types of homes and troubles. We live outdoors in tents we build out of pine trees, and the average stay is 15 months.

There is no way I could ever describe this place to anyone. I will try to tell you how it changed my life and my idea of manhood, and I will say it is probably the best program for juveniles that I know of.

Statistically, 85% of our kids never get into trouble with the system again. I'm not big on statistics but those are good, considering the school has been around for 25 years. But what you won't see is how these kids come in defiant, mistrustful, angry, and depressed and are able to turn their lives around and be genuinely happy.

The way that happens is we are able to connect with these kids on an emotional level that they have never had before. We allow kids to see our own struggles and insecurities and make it safe for them to be open with their own. We allow them to be themselves and not an image they have to put on.

Now some are more resistant than others but after 2 months they are usually well on their way. Since this is not about the school but about my experiences, let me continue with my story.

I will keep it about me. Just imagine being in a place where you are able to connect with kids and allow them to get rid of their secrets (and I have heard them all) and to just be themselves without medication or anything. It is truly amazing.

But the problem was that I had never talked about feelings before I felt different, I was not a big fan of confrontation, and I knew no one in Virginia.

Oh yeah, the job is 5 days a week for 24 hours a day. I lived, ate, and worked with the kids doing the same thing they were doing. I had my supervisor, a man named Ben. He is one of the most amazing people I have ever seen.

ABOUT BEN

He has a presence around him that made people want approval from him and worry about him. You knew he cared about you. One moment he could be confronting a 16-year-old bully, getting angry with him and going right at him, and the next minute he would be comforting a 17-year-old depressed kid in a gentle way.

All kids respond to him because he has a way of making those around him feel close to him and able to open up and talk to him. He was my first supervisor. When I first met him I immediately liked him and wanted to hang out with him.

Unfortunately, when I came to the school my idea of friendship was a little different than at the school. If I liked you I would harass you and tease you a little. Never intending any harm, just joking around, being sarcastic.

Within a week, Ben sat me down and asked me if I had a problem with him. He said he got frustrated with the way I was getting at him and didn't understand it.

I had never known anybody to talk like that and he threw me off pretty quick. I quickly told him that I liked him and that's just the way I was used to showing people that I liked them. He understood and today we look back and laugh at that story. But that is where I began a whole new way of communicating with people.

SEEING AND SPEAKING THE TRUTH

At the school we are not sarcastic with each other, and if someone is they will be confronted on it to see what the problem really is. I had never seen a place where people (kids and staff) were so open about themselves and letting people know what they were scared of, insecure about, and anything else.

My first 13 months were a roller coaster ride. There were days that I wanted to quit and there were days I never wanted to leave. I learned how to work with kids without being their buddy. I always wanted people to like me and not be angry with me, but that doesn't work well with kids.

I had to learn not to let fear control my actions. I had so much fear about doing the right thing, saying the right thing to help out, and getting the kids to like me, that I needed to learn a lot and talk a lot.

There were some kids bigger than me, and I knew that they were stronger. I did not feel like telling them they were lying and mistreating people in the group. But Ben would come along and help me out and ask me why I was so scared. Then he would tell me some of his fears when he started, and everything would be all right.

No one had ever told me they were scared of things or felt inadequate before, and I started to feel more normal and happier.

The school is based on relationships, relationships with other staff and relationships with the students. I love this idea because it breaks through all the images people put up in order to hide their true selves.

I have seen kids who come in with their hair dyed, wearing chains and big baggy pants, turn into sensitive kids who just want to be liked. Relationships were always hard for me because I was a person who had a lot of feelings of insecurities and doubts, and I wasn't used to telling anyone about these feelings.

MEN FEEL

The old idea of what it means to be a man is that men always hold it together, men don't have feelings, and emotions are for women. These old ideas got me into a lot of trouble. I had Ben start telling me that he always felt pushed away by me and didn't really feel close to me. I didn't know what that meant, but he said he could see I was depressed but didn't know what was going on with me.

I started to be able to talk about feeling less than others, being scared of having friends, not knowing how to talk to other people, and all the other stuff I had inside me that I didn't talk about before. I found out it was OK to say, "Hey, I'm scared of this and I need some help right now," and people wanted that from me.

For 13 months all of my old ideas about what a man should be were completely changed because I saw how it worked with the kids. I saw how it worked with me. I was able to have friends that I could rely on who wouldn't judge me or look at me as being weak. They would help me out with it, and the more I was able to do that the more confidence I had in myself.

After 13 months I was promoted to supervisor, which meant I got to go home at night. Now the people at the school and kids there were teaching me about relationships—how to confront problems instead of avoiding them, how to trust your instincts and how to believe in yourself.

I found out things about myself I didn't like and things I did like, and I was able to grow and learn from them. I was changing as much as these kids were changing and I enjoyed it.

AN OLD SHADOW REMAINED

But I was still drinking. While I was getting a new perspective on life and what relationships really are, I still had some feelings of difference and inadequacy. You see, no matter how much I would talk about myself, I still had secrets that I knew I would never tell anyone. They always made me feel different. At first my drinking wasn't too bad because I could only drink 2 days out of the week.

Once I got promoted I could drink every night if I wanted to, because as a supervisor, I was allowed to go home every night after work. At first I would go and have only a couple of beers at the bar, but it soon became that I was getting drunk a couple of times during the weekdays and every weekend. I would then go back to work and people would be mad at me or concerned about my drinking, depending on how I handled myself that night.

You see, no matter how much I would tell people about myself and start to feel closer to people, I always had these feelings of difference that I was less than others and that people didn't understand me. Even though I was able to talk about my thoughts and feelings more with people, and people said they understood, I never really believed them.

My drinking got worse, but I still was able to handle my job, help the kids, and help other staff. But I began to keep people from getting close to me. I started what we call "internalizing" my feelings.

The old ideas of being a man and doing it my way, not showing any signs of weakness, were still there. So while I allowed people to know some things about me, there was still a gap, a part of me, that I kept from people.

Drinking was still making me feel better or at least forget about my problems, but it was getting worse.

THEY KNEW

Every now and then Ben or someone else would sit me down and tell me they were mad at me and knew I was depressed and wanted to know what the heck was going on. I would tell them as best I could and was able to talk about my drinking some. But I loved drinking and what it did for me. Unfortunately, I was never able to control how much I drank once I started. I believe the school helped me from getting too depressed and doing something stupid—suicide was a thought every now and then—and from getting into many physical consequences.

At this point I had paid my bills off, and I never got into trouble with the law in Virginia. But I was leading two lives. One at work where I was there about 3 years now, and the other, the inner me.

I knew how to confront kids and wasn't scared of them, no matter who they were or what size they were. I was able to help staff learn about themselves and how to confront themselves and how to work with kids.

Out of the 70 some kids at our school, I had a relationship with each of them and was able to reach them on an emotional level. I realized where each kid needed to grow and change in order to be successful with their lives.

I had relationships with all of the staff, especially the supervisors, and they could rely on me to help them out when they needed it. I was being pretty successful at the school and people looked up to me.

On the other hand, those who really knew me and saw how I acted outside of work were getting more concerned. I usually watched who I drank around as best as I could so that I wouldn't get in too much trouble.

People had been telling me for awhile that I drank too much and that it affected my job and my relationships with the people I worked with.

The other side of me began to get depressed. During the day I was busy doing things and didn't have too much time to sit and think. After work, I became depressed, anxious, and withdrawn. I wouldn't answer the phone much because I was usually drunk, and the guilt of it all started to catch up with me.

The last 6 months of my drinking were pretty bad. I was blacking out 5 nights a week and I was getting to be a mean drunk. I was told that I cursed people out, became belligerent, and scared people with the way I drank. "Sorry I was drunk" wasn't working very well with my coworkers. With all of these relationships where we try to really get to know each other, we end up saying everything. People would tell me they were concerned about me and angry at me. They all wanted to help me out, and I would sometimes try to let people know how I was feeling and what was going on with me. But I couldn't stop.

THE BOTTOM

Finally, one morning a good friend of mine told me he was sick of my drinking and all the crap I pulled when I was drunk. He was tired of having to defend me to those who didn't know me as well. He was tired of all the excuses I had and didn't want to be around me anymore.

After 6 months of what I just thought was a bad string of luck, that was the final straw. I had always thought it wasn't quite that bad yet because I was still doing my job. I had also been talking to someone for the last few months about my drinking. He was in recovery and said to give him a call when I was ready. Before, I wasn't ready. Ben was there that day, and for the first time in probably 10 years, I just broke down and cried.

I was defeated and felt like I had no place to turn. The idea of holding it together and doing it my way had not worked well at all. I had no more excuses and I was just worn out. I was scared to drink again but I knew I couldn't quit on my own. I had tried to quit or control it before, and it never lasted for longer than a week or two. The problem would blow over, I would do a little better, or life would get too tense and I would drink again, and I knew it.

CLIMBING UP

So I called the guy up and started in recovery and haven't had anything to drink or a mind-altering substance since.

I also have no desire to drink, and I never thought that was possible. Recovery was tough but the idea that I could do it my way was gone. The idea that I could handle my own problems was gone.

I hated asking for help because I felt weak. I hated knowing I was powerless over something because it made me feel weak. But I did and people I worked with helped me out because all of those feelings came back, and I needed someone to talk to.

I learned that the more open I was with my coworkers, the more they respected and felt close to me. I never thought it would happen that way.

COMING BACK, A NEW LIFE

In recovery, I followed some directions and got rid of all my secrets and started to clean up my past. I found people who drank they way I did who were happy and sober. I never thought that was possible. I didn't feel different anymore and I had a new hope.

In the last 2 years my life has been amazing. There are good days and bad days, but I know it will always get better.

I have become the Program Director of my school. I am not ashamed of the past and have no secrets in my life today. I have cleaned up my past and all the people I hurt along the way. I try to hide nothing from the people I work with and I have true relationships where nothing is hidden.

I am not living a double life anymore. I am not scared to be myself, even when I'm afraid and insecure. I know how to handle it now. I'm able to relax and realize that life just happens and to enjoy it.

A REAL MAN NOW

My experiences as a man have been fun and challenging. I have had a lot of different experiences. The last 5 years have completely changed my life and I hope people learn something from it.

For too long I went around feeling insecure, scared, and weak, but having to hold it together because men are supposed to be strong.

I have been lonely and had no real purpose to life, but if you asked me I would have all the answers. I have seen so many adults and kids hide behind the image of what their idea of a man should be. The problem is once you get past that image, they are depressed, angry, scared, and lonely, but spend all their time trying to impress other people and act like they have all the answers.

I have found that it is more manly to ask for help. It is so much harder to say, "I'm scared and I'm not sure what to do." It is harder to say, "Look, I'm feeling lonely today. Do you have a minute to talk?"

What happens is that you become connected to other people around you. You get relationships that have depth and weight and people who truly care for you and you for them.

To me today, being a man means being able to ask for help and show my weaknesses to others. To admit that I do not always have the answers. To take actions regarding doing things that I do not always want to do.

I still hate asking for help but I do it anyway, and the more I do it, the easier it gets. I don't like telling people my insecurities and fears, but I do it. The more I do these things, the closer I feel to people and the happier I get.

I tried a lot of things to make me happy that didn't work. The more I let people get to know me and then try to help out others, the better my life gets. I never would have thought this all possible, but it's happening every day.

Some days are better than others, but it is happening. The most important thing that has happened is that I can look you in the eye without any shame or guilt. I can look knowing that I am not trying to impress you, and I can truly feel that I am enough as a person and a man.

CHAPTER 11

FROM GUNS TO POETRY

Daniel R. Collins

What does it mean to be a man? A tricky question, at best. Society is changing so fast it is difficult to define anything anymore. Gender roles vary greatly depending on one's geographical location, cultural background, and personal experience.

Modern men, young and old, are finding their identities challenged at all times. The predominant influences of past generations, archetypes of history, constant pressures of the media, and role models in our immediate surroundings clash to form our sense of self. It is amazing anyone can cope with the stress involved in simply figuring out who he is, or his role in society in relation to others.

Within moments of birth, children begin to identify with the world through the behavior of others and immediate influences around them. The foundation of a lifelong personality begins to form in these early years.

The desire to fit into the molds made for us as children is intensely powerful. We tend to aspire to the guidelines laid down for us by family, friends, and the media, duplicating the images of humanity around us. In some cases, we try to become the norm. Even at a very early age we learn which behaviors will elicit negative and positive responses from those around us. These models of humanity and gender continue to guide us through our adult lives, with all their strong points and shortcomings. In trying to define myself as a man and a person, I am often reminded of experiences that have greatly affected my overall perception of the world. Perhaps those moments reveal an answer to the question posed.

ONE POWERFUL MEMORY

It was fall and cold already. The sun shone red through pine boughs on the comfortable downward slope of the wooded grove just east of lake Anisagunticook, named after the beaver by the local Native American tribes, their shapes similar when viewed from high in the neighboring Appalachian hills. I was just 10, orange vested, with my shotgun crooked under my arm. Boots made soft sounds in the wind, the ground familiar, just hardening in late October. We were looking for rabbits, walking easily.

My father hunted for years and never shot a thing. I can imagine him walking into Sears & Roebuck, all of 25, smiling broadly, frightening the locals. He probably looked the part. I've seen pictures of him out in our wooded yard wearing worn denims and floppy work boots, thick sawdust flannel shirts, wandering white dreamlike chickens in the background. But his bearing must have screamed of the city. He grew up in Hoboken, Irish and poor, bread with no butter and cold coffee for supper. He married my mother 6 years after he saw her standing, shy and golden, against the padded gymnasium wall of a high school dance. They were gone a few years later, packed in a Volkswagen, heading for the hills of New England to start over.

His loud friendly voice, his New York accent—the man behind the counter hadn't heard anything like it in years, and was probably taken aback. I imagine this scene . . . I tell you the mannerisms of native Mainers are like no other, unique to the elder generations of that particular corner of the world. My father must have seemed to them like a character from some matinee drive-in film.

The woods get quiet sometimes, as if sensing your presence, guessing your intentions. The sensation is similar to walking into a crowded room at an inappropriate time and facing a wall of incredulous silence, eyes turned toward you, wondering who you are and why you've come. I'd experienced this before. I had been raised in the woods and was familiar with their strange ways. Sometimes the silence was the silence of animals, in nearly constant motion, suddenly stopped short after picking up your scent or the vibrations from your boots on the hardening ground. Sometimes it was just a lull in the wind. The end result, however, is the feeling that something, inevitably, is about to happen.

THE WEAPON

I had fired the weapon before. I can clearly remember the first time, all of 8, no idea what to expect. My father walked me out into the hot straw afternoon, shotgun under one arm and a large square sack dragging behind in the hay. When we'd reached a safe spot in the field sloping downhill from the house he opened the burlap bag and pulled out a tall skinny mirror, the cheap kind that bend in the wind, one he found out in the old carriage house perhaps. He carefully set the mirror up against an old oak stump at the edge of our field, then handed me the 20 gauge, safety on as always. If you are not familiar with firearms, you should know that a 20-gauge shotgun is no small weapon. It is capable of killing a black bear, and powerful enough to throw a grown man off balance with its recoil, if he is not prepared for the blast. My father directed me to stare long and hard at my own image in that mirror, wavering in the wind with the glass, and to fire when ready.

The explosion knocked me literally on my can, a walloping shock that struck me deaf, dumb, and down. In the short flight backward, in the periphery of my vision, was a shower of almost imperceptible shards of my own image, just instant millions of deaths shimmering and gone. I sat up stiff, saw that the mirror and a good part of the stump were no more, and burst into hot fearful tears.

"Anything you point that gun at. . ." my Father said, "dies. Do you understand?" He hauled me back up to the house in a sort of posttraumatic shock. My right shoulder and arm had gone numb, and the developing bruises from the shotgun's kick would last for weeks. He caught hell from my mother when she realized exactly what had happened. She knew he was going to teach me how to shoot that day, she just hadn't realized what would happen, that it was some large event in my life. Maybe she sensed something would never be the same for her son now, shattering his own image in the wind with a weapon that could just as easily have torn husband or child to tatters if something had gone wrong.

NEAR MISS

Now, 2 years later, in the sudden silence of nature's awareness of some strange new predator, I fired that gun again. We had all gone still, sensing the tension in the forest's silence. Just then a flurry of movement from behind a downed birch tree; something jumped and I fired. It was an instinctual reaction, an unbelievably quick and accurate movement. Swivel and squeeze trigger, and the world explodes and then silence.

This time, strong enough now to handle the blast of the weapon, I stood agape and deaf for what seemed like an hour before I heard the muffled voices of my father and brothers. "What was that? Careful, what was that?"

I inched forward, stepped over the shredded skin of the birch tree, and quickly spotted the bottom half of a small red chipmunk, torn in two when he peeked his head over the branch.

My heart was racing, my eyes wide and dry. I felt nothing but some indescribable sense of urgency, like I either had to quickly kill again, or else hide this shameful display away forever and flee.

We returned to the house, deep concern on my father's face, not quite sure how to handle this situation. It could have easily been my own little brother (only 6 years old then) who popped out of some hiding place and been tragically killed, or a neighbor or pet or who knows what.

On the other hand, he had given me the gun, taught me to use it. If there had been an accident he would have felt as if he had pulled the trigger.

I don't think we ever discussed this. I think we both knew exactly what had transpired. I spent years hunting with friends and family after that (not much else to do in Maine between October and April) but I never shot another animal. I even remember seeing a rabbit or two in plain sight, having stalked them carefully, knowing their habits, and then just watching them until they slipped away.

On one such occasion, I even fired a round into the ground a few feet away from a great gray hare. I don't know why I did it, maybe I wanted him to know what I could do but wouldn't. Maybe I needed a bullet to miss for once, break the great mystery and apologize somehow to the red chipmunk and all victims of the careless power of humanity.

THIRTEEN

The next thing I knew I was fighting to find my own identity in the maelstrom of adolescence. I was sheltered by my small-town surroundings and had little experience with the outside world, but I had begun to hear things. By the time I was 13, I knew that I would be leaving home, going to college, and fulfilling a need to explore and experience not only the joy of life, but also the hardship.

It had nothing to do with any unhappiness at home, no hatred of the nature that served as the theater of my youth. It was simply an inborn, and encouraged, desire for constant progress. I was hungry for knowledge and experience, and knew I would want more than the life my peers aspired to.

THE JOURNEY WITHIN

Books, primarily, fed my mind with images of cities and countries far beyond my grasp. Reading was always a favorite activity, an escape mechanism and educational resource of mine, ever since I was very young.

In the eighth grade, I read the *Lord of the Rings* trilogy by J.R.R. Tolkien three times, back to back. I drew great detailed maps of the imaginary land, painted battlefield scenes, designed costumes with my brothers for mock warfare in the woods, and deciphered the Rhune script invented for the fantastical world by its author.

I was absorbed, learned strange imaginary languages, and exhibited far more interest and felt more passion for such stories than for any of my schooltime studies.

As I matured, and my literature of choice slowly evolved, I carried with me the absolute admiration and desire for the written word. Poets and philosophers became my experts; storytellers and singers became my guides. And I began to write more seriously myself.

As early as kindergarten I had found a love of writing, and was dramatically recording the camping and hiking adventures that I had all through middle school. Sometimes I churned out 60-page stories about a weekend jaunt up some nearby cliffs and distributed copies to all who had participated.

When I entered high school, and began to rebel against the social cliques that even in small, primarily poor, and uneducated towns such as mine held an all-powerful grasp on young lives, the tireless writing continued.

A Poet Evolves

I started writing poetry as a joke with one friend when I was about 14, poking fun at the flowery melodrama we thought the art was, laughing for hours over sickly-sweet odes written for any number of unlucky muses. I was shocked a year or two later when the same condensed, colorful style that had warranted so much distaste and mockery suddenly seemed the most effective way of expressing the array of complicated emotions and ideas that dominated my day-to-day existence as a teenager.

Soon I would address my fears and my problems, as well as hopes and aspirations, through the medium of poetry. I wasn't interested in the traditional works of the famous poets and never felt a passion for their work. But I had found an outlet in my own form of the art, a condensed and usually improvisational rendering of my own impressions of the world (usually confined to the events of my life).

What I couldn't say to my family in the awkward years of adolescence, couldn't depend on my friends to understand, and found no answers for in society at large, I spoke of in poetry. In this way I found strength and self-confidence that I later realized had eluded those popular androids that had tortured me in my youth and stolen those traits from me in the first place.

I began to trust my own interpretation of the world around me, with the support of my expanding list of authors exploring similar issues to back me up. In the works of Albert Camus, Jean-Paul Sartre, Ernest Hemingway, and others I was able to identify the source of some underlying feelings that I couldn't categorize within the realm of my surroundings.

In their philosophy and experience I found the noise made, if you will, that now echoed, unnamed, in my own mind. I couldn't describe my own thoughts on such timeless themes as sexuality, spirituality, authenticity, and death until I understood I was just the latest in an infinite tradition of heavy-hearted and disoriented humans sitting with head on hands just trying to understand the point of being alive in the world.

Literature helped free me, for a time, from the short-term and insignificant concerns of most of my classmates, and, it seemed to me, most of the world.

Other Boys

My friends were limited to the goings on about them. They didn't strive to find out what was happening beyond the walls of our small-town existence. In some cases, their families had lived on the same plot of land, worked the same trade, and stayed within a day's walk of it all since the original settlers of the area chopped down the first pine tree nearly 400 years ago. It was difficult for them to understand my own strong desire to leave the area, to challenge their own deeply instilled beliefs about the future and the possibilities available to us as a generation.

The Journey Outside

My mother began enrolling me in summer programs starting at about the eighth grade. It was then that I was exposed to new influences, mainly kids from other towns and states with knowledge of books, music, and regional issues that had never crossed my mind. The friends I made crewing on schooners off the coast of Bar Harbor or studying American history at Bates College in Lewiston, Maine, served to bring up vague whispers of artists, musicians, political figures, and social injustices which I never knew existed.

And it didn't hurt that the people I met through these experiences saw me in a new light, allowing me to do the same. They didn't remember me as an outcast kid in the fifth grade; they hadn't seen me struggling with my weight, with my sense of self and my dignity all through the early years of puberty.

The women I met were sometimes attracted to me, a preposterous thought to most self-conscious teenage boys. I was not expected to behave in accordance with the model gender and intellectual roles established haphazardly by the collection of peers I had grown accustomed to. And the men I met respected my artistic aspirations and they encouraged invention.

Music and Meaning

Music began to surround me. It's hard to explain the eerie sense of deja vu that set upon me when classic tracks from the Rolling Stones, Beatles, and Doors suddenly brought back memories of hearing the very same records as an infant. But there was new music, my music.

Bands began to speak to me directly, and I tried to talk back by absorbing myself in the lyrics and melodies, and learning to play music myself. I had played the saxophone for years in the marching band and knew I had a natural talent for music, but had never experienced passion for it.

When I picked up my dad's guitar at the age of 13 (which I still perform with to this day), I knew something exciting would come of it.

And school wasn't a total waste, although it served mainly as grounds for my own inquiries, with skipped study halls spent in the back room of the library drinking coffee, reading, and listening to the Velvet Underground.

I began to read the works of modern writers. Allen Ginsberg, Gregory Corso, and Jack Kerouac were among the most famous; Emily XYZ, Jim Carroll, and Richard Hell were some of the lesser known writers.

Playing in bands throughout high school further increased my self-confidence as an artist, and a man. I began to look only toward my eventual escape into the world.

TWENTY AND TRANSFORMATION

Moving to New York to attend Ithaca College was a huge step in my life. It was a transition which took me as an individual who existed in my old surroundings through a tremendous period of transformation.

I learned to learn again, for one thing. I had never really studied or seemed to do anything in high school. It was all too easy. I immediately had to realize that my intellectual prowess, which had seemed an unstoppable wave of truth and rebellion by the time I left home, was actually just run-of-the-mill college-bound material with a little extra reading thrown in.

The conservative "moral" framework of rural Maine, which I had always questioned, dissolved in the diversity around me. Suddenly I was confronted with increasingly different social, racial, and sexual backgrounds. I became friendly with many people experimenting with homosexuality, with none of the outright disapproval exhibited by many people in my youth.

My friends were Jewish, African-American, Mexican, and white, as well as Irish, Italian, and Greek. All cultures echoed in our conversations. We played with drugs, with music, with each other.

For the first time I knew people who openly discussed their experiences with sexual, physical, and psychological abuse. A dialogue was opened, if you will, with the world.

CONTINUING THE OUTWARD JOURNEY

It was traumatic to leave that world, after 6 years in the upstate New York town. I had found acceptance as a musician, as an artist, and as a man.

I remember being told by one vixen who caught my attention, when she finally disposed of my heart, that I was simply too nice. She needed someone, she said, who would yell and smack her around once in a while. While that was a little extreme, the general sentiment had followed me throughout my life. "The nice guy finishes last"; "you're just like a brother to me." I had more "sisters" than a nun in any convent.

I decided I wanted to "finish last," if that was the price to pay for respect to women, and all humankind. And besides, the best poetry is written in the vague waiting that accompanies the broken heart. I have a box full of poems from high school and college, nothing I would print now, on the subject. They number in the thousands. I had learned a lot about relationships, suffering through a 2-year disaster and several misguided flings.

Finally, I found something real, and it has lasted to this day.

INTELLECTUAL MATURITY

After initially having trouble adapting to the rigorous schedule of academia, and nearly failing out several times, I was overtaken by a passion for knowledge that I had never known.

I delved into spiritual studies of Native American, Buddhist, Jewish, Christian, and other traditions and history. I read in earnest the manifestos of the existentialist philosophers. I pondered the environmental writings of modern and ancient ecologists and spent uncountable hours in the gorges of that region stalking deer and watching the sun as it set over a different mark on the horizon each day.

And I worked like hell to get my grades back up, achieving nearly perfect marks in my later years (with a few problems here and there). By the time I graduated I didn't want to stop, and I can't wait to continue my formal education, if the opportunity arises.

I have applied to several graduate programs. I had to decline one offer because I didn't want to double the $20,000 I owe for my undergraduate degree. Other programs declined my applications, looking for more experience or possibly sniffing at the few classes I failed as a wide-eyed, addle-brained freshman.

Although I know I don't need it to survive in this world, I crave the community of learning—more than the knowledge itself. And I feared the working world. I didn't want to sacrifice myself to the 9-to-5 grind that turned all of my high school friends, and their parents before them, into passionless zombies working from check to check. After the initial trauma of leaving that college universe came a 6-month period of living on a dime between Brooklyn, Burlington, Los Angeles, and Maine in fear of the eventuality of the professional world.

I finally rid myself of the never-ending string of food service jobs I'd had all my life, and landed a position as a full-time reporter for a weekly newspaper. My girlfriend of 5 years is finishing her master's degree, and we are moving ahead with the lives of the independent young people we are.

A PASSIONATE MAN

Music, art, and exploration of the mysteries of humanity remain my daily passions. I have recorded my own albums, published my own poetry, and performed all over the East Coast in various venues.

I plan to work until I can make a living from art, or at least until I pay off my school loans. Then I can take to the hills as old Gary Snyder would have recommended: living from the land we sprung from—becoming one with nature again.

The ancient Sutra of Hui Neng that turned my head around as a youth and embodies the philosophy I follow now. It is the sentiment I will close with, and live by:

> One does not need universities and libraries. One needs be alive to what is about.

That will provide an answer to any question asked.

REFERENCES

Camus, A. (1970). *The stranger.* New York: A. A. Knopf.

Carroll, J. (1994). *Basketball diaries.* New York: Viking Penguin Press.

Corso, G. (1960). *The happy birthday of death.* New York: J. Laughlin & Co.

Ginsberg, A. (1995). *The journals.* New York: Harper Perennial.

Hemingway, E. (1964). *A moveable feast.* New York: Charles Scribner's Sons.

Kerouac, J. (1971). *Dharma bums.* New York: Penguin USA.

Moore, A. (Ed.). (1990). *A day in the life: Tales from the lower east side.* Brooklyn, New York: Evil Eye Books.

Sartre, J.P. (1958). *No exit and three other plays.* New York: Vintage Books.

Snyder, G. (1969). *Earth house hold.* New York: New Direction Books.

Tolkien, J. R. R. (1982). *The lord of the rings.* New York: Ballantine Books.

VOICES THREE

MAN AS FATHER

CHAPTER 12

WHAT THE MESSAGE SAID

Joey Poole

This poem is based on a conversation with a friend in a bar.

You finally made one *is what it said.*
So the orange juice and the vitamins and the boxer shorts
instead of jockeys had worked.
You finally made one *is what her note said,*
on a yellow legal pad with vein-blue lines
on the chipped counter.
Went to get groceries. Supper's on the stove.
And me, home from rolling out
fiberglass pink insulation that scratches so
I can't tell if it's stuck to me or growing out of me,
I finally made one.

When the doctor told us,
squinting behind his glasses,
thumb in his belt loops,
holding his white coat open so his
fisherman's tie fell straight and true
to his zipper, that the diagnosis was
Low Sperm Count,
which is something they say so your wife
will know it's you, and not her,
it just made Regina try harder.
So it was orange juice and vitamins and boxer shorts
for me, monthly charts and thermometers for her.
There's still a couple thousand of them,
she figured, and it only takes one.
And I swear I could feel them
in me, swimming

The way that silver thermometer stuck
out of the tight line of her lips
I knew she didn't even want to see me.
Shaking the mercury down
just like a nurse or a mother
and spraying honeysuckle
perfume on her throat, she said
that I'd better make it quick.

You finally made one
is what the message said.

CHAPTER 13

A GENERATION

Amittai Aviram

I wrote this poem for my son, Blake.

> My child, I often long to speak with you,
> Still in your womb, ears to the water.
> I dream of breathing soft words on your skin,
> Wrinkled with wet and red in the darkness.
> I know you are a sailor, proud and wave-wise,
> You who have tested all salty quarters
> Round your globe: not guided by stars or maps,
> Pressing your way by sound and touch,
> You hear the low heart's lap, the breathing whirlwind,
> Gurgling rivers and cave-ringing voices.
> How brave you are to navigate that pitch-sea!
> Steering your body, sure in your heart,
> You take your bearings from the rosy twilight,
> Resting for moments, now heaving onward.
> Soon setting sail, you'll cut your final trip,
> Beaching for good on this bone-dry strand.
> What feast can I prepare to welcome you,
> Stark on the shore beneath the white sun?
> What party, bringing towels and warming blankets,
> Clothing your shoulders, will carry you up
> And seat you at the head of our high table,
> Set on the sand-rippled plain? And what odes
> To sing, to celebrate so bold a captain
> Voyaging far to have sight of our land?
> My child, while still you ride the waves in darkness,
> Take me on board with you, there, as a guest,
> And ferry me across that briney pool

Known to me once, when sail, keel, and sound
Were mine. And as you bear me through that old sea,
Help me to find the secret wet ways
Forgotten. You who drift so close to sunrise,
Show me the wash of the whispering dawn.

CHAPTER 14

REFLECTIONS ON FATHERING FOR THE 21ST CENTURY

Dennis R. Finger

WRITING AS A LIVING EXPERIENCE

I delayed writing this chapter. Before I write I sometimes hesitate and, finally, pour forth a stream of thoughts and feelings. But for this chapter there was much more than the usual inner delay. This experience evokes the image of a child who goes to the ocean for the first time and is both attracted to the prospect of swimming and water play and yet at the same time terrified of being engulfed by overwhelming waves. There are several reasons for my procrastination. This writing is to be phenomenological in nature, that is, expressed through my living experience. There is no preplanning done (consciously). There is a topic, but the words proceed from inside out, from within me to the page. I have written before for publication, but never in such a naked, vulnerable way. Also, the subject matter concerns fathers and fathering in the 21st century, which has affected my starting to write.

MY FATHER: MY MODEL FOR FATHERING

I know that I can never say "Dad" again, and that hurts deeply. You see, within the last year and a half, I have lost both my father and my father-in-law as well as a favorite uncle. Taking another perspective, I was fortunate to have my father alive for so many years. Recently I turned 50. Still, the world has seemed somewhat odd and out-of-kilter without my dad here. I had an absent, tough father who was also very dedicated to our family. I grew up in Brooklyn, New York, the gateway for many persons into America. I lived in a two-family house (which we owned) in a working-class neighborhood (Flatbush) across from a Sears and Roebuck department store.

As an aside, this mode of expression feels like being in a therapy session as both the patient (analysand) and analyst. As a psychologist-psychoanalyst, I feel as if I am converting a verbal free association into a written expression of anything that comes to my mind.

So many people I have met started out in Brooklyn. My father, Irving, was a very hard worker, toiling 7 days a week during my elementary school years. He had grown up in the Bronx, another New York City borough. Irv (whose birth name was Isadore, which he disliked) was the oldest of three brothers. Manny was the middle child, Al the youngest, and Abe and Gussie were their parents. They were a very poor family, and all three brothers shared one bed. My father was smart, attending Stuyvesant High School in Manhattan. Stuyvesant is one of New York City's premier specialized high schools for very intelligent teenagers. Unfortunately, my father had to drop out of Stuyvesant in his senior year to help support his family in the Great Depression. I realize at this moment what a tremendous disappointment and sacrifice this must have been for him.

Irv entered the U.S. Army during World War II and rose to the status of "technical sergeant" specializing in company communications. Stationed in England, the story goes that Al, also in the army in England, was marching and saw a guy in a jeep at the driver's wheel with his legs up on the dashboard smoking a cigar. My uncle said that he looked at the soldier and realized that it was his brother, Irv, looking "like a million dollars." After an honorable discharge from the army, Irv took a full-time position working in the U.S. Post Office. It was considered a steady, reliable job with decent pay. He worked at the post office windows selling stamps, determining the proper postage for items, and working with the public. Later, he rose to the position of information specialist. He talked often of taking the supervisor's test, but he never did. One obstacle was that he would have to take less attractive hours as a new supervisor, but also there were his own personal concerns. My father told me in one of our talks growing up that he yearned to complete high school and attend Pace Institute (now Pace University) in Manhattan to become an accountant. But this was not to be. My father stayed at his job in the post office for the next 38 years. He referred to his job as "the place."

My father developed into quite a card player, joining a group which lasted for many years. He would play cards weekly, and once each month the game was in our kitchen. There was smoking and yelling and cajoling. All of the guys let out a great deal of steam. The whole room took on an intense, exciting, emotion-packed atmosphere. Rather than a kitchen, it was more like the betting windows before a horserace when everybody is sweating, and totally engrossed in the betting. Which reminds me that my father was a horserace fanatic. He listened every night to our kitchen radio, rooting and hollering for his horse. When another horse won he would often say, "Oh, I was going to play that one!" with some expletives. When he won you could see his face beam with success and satisfaction. Once during my elementary years, he won $550, a terrific win for that time. He bought my mother a new clothes washer and dryer. She was thrilled. Of course, there were many lost bets.

Besides the post office, my father worked on Saturdays at E.J. Korvette's Department Store in downtown Brooklyn. Korvette's was a large department store chain, which was popular during the 1950s and 1960s. I remember being very surprised to learn that E.J. Korvette's stood for Eight Jewish Korean War Veterans. At Korvette's my father was a quasi-accountant, "balancing the books" as he described his job. On Sundays Dad worked in Manhattan at Whelan's Drug Store, once a large pharmacy chain in New York City. So, Dad worked many hours on behalf of his family.

To me, this was the role of the father in the 1950s. Fathers worked to ensure that their children had food, shelter, and clothing and to enable the wife to stay home and be a full-time mother. In these respects I was fortunate. Unfortunately, my father was very tired the few times when I did get to see him, which was unusual. He worked long hours. I remember when he would come home from work and sink into his favorite chair. Then he would read his newspaper while my mother cooked dinner for him. Tears come to my eyes as I realize at this moment that I rarely crawled into his arms as my own son often does with me (which I feel very happy about). Sometimes I would get my father's houseslippers and help him remove his heavy work shoes. I remember his musty smell, heavy laden with body sweat.

I remember with joy the times that my father brought home a large box of "Chinese" almond cookies for me which a customer had given him. They were fresh and delicious. I realize as I write this that I like almond cookies and perhaps this is a connection to my father. I miss him. As a window clerk, he received gifts from his regular customers. Once, he brought home a wooden baseball bat, another time a racquetball racquet. The one drawback was that they were not my size, although I appreciated my father's gifts. I also appreciated my father sending my mother and me away every summer to the Catskill Mountains, a popular summer vacation spot for New Yorkers in the 1950s. In the beginning we went to a bungalow colony, which was a small community of modest summer cottages with a pool and recreation center. Like many fathers of that generation, he came up on weekends and on his 2-week summer vacation. When I grew older, we stayed for several summer vacations at a small resort called the Kenmore Hotel on Kauneonga Lake, one mile from White Lake, New York. I had many wonderful times during those summers. I am thankful my father was so adept with our family's finances and able to provide us with many exciting summers.

I remember, though, that he would discipline by yelling and spanking. Being a good parent is one of the hardest jobs that anyone has and, unfortunately, many parents do not know how to discipline their children. They confuse parenting, providing guidance and instruction, with punishment. It is hard to believe that physical punishment is still one of the most popular discipline techniques used today in the United States. Parents need help to become better at parenting (Keith & Christiansen, 1997).

When I was young, perhaps 3 or 4, my father returned from work, and my mother as usual told him all of the "bad" things that I had done that day. My father sternly told me to go into the bathroom. I was absolutely terrified. On the way to the bathroom I slipped a book inside my pants to shield my behind. My father began spanking me and laughed when he felt the book. He told me to make believe that he was spanking me. I cried as if in pain and returned to my mother looking appropriately dejected. Oh, how I loved my father that night! During that generation, fathers were the disciplinarians. Mothers would wait for the fathers to return, and children would wait hours to be punished. That was a bad policy. It is best to provide an appropriate, immediate punishment. Let the punishment fit the "crime," and get it over with. A delayed punishment is an extra drain on the whole family. And it does not have to be a major drawn out punishment. It is effective as long as the child feels punished.

My father was a big comedian at family gatherings. He always had a few jokes to tell. His laughter could be contagious, and it persuaded others to join in. It was wonderful to see this humorous side of him, and I wish he had shared the comedian side of himself more often with me. As we both matured, a real affection and love emerged between us, and at the end we were holding hands as he lay in his hospital bed.

After he died, I had many dreams about my father. In one dream I was parachuting from an aircraft. I was descending in the sky and wondering if I would be safe. Then I heard my father say to me, "Let me be your parachute." It was a very emotional and powerful experience. I really understood how stable and reliable my father had been for me. I could depend on him to be my strong parachute. Perhaps this dream was a "curative fantasy," helping me cope with my father's death (Natterson, 1980). In another dream, I was holding my father in my arms and he felt very solid. I told him how much I missed him. In tears I awakened, and he turned into a spirit and flew out from my arms. I miss my father, and the world seems strange without him. It is so odd how someone who was such an important part of my life no longer exists. That is the way of life. That is our human destiny. One day I will no longer exist.

MY SON

My son is smart and talented. His early interest in the Power Rangers turned into a love of Beanie Babies, into playing ice hockey and collecting hockey cards. These in turn gave way to Pokemon, Nintendo, roller coasters, soccer, and lately music. He is becoming a real preteenager. The Internet has opened a world of information and contact. He is the kind of child who really delves into something in depth. Now he is researching various roller coasters around the country, their speeds, lengths, and duration. And, upside-down rides! He wants me to try the Batman ride at Six Flags. "You'll love it, Dad. It's so much fun." He is a joy in my life. At bedtime we have been reading *Harry Potter and the Chamber of Secrets* (Rowling, 1998.)

What does it take to have a good son-father relationship? What will it take in the 21st century? Time together, quality time and quantity time. Finding time for children is very challenging for busy working couples. Making sacrifices when you do not want to, being patient when you have no patience left, having energy to do things with your child when you are desperately tired. It can be very tough. Fathering includes having fun together, listening to your child's emotions and ideas, helping your child learn about life, encouraging your child to try new things, and going easy on your child's mistakes. Recently, I bought a drill and my son wanted to try drilling and using the new screwdriver attachments. He loved trying to make holes in cardboard boxes. Together we are building a desk for him.

MY ANALYST: MY SECOND FATHER

During my training as a psychologist and psychoanalyst, I had a special relationship with my own psychoanalyst. I felt that he refathered me. Therapy can be perceived as a second chance at growing up through a new, nurturing, growth-enhancing relationship with a therapist. I have been very fortunate to have a solid, warm relationship with my analyst. I have been able to draw sustenance and patience from that relationship, which has helped me to have a better relationship with my son. Through the therapeutic process, the analyst becomes incorporated into the psychic self, becoming in a sense a third parent. I have become a better parent because of my own personal therapy. My son and I have developed a friendship, and he sometimes says that I am the older brother he does not have.

MY SON AND I: THE SON-FATHER RELATIONSHIP

We have gone away for a few "Indian Guides" weekends in the mountains of New York State and on several day trips. Because my wife also works, I am able to spend time with my son each day. He teaches me about new trends in music, video games, theme parks, children's books, and other areas. I strive to be open to his perspectives and to try out his interests. It is usually a fun experience for me. I am not a lover of roller coasters but he is trying to convince me, as I mentioned earlier, to try an upside-down ride. I imagine these upside-down rides will multiply in the 21st century. He enjoys the thrill of being scared, which I do not relish. He also likes horror movies, such as the remake of *The Haunting*. I never would have seen that movie if not for my son. The movie included psychological experiments on fear, and I did like aspects of it.

Fathering does not have to be expensive. We took balloons, filled them with water, and had a water balloon catch. We played Frisbee. We played catch with a ball. We went on a "walkabout," an adventure walk together, looking for interesting things around us, whether they were plants, animals, people, houses, aircraft, or noises. We ate ice cream together. We went shell hunting on a beach, watched a movie together, went for a hike in the woods, and played soccer, baseball, and basketball. There are many activities to do together, limited only by our creativity and our imagination.

Fathers need a willingness to try. Children can suggest activities and fathers can follow their leads. Children can help us be better fathers. They can teach us about what they need and how we can meet their needs. Children also need limits, and one difficult challenge is determining when limits are needed and then putting those limits into place. Becoming a better father is an ongoing process. I think of father-son situations that went awry and how they could have been improved. I ask my son how we could have done better as a team than we did. It is an ongoing struggle of learning experiences filled with joy and tears, but hopefully a good deal more joy.

An eminent pediatrician and psychoanalyst, David Winnicott (1988), talked about the "good enough mother." We need to be "good enough" fathers, not perfect or terrific, just good enough. That perspective allows fathers to be real, genuine, and not so pressured, yet at the same time to provide enough nurturance to positively sustain and enhance the child's growth. Shortly, my son will be a teenager in the 21st century, and I wonder about our future relationship. How will his adolescence affect us? I am hoping that we have a "good enough" relationship to carry us through his teenage years.

REFERENCES

Keith, P., & Christiansen, S. (1997). Parenting styles. In G. Bear, K. Mintz, & A. Thomas (Eds.), *Children's needs II: Development problems and alternatives* (pp. 559–566). Washington, DC: National Association of School Psychologists.

Natterson, J. (Ed.). (1980). *The dream in clinical practice.* New York: Jason Aronson Publishers.

Rowling, J. (1998). *Harry Potter and the chamber of secrets.* New York: Arthur A. Levine Books.

Winnicott, D. W. (1988). *Human nature.* New York: Schocken Books.

CHAPTER 15

MAKING MEN OUT OF THEM

Gordon Grant

As a graduate student in the humanities, I was fortunate enough to be exposed to a reasonable amount of feminist critical theory, and I have long been able to understand gender as a social phenomenon as much as a physical reality. I see men performing their maleness all the time, and most of the time I can afford to be mildly caustic about this acting. I also think I have, at least some of the time, a pretty good handle on my own gender performances; I know I also like to play against type sometimes as well, especially when I can undermine a colleague's or acquaintance's unthinking masculine perspective on a movie, a political issue, or workplace politics.

My play with male identity isn't so simple, though, when it comes to my sons, particularly when I am coaching them—my older son in basketball, my younger son in soccer—and I find that the lessons I was taught as a boy and teenager about mental discipline, physical aggressiveness, individual effort, and success are the lessons I am trying to teach to them and their teammates. I'm not just teaching them how to be successful in their sport. I'm teaching them about how to be young men.

When I was a high school athlete I was okay, certainly not the best player or a team leader, but mostly a starter on a small high school basketball team. I had some natural ability and was good at picking up technical skills and thinking through the game. I liked zone defenses because they were tactical. But I was a diffident competitor—I was always somehow disengaged from the game, too aware of performing for others and not focused entirely on being inside the activity, the competition. I liked practices the best, frankly, because they were about learning about the game for its own sake, not about winning. I was always shocked, after those nights when I did for some reason get really inside a real game, that I could do some of the things I did when I played without thinking. Sometimes I could even remember things I did without actually remembering doing them; at those times—a tip in on a rebound, a hard drive to the basket, a jump shot without stopping to consider if I was open—it felt like my body had actually disengaged from my mind. I supposed I should have relished those times, but they almost seemed scary, like a blackout. I still can remember a few of them, but I think of them as if I had watched something on television, not as if I had made the moves myself.

Today, I see this distance from the game itself at times in some of the kids I coach. And I find myself yelling at them the ways my coaches yelled at me: "Stop putzing around!" "Get in the game!" "Find your position!" (One of the names we used when I was a kid for a player who was holding back was "Polly Putz." The implied insult here makes me cringe now, even though I still use the verb but never the name.) I find myself teaching all these boys in my care—this year a group of 10- to 11-year-old basketball players and 7- to 8-year-old soccer players—how to discipline themselves, how to get more competitive. The older boys are well on their way, while the younger ones are more clearly still children. Some kids from both age groups still lose interest in my lessons and drills on passing and getting open. Some of them still romp with each other like puppies, some of them wander away looking at flowers or bugs or dust balls. None of them like getting hurt or playing really physically.

I've played ball with enough really good women athletes to know that both sexes need emotional and mental intensity as well as physical toughness to succeed. But I also know that I am trying to help these boys build the shell that will encase their childlike softness, which they show to me when they cry, when they give up competing because looking at the clouds is more fun, when they hug me because they are happy—or sad. I know I am helping them think analytically about competition, about positioning and technique, about becoming, in some sense, the artisans of the physical body that real athletes are. But I also see them becoming tough, developing that ego that male athletes seem to think is a passport to all sorts of privileges. This makes me wonder if I am doing the wrong thing. Then I go out and play with them, roughhouse with them, give them a few gentle knocks, make a move on them, show them how much fun it is to play hard. And they get better.

CHAPTER 16

DUANE'S FATHER: A POEM AND A REFLECTION ON CHILD SUPPORT

Charles Weathers

Duane didn't spend much time with his dad.
He was born out of wedlock.
He lived with his mom on East Main;
His dad was just around the block.

Now even though he didn't spend time,
His child support he paid.
He took financial responsibility
For this life that he made.

He was no deadbeat
As we define it today
Because the check was always on time.
It was the first thing he'd pay.

Duane's mom was grateful,
And Duane was too,
But something was still missing.
No one really had a clue.

Duane was always laced
In the newest gear and shoes.
He had the latest games and bikes,
So many he could pick and choose.

Duane still felt distant,
Felt alone and withdrawn.
He had everything he wanted—
Why did his heart feel so torn?

He had the greatest dad around,
At least that's what mom always said,
Because dad always sent that check,
And that made sure Duane was fed.

He'd spend time with his dad
Every now and then.
But, if it was up to Duane,
It would be more time, less money that they'd spend.

With a look of despair
and a feeling oh so empty,
Duane asked his dad,
"Can you spend more time with me?"

His dad got upset.
He said, "What more can I do?
According to the courts and the system,
I'm a good father to you.

I pay my support,
You get your check on time.
You're never satisfied boy!
All you do is whine."

Duane sat in silence
With a tear in his eye.
He had upset his daddy
But he couldn't figure out why.

He said, "Sorry for whining
and being such a bother.
But today was 'bring your dad' to school day,
And I'm tired of a check being my father."

* * *

The purpose of this poem is not to dog men who pay child support. That's a good thing. But since we have so many slackers out there who don't pay their support, we get one who does and use that as the defining characteristic of being a great dad. Here's a little wake-up call: *you don't reward and applaud what someone is supposed to do.* This lowers the bar and the standards. All of a sudden minimal expectations set in and mediocrity is deemed worthy. I hear men saying, "Oh I pay for my kids," like they want a medal. That's what you're supposed to do! That's not the end of the obligation; that's only the beginning. We've defined our fathers according to the governmental social definitions. A man might say, "What more do you want?" On behalf of the kids, I'd say a lot more, a lot more. We need to stop using substandard models of mediocrity and failures as a benchmark for our achievements as fathers.

If you don't pay support, you're a deadbeat, and if you do, you're the best thing since sliced bread. Your children need the money, no doubt, but they need a daddy too! And let me just say this for the woman who believes "I don't need no man to raise a child." You don't believe that and if it hasn't sunk in yet, let that child get a little older and a little bolder and you'll believe it then. You may not feel you need the man who helped you make him, but we just have to chalk that up to your lack of judgment in allowing someone less than a man to get you pregnant. The truth be told, if the daddy was a real man, you wouldn't feel the same. This is why it is so important to do things decently and in order. Don't have the child and then determine that his daddy ain't %^*#* good.

If we'd be more concerned with keeping our pants on than getting our groove on, we'd save everyone a lot of pain—most importantly all the Duanes out there. Remember, a check can't play catch, tuck them in, go to a parent-teacher meeting, go to a T-ball game, or just sit and hold a child in its lap. If you're a dad paying support, I know it isn't easy, you have double duty, but guess what? It's not about you anymore: it's about your child. Your son or daughter didn't ask to be here. You brought your children here; now don't just pay for them, raise them. And if you want to do the world a favor, find a young brother out there on the same path you were on and do your best to help him change course. It's best for him, the child, and the world.

Spend time with your child. This also applies to many of us working fathers who come home to our intact families. Mom needs some help. And we can't buy our children's love.

Chapter 17

Like Father, Like Son:
Fear and Fatherhood

Ray McManus

I am afraid my son will grow up like me.

I am not accustomed to being afraid. I can honestly say that I have been truly afraid only three times in my life. When I was 9, I almost blew up my cousin playing with gasoline and fireworks. A bottle rocket flew and hit him in the mouth, where it exploded. Luckily he was not hurt severely, but there was a lot of blood. I had never seen that much blood before. When I was 14, I woke up to find my best friend's brother trying to molest me. He must have been 15 years older than I, and he was big. I knew I couldn't fight him, and I somehow knew what harm revealing the situation could cause the entire family. (His wife and two sons were sleeping in the rooms down the hall.) So I just rolled over, face first in the couch, and pressed myself as hard as I could against the cushion, trying to prevent him from touching me further. Seeing my cousin with blood all over his face and having an older man stick his hands down my pants seriously scared me, but I have never been as scared as I was on June 25, 2000, the day my son Sean was born.

Twice, fear came, but I eventually outgrew it. My cousin grew up with a very small scar on the left side of his mouth that can only be seen in indirect sunlight. My best friend's brother came out 7 years after the encounter. Even though being molested scared me, it didn't make me fear homosexuals. But when Sean was born the fear came, and 7 months later I don't see the fear ever leaving. I have a hard time believing that I am a father. I don't feel as if I have matured to the level that my father had when I was a kid. In many ways I still feel like a kid. I certainly have a hard time considering that another life is solely dependent on me.

I grew up in a small town in rural South Carolina. When I was 12, I smoked my first joint. At 13 I bought and smoked my first pack of cigarettes. That summer I drank liquor for the first time, tried hash, and lost my virginity. I didn't have any of the interests that many of my classmates had. I didn't want to play sports, I didn't want to study, and I didn't want to be dependent on anyone else. I was just interested in smoking pot and hanging out. I hit my rebellious teenage angst, full force, 3 years before I was supposed to. I dyed my hair blue, shaved my hair into a mohawk, pierced my ears, and wore clothes full of holes before I even had my driver's license. Within the first year of driving, I managed to wreck my father's Toyota pickup truck 11 times, hitting almost every dirt bank in Lexington County at least once.

My parents, good Southern Baptists, were ready to give up by the time I hit 17. They figured I would end up in jail or the hospital, and do damage that could not be erased. I don't blame them. The sad part of it all was that they didn't know—and still don't know—half of the things I did. I was pretty much stoned every day, tripped on acid and mushrooms almost every weekend. I was drinking regularly, sometimes in the morning before school even started. In fact there wasn't a day that I can remember, between the age of 15 and 21 that I wasn't under the influence of some kind from the moment I woke up to when I went to bed. It wasn't until I was married and in college that I realized that I needed to change. And just like that, I quit doing drugs, I quit drinking heavily, and I started studying. I blame an English professor and a persistent wife. But that's another story.

Now, things are much different. In 7 years I managed to complete an undergraduate degree, and I have just completed a master's degree. It is safe to say that I made a complete turnaround for the better. I don't necessarily regret my past because what I did has made me who I am, and I like who I am. But I have to live with regret for being so stupid when I was younger, and not just with regret, but with the thought that I could have easily done so much better or so much worse. It is that regret that has turned into fear—fear of repetition, of duplication.

I look at my 8-month-old son, who at this point is progressing faster than normal toddlers his age. He says "mama" and "da" with purpose. He can feed himself from a cup, hold tiny objects between his fingers, and shows signs of having a strong memory. He crawls and is almost walking, much like me when I was his age. In fact, talking to my mother, I have found that in many ways Sean is acting very much the same as I did when I was his age. Friends of mine who already have children tell me that most times the firstborn develops much like the father did. I don't know if that has been scientifically proven, but it is enough to scare me. I can't help but wonder what he will do when he reaches his teenage years.

Part of my fear has to do with prevention. I know my father tried to prevent me from becoming who I was. However, his advice, his lectures, his threats of what could happen unless I changed fell on deaf ears. I figured he was just old and out of touch. I knew that he didn't experience the things that I had already experienced, and I knew he lived a much more sheltered life than I did. It seemed that every time he pushed me, I pushed back even harder. I was independent. I didn't need him at the time. I am afraid that if I do the same with my son, I will get the same reaction, or if I don't push and let him figure things out on his own, he will make the same mistakes I did and realize what he has done only a moment too late.

Just as I am sure Sean will have questions for me, I am left with questions for myself. Should I take him to church? My father took me to church; in fact, he crammed church down my throat. I haven't been back to church since I moved out of the house. Do I talk to Sean candidly about drugs and sex? My father did the same with me, and my inquisitive nature only led me to experiment, since I didn't think my father knew what he was talking about anyway. Should I share with my son my testimony about the things I did and how I don't regret them, knowing that it could tarnish my fatherly image, or even worse, promote his own demise? My dad admitted his failures to me, but they seemed so minimal. Besides, it didn't warrant any further respect, and looking back, I could say that those admissions helped strip him of his hero status.

I know that I am jumping the gun here. My son has just learned to walk, and I am already playing the "what if" game. But that is what fear is for, I guess. Perhaps it is best that I fear these things now. Call it preparation for whatever should happen when he gets older. Maybe I should just back off, let him learn the way I did. After all, I didn't turn out half bad. But I'm not sure that is a risk that I am willing to take. I am afraid he will not be as lucky as I was. Besides, who knows what teenagers will be faced with when he becomes one. The progression of the last 40 years doesn't seem positive.

I guess what it all boils down to is that I'm afraid that I will receive the payback for my past transgressions, and it will be more than I can bear. Will the punishment fit the transgression? Will I lose something so dear to me, simply because I was a stupid kid? Will my son go off and never come back, simply because I spent most of his life trying to shelter him from the things that could happen, rather than just being honest and, in that honesty, loving? I guess most fathers would take pride in hearing the phrase "like father like son." When my mother was angry with me, she used to tell me that one day I would have a son and he would act just like me. If only she had known before she put that curse on me.

CHAPTER 18

CROSSING THE HURDLES: FATHER AND DAUGHTER, HOLDING ON AND LETTING GO

Robert Therrer (pseudonym)

It was a hot, July night in Columbia, South Carolina, about 4 years ago. I was exiting the local yuppie toy store where I had just purchased the latest Beanie Baby for my just-turned-teenager daughter, Amy. We were accosted in the parking lot by an aggressive person. Who would panhandle at this late hour? Sensing threat, I said, "Amy, let's get in the car and get home." But no, a reporter for *The State* newspaper flashed her credentials. She was composing a late-night story for the morning paper on the Beanie Baby craze. We chatted innocently as we held our pet purchases: my baby monkey was named Bongo and my daughter's matching monkey was Bingo. How simple and innocent life seemed on that summer night!

Four and a half years later, Amy had turned 16. Our family of three had made it to the year 2000, the millennium. But by June of that year, we began to suspect that we were on a roller coaster of familial emotions. On June 2, my mother suffered a massive stroke, from which she never recovered. On June 14—while we were on a family vacation to the Canadian Rockies—my wife's father died after being diagnosed with lung and kidney cancer only 6 weeks previously. On November 1, my mother died and the three of us attended a family funeral for a week in St. Louis, Missouri. By mid-November, we hoped and prayed that our agonies were over for a while. Life's routines were beginning to resume. It was even time for a long-postponed trip to the dentist's office.

And so, on a dull day in mid-November, I found myself confined from 11 A.M. to 1 P.M. in the dentist's chair, getting three cavities filled. When I got home, I found a message on the answering machine from the principal of the local public high school, a calm but urgent voice requesting that I call immediately about our only child, Amy. When I called, the principal assured me that

Amy was fine, but that she had been questioned and had admitted to being involved in some inappropriate behavior (was it drinking?) on a school-sponsored field trip that had occurred 6 weeks before. She had been suspended from school, so I needed to pick her up right away. She might be expelled for the rest of the academic year, depending on the outcome of a future hearing.

This wasn't a typical call: it was a wake-up call. With a stellar trajectory, it moved our father-daughter relationship from the world of childhood to the menacing world of the adult temptations and afflictions that one sees every morning on the news—drugs, drinking, and school shootings. It had hit home; it had hit us; it was our daughter.

The actual incident had taken place on a field trip to Savannah, Georgia, on the first Saturday night in October 2000. Because there was inadequate adult supervision, the 40 or so students were casually wandering around the motel premises even after 10 P.M. Shockingly, to me, Amy was in a group with four other girls who accepted the invitation of a similar group of guys to come up to their second-floor motel room and "party." I believe, as they later claimed, that the door of their room was never closed. Since there was and is no physical evidence from that night, it can never finally be determined what substances were consumed in the room. A bottle with an orange liquid in it was passed around, and the various teenagers seem to have taken a sip apiece to be "cool" with their friends. Even more shocking to me to this day is not the possible consumption of a few drops of alcohol, but the dangerous and reckless adolescent lack of judgment which allowed the girls (including Amy) to accept such an invitation from strange guys. Who knows what could have happened that night? Where was her guardian angel?

There is no point in belaboring all of the turmoil of the remainder of the month of November. We went from nights of lost sleep to endless frantic phone calls to long negotiations with our lawyer and with school officials. As never before, Amy elevated herself to a new maturity. Her testimony on her behalf before the hearing officer was honest, well delivered, and sincere. While many other students involved in the incident denied any wrongdoing, Amy—with her supportive lawyer and minister present—answered all of the questions with the truth. Again and again, we would ask: was it worth it?

I lived with Amy for the 18 or so days that the crisis went on; I lived through her growth and aspirations to put her life back together again after this humiliating setback. What could be salvaged? Would she have to find a new school? Could she get back in the school and resume her work in the district's magnet program for academically talented students? What about track as a sport in the spring? What about cheerleading for the rest of the winter season? Would she ever regain the daily routines that we had come to take for granted as good and worthwhile, the routines we depended on after months of emotional turmoil?

Somehow—and it was far from easy—successful resolution came by November's end. We owe a debt of gratitude to the helpful attitude of the principal, the skillful insights of our lawyer, and the compassion of many supportive friends, both teenagers and adults. The long November nightmare finally went away; nearly all of Amy's extracurricular activities were restored. But now the line is always there for her father: how does a father allow a daughter to develop her own interests and maturity, even while he tries to protect and direct her choices and decisions? The wavering line of withdrawal versus intervention comes into play with every important aspect of her experiences: the choice of a boyfriend, of a college, of sports activities. Allow me to elaborate on these three areas to trace out the interplays.

If my daughter goes out on a date until midnight, then it is certain that I shall receive no sleep until she returns safely that night. The terrors are innumerable: a car wreck, a rape, a mugging in a local mall. And yet, she needs to achieve her own relationships with boys, and why not start the process at a much earlier age than I did in my past dating practices. (If memory hasn't failed me, I had no dates in high school and one date in college!) I am always happier if she goes out in groups of four or six. But twice now, she has had longer relationships with older guys—two high school seniors who are now in their first years of college. And why is it that our only brief discussions of sex have been strictly in negative terms: the dangers of the AIDS epidemic; the need to wear a condom (yes, I said it once to her!). I sound like Moses on the Mount: don't drink until you are 21; postpone sex until you are a grown-up. Will she follow the tablets I pass to her or break them in pieces on the ground? I don't know.

And there is the biggest choice coming up—going out of state to college. It was a dreary January day in early 2001 that we headed as a family up to Davidson College in Charlotte, North Carolina. We took the campus tour and interviewed with the admissions counselor. I could see the tension in choice developing even as the day unfolded. To me, the college seemed like the perfect choice: a high-ranked, challenging, idyllic campus that I sure wish I could have had the opportunity to be a part of when it had been my time to select a college to attend. (Because of my parents' financial situation, I had to opt for the local branch of the University of Missouri in St. Louis.) But the choice of college to attend had to and has to be Amy's to make. My role must be to help pay the bills for college and to offer positive mediation between my wishes and hers as she explains to us how she puts various colleges on and off her selection list. We talk with each other, and I try to be helpful and encouraging in the role of listener and peacemaker.

Perhaps it is sports, though, that most brings home to me my sometimes vicarious investment in her decisions. As I write this, January has turned to February to March in one of the coldest winters that Columbia has ever experienced. On a recent cold March night in Columbia, the many male and female athletes on the field were excited to start the meet. The time was 5 P.M., time for another track meet at the local high school track. As I sat there as a spectator in the stands (which I never did when I was a student in high school), I realized the tremendous implications of the federal Title IX program in our lives—women's sports can and must receive serious attention and funding. So there I was, waiting for Amy to compete once again—in relays and in her specialty, the 400-meter race with its 10 hurdles. Her goal is to break the previously established high school record of 1 minute 8 seconds. Her best time so far (in past seasons) has always been 2 or 3 seconds off the record. Maybe tonight, I thought! But then I was also thinking how it is all a middle-aged father's ultimate fantasy: as she turned the curve and headed down the stretch for the finish line, after clearing a series of hurdles with gazelle-like grace and poise, I realized for an instant how easily I live through her experiences. It is not that she doesn't love and want to do track; however, I sit religiously through each track meet because I myself feel a chance to replay my adolescent fantasies: her track participation is the work I never got around to doing in high school. Each run she does is one that I cannot do, especially after my serious knee surgery in 1995, which put an end to my jogging career on the streets of Columbia for good. Sitting through these track meets, I live through her. Maybe she won't pick a college that is 500 miles away, and I can follow some of her track meets during her college years! But maybe not. It must be up to her.

Sometimes Amy's mother and I think, as many parents must, that our daughter tries to be deliberately different from us—just for the thrill of it. Whereas we were not especially social in high school, she is. Whereas we did not go far away to college, she will find that perfect, faraway campus on the back roads of a New England hillside. Whereas we tended to study history and literature, she will make her career in the business world. While we as parents had little or no artistic ability, she enjoys her painting and drawing classes. While we rarely watched, much less participated in, sports events, she is a valued member of her varsity track team. When I pick up the morning paper now, I turn to the sports section. I remember that late-night reporter at the toy store, and the article about a father and daughter purchasing Beanie Babies together, but now I look for my daughter in the track and field results.

The differences in outlooks and generations can be stimulating and open new opportunities. Daily, our relationship requires empathy and imagination. The best a parent can hope for is a constructive approach that fosters open communication and positive mediation as one tries to live with, and sometimes through, one's offspring.

VOICES FOUR

MAN AS SON

Chapter 19

My Father

Carl Jenkinson

His bald head. In winter, pale, and gleaming. Freckled. In summer, never fully tanned.

His whistle. Tuneless. Incessant. Its abiding knack to grate on my nerves. His
   ridiculous smile when I ask him to stop. Tell him to stop.

His midnight raids on the fridge: creeping down the stairs, believing he is unheard,
   unobserved, to devour slabs of sharp cheddar cheese.

Random books, unread, gathering dust in piles about the house.

Never needing to catch his breath: working past dusk and into the chill of night,
   harvesting potatoes.

His breathlessness, his labored breathing.

Calling out to his dead brother.

His voice on the telephone; his inability to understand, and his canny ability to guess at
   my meaning, to know my voice pattern, to know me.

The set angle of his jaw.

His eyes, which have become docile, lost; a paler blue.

His hand cupped behind his ear, a totem against deafness; a charm.

His temper.

CHAPTER 20

IT'S IN THE BOY'S BLOOD: A VERY OLD STORY

Mark Powell

This is a very old story, even if I do not understand it.

I have a memory of the memory now, something spun out from idle moments of reflection, but the truth is, I only remember sensations. Lying there on my back with only a thin cotton shirt between the chalky court and me. How the sky was the color of ice. The taste of blood in my mouth and how my fingertips were cracking and how my nails were almost blue along the edges. I remember how cold it was. And I remember my father skulking away. A grown man, I told myself. Look at him, a grown man. I sat up and dusted my hands along the front of my pants, stood slowly, gently. I was 15 years old and for the first time in my life had just beaten my father in a game of basketball.

Later, my mother would tell me the story I couldn't remember, filling in the blanks of my mind. She said she had stood half-peeking through a part in the blinds watching us. It was snowing outside. The court was swept. Only our hands and heads were visible. She told me she had seen me go chest to chest with my father. The shot would have won the game but his elbow came down in the middle of my face. I felt wet—I imagine my mother gasping at this moment, hands to her mouth—and passed the back of one sleeve over my lips. My nose was bleeding in sheets. My father looked at me very calmly, very evenly, and said, "foul." I took the ball back to the top of the key. The next shot went in though I did not see it. He knocked me down and I know now the memory I have of the quick snapping skirt of net is imagined, a scene from some useless moment, a thousand useless moments. He looked at me lying there on my back and said, "good game." Then he walked away. The game was over.

It is difficult for most to understand my relationship with my father. He is 6 feet 6 inches tall, played college basketball, and is something of a schoolyard legend in my hometown. He started taking me to the gym with him before I could walk and, of course, I hated it, hated it for spite. This is a very old story, a tired story played out in countless variations with only names and places ever changing. The boy wants to go on hating what the father loves but cannot, gives in, loves it himself. It's in the boy's blood, they all say. Look at him, that boy's got it in his blood, doesn't he? By the time I was 11 years old I dreamed basketball, heard the dull thump-thump rhythm in my sleep, smelled the wood floor of the gym when I shut my eyes. What people say is that the boy is obsessed. Boys, it seems, become obsessed; boys get things in their blood.

All the while, my father, strangely enough, watched this from afar. He never interfered with coaches, never tried to second-guess what I had learned. You dribble with your head up, you find the open man. But every night at 6 P.M. when he came home from work, he would walk back to our court—a basket hung above the garage door, net in shambles—and we would play. For my 13th birthday he put up a floodlight so that my mother had to stand on the back porch and call to our wagging shadows to come in and that didn't we know it was freezing and didn't we care we'd catch our deaths. Evenings were lost to nights. But in all the games we ever played, not once did he let me win. There was no father's mercy, no moral victories. Our games were quiet wars that dragged on wordlessly, and I lost ten thousand straight until the day my nose was bleeding and he knocked me down as I let go a shot to win the game. Then it was different, I had beaten him.

My mother watched him walk off the court and up around the house and leave. She never came out to check on me, and I still appreciate that. She simply closed the blind. Probably, she said a prayer. I wiped the blood on the inside of my coat, my hands along the seat of my pants. She was waiting for me in the kitchen.

"How did it go?" she asked.

"I won."

I said this nonchalantly, no change of expression.

"Very good."

She was drinking coffee.

"Very good," she said a second time, much quieter this time.

She held the cup with both hands, sleeves pulled down to her fingertips, never mentioning the smear of mud-colored blood down my left cheek. She betrayed nothing. But walking out, I noticed the very slightest of tremors rippling across the coffee cup.

There is a moment lost in one of John Updike's novels where Harry Angstrom is riding in a pick-up truck through the rain with his grown son Nelson on the seat beside him. Harry wants to talk to Nelson about marriage, about fate and traps and love for the sake of love, but does not. He stops intuitively and though it is unstated in the book, the moment is easily understood: some things are best left unsaid. Thoughts pass in glances.

I have often wondered since then what it was that passed between the three of us that day. I think of my mother burning with anger at my father for wounding me, then at the same time brimming with pride at my having taken it and dealt it blow for blow. Sometimes I think of my father walking away and

I remember his shoulders slouched with defeat. But perhaps this is only the echo of a memory and in truth it was not defeat that bowed him, rather it was some mottled flicker of pride and sorrow. Things change. I said this was a very old story, a tired story, but its exhaustion makes it no less true. We have never spoken of that game and probably never will. But sometimes I see it pass between us as memories must pass between all fathers and their sons, not as violence or competition, but as some implicit understanding. Thoughts pass in glances. Perhaps some boys do become obsessed, maybe they get things in their blood, but perhaps they only try to make sense of what they are given with whatever strange tool they can find. They keep pacts in a tragic, beautiful sense, keep promises and trade places with their little blood rites. You dribble with your head up, find the open man, knock down the open shot. Sons become fathers. You go on trading places, finding little ways to love each other.

CHAPTER 21

MAN WITH A MISSION: FOUR VIEWS OF MY FATHER*

Bryan Waterman

I

I was upstairs asleep that night in 1976, but still I can see my father, spread like a crucifix on worn orange carpet, thinking he was about to die. I've heard him tell the story and I remember parts: how he had contracted the mumps from the kids, stayed flat on his back for weeks, and, instead of recovering, developed (or intensified) allergies to everything, even the sugar in Campbell's soup.

Not that his health was ever great anyway. He'd been raised by a mom whose husband walked out after returning from World War II, a mom who had to be to work before he was awake in the mornings, which left him to a diet of toast and cocoa for his first 6 years. At 18 he converted to Mormonism and was sent as a missionary to Guatemala, where contaminated cola ate his insides like acid. By the time the mumps took him down when I was 6, he had no immune system, and so I grew up in his world of allergy pills, self-inflicted shots, wormwood teas, and unstable emotions.

According to my admittedly imperfect memory, the night he spent sprawled on the living room floor, he made two promises. One, he would never fail to do his home teaching, the Mormon practice of congregants visiting one another at home each month, a sort of bureaucratic fellowship. That night he had flaked out on his home teaching assignments because he was sick, but he depended on *his* home teachers to come anoint him with oil and remove his sickness. After that he was 100 percent.

When I think of my dad home teaching I think of hippies: from 1976 on, he'd teach whomever they assigned him, and we had whole communes of

---

*Essay first published as "Four Looks at My Father" In *Sunstone*, June 1999 (15–17).

rebellious Mormon kids who were living the natural life, miles out of our rural Arizona town but still in our congregation's boundaries and on the church membership lists. He milked goats while my mother helped deliver babies named Wind and Morning. He offered our phone and our faucet when they needed a place to stop in town. Every once in a while we'd get a van load of messy-haired kids to come in with us to Sunday School. It was a mission of love.

His second promise affected me more directly. I can't remember him ever saying so, but I pinpoint that night as the time he decided to give everything to fatherhood. When he saw his 6 short years as a parent spin and rock, about to escape him, he reordered whatever priorities there were to reorder and started getting ready for his first Pinewood Derby, his first tee-ball game, his first Scout-O-Rama. We were doomed to superdad.

II

My first day of first grade at the old Snowflake, Arizona, Elementary School, I walked the three-quarter mile walk from home with my dad, since it was his first day, too, if you don't count preparatory faculty meetings. He taught "special ed," and so I never expected to have him as a teacher; instead, I needed him to convince the librarian ("Mrs. Switchblade Fingernails") to let me read from the sixth-grade shelves. We'd race to school, lamppost to lamppost, past the Pioneer Market, past the old Main Street Chapel, then he'd head for his classroom and I'd head for mine.

By the time I'd reached sixth grade, though, special ed had sucked his spirit dry (his phrase). He was in a regular classroom, and I was his student. The benefits:

1. He let me run my own student newspaper, courtesy of new Xerox technology.
2. He appointed me class president once.
3. He let me organize a tournament to see who could do a Rubick's cube the fastest. (Of course he had special Chinese instructions and I had long since got it under a minute.)

The disadvantages:

1. He watched to make sure I didn't hold hands with girls during film time.
2. He pulled me outside the classroom one day and bit my head off for publicly humiliating the kid who always made up unbelievable hockey stories for the morning news-weather-sports reports.
3. He still wanted to race to school, or else when he'd walk, he'd throw his elbows out like a drum major's and imitate a tuba. I had become increasingly aware of the other kids walking to school—especially the ones wearing training bras—and I didn't exactly want to be marching with the one-man band.

I survived, although perhaps a little traumatized.

By the time I was a senior in high school, elementary school had sucked his spirit even *drier*, and he'd returned to high school teaching, where his career had begun. Somehow, though, he ended up teaching English (a political science major); it seems high schools hire only coaches (history minors) in social studies. When he got the chance to teach an advanced government class my senior year, he had a chance to regain some of the energy the previous years had drained.

I sat back and watched. He read passages aloud from *Lord of the Flies*, kept kids sitting on the edge of their seats as flies buzzed around a great pig head on a stick. He outlined the American legal system with verve, made history come alive when he played Jefferson or Hamilton. In May he scrapped the final exam, held a class mock court instead, much to the administration's displeasure. They took the course away from him the next year. He didn't assign enough homework, they said.

When graduation came, though, and the seniors sat at midnight watching slides set to sentimental pop songs, his picture came up again and again: his transcendental meditation finger exercises; his rendition of the 1960s dance craze, "The Vulture"; the stance he takes when he can't remember what he was saying, his tie flipped up in his mouth, forehead furrowed. The crowd cheered each time his picture took the screen. I realized I had seen a master teacher at work, from a higher view than had that sixth grader.

At 19, a week before leaving on my own Mormon mission, I took him to see *Dead Poets Society*, thinking his conflicts with a stodgy system mirrored Robin Williams's as Dr. Keating. At the movie's end he cried like a kid, and I half expected him to stand on his seat and shout Whitman's line: "O! Captain, My Captain!"

III

Most of my father's books are kept in his library, shelves floor to ceiling that made me so proud I once snapped a picture with a Polaroid One-Step to immortalize their grandeur. His second library, the family sometimes joked, was the bathroom. Always, a stack of half-read paperbacks stood to one side of the toilet or the other, or on top of the tank. Placemarks bulged a rainbow of cardstock, and he'd often yell out to someone passing in the hall and make them listen to a potent paragraph.

That's what happened the day I became convinced of his apostasy. I, the innocent passerby, was probably 12 or 13, intellectually innocent. He was reading Christian philosophy, something unsafe, outside channels of real (read, "Mormon") revelation.

He said, "Do you think God created the world through evolution?"

I stood, drop-jawed, ears unsure. I said, "Evolution?"

He said, "I think it makes a lot of sense," and he held the book out to me—spine spread wide—to back himself up. He resumed his bathroom business, and I left, stunned, having been forced to think things I'd never thought before.

That memory sometimes stands out to me, signaling irony like a flashing blue light signals a K-mart shoe sale. My father's love of knowledge meant this: family discussions one after another on the religious meanings of *The Empire Strikes Back*, Yoda's teachings dripping heavy off his tongue; morning family Bible study, occasionally augmented by secular poetry or his own family history research; an occasional, "So *that's* what Emerson was getting at with his transparent eyeball." Here's his love of knowledge once removed, manifest in me: my first encounter with the left-leaning Mormon intellectual community at 18—instant identification with an ex-bishop who admits he grew up in a racist church; my realization at some point that Yoda's religious insights, derived from Joseph Campbell, weren't at all exclusively Christian in meaning; a selectively eclectic theology that stretched traditional understanding of church leaders' authority, followed by a more complete abandonment of belief. He says, "Where did I go wrong?"

When I came home from my 2 years of missionary work—two thirds of which I spent in bruised-up brownstones in New Jersey's inner cities—he told the church elders with their slow Arizona drawls he was glad I'd come to doubt the Democratic party's approach to social ills. What he didn't realize was that I'd still never vote Republican—at least the Democrats admitted social ills exist. When my wife and I first voted for Clinton and my parents said, "But he supports gay rights," we said, "Well, why do you think we voted for him?"

They're still bemoaning the railroading of Evan Mecham, his being tossed out of the governor's office so many Arizona Mormons had worked so hard to get him into. When I was a senior in high school Mecham—notorious for rescinding the state's Martin Luther King holiday and for a general lack of cultural sensitivity—came through town, campaigning against his impending recall. He spoke in the Snowflake High School auditorium to an audience primarily made up of good Latter-day Saints. My father clapped along as the crowd gave him ovation after ovation (in church they'd compare him to Joseph Smith, the martyred Mormon prophet). I clapped once, when God's little governor said, "We need to be more careful who we put in office."

My father wonders if he should have told me his conversion story one more time—how his parents threw him out when he'd joined the Mormons at 18, how he'd taken a mission call on faith and someone's anonymous money. How a church leader blessed him with the promise that his parents would be baptized if he served a worthy mission. (He did, and they were.) He gives me a book of religious essays by the Mormon science fiction writer Orson Scott Card: I *hope his faith strengthens yours; he survived his intellectual phase.*

IV

I'm afraid I gave my dad an emotional beating as a teenager. Once, the night before I was to leave for a week in Puerto Peñasco, Mexico, with a group of friends, he and my mother barged in on me at a friend's house. Sure, it was

4:30 in the morning, and sure I should have been home at midnight, but we were doing the long hot highway to Mexico in the morning, and sleeping was the last thing on our minds. I argued my point in the family van on the way home, and I don't remember quite what prompted it, but I remember him sharp-tongued: "You're too damn smart for your own good, and your smartness is going to kill you someday." Of course he came forward with the scripturally mandated "increase of love" like clockwork: five, four, three, two, one. Every time. I'd count it on my fingers in my bedroom.

Six years into my own fatherhood, I evaluate my own performance through my childhood memories—sometimes in fear, but more often with increasing compassion for him, a clearer recognition of what went right.

Maybe I just never could understand the sickness that had twisted his temper. I certainly didn't understand him the morning we fought over breakfast until I yelled, "You're a fool," leaving one sister crying at the table, the other kids staring at oatmeal while I slammed the front door behind me. In time, we cleared space for each other, stayed quiet when we knew a few words could set off something bad.

He wrote calm letters to me while I was a missionary; occasionally they would reveal a doubt, a struggle—why, if he did all he could to live a righteous life, did God keep him from getting well? Like Tevyah, he'd shake his fists at heaven, say, "You're supposed to be *bound* when I do what you say."

Once, in the middle of a humid New Jersey week, I wrote him over lunch, something I'd usually save for my one day off each week. (We weren't allowed to phone home.) I sent him scriptural references, the outline of a talk by some motivational speaker, some popular Mormon self-help tips filtered through Steven Covey's *Seven Habits of Highly Effective People*. But it was timed just right, inspired. My mother wrote that he'd received the letter while home for lunch, on a day he was convinced he couldn't take an afternoon of smart-assed classes. She said he cried reading what I'd written, just those few lines.

When I call home, now that they have more kids married than living with them, my mother does most of the talking. She asks how my daughters are, how Stephanie likes her job. Occasionally my dad will ask me what I've read recently, or if I've heard a certain Stones song he just downloaded. But more often, somewhere in the background, my father breathes on a faded extension, static on the line. He stays quiet, and what rides his silence is a love that hasn't quite cast out fear. When I say goodbye, he'll say it back, then leave me on the line with that hard click.

CHAPTER 22

WITH FINGERS LACED: MASCULINITY, DYING, AND SURVIVAL

Pete Mackey

Were my father not emaciated, dying of hepatitis C, he might have been in the midst of many other moments as he leaned forward to rest his forearms on his thighs and stare down into his laced fingers. He might have been an NCAA Division I full-scholarship basketball player wishing for the final shot to fall, a father expressing gratitude for his six children's lives, or a lifelong devout Irish-Catholic praying at another never-missed weekly mass. He had been all these before, surely In this precise pose. Now he was merely fighting against the force of a deadly disease. He was merely himself trying to stand, being watched by his son.

* * *

It was Labor Day weekend, 1998, in West Chester, Pennsylvania. I had detoured there on my way home to South Carolina from Ireland because, during my vacation, my father had slipped into a coma. He had returned to consciousness and been released from the hospital by the time I arrived. But if I had thoughts of being useful, they were misplaced. Beside him, I was no better than I would be if I were far off. He had hunched back in his lounge chair and, for 5 minutes, sat nearly still, waiting for the dizziness of that slight movement to pass. He was also insisting, by steely concentration and muttered expressions, that he was okay, that he did not need help to stand. He would do it himself. For now, though, he was fighting whatever demons wailed in his mind, scraping together any scraps of will left after the previous few months. Already thinned by the illness, he had dropped another 35 pounds since June. His skin sagged around his frame like clothes on hangers. His cheek bones protruded. His eyes seemed to have retreated into caves. It was as if he were fading into some dark place inside himself, somewhere broken, and he was: into the sickened liver. He looked like what he had become: someone dying. Here, him, my father at that instant, this is masculinity. It is fighting to stand on your own, insisting that you must.

* * *

Hepatitis C is a remarkably pervasive and successful killer, living as it does incurably in the blood of 4 million Americans. Hepatitis C actually infects four times as many Americans as AIDS, according to the Centers for Disease Control. Some 7% of those suffering from hepatitis C contracted it via transfusions, some 60% from IV-drug use, and some through sexual contact or as unborn babies. Like its deadly blood-cousin AIDS, hepatitis C is also withering. With each pass of the bloodstream through the liver, it cuts the organ's ability to clean out the body's poisons. Eventually the liver becomes useless. The result? Hepatitis C kills 10,000 people a year, via such effects as liver scarring, liver cancer, and cirrhosis.

In 1984, the virus began the siege that would become cirrhosis in my father. That year, double bypass surgery let the virus into him via a blood transfusion. He might as well have been taking after his eldest brother, Tom, who had contracted it the same way, at the same hospital. Although Tom died in 1994 following heart complications, hepatitis C surely had some role, forming a dark yoke upon body and mind as it does. But heart attacks are the family way. A heart attack had killed the father of these two men, as well as his own brothers. Even in this second generation, when the heart could not kill Tom and my father, it admitted another threat sideways. Through the transfusion, it had given the virus a new place to live, in the familial blood.

That fact seems ironic. Blood, after all, is an archetypal female motif. My dad and his brother were men in the classic sense: hard working, devoted to faith and family, never far from a laugh, fiercely proud of their heritage. Yet the blood infection had entered them, secretly, with torpid power, like another masculine figure: the Cold War spy. The all-consuming heart attack would have fit better: an explosion, a burst of muscle and force, a sudden jaw-bit show of desires that do not know how to stop, or when.

* * *

As I watched my father stare into his hands, was he urging that heart to another surge of fidelity in the new struggle of rising to his feet? Had he forgotten or forgiven its collusion against him with the virus? Or was he cursing it in silent dismay, trying to understand why it had taken him to the deadly infection?

My father, like many serious athletes, had once known a heart that seemed beyond defeat. How many times had it plunged and pumped during his years on that scholarship? How many times had he asked of it, near exhaustion in a game's final seconds, for oxygen and energy? For eternity, he had counted on it without a thought of its failing him. Nor had he ever lost the love of competition that continued to make such demands on the great center muscle. Even while raising us with my mother, even while traveling tens of thousands of miles annually as a sales manager for GTE Sylvania, he played basketball every week at the Ridgewood, New Jersey, YMCA.

It was only natural, even inevitable, that he was in the middle of such a game when his heart abandoned him. Precisely, typically, he was competing with men half his age. He was 51 at the time. The windows in the gym were closed. It was summer, and hot. The action was frenetic. Dad's arm suddenly began tingling, his chest tightened, and his breaths grew short. He sat down. A fellow player who was a police officer read the symptoms immediately. My father was rushed to the hospital. He had taken his heart as far as it could go. He had found a limit, as men do, only in pain. He had also broken down on the inside first, where no one could see.

* * *

Now, as he stared past those hands to the inside, bent as if in prayer, what was my father waiting for? Another expression of will: this time, simply to stand by himself? Had he not shown enough will already during the months of decline?

Earlier that summer, he and my mother had celebrated 40 years of marriage. Their children and grandchildren gathered at a hotel to enjoy the occasion as they could, regardless of the fate lingering. We all went to the indoor pool before dinner. My father, though, should not have been there, even just to watch. He should have been upstairs sleeping, saving his strength for the dinner party to come. But with all of us together, he could not be absent. He must insist on being with us, regardless if, at times, sitting in a chair beside the water, he slumped into sleep, dragged inward against his wishes by the collapsing liver. No matter. He was at least there. He could barely have done otherwise. He had insisted on being present our whole lives. During our hectic youthful involvement in sports, when all six of us were on different teams, we often competed in various towns on the same day. Dad hardly missed a game. Now he had other games to watch: among his eight grandchildren. They were splashing and laughing, taking their first attempts at going under water, and getting piggyback rides. The pressures on Dad's mortality simply concentrated his resolve. He would continue to watch the play of his generations. He would continue on his own terms out of love for family. If 2 days later another coma took him, so be it. For as long as he could, he would not let life go.

* * *

For many years, the tenacious disease had also worked with as much will as a man can possess. It had destroyed slowly, constantly, as it always does. Fourteen years of it had brought my father to that chair. That duration is common, for the virus begins harming the body long before its symptoms emerge. My siblings and I hardly were aware such a disease existed, and could not see that it had found our family. We had shrugged off to advancing age Dad's increasingly frequent naps and forgetfulness, declining weight, and suddenly unsure steps. We did not realize that a virus was churning poisons back into his muscles and brain.

At Thanksgiving 1997, finally, the effects announced themselves too dramatically to dismiss. The family was assembled at the dining room table for one of our favorite activities, a board game. In this game, a player reads out a question that everyone else tries to answer. They write their guesses on slips of paper and pass them forward to the judge, a role each player holds in turn as the game advances. Each of us having been the judge, we all confronted a surreal moment: seeing the correct answer in our father's penmanship and then trying to convince him of it. He could not remember what he had thought seconds before. He could not recognize the marks of his own hand. We could only reach for the obvious suspect, Alzheimer's.

Days later, our parents told us about the disease. They had learned of it from blood tests in the mid-1990s but had kept the news from us. It was typical of what we had learned from our father: no one likes a complainer. Life brings pain. Bear it yourself for as long as you can.

* * *

Such pride helped my father rise at last to his feet that day as I watched. He could not walk any longer, however, without leaning on someone. My mother and I helped him move gingerly forward. He was hardly a father between us. He seemed more like an elderly grandfather: weak, small, and folding. I only helped him for several steps, though. Then my mother took over. It could only have been that way.

When, in the spring of 1998, Dad's condition began worsening, my mother entered a torturous world. Sometimes hepatitis C's last stages break slowly. In my father's case, they rushed. All the while, my mother stood by him like the most glorious of nurses: fearless, devoted, and compassionate. This is hardly an emotional assessment; it is the plain truth of how physically needful my father had become, and how much my mother proved his guardian. She later would tell me that his condition sometimes hurt so much to witness that she had to step outside the house to cry. It was seeing the mental collapse: with the toxins and medicines brewing inside him, her husband was becoming lost inside his own life. He would enter the kitchen carrying a sock and ask her what it was for. He would wake in the middle of the night screaming from horrifying nightmares. He would speak nonsense to her, needing to be coaxed back to sanity. It was seeing the physical collapse: with each passing day that summer, her husband was losing his ability to care for himself. He could not sit up in bed on his own. He could not stand long enough in the bathroom to wash his own body. Eventually he could not walk at all without her by his side, as on my visit. Numerous times his wife rushed him to the hospital as his body spun into free fall.

As I watched him stand, such a time was about to come again. Before the day ended, he would be back in the hospital. His blood pressure and breathing would become erratic. Yet it had only been a few days since he had last been in the hospital, while I was in Ireland. Time was clearly constricting. My parents, though, had made a pact. They would keep Dad alive long enough for an organ donor to be found. One of their daughters was expecting a baby in late September, a daughter-in-law one early the next year, and a son (this son) was writing a book. My father was determined to see all these things happen. Fortunately, sadly, ironically, his plunging descent had served this cause. It had earned him a place on the list of those urgently needing a new liver. The odds of finding a match were enormous. Nearly a thousand people a year die waiting for a liver transplant. But the listing at least gave my parents hope. His role was to conserve himself, turn inward, nurture a space in which to keep going. Hers was to deliver the acts of kindness and attention known only by the most loving partners amid crises. My father had grown to love someone so fully that she could help save him.

* * *

When I finally left for South Carolina on Monday, September 7, my father was no longer in the hospital. His stay there during my visit had not lasted long. There was little more the doctors could do to help. But he would be back there again far sooner than he thought.

On Tuesday evening, September 8, my mother and father were in bed watching Mark McGwire try to break Roger Maris's single-season home run record. Like the rest of America's sports fans, all season long our father had watched McGwire and Sammy Sosa chase home run number 62. Indeed, growing immobilized by disease, Dad was capable of little else. It isn't surprising either that one of our family's cherished possessions is now a quilt my mother has since made. It shows McGwire on his record-breaking swing. She calls it her "home run heroes" quilt. It is dedicated to all the great home run hitters, as well as to my father, and to a man we shall never know. McGwire's signature is on it. But the quilt matters because of what our mother was commemorating. Shortly after McGwire hit number 62, my parents' phone rang. It was the hospital. A matching liver had become available.

By the next afternoon, September 9, I was watching my father again. The transplant surgery was over, and he was unconscious in the post-op recovery room. Tubes protruded from his arms, legs, and neck. Machines connected to his body beeped and hummed. A ventilator tube curled past his lips and toward his lungs like a translucent cane. Except machines were not doing all the work. The liver's goodness already showed. Dad's face was flush with color. His skin was filling out. He looked like what he was: a man coming back to life.

Standing over him, I felt compelled to tell him so. His head suddenly shook from side to side. The nurse visiting the room to check on his vital signs noted that Dad was too far under the anesthetic to hear me. She said the motion of his head was only an involuntary reflex attempting to repel the tube in his throat. I had to continue talking anyway, regardless of whether I might as well have been signaling silently into a void. Sometimes not even the embarrassment of having such feelings can control them.

My father's pinky finger rose slowly, as if tugged by a string, and gently fell back. The nurse observed that, in such an inactive state as Dad was now sunk, muscles can move spontaneously like that. Still I could not help releasing my thoughts into words.

Within 24 hours, the tube in Dad's throat was gone, and he was upright and conscious. He told me that he had recognized my voice and had shaken his head and raised his finger to tell me so. More than that, even lost behind the tubes, suppressed behind the waves of anesthetic, he had been able to wonder why I was there: hadn't he and my mother put me on a plane to home 2 days ago? I was amazed, my shame as great as my relief. He had heard my every word.

* * *

My father seemed to have been injected with life. In only a few hours, the transplant brought him a stunning distance from that broken place where he had bent over his hands. Within days, it was evident the new organ and he had matched. The recovery would be quick. The positive course of that reversal has never changed. The truth is, a liver donor saved Dad's life. How completely had someone done so? We were later told by those who saw it during the transplant that my father's old liver was in such bad shape, it was not working anymore.

The successful surgery meant good news had to be spread. Our family began contacting those who had been waiting out the surgery with us. I called a friend of my father's. He had been the star center on their college basketball team, and my father had kept in touch with him. He told me that since learning of the illness months before, he had gone to church every day to pray for his friend. He remembered for me that during their away games in college, my father had encouraged him to go along to the Catholic church in whatever town they found themselves. He went, although he was not Catholic. Years later, alone with his memories, the friend and teammate had done again what he could in prayer.

Other gestures were owed too, from my parents, for the donor. If a life had been saved, it was because another had been lost. In keeping with standard practice, the hospital would tell them nothing about the donor. All they would say was that he had been a tall man. The description is too apt for comment. My parents could only write a letter of gratitude to a nameless family and ask the surgeon to forward it to them, which he had said he would do. It was another silent wish into a void. It also was written in my father's own hand. This time, his fingers were unlaced. He also knew what he wrote and meant to write. Like his former teammate, he was offering an expression of faith and remembrance into the darkness.

Such gestures continued the chains that link men as they always are, by action, however small and hopeful, or grand and selfless. Fate never fails to lace fingers together somehow in the end. Masculinity, at least as I witnessed it from outside a crucible, proves itself there above all: in the humility and decency of admitting these inevitable ties, beyond even doubt or death. It is accepting that in the end we will find that we are far less powerful than we might have feared, even as, all the while, we are granted more power than we can know. Masculinity? It is even one man showing another, in confronting death, how to live.

Chapter 23

Raking Leaves

Ted Wojtasik

Novelist Ted Wojtasik writes in this story about a seemingly normal father-son chore, but in the context of his father's slow recovery from a stroke.

I've been thinking of leaves, once again, of raking leaves and of my father raking leaves. These were November leaves, not October leaves or September leaves, but the final leaves of the season and of the year. These were the leaves of the sugar maple—like bright red palms against the sky. These were the last leaves to cling, the last leaves to fall. The stubborn leaves, my father calls them. The leaves of the flowering dogwood and the swamp maple and the black oak and the white ash were all gone. All these trees now stood in Connecticut as they have stood already for a good month in Maine or New Hampshire—naked and dark and lifeless. The leaves of the great sugar maple, though, were the last leaves of New England to touch the cold fall ground.

And my father, in his plaid winter jacket, white-haired and wrinkled, still tall after his stroke this past summer, stood in the backyard waiting for me. He pulled on his worn work gloves. He had the rakes, one for me and one for him, leaning against the cart.

"All you need to rake is a rake," he said, standing next to his bright yellow tractor with the old wood cart attached behind it. In the cart he had a cardboard box. "We'll rake the leaves into two or three piles or four piles and then rake the piles into the cardboard box and then dump the leaves in the box into the cart." His eyes traveled across the backyard. "It won't take too long to do this."

My own eyes traveled across the backyard, and I agreed with him. The late afternoon sky was clear, the air mild, and the scent of winter far away.

"It's a good day to rake leaves," my father remarked, glancing up at the sky, and then started to rake with deliberate slow strokes.

I started to rake, too, but quickly. I raked self-consciously. I am raking leaves, I thought, with my father on a November afternoon—a father and son rake leaves. I read and think too much. I am not used to raking leaves because

I live in the city. I did not want to finish the backyard that day or the next or the day after; fortunately, we still had the front yard to rake.

I watched my father rake leaves and listened to the scrape of bamboo teeth against leaf, against lawn, against root. I watched to see how well he raked: whether he raked as he used to rake and whether he held the handle as he used to hold it.

At one point he stopped and stared, with continued disbelief, at his left hand. He flexed it and sighed. "To think I survived Omaha Beach to end up like this."

My father has a Purple Heart and two oak-leaf clusters stuffed in the top drawer of his bureau: shot in the left knee, shot in the left knee again, shredded with shrapnel in his right hand and arm. He helped liberate the concentration camps in Dachau. He had seen a man, skeletal from malnutrition, his skull-like face astonished at freedom, totter and fall down dead.

Together, in silence, we raked the leaves. We raked them into piles. And then I held the cardboard box next to a pile as my father raked the leaves into its opening. I lifted the box and dumped the leaves into the cart until the cart was full.

My father inspected the leaves in the cart and then stared at a small pile of bright leaves in a corner of the yard, near a hedge of yews, a dark constant green.

I said, "We can get that tomorrow."

He said, "I'll come back for it."

He had to drive the tractor and the cart through the back fields to the ravine to dump the leaves.

"We can do it tomorrow, and we can do the front yard tomorrow, too," I said.

With narrowed eyes he studied the sky. "We still have time. I'll come back for it."

"But we have all day tomorrow to do it," I insisted. "Besides, you've done enough today already. We don't have to do it all in one day."

"I'll come back for it," he repeated.

"But we can do it tomorrow."

"It might rain tomorrow."

"Did Mom tell you that?"

"No. It just might. You never know when it might rain."

"We've done enough today already."

"I'll come back for it."

"Dad, it's getting dark."

"It's not that dark."

"Why can't we do it tomorrow?"

My father looked at me. "Because I want to get it done today."

He pressed the cardboard box down on the leaves in the cart and set his rake on top of the leaves at the side. Slowly he climbed into the seat and started the engine. Over the disturbing roar of the motor, he shouted, "You can go inside if you want to. I can finish up myself."

I stood holding my rake as he bumped over the exposed roots of the swamp maple and drove past the vegetable garden, filled now only with the tangled dark vines of the pumpkin. I kept my eyes on him as he drove into the back fields and disappeared over the far edge, his white hair visible to the end.

Tomorrow, I'll ride with him to the ravine. The sound of the tractor vanished into the air, now darkening with night and with cold and with resolution. And I waited in the backyard with my rake, in the twilight, for my father to return.

CHAPTER 24

ON MASCULINITY

Ben Triana

This poem deals with my frustrations, fears, and observations of masculinity, especially through the impressions my father has made on me. He is the closest thing to God, in so many ways.

> I am afraid of the male body.

> Afraid of that rim of fat,
> The only physical bastion of masculinity
> After 40.
> The gut.

> I am afraid of it,
> Of becoming.
> Of it on my father,
> On me.

> I am afraid of my father.
> Of him and his, "If you're gay,
> I'll kill you."

> I am afraid of him,
> Him in his boxers,
> His skin drooping
> (He's over 40),
> To know that to be male,
> To be masculine,
> It is only in his gut.

> But sometimes
> It's in his hands,
> In his face,
> Chiseled from stone.

Then, at that moment,
He is God, and I want
To kiss him.

But I am afraid.
I am afraid of being in the
Theater,
Of sitting next to a woman
And staring at that screen,
Of leaning over.
Of whispering,
"My God,
He's attractive,
He's beautiful."

Of having sex with her later,
With my male,
My maleness.

I am afraid
Of reading God's lips
And knowing:
"You are already dead to me."

And I am afraid,
That all I have to be masculine,
Is a gut, when I am 40.

Chapter 25

Acolyte

Jack Brannon

My father was a physician for the local university students and a sports doctor for the football program. My father was an able surgeon with a true liking for the young athletes he treated. As a child, I tagged along with my father, finding the gym to be both home and temple. After a season or two I was into full-fledged gridiron hero worship.

> *Once my father made a calculated effort*
> *to save me from the fate of sissydom,*
> *took me out to the campus gym*
> *where he worked among men's men,*
> *a healer to Saturday's warriors,*
> *so that I might be raised in the company of athletes*
> *to marvel and admire the achievements*
> *of young lords on the gridiron.*
>
> *On a sweltering September night*
> *before an altar with limed boundary lines*
> *and 72,000 celebrants,*
> *someone hands me a white towel*
> *saying, "Wipe 'em down*
> *when they come off the field,*
> *they're sweatin' like warthogs tonight."*
>
> *"How . . . should I ask if they want . . . ?"*
> *Sissy boys would never be rude.*
>
> *"Naw, boy, just wipe 'em off,*
> *they'll be grateful."*

I move off lost along the benchline
as a host returning from battle,
shuffle from one seraph to the next,
watching for the moment
between spitting and shouts
when I can make oblation
with the offer of my trembling towel.
One by one I serve the giants
amid the terrible din of the temple.

These drenched and flaming faces
with their pimply blotched terrain
smeared wide with muddy gore
under a dripping crown of butch-waxed hair,
these holy images endowed by time
and my father's adoration,
loom vast and shining
in the museum of my childhood.

I wipe the towel across each face
down the massively muscled arms
in a sacramental trance,
then soak in each, "Hey, kid, thanks,"
receiving the manna
that dared not speak its name.

VOICES FIVE

TOWARD OTHERS

CHAPTER 26

UNATTRACTIVE MALE SEEKS
HUMAN FEMALE

Joshua E. Borgmann

Straight up, here I am: SWM 25 seeking SF 18–35. Looks, race, other shit unimportant, but must be willing to tolerate fat bald man interested in music, primarily the British band Cradle of Filth; books: *American Psycho, White Noise,* and maybe *Wise Blood;* movies: *Pulp Fiction, Texas Chainsaw Massacre, Dogma, Pornogothic, Blair Witch*—digs *Star Trek* and *South Park* for sociopolitical discourse—overall a very underground black death doom grind kinda groove looking for someone who can just sit back with some Type-O-Negative playing 'cause I do that a lot when I write 'cause I'm a poet and yes I've written love poems even though I haven't had many dates. Back some years I wrote one I called "Black Is the Only Color in the World" and later, after I gave up this dancer I was seeing, I traded the poppies for telephones that never ring and even though I wasn't Alan Jackson or even Garth Brooks I felt like I needed a cowboy hat 'cause I was sure stuck writing that damn "she done gone left me and I'm so sad" song, so I moved on and wrote one on the girl I stalked in sixth grade and that one went over well but hey I'm rambling so back to business. Morally I'm for this carpe diem do as thou will shit but politics is kinda tricky 'cause really that's economics and some days I feel socialist and others libertarian so I just vote Democrat but I'm anticensorship and don't mind pornography. It's better work than McDonalds and besides how else is a guy like me going to see naked women anyway but hey don't take that wrong 'cause like I've said somewhere else sex doesn't equal success.

Note: Children tolerated, pets welcomed; however, if you're an overzealous Christian or a sorority type and you're still reading please stop (all other responses will be considered for replies).

CHAPTER 27

SOMEWHERE ON MEETING STREET

Jared Chesson

I *submit,*
my hands work our
old Charleston
ceramic sink, the
soap dish
sits fresh with soap,
our toothbrushes—purchased
after we camped Grandfather Mountain
and forgot our two
toothbrushes at home—lie
in a mirror medicine
cabinet, with
a warped picture of
our burnt cheeked
faces, smiling warm on
the beach, on
the mirror's upper right
hand corner. The Charleston
faucets squeak, leak
on rusted pipes
that bend and rust,
underneath the sink;

in bed
we tuck in close, like
two
vinyl records finding
the same cardboard sleeve,

we
talk close, drift,
drink our dreams.

In morning
I shave away my sleep,
look as my wife
stretches under sheets, she
turns, lips part
a blushing smile,
her immediate stare grips,
controls,
legs,
perfect milk, walk her
into me.
I wish her closer.
early morning,
we fix
the pipes on
our sink, clean,
quaint, close, in a bathroom,
somewhere on Meeting Street.

CHAPTER 28

LET YOUR BEAUTY CHANGE

Brad Bostian

Let your beauty always fade, my love,
Let crows dance up your neck frustratingly
Humanizing you, while strings above,
By which fate lifts your soul, lift your body
And drop it, and let your skin become papery
With ink from all the years' calligraphy
To cover the marks others remember you by,
And let your well of love dry up, each eye
Cloud over like a lake, deep and cold.
Time will strip the leaf from your gold temple
And make instead a small, homey chapel
Under split trees, hollow and old.
Let your cracked bell call companionship.
On your hard pews I'll still worship.

CHAPTER 29

A SINGLE MAN ABOUT TO MARRY

Neil Fitzsimons

BEING A MAN

When did I become an adult male? In legal terms, it was the day I turned 18 that I became an adult man. I was able to vote, a police arrest became more than a phone call to my parents, and military service became an option. I believe that at 18 I was only in the earliest stages of manhood. Thinking back, my friends and I thought we had learned all there was to know in our world, but what is the male experience? Or should I ask, " What is my male experience?" This is a question that I'm facing for the very first time in my life. So if I ramble on, please bear with me. I've lived the past 27 years as a male, and have never been asked about my experience as a male. Now that I think about this question, I'm somewhat surprised that I've never been asked about my experiences or never really thought about it myself. I have lived 27 years as a male and have put very little thought into the question or meaning. The first thought that comes to mind is that men are men. End of story. But there is much more to this question. Every man is different, and each of our experiences differs from the others. Everything from our background, social class, friends, and family affect who we are, and what we've become as men living in the year 2001. So, my experience as a male can be traced and broken down from my past experiences, both good and bad, along with my ideas for the future. In reality, some of my experiences were extremely limited, but overall, I've enjoyed every aspect and adventure that I've had as a man.

NOW

Currently I'm a 27-year-old man who's engaged to get married in 6 months. Getting married is a huge event for me. Not only will I be spending the rest of my life with my wife, I'm changing my life in many ways.

Gone are the days when the only person I'd have to worry about was my-self. When I go out with my single guy friends, I'll be the married guy who gets them drinks while they talk to the single ladies. But, missing all of these things is OK with me, since I'm gaining a great person. And I am sharing my life with another. Marriage is a huge part of the male experience for me.

When I was younger, I always believed that one day, I'd get married. Be-cause that day was always so far ahead in the future, I didn't have to think about it for the moment. I never really thought about how my wedding would be, or who would attend.

About Marriage

When I think about marriage, and what it really means to me as a male, I think of many different things. Marriage is letting the other person know that you love her and only her, and that the two of you want to spend the rest of your lives together.

It's a great feeling to have someone to plan the future with and to share ex-periences. It is in these situations that I can see the differences between men and women. Although we have the same goals and ideas about our lives to-gether in the future, we look at them through different eyes. Mine through the eyes of a man, and hers through the eyes of a woman.

For example, I don't want our bed to have flowered sheets or a brightly col-ored bedspread. We do have many differences and ideas about how things should get done, but that's what makes us work together so well. Our differ-ences complement each other in ways that enable us both to grow.

About Fears Too

Being on the verge of marriage also comes with a few fears. I have to start think-ing about our future together in many different ways. Everything from children to money and careers becomes a quick reality. In the past, children were those little people that older married people had who cried and spit up on them-selves. But now that I'm getting married, the next question everyone asks is, "When are you two going to have kids?" My polite answer is, "In a few years," but my real answer is, "When we're ready." And when that is, I don't know.

Changes

After getting married, a man has to face the next big decision: children. And the decision to have children certainly seems life altering, for the good, of course. Over the next few years I'll face what every single man faces in the course of his life, and that is change.

Looking back at my life so far as a male, change and adapting to change seem to be the common themes. At every age I've had to adapt to some sort of change or another. And these changes have come in many different forms and situations. Sometimes change was good, and other times it was bad. But, I've tried my best to learn from my experiences and grow as a man.

One of the earliest moments that I remember change affecting my life was in grammar school. Around the sixth grade, the girls started to become interested in the boys as more than just friends. This was the age when spin the bottle became a birthday party favorite, but only when the parents weren't looking.

At that time, I was very happy with the idea that the girls were just other friends, except that they wore dresses to school. But all this changed very rapidly when I had to kiss these same girls. And it was the girls' idea, not the boys', to play spin the bottle in the basements of our parents' homes.

Change came rushing in like a tidal wave, the second I had to kiss the girls in my class. At that moment, I realized that I had enough male friends to keep me happy, and that girls were much more than classmates. It was at that moment that I learned that my relationships with both my male and female friends had changed. My male friends and I would start to talk about the girls we liked and those we disliked. These events also changed how I watched television and movies, and did I ever have a crush on Daisy Duke and Princess Leia.

CONSIDERING MY CAREER

As a young man, I never really worried about what I'd become in the future, and to this day, I'm not quite sure what I want to do. The question of what I want to do not only with my profession, but also with my life, has been affected by my past.

My likes and dislikes all come from decisions I've made in the past and learned from in one way or another. And I'm not the only male with these questions. Every one of my friends has the same questions running though his head.

My career path has changed in the past, and will change in the future, and it's up to me to handle this change, and decide which path works best for me. Since I'm now engaged to be married, my decisions are not only based on my best interests alone, but also the best interests of my fiancée.

Never before in my life have my decisions had such an impact on another individual. All of my decisions today will in some form or the other affect my future family. These are decision-making changes at their best. I no longer have only my best interests in mind, but those of my fiancée.

As a man, I welcome the change, and look forward to my future with my wife, and growing a family.

EXPECTATIONS

Does society expect man to act a certain way? My answer is yes. Throughout my entire life, I've heard people tell me how men should act; I watched television to see Hollywood's version of a man in action.

And what do I think of what I've heard and seen? I agree with some things, and disagree with others. Each man is very different, and each will have his own ideas about what the ideal man should look like and how he should act.

But I cannot put into words what or who this man is, or where one can find this person. In my mind, the ideal male is a mixture of many different individuals. I take some qualities from both real-life men whom I've met, and those I've seen on television and in the movies. Then, I try to live my life by following those good qualities. And trust me when I tell you that I don't always follow my own advice. But I try my best, and always evaluate where I am in life, and where I'm going in the future.

STEREOTYPES

There are many times during the course of a day that I try to act as society sees a man. There are many stereotypes about men that have been driven into us in some form from a very early age.

Men don't cry! Period. End of story. It doesn't matter how much psychological or physical pain a man might be in, he never cries. Watch any sporting event, and you're bound to see a player go down with a painful injury, but does he cry? Of course not. We're supposed to grit our teeth and take it like a real man.

I've had a few severe injuries (nonsport-related) that have caused me extreme amounts of pain, but for some reason or another, I couldn't cry. Even if I really wanted to sit and bawl, I just could not cry.

The same goes for when a man is emotionally distressed. According to the unwritten man rules, we're not allowed to cry if something is upsetting us emotionally. The next time you go to a sad or weepy movie, look around and see how many men are crying. I'll bet not many. But look at their faces, and see the amount of effort they're putting into not crying. I can tell you from many years of experience that trying not to cry is a very difficult task.

The last time I remember crying from an emotional situation was back when I was around 16 or 17. The reason I cried was from reading the book *Old Yeller* (Gipson, 1990), and the little boy had to shoot his dog. I cried my eyes out in my room all by myself. Maybe I should read *Old Yeller* again.

MORE CHANGE

Everyday, I seem to change in some form, based on my experiences and influences. I guess this is a part of growing older, and wiser. But it's not to say I can't revert back to who I was years ago.

Every time I set foot into a toy store or amusement park, I feel like I'm 14 years old again, with no worries in the world. And it's that 14-year-old kid that shaped me into who I am today.

Thinking back to any age, I'm still the same person, with modifications and changes that come from my experiences. But my core personality has remained intact, even with the changes in my environment and life.

CARING FOR AND ABOUT

Another aspect of my male experience that has interested me in the recent past is the comment that my fiancée made. She told me that I take care of her when she is sick, much better than she does of me. Is there any truth to this comment? I'm not real sure. But when we discussed this with a few friends of ours, most of the women agreed.

Is there some unknown motherly instinct that I never knew I possessed? I am not sure of the answer, but I do know that it feels very natural to take care of her when she is sick or sad. But at first thought, isn't it the woman who takes great care of the man when he's hurt or sick? Not that she doesn't care for me when I am ill. I would say that she does a wonderful job of caring for me.

I guess that men are much more sensitive than we get credit for, but perhaps we show our sensitivity in different and sometimes hidden ways. Being a man means that you take care of those you love and protect them as best you can, while expecting that she will do the same for you in times of need.

REAL MAN IMAGE

In my lifetime, I've witnessed many men trying to put out the appearance that they're real men. How many guys do you see at a stoplight with bright red sports cars, who slam on the gas pedal when the light turns green?

I can't help but laugh, and wonder what their motives are behind the display of power and supremacy. Maybe they lack self-esteem, or they think girls like guys who can drive really fast. If this is true, please let me know.

The same holds true in every bar in America. You have the guys with big beers in their hands that look around and discuss which of the other guys they can beat up in a fight. And as the night progresses, they test themselves by picking a fight with another guy because he looked in their direction. For some reason, they think this proves that they're real tough men. But when it comes down to actually throwing punches, they usually swing like a girl! Go figure.

REALLY REAL MEN

Not all men are like this, in fact most are not of this breed. But, it's these guys who give us levelheaded, smart, good-looking, funny guys a bad name. Just kidding! Watch—some guy will want to punch me this weekend.

So as I End

In conclusion, my overall experience as a male has been great. I'm very happy where I'm at right now in my life, and can't wait to see what happens in the future.

The idea of change and how we react to change keeps popping into my mind when I think about my experience as a male. Writing this essay has helped me understand what change is to me, and how it has affected me throughout my life.

I've only given a few examples of the change that happened in my life, but there are hundreds more that I keep to myself and those people who were there with me. And every male has his own changes to deal with, and must grow from his own experiences.

But we can share with each other, and understand what the other has been through. From what I've seen, it's not the strong who survive; the men who adapt to change best are those who will really survive.

CHAPTER 30

FURTHER THAN WHERE YOU ARE: A FATHER'S ALCOHOLISM, A DAUGHTER'S DEPARTURE

Anna Blackmon Moore

This piece is the first in a series of memoir essays. It attempts to foreground patterns of thought and behavior from which the narrator cannot escape as she becomes an adult.

My mother left when I was very young. It seemed like something invisible had removed itself from our house. I started watching lots of television with Edward, if he wasn't storming through town with his friends, but sometimes I stood in the front hallway and rubbed the oak paneling, or drifted into the dining room to play Pretend Tea with my grandmother's silver. Sometimes I taught Smokey the kitten gymnastics on the living room rug. Sometimes I went over to Abbey Duke's house. Sometimes I looked out my bedroom window into the rolling backyard hills of our neighbors.

Eating became very routine. I had cereal every morning and made a peanut butter sandwich to take to school, along with a Hostess cupcake. My father made supper for us every night, after he changed into boxer shorts and a bathrobe. Waffles and bacon on Saturday, fried chicken and biscuits on Wednesday. He spent the rest of his time grading Shakespeare papers and drinking bourbon and smoking cigarettes in his recliner, which was next to the bed he had shared with my mother until her last year in Grinnell. She had moved to the bedroom down the hall to escape my father's snoring and to have a softer bed. The one in my father's room had no box spring. Bouncing on it was impossible. If my father wasn't home, Edward and I used it as a mat for Pro Wrestling, which we watched on Saturday mornings. He was 3 years older than I and much bigger. He always won.

A cleaning lady started coming once a week. First it was Mrs. Rutherford, a tiny, quiet woman in her 70s who got on her hands and knees to wash the front and back stairs. This soon became too hard for her, and my father regretfully let her go. Then he hired Mrs. Wiley, a woman in her 50s with yellow hair and enormous breasts, who didn't bother with the stairs. She told me one day that I had dandruff.

"What's that?" I asked. I was in the playroom, standing in front of the television. I turned it on. I had just gotten home from school.

"It's when little flakes of skin get into your hair," she said. She had turned off the vacuum cleaner and she was squinting at me, her fingers wrapped around the handle. Smokey ran through the dining room behind her. "You should use some Head and Shoulders."

"I do use that," I said. Shower day was Sunday.

"You use Head and Shoulders?"

"That's what's in the tub," I said, touching my hair. *Gilligan's Island* was starting. I paid it no attention.

She cocked her head to the side. "Your hair looks a little greasy, too. You might want to say something to your dad."

"Oh," I said. "Okay." She turned the vacuum back on. I could hear it rumbling on the hardwood floor beneath the rug as I walked quickly past her, sticking my fingers in my hair at the scalp and trying to pull them through. They got stuck at my ears. When I reached the bathroom I turned on the light and studied my hair in the mirror. It didn't look any different, brown and thick, hanging just below my shoulders.

I mentioned it that night at supper.

"Dandruff?" my father said, pausing over his pork chops. He let his head fall forward and squinted at me, over his glasses. Edward was somewhere with his friends.

"Yeah."

He looked into his plate and stuck his fork into a pile of rice and gravy. "You're too young to have dandruff, love. Only grown-ups have dandruff." His hair was coarse and oily, sticking up from his head in shining wires.

"Oh."

"Mrs. Wiley is just picky. And she can't see very well."

I dipped a piece of pork chop in my applesauce and watched him eat. There was a piece of rice caught in his beard. He buttered a roll and took a long swallow of iced bourbon.

* * *

School was about a mile from our house. Edward took a shortcut if there wasn't lots of snow on the ground. One morning I followed him. He kept running from me and looking over his shoulder because he didn't want his friends to see him arrive at school with his little sister. I also don't think he wanted me to know Grinnell the same way he did, cutting between houses and across backyards. None of them were fenced. One might be overgrown and scattered with tricycles, the next might be mowed and empty, and the next might have a square flower garden with glittering lawn ornaments lining one side.

I started taking the shortcut every morning. My feet got wet with dew but it was a much faster way to get to school. I always wondered if some mother or father were watching me through a window, if they used my walk through their grass to gauge the time or if I made them angry, if someone was going to open his back door and stick his head out and tell me to get off his property.

Edward never seemed to worry about it. He always left the house before I did and I caught glimpses of him, ducking behind a garage, running ahead of me and then disappearing, grinning at me if I happened to notice him crouched behind an empty doghouse or pressed behind the trunk of a maple. Some days I didn't see him at all but I could hear him, rustling and breathing.

We never saw each other on the walks home after school. He was usually with his friends, a handful of boys with blond hair that covered their ears and touched the backs of their collars. Sometimes one or two of them would be at our house when I got there. Edward would point out my dirty hair or clothes until I went to my room. Then they would leave to watch cable TV at Paul Latcham's house, or to throw acorns and apples at cars on Sixth Avenue—a busy, four-lane street that cut through the middle of town and divided the college in half—or to make out with girls under the stairs at the Athletic Complex on campus.

Right before they all moved on to junior high, one of the gang moved away. The rest of them turned on Edward, and he was suddenly home all the time. He never wanted to leave.

"How come you don't want to go?" I asked. My father was taking us out for pizza and we were in the front hallway, pulling on our coats while he was in the back of the house, looking for his keys through piles of papers and books on the kitchen counter. Mom had made her weekly visit from Iowa City the night before, to take us out for burgers. I loved eating out.

Edward looked down at me. Long coats that nobody wore hung from hooks on the door and brushed against the side of his head. He leaned down and put his face close to mine. He had a very large mouth. "God you're a dumb fuck," he said. "You are such a dumb fuck."

I took a step backwards, away from him.

"I'm going to fucking kill you," he whispered. The paneling behind him was very brown, very dark. It seemed to shimmer, around his head. "I'm going to kill you. You think I want to run into any of those guys?" He breathed hard through his nose, which was always clogged up.

"I don't know."

"Well don't be so fucking stupid." He shook his head. He made a fist and hit my arm. I put my hand over it.

"You chillens ready to go?" My father strutted in, past us, and opened the front door. He had combed his hair but it was sticking up along the part. We followed him across the porch. It was cold. The pine trees in our front yard were speckled with snow, which was packed hard in places along the sidewalk to the driveway.

I scurried behind Edward, who held his head down and kept his hands buried in the front pockets of his coat. He was nice to me some nights if I allowed him to check my weight. He only asked after my father was passed out and we were alone downstairs in the playroom, his face curious, his hands probing, television droning in the background. I watched us from a large school picture of mine, sitting atop narrow bookshelves that were built into one wall. I was wearing a shirt my mother must have bought for me, white with a yellow collar and yellow flowers. My lips were parted, my cheeks splotched with little-girl red. An old wooden lamp illuminated all three of us in the dust that coated the TV, the piano on which Edward and I practiced a half hour a day, and the rows of my father's books, on mounted shelves, which lined the other walls up to the ceiling.

* * *

My mother had been gone a year or so when we started spending one or two weekends a month with her in Iowa City. She was taking art classes at the university. She took me to her studio and showed me the sculpture she was making, a big white thing that looked like shaped paper maché.

"What is it?" I asked, pulling on the zipper of my sweatshirt. Edward had stayed in Grinnell that weekend. We had just started making the trips separately.

"I don't know," she said. It was resting on a wide counter against the wall. Other students were bustling around, scraping and painting and mixing clay. "It doesn't really matter what it is, you know."

"It doesn't?"

She shook her head. "No." Her hair was thin, much thinner than mine or Edward's. It hung to her shoulders in weak, fragile strands. She stopped styling it after she left Grinnell. "It is so good to see you," she said, squatting so that her eyes were level with mine. She no longer wore makeup, and I could see the thinness of her eyebrows, the tiny wrinkles on the outside of her eyes and on each side of her mouth. She smiled.

"Will you play with my hair when we get home?"

"Sure. After supper."

"Is Leonard coming over?"

She nodded. This was her boyfriend, whom I liked very much. He had big hands and a happy, rolling voice. My mother had started to dress like him, in khaki pants and hiking boots. We were planning to make a Chef Boy-ar-dee pizza.

I don't remember feeling much of anything when I left her to go back home on Sundays. She would sometimes drive me if I begged and cried—Grinnell was an hour away—but most of the time I took the Greyhound and bought candy at the meal stop with money she had given me for supper. She rarely said anything about my appearance; if she told me I looked pretty she said so almost gravely, as if she were powerless over some unseen force.

I thought I was pretty, too. Sometimes I stared at my school picture in the playroom and pretended I was a model.

* * *

Two years later, when I was in third grade, I approached our house from school one afternoon and saw my mother's car in the driveway, parked behind my father's. It was a warm, spring day. Our crabapple tree was in bloom and the enormous pine trees that separated our front yard from the neighbor's were rippling in the breeze.

From the bottom of the driveway, through the two baby pines that grew right in the center of the lawn, I saw my mother and Edward sitting on the front porch steps. When I reached them she stood up and hugged me and said she was there to talk to each of us for a little while. Edward was staring at his shoes.

It was almost time for my television shows—I had just bought a little black-and-white TV with my saved allowance money and years of $10 and $20 Christmas checks, which my father deposited in a savings account for me—and until nightfall I liked to watch the shows alone in my room. But for some reason I didn't want to go inside. I walked around the house to the backyard and sat on the wooden swing and plopped my backpack on the ground. There were rusted toys in the sandbox that I vaguely remembered playing with. A dump truck, a little shovel. I thought that Edward and I might have played there together. I wasn't sure.

Then my mother was walking toward me, drifting across the backyard with one hand over her eyes to block the sun. She stopped in front of me and stood very still. Our house seemed to swallow her, and I saw my father, watching us through the kitchen window. The sun snapped beams of light from his glasses.

"I want you and Edward to come live with me," she said. She held her mouth in a large, serious 'O' that made her lips look thin and wrinkled.

"You do?"

She nodded. "Yes. How do you feel about that?"

I shrugged. "I like it here."

She said that it might be better for me and Edward and that she missed us terribly. Was I happy, living with my father?

"Yeah." I said. "Edward is too."

"I think you might be happier living with me in Iowa City."

I gripped the swing chain with each hand and studied her face, the thin lips, the serious gray eyes, the wrinkles in her forehead.

"Well," I said, looking at the flattened grass beneath the swing. "I don't want to." I spoke very softly, a loud whisper over the wind. "I don't want to leave here."

She frowned and told me she loved me and asked for a hug, bending down on one knee and opening her arms. I jumped off the swing and gave her one. Her hands pressed hard into my back. Her head was on my shoulder. Then she left.

* * *

During the custody hearing, Edward was leaving the house once in a while to spend time with Jeremy Duke, Abbey's older brother. He and Abbey didn't get along very well either, but sometimes the four of us would play hide-and-seek in the Dukes' backyard. They had to talk me into it. I was afraid of getting stung by a bee, and I hated missing my television shows.

Edward was still afraid of his old friends. When he wasn't with Jeremy, he watched television with me all afternoon and evening. I had started eating bowls of Peanut Butter Crunch after supper, so he was eager to check my weight after Dad was passed out. But until 9 or 10 o'clock Dad came downstairs for fresh drinks from the kitchen cabinet, and he always stuck his head in the playroom to say hello.

One night Dad came in to watch 10 minutes of *Soap*. When he got up to leave, he stumbled and bumped his shoulder on the doorframe. Edward looked at me from the couch. I was sitting on the chair beside it, my feet curled underneath me.

"Anna."

"What?"

"What do you think is wrong with Dad?" I turned away from the TV and looked at him.

"Wrong?"

"Yeah. When he slurs and trips and stuff like that."

"He's tired."

Edward took his feet off the bench we used as a coffee table and put them on the floor and sat straight up. "W*hat*?"

"He's tired. That's what he says when I ask him."

"You think he's *tired*?"

"Yeah. That's what he says."

"Shit." He looked down and slowly shook his head. "You are so fucking stupid."

"Why?"

He raised his head and leaned toward me and slammed his hand on the couch cushion. "Because he's an alcoholic, idiot."

"What?"

"He's an alcoholic!" he whispered, like a savage. "Dad is a fucking alcoholic! Don't you know that?"

"No he's not."

"That's why Mom wants us. Ask her. Go ahead and ask her. You're an idiot. What a fucking idiot."

"He's not." I put my feet on the floor. "He's just tired."

"Idiot!" he said, shaking his head.

I stood up and put my hands on my hips. "Well I'm going to go ask him."

"No!" Edward stood up.

"I am," I said, shooting out of the room. "I'm going to ask him again." I marched through the dining room, into the kitchen, where Dad was standing at the counter, taking the cap off a bottle of bourbon.

"Daddy," I said, standing next to him.

"Yes, love?" He kept his eyes on his glass, which he had just filled with ice.

"Are you tired?"

"Yes I am," he said. "Boy am I." He was swaying forward and backward as he poured. His robe was untied and the sash slid back and forth, across the linoleum. Smokey sat at the bottom of the back stairs, her tail twitching. She was waiting for him. He was the only one she cuddled with. I tried to get her to sleep with me by sealing her up in my room, but she stayed against the wall under my bed and growled.

"Are you drunk?"

He put the bottle down. The overhead light was on, white on my father's dark head of hair, waving out in different directions. It stuck straight up on the top.

"No," he said, turning to me.

"Well," I crossed my arms. "Are you an alcoholic?"

"No love, of course not." His boxer shorts were sheer and dirty. "I'm not an alcoholic."

"You're really just tired?"

"Yes. Yes I am."

"You're tired a lot."

"Yes. Yes I am."

"Okay, then." I dropped my arms and walked out of the kitchen, brushing my hand along the sideboard against the dining-room wall. The wood felt cool against my palm. My stomach hurt. I had been to the doctor's the week before and they said I had a pre-ulcerous condition. I liked the way it sounded, but I could no longer eat Claussen pickles or my father's fried chicken.

I looked at Edward as I sat in my chair and curled up again. "He says he's not." My stomach felt empty, hollow.

He shook his head and breathed in and out like he had a cold. The TV droned. It was time for *Hart to Hart*. We heard Dad go up the back stairs, his footsteps thunking hollow through the house.

* * *

My father quit drinking shortly thereafter and stayed sober for the duration of the hearing. My mother's lawyer rounded up my father's colleagues and interviewed his Georgia relatives to gather information about his drinking habits. My mother's mother and sister were flown up from Florida to testify against him.

But I witnessed none of this activity. I went to school and went home and tried to avoid Edward. I watched television and played with Abbey Duke and chased Smokey and studied my father for signs of drunkenness and talked to my mother on the phone several times a week, heard the urgency in her voice, in her quest to get us out of there. I began to use her words and her tone whenever I talked about our situation, which wasn't very often, since Edward wouldn't discuss it.

"Idiot, shut up," he said one afternoon before Dad got home from the college. We were watching *Hogan's Heroes* and Edward was sitting on the couch, stuffing half of a peanut butter sandwich in his mouth at one time. He liked to open his mouth and show me the mass of bread inside. He washed it down with a glass of milk and smacked and wiped his chin with the back of his hand. "You're such a phony." He stood up, still staring at the television. He had gotten very tall. "You sound just like Mom."

My father didn't speak of the hearing until the day before Edward and I were scheduled to testify. He made a huge fried chicken dinner—a baked drumstick for me—with extra homemade biscuits and a chocolate pecan pie for dessert. Afterward, we all sat in the living room and my father leaned forward in his chair, his elbows on his knees. He gazed at each of us, sitting on each end of the flowered sofa he had inherited after his mother's death, and he clasped his hands and then asked what we were going to tell the judge. A glass of iced coffee sat beside him on the end table, beneath a framed picture of Chaucer.

I looked at Edward. His hands were trembling. He looked like he might be running from his friends, like Paul Latcham and the rest were right behind him, their hair combed over their ears like helmets. He kept his eyes on the carpet and rapidly tapped his foot. I looked into my lap and tried to avoid my father's face.

The next afternoon I testified that yes, I had seen my father drink in the mornings.

"You've seen your father drink in the morning?" a man asked. I was in a shimmering white room, on one side of a round table. Four or five suited men sat across from me. I was disappointed. I had pictured myself sitting in a mahogany witness stand, speaking to a jury.

"I think so." My parents and brother were outside, in the hallway.

"What did he drink?"

"I don't know."

Another man spoke. "Did you ever see your father drink beer from a wine glass?"

"Huh?" A pitcher of water and a set of glasses sat on a table behind them, against the wall.

"Did you ever see your father drink beer from a wine glass?"

I pulled one hand from the other and chewed on my fingernail. Surely he had. "I . . . I think so."

"Beer, from a wine glass?"

"I . . . I'm not sure. Probably."

"Probably? What do you mean?"

I bit off a chunk of cuticle. I pictured my father the way I always had, wobbling and pouring. It was nothing out of the ordinary; it required no explanation. Why wouldn't he drink beer from a wine glass? Or bourbon from a water glass? Or martinis from a tumbler? Or wine from a plastic cup?

They asked me a few more questions about my father that I didn't know how to answer and then thanked me. One of them said I was finished and opened the door, and I walked out into the hallway. My mother stood and smiled and stretched one hand toward me, clutching her pocketbook with the other. My brother sat in a tight wad on the other end of the wooden bench they shared. He looked like he might vomit. My father stood up from another bench, across from them, and coughed and put out his cigarette.

"Hello, love," he said gently, moving toward me, touching my shoulder. I looked up at him, at his shaggy professor beard and then into his eyes, shining tenderly behind his glasses.

* * *

My brother and I left Grinnell that summer, right after my fourth-grade year. My mother came for us in her new used car, a Dodge Vega hatchback, and the three of us loaded it up while my father stood on the back porch stairs and watched. He may have been drunk. His crazy hair blew around his head, his robe was open, and his slippers were folded and creased around his heels, covering only his toes. The house loomed behind him, empty except for Smokey.

My picture remained on the playroom shelves and I watched him from there after we drove away, saw him moving through silence from room to room.

VOICES SIX

GENDER AND SEXUALITY

CHAPTER 31

RAISING THE SPILL

Ed Madden

The shocked small face blinks at the light—
the mouse we find beneath the plastic spillway.

I look up at my cousin, his arms strong and chest
broad after a year of football drills. It's hot

out in the rice field, and we are tired.
We've been raising spills throughout the fields,

locking water behind the levees. We lift
the sheet of black plastic against the weight

of running water, insert a board to hold
the lip of spill high and stiff, to stop the flow.

We lift slowly, afraid of what might lie
beneath—moccasin coiled in fat loops

of black, the large spiders skittering across
the water's film. But here, there's only a mouse,

size of a thumb, gray fur, pale paws, the pink
of skin shining through. The air is damp and thick

with heat. He's been telling me about his girlfriend,
the cheerleader, pink and freckled. He has been

telling me about the team's trip to Memphis,
where the boys hired a prostitute—no one

told the coaches. My cousin adjusts his shovel,
says he only had oral sex, so technically

he's still a virgin. What I would say I cannot
say. The mouse looks up, its eyes black

pinpoints of panic, its tiny ears velvet
and fragile. My cousin laughs. The pale feet

scurry for purchase, the mouse disappears
in the rice, leaving behind five things,

almost embryonic, pink and unformed.
My cousin will lift his shovel; he will smash them.

CHAPTER 32

IMAGINATION IS DECAYING SENSE

Christopher Davis

Wiggling her wings in dark, cold air
around my body in this wheelchair.

My low growl half-
anxious, half-angry,

I can't get light-
ly off, siren-

aroused coyotes crying
down in my hot fault,

my huge she screaming guilty
of effeminacy, *my puppet*

masculinity howling for mercy
on my skull's stage. Behind

my hands' un-
folded prayer,

this mask ex-
plodes in tears.

Mother, turn this self-
hate into humbleness.

Her blue fruit jar
stuffed with dust,

its lip shining

like thinking,

sparks in bulb light.

CHAPTER 33

WAX: SEXUAL ANXIETY, SEXUAL HARASSMENT

Jared Chesson

My dad asked me if I was gay. I said no. And then cried because I had no girl-friend to prove it.

My freshman year I shared my toilet with my best friend and two drag queens. They are people before drag queens, of course, but if I were to ask them, "How would you describe yourselves in two words?" they'd say drag queens. We became friends. Both were very talented in the ballet; one of those two ended up directing a big show. They enjoyed dressing up at 11 o'clock every night, and coming home from clubs at 5 o'clock in the morning. I suppose they woke me up a couple of times, but I guess I woke them up, too—they slept during the day.

Sophomore year I was good friends with a gay guy. We hung out every day and talked about relationships. We loved the same kind of music. He's a huge Phish fan, and I like listening to them, but never had to buy their CD since we were always talking about them. Same year another guy, my closest confidant, tells me he's gay, and that he was most afraid to tell me—of all people—because he thought I might react funny. It hurt, mostly, but I can understand.

Both years I had been getting my hair cut every month or two—my hair gets long sometimes—by the same man who owned a small barber shop/beauty salon/gossip shack. He told me he was gay the first day he cut my hair. He told me how he would go to bars, drink and do drugs, and get into fights. I suppose he thought he had to tell these stories so I would think he was cool. It didn't matter to me. I just laughed along; he was a good storyteller.

His being gay never bothered me. Sometimes, though, there would be some awkwardness. He asked me if I was gay once. End of freshman year. Pretty much the same week my dad asked me. How was I supposed to react? I just said no. It's an awkward thing for a guy to try his best with girls who ignore him, and at the same time to be accused of being gay. He walked next to me and "led" me to my chair with his hand on my back. Once or twice his hand was low at my back. I could only think about all the girls I read about getting touched, cornered, raped, and how they were stuck in pause while everything around them was in a blur.

I remember, now, that he was doing this more on my final visit, sometime at the end of my sophomore year—actually, no, it was around Valentine's Day. I remember because that was the year I gave a valentine made out of Twizzlers to a girl named Lindsey. She told me on the 14th she was getting back with her boyfriend. I went to get a haircut about 3 days later.

After arriving at the barber shop, I waited, flipping through magazines for 30 minutes, waiting on him to get through buying products from his product lady. She finally convinced him to buy a certain shampoo that was supposed to be better because it was made of a flower from Africa, or Australia, when all the other ones were harsh and would lead to split ends. Well, she leaves, and it's just him and me. His shop is neat and clean. I think it used to be a house of some kind, and he converted it into something that looks like a dentist's office. The place above him is still for rent.

"The place above me is still for rent. That would be a perfect place for a college kid, man. Right next to Five Points."

"Yeah, easier to walk home at night."

"Exactly. Well, come this way, and we'll get started, sorry I took so long, but those sales ladies can be real bitches sometimes."

Something about the way he said, "come this way" caught my attention. He led me again with his hand low. I had let my hair grow out a bit; everything needed a trim, really. The awkwardness lifted after the usual small talk. I told him I wanted to keep it a tad long on the top, and shorter on the sides. I have these wings that curl out. I hate them. He tells me about his knee and how he hurt it in a fight.

"Me and my friend were at this bar. Some guy tries to pick a fight. Whatever, we kicked his ass. But he did hurt my knee though. I tore something in there."

"Cool. What bar?"

"Group Therapy. It was outside the bar actually."

"Cool."

I hadn't been in many fights, except cheap ones like in elementary school, so I couldn't really say much to keep his story going.

"You know I am starting up a new business. Here's the sign for it. It's going to be a 30-minute full body wax job." The sign read, "Full Body Wax Jobs."

Press pause.

"Really? You think a lot of people will want to do that?"

"You haven't done it before? Wow, it's amazing. Hey, I have an idea. You see, lately I have been practicing on a friend of mine, he's straight as hell, and I got it down to under an hour. I need to get it around 30 minutes. My friend loves it. Once he got this huge boner, and he's Italian so his boner is fucking huge, and I leaned over and said 'Hey pal, this ain't no Asian parlor.' Anyway, we laughed. But the thing is, I need a new guinea pig. Would you be interested? You are a bit hairy, we'd have to trim your leg hair a little bit. Are you hairy? If your eyebrows are any indication, we may have to shave you first. I just need someone so I can practice."

"Um, I don't know."

We laughed. He asked me if I wanted to wax my eyebrows, and I took him up on his offer. I was completely in the innocent—nothing would happen to me because I am too nice. With that attitude came some sort of expectancy about the rest of the world. As if someone handed me a golden ticket, which gave me the rights to watch everything happen, and not take part.

After he cut my hair, he led me, hand in place, to his waxing room. The waxing room looked more professional than the one I was in earlier, down the hall, and there were big windows around. I felt more comfy. He grabbed my hand.

"Hey, what are you doing?"

"It's the same as the body wax, just that this one does your hands only. Here let me see your other one."

My hand was being inserted into a box filled with a warm liquid, like hot syrup served at Cracker Barrel. When I pulled them both out, the wax hardened around them, forming immovable gloves. He had oven mitts ready.

"Here, put these on. And then these zip lock bags go over it. Ok. Now we can leave that for about 20 minutes. Here, lean back in this chair and I will do your eyebrows."

Press fast forward.

I was leaning back, with my hands unable to do much at all, and he laid a towel down like the dentist lays the radiation blanket before taking x-ray pictures of your teeth. He waxed my eyebrows, which hurt, and lifted the towel off my chest and abdomen. He said something about how he was sorry that the towel left lint on my shirt. I looked and didn't see any, but his hands were brushing already. He brushed over my chest, down to my stomach, then over my zipper. I saw everything, felt nothing.

"Ok, I think those hands are ready to be peeled."

I wasn't feeling too crazy about everything now. I was ready to leave. The wax peeled off nicely though, and my hands had never been softer. Everything about this next moment seemed orchestrated. Everything was bright, clean, and crisp, everything had texture.

He asked me about being a guinea pig again. I said I didn't think I would, but that I would consider it and would definitely try to help him find someone if I didn't do it. He said that I would definitely need to trim my leg hair. I stood up to walk out the door. He stopped me with his hand.

He asked me how my chest looked hair-wise. I told him I didn't think I had much. He lifted my shirt up, and said I might need a trim there too. He said my stomach was fine, though. He asked me about my back. I said I had no hair on my back, but he lifted my shirt up again anyway.

This guy is 6 foot 4 inches. He is intimidating. He tells stories about kicking guys' asses. He talks fast. He seems professional. I didn't want to insult him in his professional workplace. What was I supposed to do? I did nothing. I stood there. Like a mannequin.

He said my back was fine, and asked me about my butt. I said I didn't think I wanted to trim anything. He pulled at my belt, and made enough room for his large football hand to squeeze in between my shorts and back.

There was this girl I was friends with at the time, who would always make jokes about guys and their asses. She said how funny it felt to run her fingers through the hair on a guy's ass, and she would tease me by grabbing and squeezing my "cute cheeks" as she so often referred to them. But we were just kidding around. His hand wasn't teasing at all. It was technical. He was testing, making notes, investigating. His hands were cold and foreign.

He rummaged around the way I see women searching their pocketbooks—with definite intentions, trying to find something, not finding it. They always check for it again 5 minutes later.

I didn't let him. I didn't know what had just happened. Mostly I wasn't mad at all, more in fast forward. I couldn't do much. I paid him. My hands were soft, like luxury skin, and the fresh bills of money hit them hard. They brought me back. Press play. The stiffness of the bills, the texture of chalky paper exfoliating my skin like sandpaper.

Everything had been orchestrated. He said he would call to see if I wanted to be his guinea pig later. He said we could meet Friday nights around 9 o'clock, so I could go out after it was over. He said women would like it. I handed over my tickets to leave, a ten and a five. Two-dollar tip. It was a good haircut, after all.

He called a few times. I never talked to him. I didn't want to give him another chance. His answering machine messages were very unsolved mysteries. As if he was going to call the police, thinking I had been kidnapped. Since then, it's been around a year or so. The more I talk about it, the more I want to punch him. The more scared I am. Of everything. Even talking. Not just with gay men, but everyone. Homeless people asking for money, new barbers, waiters and waitresses, taxi drivers, the lady that cuts the meat at Bi-Lo.

Hell, maybe I misunderstood the whole situation. Maybe he did have good business intentions. But he never did put that sign up.

CHAPTER 34

NOTES FROM THE CLOSET: EDUCATION, FAMILY, AND SEXUAL DIFFERENCE

Sam Kennedy (pseudonym)

Somehow I thought my life would be different from what it is today. I suppose when I was younger, I thought I would have the traditional life with a wife, two kids, and a dog. After all, society teaches all kids that this is expected, that this is the norm. Here I am, an adult in my early 30s, and my life is far from what I thought it would be. It is hard for me to think of myself as an adult when a part of me is still that quiet, studious kid, being taunted by the boys I had been in school with since kindergarten. And it is hard for me to feel like a normal guy when I am not married, and I don't have children or a dog. I walk around daily with a huge secret.

I am a closeted gay white male living somewhere in South Carolina.

There are a couple of reasons I stay in the closet. First, I am in education in the public schools, so my closet doors, out of necessity, must remain tightly sealed. It bothers me to live this way, because I know I could be a positive role model for those students who are struggling with the same issue I struggled with back in the late 1970s and early 1980s. However, I am a realist. I know that my sexuality would become too much of a distraction for conservative parents and closed-minded students.

Second, I am closeted due to my relationship with my family. I grew up in a very stable household, with loving parents and two brothers. I was the middle child, always trying to be the peacemaker. I hated arguing, and I bottled things up inside so that I did not have to confront them. This is a bad habit that still plagues me to this day. My parents have always supported us in anything we chose to do. Being fairly close in age, my brothers and I were always very competitive. We competed for our parents' attention. I always felt that my brothers were closer to my dad. They had sports and cars in common. I was closer to my mom, as we had music and reading in common. There seems to be a very delicate balance in my family, and I am not about to tip it by outing myself. However, I feel like my parents must know that I am gay. It has been many years since I was last asked whom I was dating, why I was not dating, or given suggestions as to whom I should ask out on a date.

So I live my secret life, lurking in chatrooms online, subscribing to gay magazines, and secretly lusting for hunky guys in leather or uniforms—law enforcement, military, or athletic. At the same time, I hope that I will find the right guy, the guy with whom I can spend the rest of my life, a guy who loves me more than he loves himself, a guy who will love me for who I am and not leave me. Lofty and romantic dreams I know, but I keep on searching, even though the odds are against me, even though I have been told over and over that I am way too romantic and idealistic for my own good. And when a guy walks out of my life, it hurts so much that I can hardly breathe.

This fear of rejection has deep roots in my childhood. My family had stability; we never moved, staying in the same neighborhood. Other friends were not so lucky. I had one very good friend who moved away when we were in second grade. We corresponded by letter and I visited him a few times, but we lost touch. For many years thereafter (even today), I wondered where he was and what he was doing. I still feel his departure from my life.

I grew up in an average size county-seat town in the upstate of South Carolina, a town once dominated by a textile mill. By the late 1970s, Chinese textile imports were taking a toll on the mill. There existed a definite difference between those who grew up on the mill and those who lived in the two major subdivisions in town, Forest Acres and Arrow Creek. I lived in a neighborhood close to town, comprised mainly of retired schoolteachers. Our neighborhood, Shady Hills, sounded more like a retirement home than subdivision. The homes were constructed in the late 1940s and early 1950s; they were not as modern as the ones built in the newer subdivisions of the 1960s and 1970s. Certain peers often pointed out that I did not live in the best part of town. Although I liked where I lived and did not resent it, I always felt inferior.

I knew at an early age that I was different from the other boys. It was never pointed out to me, but I think it was obvious. At recess, the boys ran around tackling each other, and the girls jumped rope and sat under the trees and chatted. I had had the breath knocked out of me a time or two and did not much like the feeling. I suppose I had (and still have) a low tolerance for pain. I was painfully shy and had few friends, so I avoided large group dynamics. So as a result, I pursued activities where I was less likely to be injured: freeze tag, the sliding board, and the jungle gym. In those early elementary grades, kids were less judgmental. I had friends, both male and female, and this pattern would continue until junior high school.

I was too small to play football and too clumsy to play baseball. While other boys waited with anticipation for the start of football or baseball season, I dreaded it. I knew that the games on the playground would turn to these pursuits, and I would be outcast yet again. I did, however, excel at soccer.

I enjoyed running up and down that field behind a soccer ball. In our games, there was not much coordination involved. Boys and girls played on the same teams in the community league, so I knew it would not be that rough.

My world began to change in the sixth grade. I can't really pinpoint a reason for the change in my peers, guys with whom I had been friends since kindergarten. Maybe it had to do with the early stages of puberty. I began hearing the word "faggot" batted around on the playground in the sixth grade. I am ashamed to say now that I used the word myself, not knowing what it meant. "He is such a faggot." Clothing began to be associated with the word. The little loop of fabric on the back of a dress shirt became a "fag tag." Blue jeans of brands other than Levi's became known as faggy jeans. (I had a pair of Calvin Klein hand-me-down jeans and wouldn't be caught dead in them. Today, as a fashion-conscious gay male, I would wear them without problem.)

One day, I returned to my desk after reading class. I was in a regular class, not the gifted and talented class, since my standardized test scores were not high enough. As I sat down, I noticed writing on my desk. I was scared at first because I didn't want my teacher to think I had written on the desk. But then I read it, and my face turned red. "Sam Cannadee is a faggot" was scrawled in large letters in blue ink across the top of my desk. The first thing that struck me was the spelling of my last name. "It's misspelled—why can't people spell my last name right?" I quickly pulled things out of my desk to cover it up.

Not long after that, I was called a faggot to my face. *The Facts of Life* was on prime-time television when I was in the sixth grade. On the days after the show aired, my friends would sit around in class during our free time and discuss the previous evening's episode. I was not able to watch it, since it coincided with my bedtime, so I generally remained quiet. When I was quizzed about my thoughts on the actions of Jo, Natalie, Tootie, and Blair, I told the group that I didn't watch the show, and why. "You are such a fag for having a bedtime," said Ricky Paolucci. I brushed it off. I did not really like Ricky. He was a Yankee, an outsider. His mom had fled to the South from up north somewhere, after her divorce, and she taught in our school and had a loud, shrill voice. He was too aggressive. He thought he was the best thing in the sixth grade.

That afternoon, Jamie, a kid who lived down the street, was over at my house. He brought up the word "faggot." He said that if you were called a faggot it meant you liked other boys. I begged to differ, saying that I had looked the word up and it meant a small piece of firewood. Of course, since he was a year older, he had to be right and proclaimed again that if you were called a faggot then you liked other boys. Well, I kept to myself that the word *faggot* and my name had been scrawled across my desk a few weeks back and that a kid called me a faggot in class. Even then, I suppose I was learning how to hide things from the rest of the world.

Eventually, I discovered that it was indeed Ricky who had written this on my desk. During the last days of school, we all created books to gather the autographs of our classmates. I remember vividly my reaction to Ricky's signature. I cannot tell you what it said beyond the first line, "To Sam Canadee." It was then that I realized that it was Ricky who had written on my desk. I was too shocked to say anything. Thus began the victimization of Sam Kennedy.

I entered White Street Junior High School in the fall of 1983. There would be kids from two other elementary schools thrown into the mix. I hoped that all of that faggot business would be behind me. I remember walking the halls that first year looking at the older guys. I never looked at the girls. I just thought that I was looking at the boys because I wanted to be them, be like them, all cool and self-confident. I kept thinking that any morning, I would wake up and like girls. And each morning, I would go to school, and as I entered the gym, I would scope out the upper classmen. They looked so much older and bigger than I. In the halls, I scanned their faces and began looking at their crotches. But I kept thinking to myself, "There is no way that I could be a faggot. This must be a phase."

I am not sure when I stopped being just Sam, the quiet kid that most people liked, and became Sam, the kid that all the guys wanted to pick on. I was not an athletic kid, but I was not what one would call a sissy either. I was studious, in the band, and quiet. That made me a lightning rod for harassment. This was something my mom could not understand. "I cannot understand why kids pick on classmates, just because they aren't into sports."

When I think of my years at White Street Junior High School, there are few pleasant memories. I had favorite teachers and a few close friends, but that was about all I had going for me. The first 6 weeks of my seventh-grade year were absolutely horrible. Guys who had been my friends cornered me daily after lunch and in the bus lot after school. I synchronized my watch with the bell, to time my advance from the playground after lunch, in hopes of avoiding the torture.

"Hey Sam, you faggot," was generally how it started. I would drop my head and act like I didn't hear them.

"Hey Sam, you faggot! You heard me!" I walked a little faster, making my way to the bus lot. Three or four guys then surrounded me. I looked up, dreading what was next.

"Oh, I didn't realize you were talking to me."

"Your name is Sam, isn't it?" Here Scott Smith, whose father was president of the bank, addressed me. "You are such a faggot. What kind of blue jeans are those?"

"They are Lee jeans."

"Only faggots wear Lee jeans."

"I am not a faggot!"

"Yes you are," shouted Billy Burch. Billy lived with his mom. His father ran out on them when he was 6.

"You're the faggot!" I shouted back.

While this was going on, Ricky Paolucci sneaked up behind me and pulled my wallet from my back pocket.

"Hey, I have the faggot's wallet!" They began tossing it back and forth. It was an orange nylon wallet with a tiger paw on it. At most, it had a dollar and a couple of quarters in the change compartment. It was tossed about; all the while I was doing my damndest to get it back. The next thing I knew, Scott dropped it into a mud puddle. They scampered off to their buses while I retrieved my wallet. I held it together in the face of that torture, and while I was on the bus. When I got home, the torrent of tears started. I never let them see me cry. I knew that would be a fate worse than death.

This cycle repeated itself daily.

One afternoon, Billy Burch showed up at my house. He had wanted to fight me at school and I refused. I was taught that you did not cause a disruption at school. And if you did, the punishment you got at home would be even worse than what you got at school. I refused to fight him and went into the house. He pedalled off. About 20 minutes later, my father got home from work. I was barricaded in my room. My younger brother met my father in the backyard and told him of the scene in the yard. Dad came in and questioned me about it. I told him what had happened. He flew into a rage.

"I can't believe that kid came all the way over here to pick a fight in my yard! I am not going to have that. I am going to take care of this." He grabbed his keys and walked out the back door. I chased after him, begging him not to confront Billy. He got in the van and made me get in, and off we went. We caught Billy about a block from his house.

"Hey, what do you think you were doing when you came over to my house to try to pick a fight with my son?"

This was the first time I saw Billy scrambling for words. He finally came up with some lame excuse about it all being a joke.

"Well, for some reason I find that hard to believe. I've heard your name brought up too many times in connection to picking on my son. If I ever catch you in my yard again or hear of your picking a fight with my son again, you will have to answer to me."

Billy took off, and we turned around and went home. I was very shocked by it and was scared at what the other kids would say at school the next day. "Faggot Sam has to get his dad to fight for him." At the same time, I knew that my dad really loved me, and that he would do anything in his power to protect me. I never suffered any retribution at school from my dad's actions. Billy kept his distance. The taunting was there after school, but lunchtime became safer. At the end of the first 6 weeks, I had performed so well in all of my classes that I was moved to level-one class in science. As a result of this change, my lunch period changed, and I met a new set of friends, and the taunting lessened. I actually made friends with some upperclassmen. They did not judge me and helped, in some way, to improve my safety after school. Being seen with them caused my tormentors to back off.

Then physical education hell rolled around during second semester. I had Coach Tom. He was a young man, with blond curly hair and blue eyes. He was probably in his late 20s, and I had a huge crush on him. I would sneak glances at him and looked forward to days when we had health class. He would sit at the desk in front of the room. When he rocked back in the chair, his gray coach's shorts would ride up a bit, exposing the edge of his black nylon boxer shorts. As we watched a filmstrip on proper nutrition or the dangers of sexually transmitted diseases, I would stare at his legs and that hint of his boxers. I wondered what they felt like and what it would be like to rub my hands across those muscled thighs, covered in downy blond hair.

Coach Tom was so patient with me. I tried my best to master any task he assigned us. I put in 100%. But I was still fighting a losing battle. When the class had to divide up and pick teams, I was invariably picked last. "You take Sam and we'll take the girl." I heard that often. I hated playing basketball because I could never score a basket. Baseball was not my thing because I could not catch a pop fly, and very rarely could I hit the ball when it was pitched to me.

After we returned to the locker room to get dressed, I would sneak looks at the guys. I observed that they were not as hairy as I was becoming, and wondered about the size of my penis in relation to what I imagined to be larger ones covered by white jockeys. I was very thankful that I was spared the humiliation of having to take a shower. In those days we were not required to do that. Looking back, I think it must have been due to the fear that a student could accuse an adult of impropriety. The school wanted to avoid that liability. As we waited for the bell to ring, signaling the change of classes, Coach Tom would play four square with the students. All of us loved to try to beat him at the game. This was a game that even I was good at, so I would stand in line. It was fun to make him run back and forth, and I would always advance and end up in the square beside him, but I never beat him. He was just too good. However, when he eliminated you from the match, he never made you feel bad about it. He always offered words of encouragement. I often thought that he let me progress further in the round than some of the more athletic kids, because he knew what was going on with my classmates.

Seventh grade ended, mercifully, and eighth grade began on an eventful note. The night before classes began, I shaved for the first time. The whole time I was being shown this manly task by my dad, I wondered if the kids who had called me faggot would do so now. The first day proved to be a good one. I was a bit taller than my tormentors and as a result looked older than them. The taunting stopped. But they did not speak to me, nor I to them. The damage had been done. I was shunned by their little circle, the very circle I had been part of only 2 years before. As painful as that was, I moved on and made new friends.

As I look back now, I do not remember many adults being around. There were no teachers on bus duty, who could have prevented my harassment. There were few teachers on duty at lunch. I did not want to go crying to a teacher to try to stop this, but at the same time I wanted them to be observant of what was going on and maybe put an end to the nightmare. To try to right the wrongs from my childhood, I have always tried to be very cognizant of what goes on in my classroom, the hallways, and on the playground. I do not tolerate name-calling, and I have tried to be a presence in all areas. If I see a group massing around a kid, I walk right through it. I know that there are kids out there just like me, kids afraid to ask for help from a teacher for protection from the bullies.

In recent years, the effects of the absence of caring adults have become all too apparent. Students who were bullied and made to feel different are returning to school and retaliating in ways I would have never conceived—by taking guns and pipe bombs to school to destroy their tormentors. I do not mean to say that the teachers in these schools are not caring. On the contrary, one teacher in particular took a bullet trying to shield his students from the anger of the disenfranchised students who went on the rampage at Columbine High School. Most teachers are simply unaware of the bullying that takes place, or some may feel that it is something that will build character and make the weak strong. And yet others try to get to know their students as individuals. But that is often difficult in a school of 1,200 students.

As I get older, it is getting more difficult for me to look at life from the crack in my closet door. My parents have always told me that they are supportive of whatever I want to do. Would this include telling them that I am gay? I jokingly tell my gay friends that I am Presbyterian, and that God predestined that I should be gay. Would my brothers buy into this? I know that living a lie is a terrible thing, but I also think it would be terrible to spend the rest of my life without my family.

The events of junior high school have shaped my life, and continue to affect my dealings with other people. I constantly fight for the underdog, and I am not very tolerant of people with closed minds. I hadn't really thought about these events much until recently. When I did, the memories came back like a flood. This time, I am not allowing them to drown me; instead, I am surfing on the crest, and I want to be a better person, as a teacher and as a man, because of what I have experienced.

CHAPTER 35

CALLING: CONVERSION, COMING OUT, AND COMMUNITY

Ed Madden

I will always be there.
When the silence is exhumed.
When the photographs are examined

. . . .

I am the invisible son.

—Essex Hemphill

Lately, I have been telling my friends a story. It is a story I find myself repeating, as if it could begin to mean what I want it to mean only through repetition. It is a bit like saying "I love you"—which I say over and over, hoping that if I say it often enough the words will begin to mean something. That is, I suppose, the nature of repetition. And of remembrance. The story is about my hometown. It is about going home, and about not being able to go home. It is a story about being gay.

One summer before I came out to my family, my mother told me about Paul on the phone. It was after he had died, and it was simply another story in the litany of stories she told me as she recounted local news. Paul was about 8 years older than I, and went to the same church I did, the Beedeville Church of Christ. He joined the Navy after high school, and I can remember his coming to church, an officious and beaming figure of manhood and respectability, in dress whites and military crewcut. But a few years after that, he seemed to disappear from the local conversation. I had, in fact, forgotten about Paul, until my mother told me he had died. At some point, between his proud homecomings as a military man and his remembrance on the telephone as a dead homosexual, Paul had come out of the closet, dropped out of the Navy, and moved to Austin. No one talked about him at home. His father disowned him. He was a prodigal, and we were all, whether we knew it or not, properly silent elder brothers. He moved further away from Arkansas, to San Francisco. And he got AIDS.

Sometime during the summer of 1991, his brother and sister drove to California and brought him home to die. He died there a couple of days later. The funeral service was in his parents' house, with no one but family invited. I was in graduate school in Austin. I do not know whether he was ever reconciled with his father. I do not know how the community mourned, or if they mourned. All I know is a gay man died at home, and no one was invited to remember him.

When my mother related this story to me, I had been to only six funerals in my life: a high school friend, my cousin's fiance, two grandparents, an aunt, and, only months before the phone call, an Austin man who had died of AIDS. Ashley died in an airplane accident a few years after we graduated—a small plane, probably a crop-duster, a daring pilot flying too low, the wheels underneath the plane catching the utility wires that crisscross the farms of Jackson County. Like all funerals, his was a community ritual; for all those fledgling adults, it was a naming of our common mortality and our common home, even as we were letting go of our hometown and finding other communities. Ed, my cousin's fiance, died only months before their wedding. Coming home from working on their house one night, he fell asleep at the wheel. I remember most that Tara refused to call me by my name, Ed, his name, and I remember her screams at the cemetery, her distress because she couldn't see him. It was a closed casket funeral, because of the accident. We buried, each, our own private images of him. I fumbled with a name.

* * *

When I entered graduate school, I changed my name. I became "Ed," not "Eddie." It is the nature of growing up. We try to lose the diminutives, the nicknames, the identities we could not choose for ourselves. Names are not easy, particularly the name "homosexual." It took me over 20 years to name myself, and it was not a name I accepted easily, or willingly. It is to call myself an outsider, deviant, queer. There does not seem to be room for queers in a small southern town, on the family farm, in the fundamentalist church, among the honeysuckle and dewberries and soybean fields of rural Arkansas, all the places I called home. I am both inside and outside, the imposter in all the taxonomies. Being gay is the wild card, the anomaly, the unknown factor, its origins and explanations far too numerous and obscure—the little farmboy who wrote poetry. How can I explain it? How can I not try?

The coming-out story has its common features, no matter how many times it is told. The sense of difference. The feeling of being an outsider, no matter how much a part of the community you are. "How long have you known?" we are asked. Always, and yet never. I have known and not known for so long, it is hard to tell where remembrance ends and repression begins. Like winter wheat, the green in the midst of fields of gray, the seasons and meanings blur in the life of the tale itself, the tale of a life. Only when I finally had a name for it, and gave myself that name, did I know. And then nothing was changed, and everything.

Now it seems a way of knowing, a way of seeing and reseeing. I am taking a friend home, and I am seeing everything through his eyes. I see the long dirt roads. I trace the family histories in the portraits hanging in the hallway. I am hugging my father and mother. I am at my brother's wedding, singing. I am tracing the roots of the mulberry in the front yard, its seedlings sprouting all around the house. I am no longer at ease here, no longer at ease.

There is a consolation in knowing from a distance, both literal and figurative, nostalgia scarring the horizon. And there is a certain pleasure to be had in the act of confession, like grace, the smell of wet earth and winter wheat under a cold green sky. The consolation of distance and the intimacy of confession meet in the act of remembering, the act of telling stories. The theologian Fredrick Buechner has written of our need "to enter that still room within us all where the past lives on as part of the present, where the dead are alive again, where we are most alive ourselves to the long journeys of our lives with all their twistings and turnings and to where our journeys have brought us." There is a room called remember, its windows each a narrative, its anteroom regret. We enter the room in the past tense; we exit in either the present or the conditional. What we remember, the reasons why, the way things might have been.

* * *

June 5, 1987. Redwing blackbirds shout themselves hoarse from the oaks of the cemetery. A crop-duster drones above a nearby rice field. The long caravan of cars that left the church is still arriving, the dust drifting in waves that coat the dull green rows of grain sorghum and soybeans, dust still hanging in air hot with the smell of Arkansas honeysuckle and vetch and the sweet maroon ferment of funeral roses. I breathe deeply: the summer grass rich at the verge of brown, freshly mown, the musty, almost acrid earth of this sandy hillside piled by the grave. These things must be remembered, like the daffodils in solemn yellow clumps that marked my grandma's death, standing in silent clusters of mourning at the cemetery, dotting her yard like relatives, nodding, touching, like cousins laughing, flaring their bright lives against the gray spring wind.

Grandpa's flowers are scattered down the line of tombstones, decorating the graves of his wife, his children; it seems the office of aunts to gather the blooms, to drape these odd dots and splashes against brown earth, gray stone. We the men, the sons and grandsons, take the shovels in groups of three, marking our ties with the thuds that fill the grave: it is love, it is family, it is something of God. There is no word for the hole that it creates.

* * *

In Jackson County, my home, in places like Cowlake, Hickory Ridge, and Beedeville, the funeral service is almost always in a church, rarely a funeral home, and the community acts as a community, showing up for visitations at the funeral home, turning out for both church and graveside services, making food for the family. I think that is what disturbed me about Paul's funeral in his parents' home—the community was not invited to be a community. Nor was the man affirmed as part of that community. The gay man's death was a marker, there, of rupture, of dysfunction.

When my Aunt Etta was dying, she chose the hymns for her funeral, and I think she chose the short inspirational verse that appeared in the program at the funeral service. I do not now remember that poem. What I do remember is the graveside service. Uncle Henry had planned ahead, brought shovels to the cemetery in his pickup so that we could bury her ourselves, an act that seemed both personal and final. What was not planned was the watermelon. It was hot, a July afternoon, and Uncle Henry sent my brother and me to the farm shop, just down the road, to get a watermelon that was chilling in the freezer there, along with an ice chest full of cokes. We returned, our arms full of grace—the chunks of pink sugar, the sweet juice, wet seeds and rinds like green jewels on the cemetery lawn.

When I went to an AIDS funeral in Austin with a friend, there were three visible communities: the dead man's friends from work, his gay friends, and his family. Except for the man's lover and his nurse-caseworker, who mingled freely, the three groups did not mix. Their only communion was the act of remembrance, of standing up before the group and telling stories about Norbert.

Norbert's sister had written a poem, which was read by someone else, since she was emotionally unable to read it. Like much funeral poetry, like all those memorial tributes in the daily newspaper, it was aesthetically forgettable. That is usually the nature of occasional verse. But it was nonetheless powerful, even when the reader lapsed into a singsong reading and the meter slipped awkwardly into unaccented gallops, even when the individual and personal was spoken through cliche. That, after all, is the nature of language: the inevitability of the cliche, the used. It is why we must say "I love you" over and over again, repeating it with dumb fingers, mute skin.

* * *

Everyone dies: that is a statement both tragic and banal. But the name of that death is important; we write it in stone. Poems and obituaries like tombstone rubbings repeat the name. We remember.

* * *

My grandpa's little brother, Oscar, died when he was 8 years old. I know little about him, though I do have a couple of his elementary school textbooks, and his copy of *Pilgrim's Progress* (subtitled "In One Syllable Words for Young People"). After Aunt Etta died, my parents and I went through some of my deceased grandparents' belongings, stored away by another aunt, and we found a box of photos and memorabilia from my great-grandmother. There were photos, most of them of people we did not know, though we did recognize family resemblances—my invisible ancestors, the pictures unlabeled, faces unnamed. We also found a prayer cloth, a square of moth-eaten green felt, embroidered with harps and swirls and arcane symbols.

My dad told the story he'd been told, that Oscar's grandmother, my great-great-grandmother, had gotten the cloth from a faith healer, who had prayed over it, or perhaps it was one of the "tinkers" who came through each year with their tools and their charms. It was kept in Oscar's sickroom, a fetish, or a quilt perhaps. My great-grandmother, Oscar's mother, who hadn't liked the cloth, had allowed it in his room, but probably not on his bed. But, strangely, she kept it. Its symbols are now impenetrable, a code both intensely personal and part of some obscure regional religious language. Other than a few books, it is the only reminder of Oscar, a piece of cloth, a text stitched with history and disease and hope.

As we were sorting through photos and newspapers, my mom also came across a small leather journal. For the most part, it was the account book of a distant Irish ancestor, a handyman who shoed horses, forged clappers for bells, and built coffins. But it had been recycled, for in the margins were the notes and poems of a little boy. Near the end of the book, after the short love poems to several little girlfriends, after the repeated refrain, "Flowers may fade, Leaves may die, True friends may forget you, But never will I," there was the final signature, "Scribbled by John Jay Madden." My great-grandfather, a farmboy who wrote poetry.

* * *

When I was baptized at the age of 8, I was told that I was to become a new man. It is what we are taught. At baptism, the old man of sin dies and a new man comes up from the grave, like Jesus. We are buried in water and raised in the language of a new life. The language is still familiar, even though the occasion is now so distant. I do wonder what I was thinking then, during that gospel meeting, a revival at my home church. I know that I was terrified of hell. I know that I was just realizing my sexuality, my sexual feelings, and I'm sure that discovery had a great deal to do with my consciousness of sin. I remember walking up the aisle during the invitation song—I can still recall how I felt—and I still feel in my dreams, sometimes, that sense of being someone else, of watching yourself, the singing, the heat, the fear of hell.

Everyone was singing, one of those many hymns of homecoming, "Softly and tenderly Jesus is calling, Calling for you and for me. . . . Come home." My brother followed me, though I don't remember being especially aware of his being there. We were asked for our confessions, standing in front of the congregation. "Do you believe that Jesus Christ is the Son of God?" "I do." We were led into a classroom behind the pulpit, where my dad and uncle dressed us in white baptismal robes. Then we were led to the baptistry, a fixture in Churches of Christ. Ours, like many others in the South, was decorated with a primitive painting of a river and sunset, probably emblematic of the Jordan River, though it always reminded me of the White River, which ran through my hometown. The preacher placed his right hand on the small of my back, his left hand holding a handkerchief over my nose and mouth, and he leaned me backwards into the cold water. . . .

For years, the dead man I left in that baptistry haunted me. He grew up. I pretended not to know him, when he showed up at parties or in dreams. But he refused to die. The summer I turned 29 years old, he told me his name was David. I stopped running away from him. I held him in my arms.

* * *

My first love was HIV-positive. We would talk about our hometowns, our families, our memories of growing up, aliens in a familiar land. He placed his hand in the small of my back. In my sleep, now that I have given my sexuality a name, I exchange my fantasies for fears, dreaming of the prodigal son's father, his open arms full of grace, imagining the hateful brother, ever mindful of appearances and the improprieties of love. "*My son who was dead is alive again.*" How can one predict the plots of exile and reconciliation? How did he tell them where he had come from, where he was going?

* * *

After I told my father I am gay, he wrote me a series of angry letters. I know that was something he had to do. He wrote to me saying that he would rather I was in jail for killing another man than admit that I loved another man.

When I told my father that I am gay, I killed the boy he knew. His anger was a form of mourning. *What is* reverberates against *what might have been.*

* * *

The summer I turned 29 years old, I went to England to study poetry. I did not go to fall in love or find myself. I went to learn more about an obscure turn-of-the-century poet named Charlotte Mew. She was a woman who refused to choose. A repressed lesbian—though I know that is really a historically inaccurate name in early 20th-century England—she never fully accepted or acted upon her sexual desires. A devoted churchgoer with a passion for nuns and other figures religious, she would never convert or confirm herself within a church. A poet, she consistently chose male, romantically obsessed, and often psychologically unstable persona—madmen, fairy children, farmers, a man going mad at the burial of his lover. She took care of an invalid mother and dying sister, and after their deaths, she killed herself.

While I was in London, I decided to visit her grave, at Hampstead Cemetery, just west of Hampstead Heath, that notorious cruising ground for gay men. I visited the cemetery once, but found it was unattended. It was far too big to simply wander through, entering the circles of each era, Dante without a Virgil, hoping to chance upon Mew's grave. So I called a county cemetery authority, who arranged to be in the grounds office for my visit. He found her plot in the records, next to her sister's, and drew general directions for me on a cemetery map. Mew had bought two plots after her sister's death in 1927, and had arranged to be buried beside her before she killed herself in 1928.

The map led me to a slightly overgrown Victorian section of the cemetery. There, over her sister's grave, was the gravestone. Mew's grave itself was unmarked, her name an addendum to her sister's stone, followed by the epitaph she chose, "Cast down the seed of weeping and attend" (the words of Beatrice at the entrance to Paradise). Although she spoke thus from her sister's tomb, her final resting place was a bare spot in the line of crosses and stones, an absence, history's invisible daughter. At the foot of her grave grew a blackberry bush, pendulant and prickly. I pulled several berries, kneeling beside the grave, ate them, the grit in my teeth, the juice warm and sweetly sour, like a name on my tongue, like the sting of memory. The air smelled of wet earth and rain, of who we could have been. Far from home, I took her into my mouth, so I could remember, and so I could speak.

* * *

The old places are gone, torn down to make room for the new. New desire, new prayers spring up in the rubble, like ivy, like Jonah's gourd vine, dark leaves like names. Some things never change. I take the names on my tongue, the bitterness. There are blossoms shining in the rubble and ashes.

* * *

There is always a child left behind, or the face of a distant friend translated into a voice. When the telephone rings, there is a face, a memory, a place, a voice that calls us into relation, into the unprecedented community of long distance. I return to the story. When my mother told me about the death of Paul, it was the simultaneous transmission of his homosexuality and his death, and what was left unsaid, his place in our community. Because of AIDS, I suppose the cultural mingling of the images of homosexuality and death at that time were unavoidable. But that, in itself, is not the point of the story, it is not why I find myself retelling it, over and over again. It is a story about being left out, about being the invisible son. It is a story about how we remember, and how we love. And more than anything else, it is the story of a call from home.

CHAPTER 36

A CONSIDERATION OF THE SOCIAL CONSTRUCTION OF MEN'S RESPONSE TO WOMEN'S STUDIES

PRESENTED AS A PUBLIC SERVICE ANNOUNCEMENT FROM GUYS UNITED TO MAINTAIN PATRIARCHY

Hayes Hampton

Guys: if a guy tells you he's a "feminist," it's a cry for help. And it's your duty to do something.

Self-emasculation isn't just a New York or a New Haven problem anymore. It's a problem that's on the rise nationwide, and it may have already happened to someone you know.

How can you spot male feminism? Here are the warning signs:

* He doesn't laugh at dirty jokes—not even Bill and Monica jokes.
* He grows quiet or appears nervous when you point out a girl's assets.
* He uses weird slang, like "gender" or "phallic signifier."
* He reads chick books or watches films like *Thelma and Louise*—even when it's not for a class or a girlfriend.
* He stops giving date reports.
* He listens attentively to women—even in mixed company.
* He is isolated or withdrawn from other men.

You may think he's got the best of reasons. He's speaking their language to try to get babes, right?

Or are *they*—trying to get *him*?

He has to know he's playing with fire. There's no such thing as "casual" or "recreational" feminism. It's a lifestyle, it's addictive, and no one is immune. Plus, by giving in like this, he makes things harder for all of us.

Here's how you can help:

- Take him to neutral ground—a Hooters, say, or the gym—sit him down, and level with him.
- Show him some positive role models. Rush, Howard, and Jesse can be your best friends at this stage.
- If he's in advanced self-emasculation, he may only listen to women: Camille, Katie, or Ally.
- Above all, don't hesitate to confront him. Don't worry about losing a friend—you're saving his life. He's not "living" as a male feminist; he's a shell of a man. He won't function for long in our society if he keeps going against the natural order of things.

Remember, you don't have to tolerate what he's doing, and you shouldn't. Feminism isn't about "equality"—it's about female domination. Once it starts, there's no telling where it will lead. Today, it's woman-only judo classes. Tomorrow, federally-mandated unisex bathrooms.

He doesn't have to be a victim of feminism.

He's a man—help him act like one.

VOICES SEVEN

RACE

CHAPTER 37

YOU DIDN'T SPEAK: BROTHER TO BROTHER

Charles Weathers

I saw you today, but you didn't speak.
You barely nodded your head as we passed on the street.

I thought maybe you knew me or I you.
I figure there's gotta be a reason we do what we do.

Then I saw another, all he did was stare.
We just turned our heads—was that fear?

I don't know him and he don't know me.
What could the source of this static be?

How far have we come in this journey of life?
Too far to continue some petty strife.

You'd think of all the people in existence
We would be the ones with no inner resistance.

Our history is long, tried and true.
The fact of the matter is someone died for me and you.

Why, for us to clown and disrespect?
Now do you really think this is what they'd expect?

I don't know about you, but I'm tired of this mess.
It's time to recognize that together we're blessed.

No fear of each other, no getting what you got.
No scams or schemes that we're trying to plot.

Just sharing, advising, maybe a little concern,
A polite exchange, who knows what we'll learn?

So the next time you stop and look at your brother,
Remember that you're each a part of the other.

We can't grow or gain, we won't reach that peak,
If we can't even take the time to stop and speak.

* * *

It amazes me that brothers, in 2001, are still hating brothers. It blows my mind that we not only kill each other with knives and guns, we kill each other with our looks. Brothers have got to lose the rage, anger, or whatever it is we hold in contempt of each other. We've got to get beyond the "you're trying to get what I got," "there's only room for me here," and "he probably wants my woman" attitude.

We have to stop associating speaking and being cordial with being "white." The truth be told, we wonder why the world treats us so hard, yet we walk around the world all hard. We try so hard to be hard that we make life harder than it has to be. Every brother out there has an example of something happening to him. We can't be responsible for others; all we have to do is be responsible for ourselves.

Now some people don't have this problem, and these are the positive, proactive men who will speak directly, confidently, and pointedly. They aren't rude but they are examples of the law of reciprocity. We receive what we give. So the next time you see a brother who appears to be harder than stone, look him in the eye and genuinely speak and acknowledge the brother. There's enough stress and requirements placed on us by the world. Let's not require brothers to belong to our frat, lodge, or clique just to speak. He may blow you off, curse you out, or he may speak back. The one thing he will do is know that someone spoke.

Be proactive in your encounters. Speak to a brother. The world is hard enough on us, without us being hard on each other.

CHAPTER 38

THE RIVERS OF MY SOUL: THE ODYSSEY OF AN AFRICAN-AMERICAN MALE

Richard E. Barber, Sr.

The song "A Change Is Going to Come" by Sam Cooke, describes my birthplace in Jones County near Trenton, North Carolina. Sam Cooke sang:

"I was born by the river in a little tent,
just like the river I've been running ever since;
it's been a long, long, long time coming but I know my change will come,
oh yes, it will."*

I was born on December 22, 1939, a couple of football fields in distance from Trent River, the seventh child of John and Mamie Barber. Our family was four boys, Fletcher, John Haywood, Elbert Franklin, and myself, and five girls, Luverna, Lila Mae, Lillian Arlene, Loretta, and Linda Carol.

My parents were farmers and lived about a mile from the little country town of Trenton, with a population of about 500 people. My father was born in Jones County in 1898, and spent several years of his youth as a cook at Dix Hill Hospital in Raleigh, about 100 miles west of Trenton. Upon his return to Trenton, he became a sharecropper on a nearby farm about 2 miles from the shack where I was later born.

MY FATHER

In 1934, near the end of the economic depression of 1929, my father made a great crop of tobacco as a sharecropper, but was put off the farm for refusing to buy an automobile from a friend of the farm's owner. A basic unwritten

---

*© 1964, renewed 1992, ABKCO Music, Inc. (BMI). Used with permission.

principle of sharecropping was to keep the sharecropper and his family financially impoverished and, therefore, economically dependent on the farm's owner. Sharecropping replaced the slave system in the South in 1863 and was considered a slightly improved form of slavery.

Being put off the farm served as an invaluable economic lesson for my father. It motivated him to land ownership and to start making plans for his children to attend college. As we were growing up, he would often relate that sharecropping experience to us, and would conclude by saying, "I don't want my children to go through what I have been through." That became an important lesson instilled in my brothers and sisters and has served us well.

Our Farmland

With $600 from that 1934 tobacco harvest, my father bought 100 acres of woodland located about a mile from the farm where he had worked as a sharecropper.

He sold part of the land to his brother, my Uncle Gus. My father cleared about one half of the woodland and started his own farming operation of tobacco, corn, peanuts, and sweet potatoes. He also raised cows, hogs, and chickens.

My mother always had a beautiful and productive garden, which provided fresh food for her quite sizable family.

My earliest memory of the farm was in 1942, when my father cut the timber on the land and with the help of Uncle John Jones, built our first real house. He would bring me to the building site and place me upon a stack of lumber. The newly built house was about a half mile from the shack by the river and on the main road into Trenton. Eleven years later, I, with the help of my father, transplanted five pine seedlings as a 4-H project to reforest the woodland.

Pennies

The second earliest memory of life on the farm, which would later become an important part of my adult life, was centered around "the penny."

When I was 3 or 4 years old, for some unknown reason, I swallowed five pennies. I still remember picking up those pennies from the corner of a foot-pedal sewing machine and swallowing them one after the other.

What possessed me to do such a foolish thing, I'll never know. But it was probably the same thing that possessed college students in the 1960s to swallow goldfish, crowd the telephone booths, streak stark naked in public places, and chug-a-lug beer until they passed out. "The devil made us do it." But seriously, whatever it was, in the spring of 1984—42 years later—I was awakened around 2 A.M. from a deep sleep by the hand of God with the inspiration to write the following essay, "A Penny Speaks." It was recorded on video by the actor Ossie Davis in 1985. These words, expressed by a "penny" itself, convey a burning desire to unite with other nonproductive, abused, and seemingly worthless pennies to make positive contributions to society and improve the conditions and the quality of life for our people through united "penny power." My father always told us: "Take care of the pennies, the dollars will take care of themselves."

Give the Penny Lovers of America your isolated, abused and trampled on, lonely and hidden pennies yearning to be loved and useful. You will find us in desks, kitchens, and dresser drawers, in closets, behind and under furniture, in shoe boxes, under and between car seats and in piggy banks, forgotten and therefore nonproductive.

We lead a humble and hermit-like existence, not fully appreciated and therefore not circulated as the other coins. My individual purchasing power is practically nil. What can you buy for a penny today?

There's no more penny candy, bubble gum, or baseball and football cards! Children used to want me, but no more. Why do I really exist? What is my purpose in this society? The answer, I believe, is in unity; for in unity, there is strength, and through strength there can be great and significant achievements. Therefore, pennies of the world, let us unite and we will become a powerful and creative economic force in this society.

Let the pennies come forth from the North, the South, the East, and the West. From the great cities of America—New York, Chicago, Milwaukee, Seattle, Portland, Los Angeles, Boston, Newark, Philadelphia, Pittsburgh, Baltimore, Washington, Richmond, Charlotte, Atlanta, Miami and Orlando, Dallas and Houston, New Orleans and others, to small country towns such as Trenton and Seaboard, North Carolina; villages and sleepy hamlets in Virginia, North and South Carolina, Georgia, Alabama, Florida, Arkansas, Mississippi, Louisiana, Texas, Oklahoma, New Mexico, Kentucky, Ohio and Indiana, Iowa and Wyoming, the Dakotas—all the states and territories. From prison cells to military installations around the globe, let the pennies come!

Let Penny Lovers shout PENNY POWER throughout the land and countryside, across hills and vales, meadows and brooks, mountains and valleys, from sea to shining sea!

With organized PENNY POWER we will send kids to computer and recreational camps; we will provide scholarships to disadvantaged, underprivileged, and handicapped young people; we can bring joy, happiness, and companionship into the lives of senior citizens.

United, we represent meaningful community and economic development projects, food, clothing, and shelter for the homeless. United, we represent cultural, arts, and crafts programs, laughing and happy children in day-care centers, educational and training programs for the unemployed and underemployed, and health and human services for our citizens. Yes, there is no limit to what pennies can do united with a sense of purpose and devoted to an agenda of progress for our people.

So all you Penny Lovers, on your mark, get set, come and get us!

The message conveyed in this monologue—"A Penny Speaks"—provides the primary mission of my cause to implement a national "grassroots self-help movement" for African-Americans through the Penny Lovers of America organization. Our website is www.pennylovers.org.

My School Years

I started school at the age of 5 and thanks to an older sister, Lillian Arlene, I had already learned to read. She was my babysitter since I was too young to work in the fields, although willing. In the third grade, I wrote one of my first "love letters" to Martha Mills, a seventh-grade student in Lillian Arlene's class. I passed the letter across the aisle to my buddy to read and help me decide if it was "romantically deep enough" to get Martha's attention. As he passed it back to me, we attracted the attention of our teacher, Miss Hazel Mallette. She promptly invited me to the front of the room to read this "masterpiece" to the class. I survived that ordeal very embarrassed, but I gained the reputation as a "real Romeo," which became known throughout the school in just a few days.

During the fourth and fifth grades, the church, the 4-H Club, and the Boy Scouts began to play very key roles in my leadership and personal development. By the sixth and seventh grades, I had acquired a reputation of being a serious student, fully committed to my studies. That was partly true since I did not want to disappoint my parents and their expectations of me. Also, I realized early on that my father and most of my teachers were very handy with a paddle and strap to maintain discipline for any misconduct or misbehavior. I didn't see the wisdom of risking a double dose of punishment from both my teachers and my father. In addition, Lillian Arlene had set an extremely high academic standard for me to emulate, graduating high school with a 98.6 overall average. She was a hard act to follow. Her teachers, with their "Aren't you Lillian Barber's brother?" memory, had great expectations of me. Therefore, for the sake of the family name and honor, I felt duty bound to give school my best shot.

Segregation

It was also during those early years that I became more aware of the apartheid and segregated society in which I lived. Our parents protected us from the evils of segregation and discrimination as much as possible. However, as I delivered newspapers on my paper route, the reminders of a segregated society were very evident. I noticed that Negro children (we were Negroes back then) were not allowed to sit down at the local drugstore and drink a soda or a milk shake—we had to take them out.

I remember a bus ride with my father to Goldsboro, North Carolina, about 50 miles from Trenton, for a dental appointment and that "white line on the floor of that bus" behind which Negroes were expected to be seated. I remember the separate waiting rooms and "white only and colored" signs over the water fountains at the bus stations. To a 13-year-old farm boy, that made no sense at all, nor did it to my father. But he would challenge us to get a good education and help change things. "No one can take education from you," he would often remind me and my siblings.

I became acutely aware of the used, hand-me-down books and pieces of broken chalk from the local white schools and our poor and dilapidated school buildings, and outside toilets. We had the potbelly stoves in our classrooms, and the white kids sat in steam-heated classrooms with inside plumbing, good books, and instructional materials. When coal was not available for the stoves, we went into the forest behind the school and cut wood and gathered tarpaper to keep warm.

Despite these glaring inequities in our school facilities, we had concerned, dedicated, and committed teachers determined to make a difference in our lives, for most had come through that same so-called "separate but equal" public school system. A school system that was in fact "very separate, and in most ways definitely unequal." Negro children were not expected to amount to anything anyway, reasoned the board of education, and the school budgets for Negro schools conveyed that message very clearly.

My High School Years

In the fall of 1954, I entered Jones High School, a newly constructed school near our farm. I was faced with new teachers, new friends, and greater learning challenges and self-development opportunities.

Students from other rural communities—Pollocksville, Maysville, Comfort, Oliver Crossroads, Wyse Fork, White Oak, and Black Swamp—provided greater competition for all of us. The increased competition made us all better students, and more prepared for college, which was on the horizon for most of us.

Some of the highlights of my high school years were:

* Meeting Jackie Robinson, the first black major-league baseball player, as part of our NAACP youth activities.
* Being elected state president of the North Carolina 4-H Club.
* Earning my Eagle Scout badge and having it presented to me before the entire student body.
* Making the varsity football team as center.
* Graduating third in my class of 54 students with an "A" average, with fewer than two points separating the top three students.

My Personal Role to Gain Civil Rights

During the 1954–1957 school years, things were happening. Dr. Martin Luther King Jr. was on the national scene with the civil rights movement; the Supreme Court handed down the *Brown vs. Board of Education* decision in May

1954, outlawing "separate but equal" public schools; and Russia launched the *Sputnik* I spacecraft in 1957.

We (my classmates) seriously began to question the second-rate facilities and teaching materials in our school. With the national emphasis on mathematics and the natural sciences at the high school level, we began to compare our school resources with those in Jones Central High School (the white school).

We would get firsthand reports from Eva Mae Berry, a fellow classmate, whose father was custodian at Jones Central, and she and her brother helped him after school. Eva Mae was the top student in our class and became the valedictorian, and my prom date my junior year. Our school had poorly equipped science laboratories and did not offer a course in physics. My cousin Donald Jones and I were determined to do something about this obvious inequity or, at least, an inadvertent oversight.

We went to see Mr. C. C. Franks, our principal, about this intolerable situation and I requested that it be corrected. He informed us that the decision was made by the board of education, and we would have to take the matter up with Mr. W. B. Moore, the superintendent of schools. Donald and I made an appointment to meet with Mr. Moore, our primary strategy and fallback strategy firmly in mind.

As we walked to the superintendent's office about a mile from our school, we discussed the fact that the federal government and the Supreme Court were on our side. His secretary ushered us into his office with an expression of great concern on her face. We expressed our concerns to Mr. Moore and the need to upgrade the science facilities and include a physics course in our curricula at Jones High School. He was quick to point out that due to limited funds and other budget priorities that would not be possible.

At that point in our conversation, our fallback strategy came to the rescue, and we informed Mr. Moore that we would like to enroll in Jones Central High School the following September. After he regained his composure from a temporary state of shock, he promised to consider our primary request and get back to Mr. Franks.

We left his office laughing under our breaths because we were quite confident that he would find the necessary funds. We concluded that he would have provided us nearly anything within reason to keep us from enrolling in Jones Central, even though the Supreme Court was on our side. Sure enough within a few weeks, he had found the funds for a physics teacher and new laboratory equipment, including photography darkroom equipment, which we had not even requested.

That situation taught me another valuable lesson. Always leverage the current circumstances to your advantage and best interest. I later majored in physics in college.

The Farm's End

During the 1952 school year, an incident that had a great impact on me happened just down the road from our farm. One Sunday as my brothers, sisters, and cousins walked home from Sunday school, emergency vehicles passed us at very high rates of speed. We learned later that day that the farmer who had put my father off his farm in 1934 had committed suicide. It was rumored that he had become heavily in debt and had become quite despondent.

I have sometimes wondered over the years that had my father made the decision to buy that farmer's friend's car in 1934 how different my life and the lives of my brothers and sisters might have been. Most likely, we would have grown up as the sons and daughters of a sharecropper and might have remained on that farm. But my father realized his dream by becoming a landowner, and he lived to see seven of my nine brothers and sisters complete college and post secondary training by earning our own way. I learned from that experience to always set goals and work to achieve them, and never allow anyone to deter you from "marching to the drum beat of your own heart." I did just that.

SUCCESS

In my senior year, 1957–58, with Jerry Butler's R & B song, "Your Precious Love" sweeping the country, I maintained a very hectic and yet focused routine with plans to enter A&T College in Greensboro (now North Carolina A&T State University) the following year. I worked two part-time jobs while maintaining my newspaper route. The year passed very quickly and graduation was just a few weeks away. Proudly I walked across the stage to receive my high school diploma with my parents, brothers and sisters, other family members, and friends looking on. The rivers of my soul had expanded, for now I had completed high school and was ready for a waiting world.

I worked in the tobacco fields that summer, as I had each summer since I was old enough to work on the farm, and my part-time jobs and newspaper route increased my savings for college. With everything that I needed, or could afford, in a brand new footlocker, I was off to A&T College in 1958 to start my college experience. I still have that footlocker as a reminder to my children of my possessions during my college years, and to contrast the U-Haul trucks I used when I took them off to college.

COLLEGE AND LOVE

My college years involved the serious study of physics, Reserve Officers Training Corps (ROTC), extracurricular activities (student government, NAACP, Phi Beta Sigma Fraternity, the student newspaper, and several other activities), the sit-in demonstrations in downtown Greensboro, and meeting Betty Jo Witherspoon, a sophomore nursing student and my future wife (and the best decision I've ever made, according to my oldest daughter, Vicky).

I met Betty the spring semester of my freshman year and she became a very important part of my life, as she has been now for over 40 years. It was during the fall of my junior year that I fully realized I wanted Betty to be the mother of my children. As Betty's senior year neared an end in 1961, we were engaged at my spring fraternity ball as we danced to the song "For Your Love."

Betty graduated and went off to her first job as a staff nurse at Fort Howard Veteran's Administration Hospital in Maryland, and I went off to ROTC summer camp at Fort Bragg, North Carolina. After summer camp, I went to Washington and worked two jobs for the remainder of the summer.

DR. PROCTOR

It was during my sophomore year that Dr. Samuel DeWitt Proctor, a young, dynamic, and talented educator, was named the new president of A&T College. Dr. Proctor came to A&T with an agenda and a plan. Academic excellence was a top priority parallel with the proper behavior of students, both male and female.

On a spring evening in 1961, legend has it that Wallace Wortham, our class president, was caught red-handed by Dr. Proctor outside of Holland Hall, the freshmen female dormitory, participating in a "panty raid." Wallace was promptly expelled from the institution, and aggressive efforts for reinstatement by his parents and friends proved futile. As class vice-president, I became president and was formally elected president of the senior class later that spring.

I would occasionally remind Dr. Proctor over the years that his stern disciplinary action of Wallace greatly advanced my college political career. This story, however, has a happy ending for Wallace. He enrolled in Penn State University, graduated, went on to law school, and now serves as city attorney in Denver, Colorado. He reconciled with Dr. Proctor several years before Dr. Proctor's death in May of 1997.

In our annual class meeting during the Homecoming Weekend of 2000 with Wallace present, a resolution was unanimously adopted making him an honorary member of the Class of 1962.

I was greatly blessed that Dr. Proctor came into my life in 1960. He became my friend, confidant, mentor, and hero for the next 37 years. He played a very significant and important role in my life. Dr. Leonard Bethel of Rutgers University and I are currently leading an effort to establish the Samuel DeWitt Proctor Society: For Moral, Educational, Economic, and Community Development at Rutgers University, where he held the Dr. Martin Luther King Jr. Distinguished Chair on the faculty of the Graduate School of Education for over 20 years. This institute, through scholarly speeches, seminars, and forums, will honor Dr. Proctor and serve to recognize his many outstanding contributions to the academic, religious, social, and community entities across America and the impact of his ideas and deeds around the world.

His national and international reputation has placed him in the forefront of higher education and scholarship, as well as theological understanding on moral and social issues, for this creative visionary was one the leading educational minds of the 20th century.

MY BETTY AND GERMANY

With Betty in Maryland, I entered my senior year focused on my studies, Army ROTC training, and various extracurricular activities. In a few short months, I would graduate with a degree in physics, and my mother and Betty would pin on my Second Lieutenant's bars.

The rivers of my soul continued to flow, and my military assignments took me to Aberdeen Proving Grounds in Maryland; Sandia Base, New Mexico; and to Europe (Germany) for three and half years. My last assignment was to Redstone Arsenal in Alabama in October 1966 as commanding officer of the 599th Ordnance Company. I had requested an assignment to Germany prior to graduation and was especially happy when it was approved by the Department of the Army.

I wanted an assignment in Europe in order to study the Holocaust and the Marshall Plan close up. In preparation for my assignment to Germany, I enrolled in a German language course my last semester at A&T College, taught by Dr. Berwin, an 80-year-old German professor. She taught German the old-fashioned way; you had to actually learn it. I became quite conversant in German and would later take an advanced German language course at the U. S. Army Language School in Garmisch, Germany.

Upon our arrival in Germany (Betty accompanied me), I was assigned as platoon leader in the 28th Ordnance Company in Zweibrucken. I focused on the mission of the platoon and Betty made the necessary adjustments of a military wife in a foreign country. She became a volunteer with the nursing staff at the post dispensary. A few months later she was employed as a staff nurse at the Royal Canadian Air Force Hospital, and subsequently took a staff nurse position at the Landstuhl Army Medical Center.

VICKY

On June 25, 1964, the stork arrived at our quarters bringing our first-born child. She remained unnamed for a day or so, for we had only selected the name Richard Jr. and sonograms were not available. I was comfortable with the name Richard Jr., but I could not convince Betty, so we settled on the name Victoria Lynette. This was a happy and blessed occasion for us, and we assumed our new roles with great enthusiasm and a lot of help from Dr. Spock's parenting guides. After a few months at home with Vicky, Betty returned to work at the Army Hospital. We hired a live-in German babysitter, Frau Geisler, to look after Vicky. Frau did not speak any English, so I became the interpreter for her and Betty. She was great with Vicky and would often take her to visit her German neighbors and their children. German children began visiting Vicky at our quarters, and with Frau Geisler's tutoring, Vicky was soon on her way to becoming bilingual. We were simply doing our part as one American military family to improve international relations with our host country.

CHECK POINT CHARLIE

It was always a sad time for Frau Geisler as German holidays approached, for her brother lived in East Germany and they could not visit each other. Too often, as Americans, we seem to take our unrestricted freedom of movement for granted rather than as a privileged blessing. Our visit to Check Point Charlie at the Berlin Wall of Shame was a sobering experience, for one quickly realized that not only was the country divided geographically, but also that real family members and friends were separated as well.

As Americans, we should be forever grateful to President Ronald Reagan for his leadership in bringing down the Berlin Wall.

TOURING

During my years in Europe (1963–1966), Betty and I traveled throughout Germany and 15 other European countries. It was an educational and rewarding experience which we will always cherish. My one regret is that we did not travel to Norway in 1964 to witness Dr. Martin Luther King Jr. receiving the Nobel Peace Prize.

We had the pleasure of meeting the Honorable Patricia Harris, United States Ambassador to Luxembourg, and her husband at a reception in her honor at the Kaiserslautern Officers Club, arranged by my brigade commander, Colonel Stanford Hicks. I would later serve with Ambassador Harris in the Carter Administration.

RETURN AND REFLECTION

As our departure date from Germany drew closer, we completed packing our household goods, purchased a new 1966 Pontiac through the Army Post Exchange for only $2,675 with delivery in New York, and happily looked forward to coming home after three and a half years. Coming home was special for it meant seeing our parents, family members, and friends, and the chance for them to see our beloved and bilingual Vicky. After a month of joyous reunion with our families, I reported to Redstone Arsenal in Alabama for a 1-year assignment.

It was during my last few months at Redstone Arsenal when the rivers of my soul took on a larger dimension and a greater meaning. I sat in my quarters one spring night in March 1967, reflecting on my 5-year military career, which would come to a close on June 1, 1967, just 3 months hence. I reflected on what I would do with the rest of my life; what causes I would support? How could I use my time and talents to help right some of the wrongs in our nation? What contributions could I make in our struggle as a people for full and equitable participation in the American Dream? Where would I find my place in the sun? I reflected on key events over that 5-year period and the impact those events had on me.

I thought about my graduation from college in 1962 and being commissioned a Second Lieutenant in the U.S. Army. I thought about July 18,1962, my first day on active duty at Aberdeen Proving Grounds in Maryland, and how I was refused service at several local restaurants notwithstanding the fact that I had just taken the oath "to uphold and defend the Constitution of these United States."

I thought about my marriage to Betty on September 30,1962, as James Meredith was trying to enroll into the University of Mississippi. His attempt to enroll caused a riot, and President Kennedy had to dispatch federal troops to protect Meredith and to quell the riot.

I remembered with fond memories the 9-day voyage on the troop transport ship *General Patton* in March 1963 in route to my first duty assignment in Germany, accompanied by my young bride.

I reflected on the shameful racial incidents and tragic events at home during 1963, which caused me to seriously question why I was in the army 5,000 miles from home, when the real battle was back in the states with the civil rights forces challenging the age-old barriers of discrimination, segregation, and unjust laws against black Americans.

I remembered the racial incident at the Heidelburg Officers Club in June of 1963, when four white American military officers entered the club dressed as KKK Klansmen. This was truly an insult to all black military personnel serving our country around the globe (I wonder where they are today).

I remembered with a heavy heart June 12,1963, when Medgar Evers, field director of the NAACP in Mississippi, was shot down in his driveway as his wife and children looked on in horror. I remembered with pride the March on Washington on August 28,1963, when Dr. Martin Luther King Jr. stood at the foot of the Lincoln Memorial and told the nation of his dream.

I remembered with great sadness the morning after those little black angels were killed by a dynamite blast on September 15, 1963, while sitting in a Sunday School class in the Sixteenth Street Baptist Church in Birmingham, Alabama. I remembered when Sergeant Robert Jackson, my platoon sergeant, came to my office to inform me that one of those little angels, Denise McNair, was his niece. He sat before my desk and wept, and I cried with him.

I remembered November 22, 1963, with a great sense of personal loss and how time seemed to have stood still when as duty officer of the day, I received a message that President Kennedy had been shot in Dallas, Texas.

I remembered the riot in Detroit, the demonstrations and civil disorders in cities and towns across America. I reflected on the needless loss of life and the destruction of property. I thought about the lunch counter sit-ins and picketing in Greensboro in 1960, and my own participation as a student.

I remembered the "hippie movement" and the rebellious young people of my generation in the early 1960s; the marches and demonstrations, the freedom rides, the rejection of traditional values, the conflict and breakup of families with the rise in cults and other seemingly attractive options for young people.

I remembered that unpopular and seemingly senseless war in Vietnam, where many of our military personnel were either killed, physically maimed, or psychologically damaged for life.

As I sat in the quietness of my quarters that March 1967 night and reflected on the events, crises, protests, and conflicts during that period in our history—a period in retrospect when it seemed that America had lost her way—I was inspired to write these words, entitled *Before I Die*, which represent my philosophy and personal ministry.

Before I Die

I want to drink from the fountain of freedom
and pass the cup to future generations.
I want to inhale the sweet air of liberty
and breathe new life and hope into a faltering people.
I want to replace promise with performance, and replace
rhetoric with results.
I want to push back the dark jungles of suspicion
that tend to separate men.
I want to remove the barriers of distrust and unite
men in a common cause.
I want to conquer new horizons with love
so that God's will can truly be done on earth.
I want to silence the guns on foreign battlefields
and promote understanding
and brotherhood among nations.
I want to extend the frontiers of freedom
so that people the world over may have
the freedom of choice.
I want to pick up the broken pieces of the
shattered dreams of our youth
and mold them into a living reality.
I want to comfort some worried and disillusioned
mother when her spirits are low and burdens heavy.
I want to instill pride and respect in some alcoholic father.
I want to rekindle the love of God in the
hearts of men and women and return humankind to
God's paradise.

The vision and challenges of this writing have become a lifelong mission for me, and are an integral part of my church, community, business, and professional activities.

TRANSITION TO CIVILIAN LIFE

Shortly before I was honorably discharged from the army at Redstone Arsenal on June 1, 1967, I accepted employment with the Westinghouse Electric Corporation in Pittsburgh. Betty and I, with our young daughter, relocated to Pittsburgh in July 1967.

We settled in an apartment in the Squirrel Hill community about 10 minutes from my office in Homewood. We sought church membership at the Central Baptist Church in the Hill District and became very involved in community activities.

Vicky attended nursery school on the campus of Carnegie Mellon University, and kindergarten and grade school at Falk School adjacent to the University of Pittsburgh. Betty once again was employed by the Veterans Administration at the Oakland VA Hospital, and received a fellowship for graduate school at the University of Pittsburgh to study medical-surgical nursing. She completed the program in 1971 and joined the nursing faculty.

DR. KING

I was on my way to an NAACP meeting in the Hill District on the evening of April 4, 1968, when a special bulletin came over the radio that Dr. King had been shot in Memphis. When I arrived at the meeting, I learned that Dr. King had died and the meeting was cancelled. I returned home and watched newscasts of this tragic event well beyond midnight.

I watched as city after city exploded in riots, looting, and violence. In Washington, D. C., the nation's capital, the riot area looked like a war zone. Pittsburgh did not escape this national turmoil. Three months later, another assassin's bullet would ring out in a Los Angeles hotel and Senator Robert F. Kennedy, a presidential candidate, would lie dying on the kitchen floor.

DIFFICULT DAYS

With an unpopular war raging in Vietnam and protests here at home, these were truly dark days for America. On March 27, 1969, the stork once again paid us a visit, but this time got it right and delivered a boy, Richard Jr., to McGee Hospital.

Three months later, on Vicky's fifth birthday, we moved into our new home in Allison Park, a suburb of Pittsburgh. Shortly after we moved in, a neighbor several houses down the street let me know that we were not welcome in the community by informing me that "the neighbors are upset by you moving into our area." I replied, "Go back and tell the neighbors that's their problem." I heard nothing more about their problem until 2 years or so later when again racism raised its ugly head.

A lady in the neighborhood was calling all the neighbors to inform them that Ryan Homes, a local developer, was planning to build low-income housing nearby. "We had an agreement with Ryan Homes not to build low-cost housing in this area and not to sell houses to blacks," she blurted out to Betty. Realizing that she was speaking with an African-American, she promptly hung up the telephone. Vicky later told me that a few months after we moved in she was called "a nigger" for the first time in her life.

As a Corporate Executive

Most of the neighbors were quite friendly and we had much in common, including working to pay the mortgage. In July 1969, I resigned from Westinghouse Corporation and joined the Opportunities Industrialization Centers (OIC) of America founded by Dr. Leon Sullivan of Philadelphia. Dr. Sullivan became my economic mentor. In 1971, I along with Brady Keys, a former Pittsburgh Steeler cofounded the Urban Talent Development (UTD) Corporation, a manpower training and business orientation center.

During my 7 years as president, UTD trained and placed more than 1,400 unemployed and underemployed persons in meaningful employment. The UTD story is a classic in manpower and management development and was cited in the Congressional Record in 1974 as one of the nation's most effective manpower development programs.

In June of 1973, I was elected chairman of the board of a group organizing New World National Bank. A steering committee of ministers headed by Dr. Brannon I. Hopson, pastor of Mt. Olive Baptist Church in Rankin, Pennsylvania, Bishop Roy C. Nichols of the United Methodist Church, and Dr. David Shannon, dean of the Pittsburgh Theological Seminary, assisted me over an 18-month period in raising the $800,000 needed to capitalize the bank.

Due to the enthusiastic leadership and support of the church community, a cross-section of the entire Pittsburgh community became involved in this bank organizing project, including professional athletes, block clubs, sororities and fraternities, the local chapter of the National Postal Alliance, federal and state employees, community organizations, civic and professional groups, the private corporate sector, and the foundation community.

Finally on March 17, 1975, New World National Bank held its grand opening with a tremendous crowd of supporters. Local and national dignitaries attended. Some time during the week of celebrating the bank's opening, our third child was conceived, and 9 months later, a beautiful baby girl was born on December 29, 1975. We named her Sharon Elizabeth and referred to her as our "IRS baby" for her timely arrival as an exemption on our tax return.

My Community Honors Me

Also in 1975, I received numerous awards and recognitions for my civic, community, business, and professional achievements, including being named one of the 10 Outstanding Young Men of America by the U.S. Jaycees for 1975. October 30 was declared "Dick Barber Day" by the Allegheny County Commissioners.

In January 1978, Dr. Benjamin L. Hooks, the newly appointed executive director of the NAACP in New York, selected me as his deputy executive director. I joined the national staff in May 1978 and relocated the family to Somerset, New Jersey, in September.

Family Honors and Losses

Betty joined the nursing faculty at Rutgers University in Newark and remained there until 1986, when she took a position at Kean College (now Kean University) as assistant dean of the School of Natural Sciences, Nursing and Mathematics. Two years later, she was promoted to dean and currently serves in that capacity.

Vicky enrolled in Rutgers Prep School in Somerset. Ricky and several other students from the area took a Suburban Transit bus each day to a school in Princeton. Sharon, who was now 3 years old, stayed at home and looked after the babysitter.

Shortly after I moved to the New York area, our family was engulfed in sadness with the death of Loretta, a younger sister, in July 1978. My father died on July 18, 1985, which created a great void in my life. He had taught me to fish in Trent River as a youngster. He had placed me in a pew for Sunday School before my feet could reach the floor. He taught me to plow a straight furrow with a mule. His lessons, wisdom, and steady hand of guidance have continued to manifest themselves in the lives of his children. He demonstrated family values long before the term became a political cliche.

Five years later, on March 25, 1990, my mother died. Very rarely do I visit Trenton without going to their gravesites to whisper a prayer of gratitude for their love and nurturing ways.

My Career and Life Flourish

From 1981 until 2000, I worked in real estate development, first as the regional administrator of the Small Business Administration in Philadelphia, then as deputy secretary for procurement for the Commonwealth of Pennsylvania in Harrisburg, and then as the contract specialist with the Resolutions Trust Corporation in Somerset, and finally, as the director of purchasing at the University of Medicine & Dentistry of New Jersey. Currently, I am engaged in several entrepreneurial and consulting projects.

Over the years, I have enjoyed watching our children grow up and go off to college. Vicky entered undergraduate school at Yale University in 1982, graduated in 1986, and then remained there for medical school, graduating in 1990. She completed an orthopedics surgery specialty in 1996 in San Francisco.

Ricky chose to return to my native state of North Carolina to attend North Carolina Central University and graduated in 1994 with a degree in public administration. In July 1998, he took Paula McDonald, a college classmate, as his bride.

Our "IRS baby," Sharon, is currently enrolled in Rutgers University in New Brunswick. I am very proud of our children and thank the Good Lord for these special blessings.

RIVERS EMPTY INTO THE SEA

I do not and cannot know how much farther the rivers of my soul shall flow into the future. I am comforted by the thought and hope that my children, and hopefully their children, will embrace the cultural values and a genuine sense of community to which I have devoted the greater part of my life. I hope and pray that they truly treasure the fruits of liberty and the blessings of freedom of this nation, and use their gifts and talents to help maintain them, and always seek to achieve an even more perfect union. In so doing, the true purpose and meaning of my life will be completely defined and shall forever manifest itself with every rising and setting sun.

FOR YOU

A message for my fellow travelers on the banks of the rivers of their souls is simply to be good to yourselves and kind to your neighbors. Together let's make America truly work for all of us. I retreat to the banks of the rivers of my soul and conclude this part of my odyssey.

CHAPTER 39

GROWING UP IN AN ORDERED SOCIETY: HOW HISTORY HAS SHAPED A GENERATION OF BLACK MEN

John R. Spann

As thinking creatures we are influenced by our primal atmosphere. The men of the 21st century, as are men of any era, are shaped by the influences in which they grow up as children, influences such as family, culture, society, and the events of history. To get an understanding of the male of today, we must revisit his past. In this chapter I will discuss some of the events of history that shaped the society into which I was born and reared and some of the events that shaped my development and ideologies as a black man today.

THE BLUEPRINT OF SOUTHERN SOCIETY

White immigrants from Europe, especially England, who were themselves fleeing a strict class-structured society, settled the original 13 colonies that became the United States. This migration began with the settlement of Jamestown, Virginia, in 1607 and continued through the founding of Savannah, Georgia, in 1733 (DeSantis, 1974). Among these immigrants were many who were fleeing the reign of King George and/or seeking the opportunity for a better life. A majority of these were themselves second-class citizens. However, after these immigrants settled the new world, they accepted the belief that they were "ordained by God" under the theory of natural law to be the dominant entity of society.

Settlers in the colonies were often escaping the consequences of a repressive social order. However, once in the new world they seemed to bring with them ideologies or beliefs about social structure and the "proper" society from a Europe that was characterized by kings, royalty, and inherited privilege based on family wealth. Consequently, the society they structured in the new world was of property-owning white males, by white males, and exclusively for white males. The influences of the social structure established in colonial America still exist and serve as a basis for racial divisiveness in American society today. The social order that evolved from the early settlers, while professing religious tolerance and the value of individuality, has demonstrated a lack of tolerance for groups and beliefs that were different from those of the white majority. Historically, acceptance and equality have been reserved for those who were or looked like Europeans. Even today, we have become a society that is growing less and less tolerant of diversity even as we become more diverse. If our neighbors don't look like us, act like us, and embrace our ideologies, we fear them. This is not only true for white Americans, but is also true for members of other racial groups. In many instances, mistrust, fear, and hatred among different racial and ethnic groups has its roots in the collective experiences of these groups in the evolution of the American society.

To understand the society that exists in America, we must first have an understanding of its foundations. In many cases, the men and women who immigrated to North America were themselves from the lower classes of European society. Many of the new world settlers came to the colonies to avoid going to jail or to get out of jail. For example, Oglethorpe settled Georgia in 1733 with individuals who were released from debtors' prison in England, in order to establish a buffer between colonial Charleston, South Carolina, and the Spanish in Florida (Eibling, King, & Harlow, 1966). By the time Georgia was founded, South Carolina was well on its way to becoming a wealthy colony with much of its wealth coming from importing and selling slaves (Franklin, 1969).

In America the elite class was self-created. Among colonial America's elite, neither wealth, honor, nor power was equally distributed. The creation and retention of wealth became a guiding factor in all activities of the elite class. I have observed that there has been very little change in this situation. Today, the economic divide continues to be a problem of society. The barrier of racism continues to prevent many from moving up the economic ladder. This is especially true for black males. While white males continue to control corporate America, black males have high rates of unemployment, and even when employed are for the most part clustered in low paying jobs. If I had not educated myself and remained focused on my goals with the determination to overcome the barriers of racism, I might have ended up in a dead-end job with little future.

The southern planters came closer than any other group to achieving a way of life in the new world that simulated that of the upper classes of Europe. Operating large estates supported by slave labor, the southern planters built impressive homes and initiated the English "squirarchy." Yet, such a position of dominance over other groups brought with it an underlying insecurity and the sense of the need to fight to maintain such dominance. It was clear that in order to have a class-ordered society, there had to be someone at the top and someone at the bottom. In the established social structure of the colonial South, white, male landowners became the top of the social order and black slaves became the bottom. The laws of "progenitor and entail" helped ensure that wealth passed from father to eldest son (Spruill, 1972). This system insured that even white women from prominent families could not inherit wealth or challenge the dominance of the white male in the social order.

Many white immigrants who came to America came as indentured servants. A large number of these individuals settled in the northern colonies and were able to move from servant status by purchasing their freedom. Those who were able to make the transition became the businessmen or the middle class. In contrast, black slaves, who were primarily imported to the southern colonies, arrived as property and were thought to have no human qualities that would allow them to advance beyond slave (property) status. The class-structured society that evolved in the southern colonies (now the southern United States) did not come into existence by accident. Extensive effort was put forth to ensure that the status of privileged whites was maintained.

Because the South became an agrarian-based society, there was a need for a cheap source of labor to support the plantation system. The institution of slavery provided a source of this needed labor. The invention of the cotton gin made cotton the chief crop of the South. This invention resulted in an expansion of the plantation system, thus increasing the importation of slaves.

My own family can be traced backed to the plantation system as slaves in South Carolina. While researching my family's genealogy, I discovered records indicating that my great-great-great-grandfather was listed among the assets of a white farm owner. Seeing those records and actually seeing the name of my grandfather listed as the property of another human made the cruelty of the plantation system very personal. I could only imagine what he had to endure to survive that system as a child. On one hand this gives validation to the sense of anger that I as well as other black males feel toward the "system." In many aspects, our social system has not changed that much since slavery inasmuch as it continues to exploit blacks.

Several years ago Alex Haley's book *Roots* was made into a miniseries for television. The movie caused ripples throughout American society. For the first time many people were able to see firsthand a portrayal of the cruelties of the system of slavery. As I watched black people in the series being treated as objects, it caused feelings of deep-seated anger to surface in myself. From my discussions with other black males concerning the televised version of *Roots*, many of them had the same reactions. The anger that many black men felt made us want to strike out or seek revenge for the cruel acts committed against our ancestors. As the institution of slavery evolved with growing numbers of slaves being brought to the South, there was some acknowledgment that, although remaining property, slaves possessed basic or childlike human characteristics. In his book *Slaves Without Masters: A Justification of Slavery*, George Fitzhugh (1857) wrote, "He the Negro is but a grown up child, and must be governed as a child, not as a lunatic or criminal. The master occupies toward him the place of parent or guardian." Additionally, James Henry Hammond, a wealthy plantation owner of South Carolina, in a Senate speech on March 4, 1858, set forth the "Mudsill Theory," the theory that a viable society is divided into two groups, one exercising superior functions, and the other group exercising inferior ones (Fisher & Quarles, 1968). The thoughts expressed by Hammond and Fitzhugh were the common perspective concerning blacks held by the majority of whites in the United States in the 1850s. Further, this perspective has remained a dominant view of blacks into the 21st century.

THE SOUTH MEETS JIM CROW

When slavery ended in the South, this caused a dilemma for southern leaders. Because of the number of slaves imported as free labor, the population of blacks in the southern states eventually outnumbered whites. By 1870, there were 4.9 million blacks in the United States. Of that number, 3.8 million lived in the states of the former confederacy (Fisher & Quarles, 1968). Consequently, after the Civil War, whites were pressed to come up with a system of retaining control and controlling the large black population. The need to control society led to the implementation of the system of "Jim Crow" laws in the South. The primary objective of those laws was to retain the structure of society in the South as it had existed before the Civil War. Those laws also helped ensure that political and economic power would remain firmly in the hands of white males. In South Carolina as late as 1900, blacks remained the majority population. This created enormous tension between the races. One of the methods used to control the situation was fear and intimidation. This also gave rise to terrorist groups such as the Christian Knights of the Ku Klux Klan. It was a common experience of blacks who grew up around this time to witness a Klan parade and fully realize the threat to their safety. The Klan represented a means for whites to exert social and economic control over blacks through the threat of physical violence. Until the late 1960s, I can still recall the Klan parades through the small town in which I lived. For a child, it was a frightening event knowing the purpose of this group. It also caused me to wonder how many of the whites that I saw in town on a daily basis were hidden under those sheets. The experiences for blacks, especially children growing up in such a society, can be equated to that of growing up in enemy territory or that of being captives in their own country.

When the Klan paraded through our town, my parents explained to us that the Klan were whites who hated blacks because of the color of our skin. They also explained to us that members of the Klan were dangerous and known to have committed violent acts against black people. While I was young and did not fully understand why Klan members hated black people, I accepted my parents' explanations that these were people to avoid. Society in the South, during the period from the Civil War up to the civil rights movement, remained two societies, separate but very unequal. As long as the two re-mained separate and blacks "knew their place," white community leaders and politicians were willing to allow blacks to exist on the terms of white leaders. However, the black leadership base that was evolving realized that conditions in black communities would never improve as long as the strict division of society remained in place. This was the impetus for the push for equality to include integration.

SEPARATE, BUT UNEQUAL

One method to achieve equality was through quality education. In the South, the education systems exemplified the idea of separate, but very unequal. I can still remember that during my primary school years the textbooks sent to our school were used books. The new materials were given to white schools. Teachers bought many of the supplies used by students in our school using their personal funds. Because the school district did not fully fund the black school, if teachers had not bought the supplies, children would have done without essential tools for education. I had always been eager to learn even before entering school. However, if my teachers had not taken the initiative to fill in the gaps and insure that our education was not deficient, my formal school years and what I have been able to achieve in life perhaps would have been very different. Disparities such as these inspired the parents who were the initial litigants in the *Brown vs. Board of Education* lawsuit to take this legal action. Interestingly, these parents were from Clarendon County South Carolina, the county adjacent to the county where I attended school (Davis, 1976). This landmark court decision, *Brown vs. Board of Education*, was handed down May 17, 1954 (Franklin, 1969). Although I was only a year old when this decision was rendered, the decision would have a profound impact on the rest of my life. During my senior year of high school, I was among the group of black students involved in the full implementation of the Court's ruling integrating the school systems in South Carolina. In 1970, our black high school was converted to a middle school and grades 9 through 12 were merged with the white school in our community.

Many people, especially whites, still fail to grasp the impetus behind that lawsuit. Black parents were not interested in simply having their children sit in the same class with white students. Rather, they realized that if they could not persuade community leaders and state politicians of the need to adequately equip black schools, then the next logical course of action would be to have all children educated in the same setting.

The matter of school integration was an issue that continued to divide the country for a number of years, especially the South. This division was exemplified by the fact that when Chester Travelstead, then dean of the College of Education at the University of South Carolina, spoke of the need for South Carolina to comply with the Court's decision in August of 1955, he was immediately fired

(Schweickert, 2001). It would not be until much later, in 1963, that any institution of higher learning in South Carolina would be desegregated. Three black students—James Solomon, Henrie Monteith, and Robert Anderson—broke the color divide in South Carolina when they registered for classes at the University of South Carolina in Columbia under the protection of federal marshals. Later that same year, Harvey Gantt became the first black to enter Clemson University. The presence of federal marshals prevented overt acts of violence against these students. However, white students did harass the black students entering South Carolina's previously all-white universities. Additionally, the actions of some faculty and other members of the universities demonstrated that black students were not welcome. There was intense fear that these young people would be physically harmed or even murdered. The rhetoric of hate from the elected leaders was so intense that it was expected that any actions necessary to prevent integration of white universities and colleges would be undertaken. Because of the hostility directed at the first black students entering the University of South Carolina, I would not have anticipated wanting to attend the university. However, as a result of the improving environment for blacks at the university, I received a masters degree from the University of South Carolina in 1977. My undergraduate studies were done at Morris College, a predominately black private college located in Sumter, South Carolina. I was encouraged to attend Morris by some of my teachers who were alumni of the college. Morris College was close to home, and it was a church-affiliated college. I felt it would provide a safe environment in which to study.

Based on the resentment and implicit hostility toward Integration in the South, black parents and teachers viewed the events at southern universities as a prelude to what they felt was likely to happen when the state's public school systems were integrated. As a teenager, I can remember my parents discussing how such fears were born out when in Lamar, South Carolina, a small town within 50 miles from where we lived, a school bus transporting black students was overturned by angry white parents. My parents were clearly concerned about this incident because my sister and I had been assigned to a new school that would require us being transported by school bus. After the events in Lamar, my parents, along with other parents from our church, formed a group to discuss ways of dealing with the situation if similar events occurred when it was time to integrate our community schools. While all parents were angry, including my parents, they felt that integration of the school system was necessary. To allow the threats of violence to stop integration was, as my father said, "Just the reaction the whites want." Although my parents were concerned, I did not think there would be any trouble, because many of my white friends attended the school to which I was reassigned and would be riding the bus with us.

The rhetoric of hate that resulted from desegregation had a negative effect on many aspects of life for blacks in my community. In some instances, black farmers who openly fought for desegregation suddenly found themselves unable to buy supplies needed to operate their farms. Local white business owners refused to do business with them. Blacks who lived and worked on white-owned farms were told that if they attended the meeting or supported groups advocating desegregation, they would be evicted from their homes. This was a real threat for many black families in our community because they lived on white-owned farms. These threats by whites resulted in more polarization of the community. The thought of imminent integration caused a strain on friendships that had existed across racial lines.

In return for being allowed to live on white-owned farms, it was required that black family members work the farm. I can recall that many of my classmates missed many days from school because the families were pressured to keep the children home to gather crops from the fields. It was not uncommon for a family to be forced to find another place to live if the white owner felt that a black family's kids were attending school too often at the expense of gathering "his" crops from the fields. While this was not actual slavery, this practice had overtones of a system that placed value on blacks based on their potential as a source of physical labor. This system forced black parents to put the education of their children in jeopardy by forcing them to choose between a child's education and the family's welfare. This situation also increased the likelihood that such black children would be destined to repeat a cycle of dependence and poverty due to the lack of an opportunity for a good education.

Discrimination and exploitation of blacks were not confined to agricultural workers. Even those persons who did not live on a farm but worked in the factories were not immune from the divisions of society. Since whites controlled the hiring and firing at practically all facilities, blacks were often terminated without cause with no avenues for redress. Further, it was common for black workers when hired to find that they were paid far less than their white counterparts. Even more troubling, black workers had to accept these conditions because there were very few opportunities for them to work. Black men in my community would often talk about the difference in their pay as opposed to that of whites when they were doing the same duties at work. There was a lot of anger in their voices. Yet they knew that there was very little they could do to change the situation. Even the slightest complaint or expression of opposition could lead to being fired. A slogan they used was "last hired, first fired." Because of these conditions, my parents demanded that we study and do well in school. They would say that the only way we would be able to advance beyond agricultural or factory labor and have the opportunity to reach our potential would be through a good education. Additionally, we were told that we would not only have to be as good as whites, but we would have to be even better than the whites, just to get in the door. Education will give you a certain degree of independence.

The reality was that even those blacks who acquired a good education and a profession were not immune from discrimination. There were doctors and lawyers in my community who were prevented from practicing their profession because they could not get licensed or were not allowed access to the benefits of their profession as were whites. Whites often feared black professionals;

therefore, efforts were made to exclude them from professional groups and organizations. For example, the first black Supreme Court Justice of South Carolina, Justice Earnest A. Finney Jr., a family friend, completed law school in the early 1960s and was admitted to the South Carolina Bar. However, even though he was a certified member of the bar and was required to pay his dues, he was not allowed to attend the meeting of the bar because of his race. Justice Finney shared that he attended the first meeting of the South Carolina Bar Association as a waiter. However, Justice Finney further shared that when he attended his last meeting of the bar, he did so as the Chief Justice in 1999. While this demonstrates the amount of change that has occurred in the South, many challenges continue to face blacks, especially black men.

MY LIVED EXPERIENCES

While I experienced much of the discrimination focused on blacks while growing up in South Carolina, I now realize that my family was blessed in many respects. Even though my great-great-great-grandfather was a slave, he was given 50 acres when the Civil War ended and was able to develop them into a future for our family. By the early 1930s my family owned one of the largest farms in Sumter County, the county in which I grew up. We were one of the black families in our community with some degree of financial independence. Because of my grandfather's foresight and planning, we were shielded from many of the negative conditions that other black families had to endure.

Still, I was always cognizant that as a black child I was treated differently from white children. This was a difference that could be deadly during a time when blacks were demanding equality and respect. I can remember in the early 1960s when the Civil Rights movement was getting under way that there were teachers in our school who were terminated for belonging to the National Association for the Advancement of Colored People (NAACP). I also recall the Orangeburg Massacre that took place in 1968 when college students from South Carolina State College (a traditional black college) attempted to enter a local public bowling hall in Orangeburg, South Carolina. State Highway Patrol officers attacked a group of black students and shot them to death during this incident. These killings demonstrated, in tangible terms, to the black population of the state that state officials were willing to use whatever measures necessary to keep blacks "in their place." This helped to galvanize the civil rights movement in the state, because now there was a realization that even black children were potential targets of deadly force to maintain the status quo. No longer could they trust their government to protect them from the hatred of those in the general population when state leaders were part of the mob. Any degree of trust that had been established between law enforcement and black communities in the state was certainly placed in doubt following the shooting of unarmed students in Orangeburg. It was chilling to think that had I been older, I could have potentially been one of these students. The events in Orangeburg demonstrated to me in tangible terms that the black population was under siege from the state, and white leaders were willing to use deadly force to maintain the status quo.

In recent years, while listening to the news accounts of the events in Bosnia and Kosovo and the treatment of the Albanian people, I realized that I could relate to the plight of these people. The situations that I experienced growing up black in white America were very similar to growing up as a captive in enemy territory. Though we had committed no crime or other offense, we were being punished for being born with black skin. Some of the tactics used against black citizens prior to and during the civil rights movement were motivated by a similar mentality as was the "ethnic cleansing" used against the Albanians under the regime of Slobodan Milosevic.

I can recall as early as 12 or 13 years of age visiting the local doctor's office and noting there were two waiting areas, one clearly labeled "Whites" and the other "Colored." Simply seeing that we were being separated because of our race caused me to wonder at that age why were we required to wait to see the same white doctor in a separate waiting area. I was a person—not a "colored" person. This same practice of separating the races was applied to the local swimming pool. The maintenance of the pool was financed with all citizens' taxes; therefore, it should have been a public pool. However, the pool's use was reserved for whites only. Day after day during the hot southern summers my black friends and I would see whites enjoying the pool. We were forced to confront the fact that because of our race we were not allowed to swim in the very pool our parents were forced to support with their taxes. Despite how humiliating this was, we realized that we could not change the situation at that time. We moved on and found another place in the community to swim. However, that experience was something I never would forget.

Having experienced such discrimination instilled in me at an early age the idea that I was living in a society that was unfair and did not treat all persons with equal respect. As I grew up and became an adult, my life experiences continued to reinforce the idea that there was a lack of equality and justice in society. When I entered the workplace, I soon discovered that it was not a place where qualified black males were welcomed. After college, armed with degrees, young black men were again confronted with the fact that skin color determined the type of jobs available. I personally observed whites with fewer qualifications being given positions through the "good old boy network." As my parents had told me, I had to work harder "just to get in the front door." Efforts to level the playing field through affirmative action programs were attacked as showing special treatment or requiring quotas. It continues to be astounding to me that conservative white males (and females) who themselves are beneficiaries of all sorts of special treatment continue to make such an argument.

Affirmative action is not simply quotas, or giving positions to unqualified individuals. Affirmative action is a program that strives to address decades of discrimination against blacks. The goal of the program is to ensure all persons are made aware of opportunities and given equal access to compete on their merits and without prejudice. Whites have a program of affirmative action called "connections." They are able to get top-level positions based on connections, yet we don't hear arguments about the need to abolish the system of gaining access based on "connections." The concept of access based on "connections" is the basis for many wealthy families financing expensive education at Ivy League schools. The connections made during college may be more important to future success than is the education received. For example, family connections led to the appointment of our current president, George W. Bush. Mr. Bush is clearly the most intellectually challenged president this country has had. His appointment to the office of president is to a great degree due to family wealth and connections. Certainly this is a glowing example of the affirmative action program for whites—the "good old boy" system in operation. His appointment of "selected blacks" to positions in his administration does not obscure the fact that elitist whites have retained control of the system in this country. It is only in recent years that a few privileged blacks have been able to become part of this connection system as is exemplified by those blacks Bush has made a part of his cabinet in an effort to appear "inclusive."

As is the case with other black males of my generation, the experiences from my childhood help to form my opinions and the thoughts about the world that I have taken into adulthood. The prejudice and inequity experienced during our adolescent years demonstrated to us that America was not "crowned with brotherhood from sea to shining sea." We learned that because of the color of our skin we would always be considered the "outsider" in society. Such an understanding is the source of a great deal of anger for myself as well as other black males. It serves to keep us ever suspicious of the "majority" society.

SOUTHERN SOCIETY AT THE CROSSROADS

The black male of the 21st century is likely to be characterized by a sense of anger resulting from past experience with prejudice and discrimination. Today white males continue to hold 95% of the top-level jobs in corporate America, as well as governmental positions. Most likely, this is not always a result of their being the best qualified for such positions. Often they acquired these positions based on preferential treatment to a great extent based on race. Even when it is necessary for blacks to be hired or promoted, it is often the black female who is targeted for such hiring or promotion. One possible explanation for this is that white men find black women less threatening. Such comfort with black women may have its roots in a historical social system in which many white men had black women as caregivers when they were children. In contrast, black men such as myself may be stereotypically perceived as physically aggressive.

Like every black male of my age group, I have experienced the fear of "driving while black." There is no question that many police continue to use racial profiling to stop a black male for questioning. It is not uncommon for some police officers to intentionally insult black males during such stops in hopes of provoking a negative reaction, thus creating "justification" for the use of deadly force or to take them to jail. While it is true that black males commit far too many criminal acts, the percentage of black males to white males in prison remains excessive when actual crime rates of both groups are compared. Additionally, the punishment for drug convictions given to black men is far more severe than that given to white men who commit the same crime. In my experience, the black male is considered a suspect first and a citizen with rights second.

Take for example the recent case of a young white woman from Union, South Carolina, who killed her two children. The mother killed her children in cold blood, and to cover her crime offered the explanation that a black man had abducted her children in the process of stealing her car. Without even bothering to check the facts surrounding the report, the local sheriff and state authorities began to round up local black men for questioning. For black citizens of South Carolina, this again exemplified an all too familiar situation. It was clear to black men in the state that the mother reported a black man as the perpetrator of the crime because she knew local law enforcement officials would readily accept the idea of a black man committing such an offense. What is even more disturbing is the fact that her plan worked. I can recall vividly that when I heard the news that the mother had confessed to murdering her two children, I was at a meeting that included a number of black men. The outrage we all felt about this case could easily be seen on each of our faces. There was a common understanding that we as black men had all been victims in this case. Clearly, we all could relate, yet again, to an incident in which "the black male" was demonized by a white person as a tool of convenience.

In the new millennium there continues to be a lot of work needed in order to bring the races together. Of those groups that are singled out for discrimination and negative stereotyping in society, black men are particularly the targets of such actions. Black men are often viewed as the ultimate "boogie man." Because of such views, many young black males have developed a sense of contempt for white-structured society and elect to separate themselves in "black only" groups. Many of these young men are not the stereotypical ghetto gang member, but rather the products of middle-class families who continue to experience racism either overtly or through subtle actions that attempt to keep them "in their place." Clearly separation is not the solution to the problem, but continued engagement with society at all levels is needed.

In my experience, southern society is characterized by a "Jekyll and Hyde" pattern. While conditions between the races in many cases are severely divided, true and honest friendships exist across the racial divide. Further, while many in the South have often adhered to a principle of separation, there are those individuals, black and white, who refused to accept the structured society. It is this spark within such individuals that will ensure a continued positive transition into the new millennium. It will be important for young black men not to lose their sense of history. Black men (and women) have struggled and suffered to build this country from its very beginning.

Growing up black in a white-dominated society in the South has given me a deep sense of strength and confidence. I realized early on that many people would attempt to judge me not on the content of my character, but by color. Such stereotypes would attempt to define who I was and determine my destiny. However, when someone attempts to box me in or define who I am based on negative stereotypes, it makes me more determined to prove them wrong. I have seen firsthand how such negative ideas about a race of people have been used as tools against them. This is why I am so involved in the political affairs of my community and state. I have consistently worked to help ensure that blacks are aware of their rights, and that they are able to enjoy all of the rights and privileges citizenship entitles them to enjoy.

My experiences have also given me a strong sense of independence and the will to remain focused in spite of the many distractions. I have internalized the wisdom of my parents and former teachers who instilled in me the fact that I would have to be twice as efficient just to be considered as equally qualified as whites. This attitude and the tenacity to determine my own destiny have enabled me to achieve a certain degree of financial stability and upward mobility. Over the past 20 years in my job with state government, I have become a recognized expert in the areas of the financial management and development of affordable federally funded housing in South Carolina. I frequently travel around the state to offer seminars to low-income families in order to help them prepare to transition to home ownership and a better life. My past experiences in facing discrimination have reinforced the importance of helping those trying to make a better life for themselves, regardless of their race, to make that first step to financial stability.

Black churches have historically been a focal point of spiritual guidance and community activism. The church has had a major role in helping me to remain focused and has given me the strength to reach my goals. Through the church I have maintained a strong faith in the ultimate "goodness" of people, but have, also, worked to be sure that the voices of black men and women are heard. Clearly, the experiences from my past and my awareness of history have shaped me into a self-reliant individual. I have become one black male who is determined to use my education as well as the opportunities I have been afforded to exemplify what black men can achieve if they do not let themselves be defined by the negative stereotypes of others. How black men remember and value the lessons learned in the long struggle our ancestors have made from slavery will help determine the future and character of the 21st-century black man.

REFERENCES

Davis, M. W. (1976). *South Carolina's Black and Native Americans: 1776–1796.* Columbia, SC: South Carolina Human Affairs Commission.

DeSantis, V. (1974). The age of industrialism and urbanization: 1865–1900. In
C. Degler, T. C. Cochran, V. DeSantis, H. Hamilton, W.H. Harbaugh, A. S. Link,

R. B. Nye, D. M. Potter, & C. L. Ver Steeg (Eds.), *The democratic experience*. Glenview, IL: Scott Forman and Company.

Eibling, H. H., King, F. M., & Harlow, J. (1966). *History of our United States*. River Forest, IL: Laidlaw Brothers.

Fitzhugh, G. (1857). *Slaves without masters*. Richmond, VA: A. Morris.

Fisher, L. H., Jr., & Quarles, B. (1968). *The Black American documentary history*. Glenview, IL: Scott Forman and Company.

Franklin, J. H. (1969). *From slavery to freedom—History of Negro Americans* (pp. 342–345). New York: Vantage Press.

Schweickert, C. (2001, January 10). USC integrated peacefully in '63—has quality Black history program. *The State Newspaper*, 110, B–1, B–5.

Spruill, J. C. (1972). *Women's life and work in the southern colonies*. New York: W.W. Norton & Company.

CHAPTER 40

GROWING UP WHITE IN BLACK AMERICA

Preston Jones

In the first scene of his abysmal film *The Jerk*, Steve Martin says that he was born a "poor black child." Soon thereafter, viewers see Martin trying, unsuccessfully, to keep the rhythm as the southern black family—into which he had been adopted as a baby—fiddle funky tunes. It isn't true that white men can't dance, nor is it true that all black men can, though American popular culture seems to suggest otherwise. So there's poor Steve Martin, fanning the flames of stereotype, trying to be a black guy and making a fool of, one might say, himself.

Despite the fact that I myself grew up the sole white boy in a overwhelmingly black neighborhood, I never considered myself "black," though I inevitably absorbed much of the lower-class black culture that existed in the Bench Area in San Bernardino, California. When the white boys across town were listening to Led Zeppelin and Aerosmith, I jammed to Lakeside, Parliament, and other soul bands. I never tried to be agile on my feet, let alone to "pop" or "breakdance," but I did speak a form of what I later learned is called "black English" or "ebonics." I spoke it well enough, that is, to signal to white folks that I lived in a black part of town, but I never spoke it well enough to fit in among the "players" (i.e., "playboys") in my neighborhood. To this day, black English is my preferred tongue, though it's been a long time since I've spoken it. And since it's the language of the guys who made life so hard for me until I joined the U.S. Navy in 1986, I can't but hear it and be reminded of the violence that my sister and I endured on account of our skin color.

I don't know how many times I've been asked why in my adult academic life I study and write on French Quebec and Welsh-speaking Wales—even to the point where I read Welsh almost daily and speak French with a Quebecois accent. Several years ago I used to say that I didn't really know where this interest came from; I said that I just possessed some abstract interest in small groups who were compelled always to struggle to preserve their language and culture. A few years ago, though, it finally occurred to me: I study the Quebecois and the Welsh because at some level I identify with their experience as small people surrounded by powerful and very different neighbors. I wasn't born a "poor black child," but I grew up a lower-lower-middle-class white boy in a black world, and that experience has made me into a man who is at all times uncomfortable with the world.

I am obliged to confess that because of the things I endured as a white boy in a black world, I bear some resentment against black America. There is little that angers me as quickly as African-American men who are unwilling to see or to admit that racism is just as endemic in segments of black America as it ever was in any precinct in the Deep South. But because of the atmosphere in which I grew up, I am also uncomfortable with middle-class white America, its niceties and pretensions. There was a frank openness about feeling in the Bench Area that I have missed since leaving it, though sometimes that openness manifested itself murderously: four guys I knew growing up had been gunned down or beaten to death by the time I left the Navy in 1990. And while I have never figured this out, I always thought it interesting that before I was to be "jumped" by a mob of black boys, I would usually be given a lecture on why I was about to get hammered. "What did you say about my mama?" was the usual rhetorical question put to me by a kid I hardly knew or had never seen before. One time I was told that I was going to get thrashed because Jesus was black and hated white people.

Of course, I was sometimes rescued by older black folks (usually middle-aged women) who, perhaps remembering the difficulties faced by blacks in the Deep South in the 1960s, saw the irony in their younger counterparts' actions. Once an elderly woman let me run for safety into her home and there wondered aloud how it was that Martin Luther King, Jr., was everywhere a hero and nowhere a role model.

In all my years, I have met only one other white guy who grew up in circumstances similar to mine. Unlike me, he had become associated with a gang in Washington, D.C., and even in Navy technical school he "acted" much more "black" than I did, though both of us gravitated toward the black guys in our division. And it seemed that, to some extent, he had experienced much more acceptance than I had. His girlfriend was black. His good friends were all black. His swagger was black. For my part, I could, and still can, put a slight black intonation and accent into my voice, but I can't say that I really had any black friends in my neighborhood. In fact, I've never had a good black friend at all.

Sometimes I played football or basketball with the black boys back in the old 'hood, but they always kept their distance from me, and I kept my distance from them. We understood that we could never be "brothers." That's because I was associated with "The Man." Even the black guys I associated with the most never came to my defense, and I admit that I hold that against them to this day. Were I ever to hear one of them say aloud something about racism in white America, I don't think I'd be able to keep myself from punching him in the mouth.

But wouldn't it be nice if those guys and I could get together some day and shake our heads at our foolishness? Perhaps, swallowing their manly pride, they could admit that they should have defended me—words would have been enough—but that they didn't because they didn't think that I, being white, was worth defending. And I could apologize to them for nursing a low-grade, simmering grudge (men are good at that). I could also admit that I understand that there are historical reasons for the anger they nursed. Then maybe they could recognize that I personally had nothing to do with slavery or the Jim Crow South. Then perhaps we could agree that, at bottom, we're all made of the same old dirt.

And then we could shake hands (black style, or white) and get on with our 21st-century lives.

VOICES EIGHT

VIOLENCE AND ABUSE

Chapter 41

Touch

Charles Weathers

To be touched is what some long for.
To be touched is what some hope for.

To be touched is why some cry.
To be touched is why some want to die.

As a child I felt the touch
Of a loving mother holding me close,
Of a father who cared and would give all he had.
There was the teacher who comforted me during a test.
There was the coach who assured me in the midst of the game.
There was that first love, a touch I'll never forget.
All touches I felt, even when they used no hands,
These are the touches that I remember and focus on.
These are the touches that helped make me who I am.

Others touched me too. No one knows of course
Because not all touches are meant for public knowledge.
Not all touches are meant to be seen.
It took 35 years to admit it, face it, and say it.
I wasn't at fault but that still doesn't change it.
I never told Mom or Dad, the coach or the teacher
That other boys had touched me and tried to hurt me.
I guess if they were just other boys, I might have said something,
But they were related, and how do you tell a parent that?
I don't know.
And how do you say it now? I mean after all,
I have an image to uphold, don't I? At this point who cares?
I guess this is what people mean when they say, "Do it for someone else."
I often wondered why I treated women the way I do,

Why I seemed to try so hard to prove that I was a man.
Why was sex the definition of my manhood?
I believe I was trying to do all I could to prove that I
Liked girls and not boys.
I guess these touches helped make me too.

I hope this touches you the right way.

To be touched is what some long for.
To be touched is what some hope for.

To be touched is why some cry.
To be touched is why some want to die.

CHAPTER 42

WHISPERING IN THE WIND: GARY'S STORY OF CHILDHOOD SEXUAL ABUSE

As told to Julie Evertz

The action of the secret passes
continually from the hider of
things to the hider of self
>   Gaston Bachlard, The Poetics of Space

SILENT SORROWS

As the proud father of two sons, ages 7 and 9, I thank God for letting me live to see them grow into the wonderful young men I am sure they are to be. There was a long time in my life when I never thought fatherhood a possibility. A victim of sexual abuse by my stepfather when I was 8 years old, I kept silent, buried the shame, hurt, guilt, anger, and fear that surrounded the experience for years. At the time, I told no one. Thirty-two years ago, who would have believed an 8-year-old boy's claims of such an evil act? I was alone in every way. Aloneness was the worst form of despair for me. Unlike today, child abuse was not widely acknowledged, let alone discussed, when I was victimized. It was and still is even less acknowledged if you happen to be a boy. Most of society still clings to the illusion that evil acts of sexual abuse happen only to girls. Society expects men to be strong, aggressive, and able protectors even as little boys. Even today, reminders of those social constructions prevail, which is why I choose to remain anonymous. I want to protect my boys and perhaps myself. I suppose I am afraid. As a rule, the world does not hand out compassion without conditions. However, I also realized that I had an opportunity to share my story with others, to put my past abuse and pain not behind me, but right in front of me, not to try to forget, but to try always to remember. Secrecy only results in despair. This is also an opportunity for me to wake up society to the reality that little boys are viciously abused too. The effects of such abuse are experienced and felt forever in one way or another. I am fortunate and I never forget it. It is only through intensive and continued discussion of my experience within the context of a therapeutic relationship that I survive my childhood memories and that I continue to create and re-create my adulthood. I consider childhood sexual abuse a chronic experience that relives itself consciously and unconsciously over and over again. There is no cure. It can not be forgotten, nor do I believe it should be forgotten, but it can be disarmed of its potentially life-damaging consequences within the context of a therapeutic environment. I have worked hard at disarmament and continue to do so with the support of my wife and children.

Gary's Story

As a child, I grew up on a farm in an area of the country that is quaintly called the heartland of America. The societal and local community "rules" of the time were, and to some extent still are:

Keep to yourself.

Family problems stay in the family.

Don't let anyone know what you have.

Don't be a burden to anyone in your family or community.

Contribute to the family.

Maintain a quiet, plain, and pleasant image at all times.

Solve your own problems (or bury them).

Don't bring attention to yourself or your family.

Spirituality is something for church every Sunday.

I lived these "rules" for years. They nearly destroyed my life.

I don't remember my biological father. I was told by my mother that he died in an automobile accident when I was 3 years old. I never doubted her. I grew up an only child. Until I was abused by my stepfather, I often wondered why my mother never had any more children. Afterwards, I was grateful. My mother was very kind and gentle but lived her life as a farmer's wife with duty and honor to her husband and few questions. My mother was also practical. She knew a farm could not tend itself and without a man around the house, we would be forced to leave it to face an uncertain future. She couldn't leave. It was her entire life and all that she knew. My mother had little family support or options. Within a year of my father's death, my mother met and married my stepfather Hank.

Hank had moved to our town from another farm community not far from ours. Considering the "rules," it was not unusual that my mother knew little about him before she married. As an adult, I learned that Hank had been abused and beaten as a child by his own father, an alcoholic who eventually left town. So, Hank grew up alone with his mother. He was an able farmer and worked hard. He did not drink or smoke. He was stern. His voice had a fearful tone to it. Despite the thousands of hours I have devoted to reliving this time in my life, I never expected him to molest me, to violate my body and mind in such an evil way. I have searched my mind for signs that I missed, reasons for his behavior, and blamed myself. My mother, also an only child, worked the farm with my stepfather. She was responsible for the inside of our house and making sure the meals were prepared. As I think of it now, it was terribly oppressive, but oppression was acceptable or at least not challenged.

I was always considered "a good child" who did my chores without question. Besides, living on a farm doesn't allow much opportunity for rebellion. My days were grueling; at least they seemed so to me. I woke up at 5 A.M., collected the eggs from the chickens (an acquired skill over time), swept out the cow stalls, had breakfast, walked to school, then returned home for more chores before supper, homework, and finally bedtime. Each day went into the next and life was fairly routine and boring. As the "good child" I never voiced a complaint. My mother would ask me about school but in a vague and hurried way that tried to express interest. She was always busy doing something as if on a schedule with little time for contingencies. It was a lonely life for a child. It is a lonely life being a contingency.

I will never forget the one evening my stepfather called me to the barn. I was 8 years old. That particular evening changed my life forever. It would be the last time I trusted for years. I assumed that he needed me to perform some chore. When I reached the barn he asked me to put some clean straw in the cow stalls. As I was doing so, he came up behind me and asked me to take off my clothes. He explained that I should feel the straw against my skin as the animals do in order to appreciate how they lived and to emphasize the importance of taking care of them. He told me that he would do the same so I wouldn't feel strange. Obedient, I did as I was told and lay in the straw without my clothes. My stepfather laid down next to me without his clothes. Suddenly, he began to touch me all over my body. He then asked me to do the same to him, even putting my hand on particular body parts. He explained that he wanted me to know about being a man and that it was his responsibility as a father to teach me about what a man's body could do and how it was different from a woman's body. He told me that I could not tell my mother because this was something that boys and their fathers kept secret. He convinced me that he was trusting me with this "tradition." He made it seem like an honor. I kept thinking that I was only a boy. Why did I need to know how to be a man and in this way? Still, I said nothing to my mother. I respected and feared my stepfather though I never showed any fear with him.

His "lessons" continued for almost 2 years. Over time, I came to dread our meetings in the barn and his "lessons" on how to be a man. I started feeling uncomfortable with it, as my friends never mentioned anything about having experienced such a thing in any of their conversations. Was this really a tradition between fathers and sons? Was every boy and father doing this and was every boy sworn to secrecy? These questions kept haunting me over time. Finally, one evening, I flat out refused his "lessons" and told him that I didn't want to do this anymore. I told him that I believed that I had learned enough. I was punished with more chores and he rarely spoke to me after my proclamation. Abandonment was my punishment. It was as if nothing had happened. Two years later, my stepfather had a sudden heart attack and died. Secretly, I was relieved. Our secret "lessons" died with him, or so I thought, but I was never quite the same. My mother sold the farm and we moved to "the city." My mother found a job working for a local church. She seemed to like the work, and I was thankful beyond words to leave the farm.

I had fooled myself into thinking that I could erase my past, or at least forget it, and start fresh in a new city surrounded by new people. As I later learned, nothing can be erased. I buried myself in my studies and finished high school with very decent grades. I applied to a college as far away from home as I could find. I wanted to be an engineer. I was good at building and math and both had always fascinated me. I attended college on the east coast of the United States, having received a partial scholarship. The remainder of my expenses were covered by loans and various jobs. Though I spoke to my mother on the phone, I only saw her twice after leaving for college, and I have never been back home. She died of pneumonia before I graduated. If I could have asked her one question, it would have been, "Did you know?"

ONLY A CHILD

It is amazing to me how life's distractions such as school, homework, chores at home, part-time jobs, friends, families, and professional responsibilities can keep us from really living. In truth, those distractions serve a purpose. The purpose for me was to keep me alive, but I was not really living. I was unconsciously existing and functioning to fit societal expectations and keep my secrets hidden from myself and from others. I was unconsciously pretending to live. Soon after graduation, I was offered a good job as a structural engineer. It was then that my emotional problems developed. At first, I was excited about my job and immersed myself in it. However, my distractions were now down to one, and I found it harder to function every day. I was increasingly anxious and seclusive, even discouraging potential friendships. I felt sad and alone and began to see my job as perfunctory. I was on my way to self-destruction through my self-imposed isolation. I was too scared to trust anyone for fear of being abandoned again, so it seemed natural to avoid relationships.

A colleague from work noticed my apparently visible decline and suggested over dinner that I see a psychologist. She went on to say how it had made a huge difference in her life. My first reaction was skepticism since this idea went against everything I was brought up to believe. My colleague had recommended a particular female therapist. After careful thought and my continued emotional decline into depression, I followed her suggestion, and, as if begging for help, began therapy. I have to admit, I felt completely awkward and out of place at first. I was the only man in the waiting area. All I could think of was that I was definitely breaking the "rules." I am glad that I did. I will never forget my first session with my therapist. She asked me only one question: What was my biggest secret that I could share? That one question opened up a dam of emotions that had been pushed down since childhood. I discovered that secrecy and all that it entails was dangerous and hurtful and ruining my life. No one had ever paid attention to me. No one had ever taken the time to listen. No one could see or feel my pain. I had become adept at hiding it in order to take care of everyone but myself. At home, I was silenced by expectations, shame, guilt, anger, betrayal, a lack of protection, and distrust. I wasn't aware of any of those feelings until I began reflecting on them and my abuse.

Over the next several years through counseling, I related all of my experiences with my stepfather, the questions I had about my mother's knowledge of those times, which at the time of my abuse I dared to entertain in my mind. What I now understand is that my stepfather was a mentally ill man. That he exploited my unconscious fear of abandonment by yet another father and used me for his own sick purposes was child abuse. It was not my fault. I was only a child. He had power over me. I trusted him to protect me and instead he hurt me. My mother did not protect me. These are not easy things to admit or speak about, yet I live with those revelations everyday and I feel much healthier having revealed them. I have been married 10 years now to Angela, my colleague, best friend, and soul mate, who helped me find my way out of my childhood and into adulthood.

PREVALENCE OF MALE SEXUAL ABUSE: WRITER INTERJECTS

Our understanding of child sexual abuse in general, and of male sexual abuse specifically, is obscure. Child sexual abuse is not often differentiated. Children still remain powerless with adults in control. It is important to distinguish the sexual abuse of children from the general category of child abuse, if we are to help these innocent victims heal into healthy adults.

Every child is vulnerable to sexual abuse. Research indicates that one out of every four children will be the victim of sexual abuse. Specifically, reports estimate the prevalence of childhood sexual abuse to range from 6% to 62% for females and from 3% to 31% for males. In a 1985 survey of 2,626 adult men and women, 16% of the men reported having been sexually abused. As with all forms of child maltreatment, reported cases are assumed to be underestimates of the true extent of sexual abuse.

Very young children as well as teenagers are victimized. Almost all of these children will be abused by someone they know and trust: a relative, family friend, or caretaker. Sexual abuse can be physical, verbal, or emotional and includes:

Sexual touching and fondling.

Exposing children to adult sexual activity or pornographic movies and photos.

Having children pose, undress, or perform in a sexual fashion on film or in person.

"Peeping" into bathrooms or bedrooms to spy on a child.

Rape or attempted rape.

Sexual abuse involves forcing, tricking, bribing, threatening, or pressuring a child into sexual awareness or activity. Sexual abuse occurs when an older or more knowledgeable child or adult uses a child for sexual pleasure. The abuse often begins gradually and increases over time.

The use of physical force is rarely necessary to engage a child in sexual activity because children are trusting and dependent. They want to please others and gain love and approval. Children are taught not to question authority and they believe that adults are always right. Additionally, social, cultural, and religious traditions and beliefs hold power over children. Perpetrators of child sexual abuse know this and take advantage of these vulnerabilities in children. Sexual abuse is an abuse of power over a child, an act of violence, and a violation of a child's right to healthy, nurturing, and trusting relationships.

Most children—especially boys due to the social expectations placed on them—do not tell about being sexually abused. Often children do not tell anyone about sexual abuse because they:

Are too young to put what has happened into words.

Were too threatened or bribed by the abuser to keep the abuse a secret.

Feel confused by the attention and feelings accompanying the abuse.

Are afraid that no one will believe them.

Blame themselves or believe the abuse is punishment for being bad.

Feel too ashamed or embarrassed to tell.

Worry about getting into trouble or getting a loved one into trouble.

Silence enables sexual abuse to continue. Silence protects sexual offenders and hurts children who are being abused. Sexual abuse is an extremely complex and damaging experience. Sadly, the damages are usually lifelong.

Physical evidence of sexual abuse is rare. Therefore, behavioral signs should be given attention. Unfortunately, there is no one behavior alone that definitely determines that a child has been sexually abused. Many general behavior changes, such as depression, sleep disturbances, school problems, low self-esteem, self-destructive behavior, drug or alcohol abuse, hostility or aggression, anxiety, delinquent acts, and eating disorders can be attributed to a myriad of illnesses or experiences. However, children who have been sexually abused frequently have some specific symptoms:

Copying adult sexual behavior.

Persistent sexual play with other children, themselves, toys, or pets.

Displaying sexual knowledge, through language or behavior, that is beyond what is age appropriate or developmentally expected.

Unexplained pain, swelling, bleeding, or irritation of the mouth, genital, or anal area; urinary infections; sexually transmitted diseases.

Hints, indirect comments, or statements about the abuse.

Children who have been sexually abused feel many different and often overwhelming emotions that include:

Fear of the abuser, of causing trouble, of losing adults important to them, of being taken away from home.

Anger at the abuser, at other adults around them who did not protect them, at themselves (feeling as if they caused trouble).

Isolation because "something is wrong with me," because they feel alone in their experience, because they have trouble talking about the abuse.

Sadness about having something taken from them, about losing a part of themselves, about growing up too fast, about being betrayed by someone they trusted.

Guilt for not being able to stop the abuse, for believing they "consented" to the abuse, for telling—if they told, for not keeping the secret—or for not telling.

Shame about being involved in the experience, about their bodies' response to the abuse.

Confusion because they may still love the abuser, because their feelings change all the time.

It is important to note that many of the emotions described above are, in fact, unconscious. Left in unawareness, the abused child grows into the abused adult, manifesting many of the symptoms described earlier and proceeding down a path of suffering with seemingly no visible relief. As with Gary, this was particularly true until he sought psychological help in understanding what had happened to him as a child and how that was affecting his adulthood, and was allowed the opportunity to express his emotions in a safe and therapeutic context. Back to Gary now.

BOYS DO CRY

For the past 32 years I have lived knowing that someone I loved hurt me and continues to hurt me even though he is dead. Of course, as a child, I was unaware that I was being hurt. I was trying to be the "good child" that I had always been. My stepfather had also been a victim of child abuse. Unfortunately for both of us, he remained in denial of his own abuse by his father and the abuse he did to me. Though never violent as a result of my rejection of him, my stepfather virtually broke all communication with me. My mother never noticed. I find that incredible. What I understand today is that my stepfather used me at a time when I was vulnerable and desperately in need of comfort. I wanted a father. In the beginning, he was seemingly harmless and a good provider. My mother was happy, so I suppose that made me happy. If I had seen any sign of violence or felt any discomfort around him prior to my abuse, I would have tried to warn my mother or run away, but that was not the case.

As a result of his abuse toward me, I grew up feeling unworthy of love, isolating myself from others. Books were my friends and school was my escape. I even tried running away from my emotions by putting as much physical distance as possible between myself and that farm when I attended college. Eventually, the emotions won and I started what I called "melting." What might seem crazy to those who have not experienced sexual abuse as a male child is that melting seemed okay at the time. It was preferable to being mentally tortured by the memories, guilt, anger, and shame. It was preferable to crying, since boys are not supposed to cry in our society. I broke that rule too. There were times when I felt like killing myself, the last attempt I suppose, at escape. I am forever thankful to God and to my wife Angela who, at my lowest, felt my pain and urged me to seek help. I don't know why I took her suggestion but I am so glad that I did. I realize that I am one of the fortunate few who live through and with such childhood atrocities. It has only been through continual self-reflection that much of these connections and emotions became a part of my awareness. Once aware, I could disarm them.

WHISPERS

One way or another, my stepfather silenced me, beat me, and won. He beat my spirit, my trust, my innocence, my sense of safety, and my love and feeling of connectedness with the world and those who espoused to love me. They were silent beatings but they did as much damage, if not more, than any physical violation did. One might think it cowardly that I kept silent. I considered it survival. Feeling invisible and knowing I was unheard as a child made me afraid and kept me quiet. Being quiet became reflexive. No one around me or our family knew what he did to me. I had been well taught in the art of secrecy during my many "lessons" with my stepfather. Over time, I was brainwashed into feeling like I was someone's property, his property, an object to be used at will by someone more powerful than I. The mental control he had over me was very strong and I never tried to speak out of fear. He made me doubt myself often. I hated that feeling the most.

My stepfather often told me that he wasn't going to hurt me. Maybe he really meant what he said. Words can be empty. He did hurt me, not only as a child but for many of my adult years. What angers me the most is that I can not hurt him back because he is dead. My stepfather's control over me was pervasive, yet he saw none of it, or if he did, I suppose he didn't care. Most of the people with whom he associated and those who knew our family believed him to be a good man, an honorable man, and a hard worker. But he was not good to me. How does a young boy fight that illusion? Public persona is powerful and frightening. It is another form of silencing another. That ability to silence can be deadly.

For most of my childhood, I lived in fear of my stepfather but no one would have known it. As a child, I used to dream of what it would be like to live without that fear, to come home from school relaxed and happy, to not have to go to that barn. My stepfather was a regretful and negative person who I know also suffered. He suffered from unawareness until the day he died.

I can't fully reconcile my feelings of fear, intimidation, and anger at his memory. Deep down, I fear the anger. I suppose I am afraid that if I allow myself to be really angry, something bad will happen to me. That was reinforced every time my stepfather sexually abused me. What also haunts me is that I believe that he felt he had the right to do what he did to me or that it was justified somehow. As sick as it sounds, I believe that unconsciously, my stepfather enjoyed having the power over me at the time. I felt and was helpless. Sometimes when I close my eyes, I can see the expression on his face during our "lessons" in the barn. I can't forget those times. I can't forgive them either. Never once did he admit remorse or responsibility for his actions. I believe that in his mind, he did nothing wrong. Lessons that I had learned as a child, the rules of the community that I obeyed, kept me a prisoner of my own abuse.

Fear had been an effective form of discipline. I never realized how much power there is in social constructions. They are hard to change. Boys are to be strong, tough willed, protectors, and providers. They are to show no emotions. Those were the messages given to me and to a great degree, still remain today. Guilt was also an effective form of discipline and regulation with me. Though I was not aware of it at the time, my stepfather was the one person with whom distance in every way felt comfortable. As a result of his abuse toward me, I lost another father. I almost lost myself. What my stepfather and perhaps others could not understand is my experience of emptiness as a result of such a violation, of one minute being innocent and the next having that innocence taken from me. I wasn't asked. I was completely dehumanized. Sometimes it is difficult for me, let alone anyone else, to believe what I endured as a child, and I lived it. As my new friend so eloquently put it, abuse is a private hell. No statement is truer for those who have been sexually abused. It is even more so for men in that we must carry on the facade of societal expectations, pushing our feelings down at the expense of our physical and mental health. That expectation is also abuse in my opinion. I refused to be victimized again. That is why I sought help to cope with what had happened to me. I was not going to let Hank or society win.

I have to say that my emotional abuse was greater than my physical abuse. It slowly ate away my self-esteem, which has required much rebuilding. It caused me years of self-imposed isolation for fear of being "found out" as having been sexually abused. I hid from myself. I hid from others who cared for me. Ironically, I now know that you cannot hide and it was all an illusion to try to do so. Knowing that I was sexually abused as a child is a cognitive awareness. On a feeling level, it hurts to the core of my soul. However, over time and with much help from my therapist and the loving support of my wife, I began to replace the experiences of abuse with experiences of safety, trust, love, and care. It is an ongoing process that will never end. I try to show my boys love and compassion always and to provide them with a safe place to be, physically and emotionally.

READING BETWEEN THE LINES

As an adult, I felt compelled to play the role that society expected. I was a functional professional who followed the law and tried to contribute to society in a positive way. I was strong and showed no weakness such as emotions. All of this is insane. Men cry. I cry. It doesn't make me weak to do so either. Society needs to cry for all the sexually abused children who go unreported and are forced to live in "hiding," silenced by the social constructions regarding the male role in western cultures. I was told once that there would be a time when I would cry. In truth, I was crying for years and in all that time, among all the people I have known in various contexts, only one person, Angela, saw me crying inside. Maybe it is my fault for not crying hard enough to get anyone's attention. It is hard to cry as a man when you are told your entire life that it is wrong to do so. It is tiring to cry when you feel beaten down and wounded inside. Over time, my cries became almost inaudible. I withdrew as a protective mechanism. In short, I was disappearing in every way possible. I felt lost and alone.

I don't feel either anymore. What stopped me from crying for so long was the fear that no one would believe me, no one would believe in me. That fear distanced me from myself and from others. Distance can kill. I wonder how many other young boys and men suffer from sexual abuse while society and individuals close to them don't see or hear a thing? It is frightening to cry alone, trying to hang on to hope with all the strength and faith you can create, yet continue to feel like you are disappearing. Most sexual abuse victims expect to remain unseen, unheard, and untouched by human kindness. They expect others will give up on them, even trying unconsciously to push them away. Many have already given up on themselves. In that expectation is great despair and suffering. In that suffering there is the perpetuation of distance.

In closing the distance, trust builds, hearts open up to the possibility of accepting love, and healing begins.Sometimes we can best help others by remembering that what we believe about them may be reflected back to them in our own presence and affect them in ways that we do not fully understand. Society's response to men who openly cry is significant. It can be a silencer or a mechanism for relief and compassion. Similarly, the places where we are genuinely seen and heard are sacred and important places for us. They remind us of our value as human beings. They give us strength to go on. Eventually, they may even help transform our suffering from abuse into wisdom.

THE WRITER SUMMARIZES

As Gary so courageously stated while describing his experience of sexual abuse, closeness is what heals and allows for the possibility of greater understanding, empathy, and humanness. Isolation only brings on despair and further distances victims from themselves and others. In order to really understand, I believe that we must immerse ourselves in the world of those who suffer in the context of sexual abuse as a distinct entity and let those who experience such atrocities teach its realities. It is only through genuineness and the capacity to endure a prolonged empathetic connection with all its inherent ordeals that those who suffer find comfort and those who comfort begin to understand the individual's experience. Simply, we must engage in experiential knowing. We cannot offer help or suggestions to those who suffer until we know, to the extent possible, their suffering.

The greatest gift we bring to anyone who is suffering is our wholeness. Listening is a powerful tool of healing. It is often in the quality of our listening and not in the wisdom of our words that we are able to effect the most profound changes in the people around us and in ourselves. It is a relationship of reciprocity with the world. When we listen, we offer with our attention an opportunity for wholeness. Our listening creates a sanctuary for the homeless parts with the suffering individual. Victims of childhood sexual abuse need to be heard and seen in order to alleviate the suffering of the experience. That which has been denied, unloved, devalued, abused by themselves and by others; that which has been hidden can find comfort in our silence and simple presence.

Healing of suffering—in this experience, that of male child sexual abuse— begins with our being real with ourselves, with others, and by having the courage to communicate our realness without preconditions or assumptions; it is giving of ourselves without boundaries. It is only through closeness and greater awareness that we can hope to cocreate with those who suffer, strategies that impact the effects of child sexual abuse. We can also educate our children about sexual abuse In order to increase their awareness and coping skills.

MAKING CARING VISIBLE
THROUGH AWARENESS

We have the ability to provide children with appropriate safety information and support at every stage of their development without frightening them. Although even the best educated child cannot always avoid sexual abuse, children who are well prepared may be more likely to tell if abuse has occurred. This is a child's best defense. In order to protect children we must teach them:

> To feel good about themselves and know they are loved, valued, and deserve to be safe. The difference between safe and unsafe touches.
>
> The proper names for all body parts, so they will be able to communicate clearly.
>
> That safety rules apply to all adults, not just strangers.
>
> That their bodies belong to them and nobody has the right to touch them or hurt them.
>
> That they can say "no" to requests that make them feel uncomfortable even from a close relative or family friend.
>
> To report to someone they feel safe being around (ideally, mother, unless she is the abuser) if any adult asks them to keep a secret.
>
> That some adults have problems.
>
> That they can rely on you to believe and protect them if they tell you about abuse.
>
> That they are not bad or to blame for sexual abuse.
>
> To tell a trusted adult about the abuse even if they are afraid of what may happen.

If a child trusts enough to tell about an incident of abuse, that experience must not be ignored. That child's future depends on responsible and loving adults who are willing to be present in the victim's life as a source of safety, compassion, protection, and stability. Our responsibility is to listen and to take action to protect those who can not protect themselves.

CHAPTER 43

CROSSING THE BRIDGE: MILITARY MEN AND THE FILIPINO SEX TRADE

Preston Jones

In war men have died to keep bridges out of the hands of an enemy. Recall the last battle scene in the nearly womanless *Saving Private Ryan*: all that blood spilled for the sake of a short bridge. Private Ryan himself could have gone home (his three brothers had all been killed in combat), but he chose to stay and defend the bridge, to keep it out of the Germans' hands. Consider also the titles of two major war films: *The Bridge on the River Kwai* and *A Bridge Too Far*.

For obvious reasons, in civilian life bridges are metaphors for human divisions and relationships. "We're building a bridge to the 21st century," said Bill Clinton, as if the future were there already, beckoning. "I'll cross that bridge when I get to it," says your neighbor who has enough on his proverbial plate to worry about than something that can safely be put off a month or two. And civil rights activists say things like, "Let's see if we can build some bridges between our communities."

I believe that when women speak of bridges, they are usually thinking in terms of relationships. Such and such friendship has gotten rocky, my wife might think, so she wants to see if she can "rebuild" the creaking bridge between them. But when men speak of bridges, they often seem to have conquest in mind. Bill Clinton's "bridge to the 21st century" helped to conquer the Republicans in the presidential election of 1996; in comparison, the bridgeless conservatives were made to appear as if their gaze was set only on the past. Even when men do try to establish relationships, employing bridges as metaphors, it seems that they see it mainly as a job to be done. *Make 10 phone calls in the morning, attend the business meeting at lunch, work on forging a bridge with local environmentalist groups later on, get in the evening jog, chat with the wife, go to bed—all in a day's work.*

Perhaps bridges are of greater significance in my own mental world than they are in others'. In the city where I grew up there were clear boundaries—some of them bridges—between neighborhoods. On the west side of Pepper Avenue I

233

was relatively cheerful and easygoing; on the east side (literally when I set my foot on the sidewalk) I became mean-faced, sullen, and had whatever small weapon I'd been carrying in my pocket at the ready. It wasn't a matter of survival: I wasn't afraid that I'd be killed, though I had been shot at. It was rather a matter simply of being fed up with getting pushed around by bullies. I crossed the road and amended my demeanor accordingly. And although the west and east sides of Pepper Avenue weren't linked by a bridge, I thought of the street as such; and since those young teen years, borders, and especially bridges, have figured prominently in my life.

During the time I lived in northern California, after visits with friends in the Silicon Valley, I was always glad to cross the Golden Gate Bridge, because that meant I was making a definite move away from the rat race of the money men and toward the slower world of the coffee men of the Sonoma County wine country. For me, the bridge was the gateway to civilization; crossing it south to north was a happy conquest. For the Silicon boys, on the other hand, it was a gateway to ease, sloth, or, at best, a weekend away from the real world. Either way, the bridge was more than a physical, architectural marker. It was a psychological boundary.

And so it was during the years I lived in Quebec, just two blocks from a bridge that connected that French-speaking province to English-speaking Ontario. In late 1995, when Quebec had its second referendum on independence, I purposely watched the returns on the English side, hoping that later that evening I'd walk home, crossing the Ottawa River, to a new nation. That was a political victory that ended up not coming about, and the trek across the bridge that evening was demoralizing.

During my time in the navy (1986–1990), when I was stationed in Coronado (across the harbor from San Diego), the great Coronado Bridge symbolized to me the border between rush-and-tumble city life and the quiet life of the island. Most of my sailor friends, being good sailors (shipmates were all guys back then), regularly crossed that bridge to get drunk and seek girls and other rewards. I stayed in Coronado, drank coffee, and hung out in the library. That wasn't a very manly thing to do, I suppose, and my buddies told me so. ("Just have some fun! Lighten up!") But I rarely crossed the Coronado Bridge for any reason other than to get out of the San Diego area altogether. In the city were battles I didn't want to fight.

Which brings us to the greatest bridge in my life, which also happens to be the shortest. It was perhaps 30 feet long, and it was the bridge that linked the U.S. Navy base at Subic Bay in the Philippines and the city of Olongapo, a vast village whose chief income was derived from the great brothel industry that had flourished there since the conflict in Vietnam.

I don't know if the bridge had a name, though I do know that it crossed a body of water appropriately called "Shit River." In the river swam Filipino kids who called on U.S. military men to chuck coins at them, and thus black and white and brown American boys pitched their pennies into the muck, watched the Filipinos dive for them, and feasted on their national superiority. Once or twice—I went to the Philippines four times during my enlistment—a legless boy sat on the bridge, his stumps festering, begging for money. From what I saw, he was too much for the American warriors; no one gave him anything. (Strike one up for the Asians.)

And now, I shall take you there.

Cross the bridge over Shit River and, instantly, you're being hit up to buy t-shirts or hats or sunglasses or "monkey meat" from street vendors: it's enough to make a nice guy mad. Or you're being grabbed in the crotch by Filipinas who work in the brothels, have massive debts to pay (though they don't tell you that), and thus need your business ("short-time" or "long-time"): it's enough to make a righteous man blush. Cross the bridge and meet grinding third-world poverty face to face: it's enough to make an enthusiastic free marketeer think twice, for if the market has been unbridled anyway, it was so in Olongapo, circa 1988.

Next, sit down to play a game with your sailor buddies wherein bar girls dispense blow jobs under the round table you're seated at, and the first to crack a smile (the sailors, not the girls) has to buy everyone a drink. Then go to a ship's party and watch your divisional officer pour icy water on three teenage Filipinas and see their nipples pop out. Gosh, what a hoot. It's enough to make a man long for the good old days of flat-out imperialism, when meaty infantrymen could just cut off a troublesome native's hands and no one, save a pesky do-gooder or two, would much care.

Unless, of course, you had grown up a Protestant fundamentalist, and had developed a deep if idiosyncratic faith, and knew the Bible (King James Version) inside and out. Unless you were the kind of guy who hung out in libraries, read books about Quebec nationalism and the functioning of the human brain, and drank coffee as a hobby (before doing so was a fad). If you were that kind of guy in Olongapo in the late 1980s—the base at Subic Bay closed in the early 1990s—then you were pretty much out of luck. Guys like you didn't fit in.

"Dear Jesus," I said, handing a cheap ice cream cone to a little boy, "this is for you." At that moment I was hung over, desperately depressed, and sure that God didn't exist. I gave the ice cream to the boy, without thinking about it, as an act of faith, hoping that somehow what I saw in Olongapo made sense in the divine economy I thought I knew.

Yes, God could exist back in the neighborhood I grew up in; what went on there wasn't his fault. The thugs who got killed there, the families that unraveled there, the lives that were wasted there—all that, it seemed to me, came about as a result of the stupid decisions made by the people who lived there. But I didn't see how God could exist in Olongapo where there were few choices available: beg or starve, sell yourself to the brothel industry (supported by the local government and police force) or starve.

The legless boy on the bridge . . . the legless boy on the bridge—I can picture him there. The few seconds it took for me to see and pass him by have replayed in my mind all these years. And now I can see Jesus there with him, saying, "You're almost home." But at the time I couldn't see Jesus, only Shit

River, the California Club, the young outcasts who had been fathered by American sailors long gone and oblivious to the fact that they were fathers. The place was God-forsaken. All at once what it meant to be a Christian and a man was unclear.

Do real men boink desperate girls in third-world countries and, handing their $20 to the mama-san, justify themselves by saying, "These girls like their jobs?" Do real leaders—the kind who aspire to direct the testosterone-laden "few good men" who've enlisted for 4 years of service—pour buckets of ice on little girls, howl, and make onlookers promise not to say anything when the ship gets back to the states? (How odd, by the way, that these bold critters should be so worried about what would happen if their wives knew what they were up to.)

Well, maybe I failed to be a real man. When I should have been getting a BJ at a back road club, I was contemplating the justice, or injustice, of God. When I should have been at bars watching young women eject ping pong balls and razor blades from their reproductive organs, I went to the cathedral in Olongapo with a Filipina acquaintance—who is still, after all these years, a friend.

Maybe I missed a great opportunity. But maybe not.

To this day, whenever I meet other navy veterans, the conversation inevitably turns to overseas ports. Say the words "Olongapo" or "Pattaya Beach" (Thailand) and there is an instant understanding. The topic shouldn't be broached in mixed company—that is, among women. (Once again, the bravery of misty-eyed sailors in the presence of their wives comes into bold relief.) But, in the absence of women, push the issue. Oh, yeah, the BJs under the table! Ping pong shows! Different bar girl every 4 hours! They knew how to treat a man! Ancient Asian secrets! Wore me out!

Then keep digging, and most of the time what you'll find is an empty coward who knows that what he did overseas was evil but is too afraid to admit it.

CHAPTER 44

HANDS

Patrick Pinnell

Pinnell says this story was inspired by a conversation with some of his male friends "about their fears and expectations of having to defend themselves." He suggests "Self-Defense" as an alternative title.

I remember looking at my hands, and wondering if the smoke from the bar was going to chafe them. Right now they're so delicate looking: slender fingers and skin that is—how do those lotion ads describe it? Supple. Even the cuticles are perfect quarter moons, no unsightly fraying and no mortal truth of dead skin.

Let me clear up right away the matter of my gender so that upon reading the next paragraph our more chivalrous readers don't become upset: I am a guy.

And I am thinking about my hands because they are now cracked and iced in crusty blood that almost makes them look like some sort of bad prop from a horror movie. No bones are broken, but I've never broken a bone so I don't really know. They hurt but none of the pain is located specifically—it's as if all the pain I should have felt until now in my life is concentrated right here on the once beautiful caps of my arms.

Smoke, apparently, will not affect your skin in such a brief period of time, but fast contact with another skin-covered-blood-and-bone sack will do quite a job. And that's just what happens when your friend decides that tonight appearing dumb in front of a large group of people is more important than years of camaraderie and he picks a fight with you. And then you react instinctively. Having never done this sort of thing before, you think it's your life on the line (and maybe it is) and so you slam your fist into his beer-slowed body. Then he's down and you whack at his head some till you can't tell whose blood is whose, and then you see the bartender on the phone. Was he on the phone a few minutes ago? You can't remember but you think maybe he wasn't and maybe now he's calling the cops and maybe you'll spend the rest of tonight in jail with a bunch of guys who've never seen skin so soft and supple—yes, supple—on a guy before and maybe you'll be too popular to ever forget that night.

So you run.

* * *

And now I'm at home looking at my hands. This is the third day of looking at them. A lot more of the blood than I thought turned out to be mine. There's a reason boxing gloves are never marketed as "supple."

Three days and I haven't heard from my friend. This is abnormal. We've fought before—never physically but words can be a lot worse than the beating he took—and he's always called. Or maybe words can't be worse. I've never actually done this sort of thing before; I didn't even know that I had it in me.

You always think that even though you don't fight a lot that if it came to it, you could do it. If it was your life on the line, then you'd come through; your will to live would be stronger than the body challenging you and you save yourself at the expense of another. But you never think about what that expense is or who the other is. Usually your assailant is just a dark figure in your mind. If you look close maybe you see that he—it's always a man, no matter whose mind, I'm sure—is quite large, and bald and tattooed. And if you're white, he's black, and if you're black, he's blacker, and if you're other he's probably *other than you.*

You don't ever think this is going to be your friend. The first guy you smoked pot with, the guy who showed you your first *Playboy.* The shoulder you cried on if you did that sort of thing. But it was, and so now I have to think about how much damage I did.

I always assumed it would be enough to save myself, and there was that macho hope/fear that maybe I'd go that much farther and do some real damage, maybe kill him—but not go to jail; this was self-defense after all.

If you kill a man with your hands, and then put them in your pocket, are they considered concealed weapons?

* * *

Day 4. No call. I dreamt last night that I was standing over his dead body and there was lots of smoke and I was wondering if smoke was bad for my skin. Then I see the smoke is coming from me, from the two pistols that have replaced my hands and recently emptied their clips. His body sits up and says, "I wish you hadn't killed me. It was just a show for the ladies. I get the dumb chick that likes stupid bravado; you get the keeper that respects a man who walks away. You were coming out the winner, then you went and you killed me."

Fucked up dream no doubt. More fucked up than the one where my mom is always switching the cushions on my sofa while I stand in the background screaming that it's my sofa and she should move her own damn cushions. That's the dream where I need the gun-hands.

It's afternoon. I'm thinking about my gun-hands. Maybe I really did kill him. Normal people can do insane things when they feel threatened. There are TV shows about it all the time. A mother picked up a boulder off her car to free her baby. I saw it. So it's not too hard to believe that a little guy with supple skin kills his larger friend when he feels his life is threatened. I mean I knocked him down. Sure, he's no boulder, but he is almost twice my size. If my fists could knock him down, what could they do to his unprotected head?

People die of head trauma a lot. It holds the brain, and if you know anatomy you know that that's kind of an important organ.

I look at my hands, like two malformed day-old cherry-flavored confections. And *they* knew what was coming; *they* were prepared. The brain told them, "We are going to experience fast, hard, impact repeatedly with a solid object." His head wasn't prepared. Not till about the fifth punch probably. The eyes knew, they were sending the message, but alcohol plays hell with response time.

I look at my hands, and I think about his head. He must be dead. He would have called. I call the hospitals but they haven't received anyone in his name, or any anonymous drunk with a stale, malformed confection-head. But how would he have gotten to the hospital? The other drunks probably put him in a cab, gave the driver his wallet, and told him to get the address from his license and keep all the cash as payment. He's probably lying dead on his front step. His neighbors might have called for help but how could they see him— I always told him privacy bushes in the front yard were a stupid idea.

So he's dead on his front porch. Worse yet, he's 4 days dead on his front porch. I am a murderer and I have a body on my hands.

Your Honor, I blame society—that great nebulous institution that trained us to be real men incapable of expressing ourselves outside of violence. But it's society that will be judging me.

The phone rings.

It's going to be the police—they'll have a few questions to ask me; no, they're not accusing anyone. Can I come down to the station? At my convenience, of course.

It rings again.

I could pretend I'm not home. But then they'll come and not accuse me at my door, and see my hands and think they're mighty suspicious on a guy who knows nothing about his dead friend's busted-up head.

Halfway through the third ring, I've answered.

"Hey man!"

So he's not dead. He says he's already forgotten about the other night—just wishes the bar stool hadn't slipped out from under him when he dodged my punch, said it left his head hurting for hours. How's the face? I ask. I'm hoping he says it's terrible, that he's going into consultation for plastic surgery (I'm suddenly crushed that he's not dead). He says the face is fine, just a little shiner and a split lip. He assures me it's pretty much already healed.

I hang up.

So he's not dead. Not even a scratch really. The asshole.

I'm no longer a murderer, but I have to remain in hiding for a while anyway. He can't know my hands took the worst of the beating they dished out. But I guess I should have expected this. On the shows where ordinary guys like me become murderers the neighbors always say, "Oh, he was so quiet," or "Oh, he was so polite." Never "Oh, his skin was so supple."

VOICES NINE

LOSS AND PAIN

CHAPTER 45

AN EROSION

Joey Poole

Novelist and poet Joey Poole writes about the experience of abortion from the point of view of the man in a romantic relationship, speaking to his girlfriend.

I.

You said the silver needle was not
as cold as Doctor Welder's comforting hands.
The illustrations on the wall were bright
depictions, showing babies hanging breach,
awaiting latex hands that will pluck
them, peachy apples from the womb. And you
remember still the glutted way it purred,
a kitten, hunger sated, belly full.

II.

This river sucks, insistent, at its banks,
and silver cirrus, clouds that cannot rain,
are crowding, lowering, mirrored in its glass.
These fish can pock the surface all they want,
and still they'll never eat the sky that floats,
the ceiling over which they'll never see.
This sliding water, cold and ankle deep,
gurgles, pulling at the sand beneath your feet.

CHAPTER 46

DANGEROUS WORK

Deaver Traywick

As if breath and sound
could bring life to dreams,
we never spoke what we all knew,
that he wouldn't live long,
that owing to dangerous work,
he wouldn't live long.

It would be simple,
a misstep on soft ground,
a loss of precious balance,
a short plunge into the combine's throat,
and as a sheaf of grain is separated,
the good parts would rise to the top
and the chaff spread out behind,
refused.

At night, in separate beds
we shared the inevitable truth,
that he would be gored
through the side by a wild steer
with one shattered horn,
plowed up
by the Minneapolis-Moline propane mule
he used to clear new ground,
a stiff rope tied
from one wrist to the hand-clutch
in case he fell from the seat
the tractor might stop before the notched disk-
blades sliced his flesh.

We also knew, but never spoke
a word against the fevered pace
of shelling corn in August heat
or the long hours
baling hay after dusk,
knowing one day he would lie down,
and go no farther,
his body worn out past repair,
the moving parts seized with rust
from the sweat of endless afternoons.

Living in the shadow of dangerous work,
knowing the day would come,
we also knew without sharing a word,
we would survive,
and manage the thing
with a plan envisioned
in early-morning dreams
but as real as if he
had made it himself.

Sell off stock and machines,
the outlying land. Pay back loans,
but save the house and the barns.
Consolidate
until all that is needed
is close at hand,
can fit in the carriage shed.
Stack the walls from floor
to ceiling with treasures:
tool boxes and coveralls,
high school jackets and rings,
antique mill stones
and hanging swings
for the garden.
Gather these close,
let the rest go,
survive, and manage.

There were nights when he sat at the table
eating a late supper of fryer, tomatoes,
and cold Kentucky Wonders
when all we could see through tears
was his already lovely,
broken shade whispering
across the blue-checked cloth.

So when she died, unexpectedly,
before the combine
or the steer or the tractor
or exhaustion took him, we were lost.
There was no plan, unspoken,
for what we'd do with him.
Having survived all that we knew was true,
we go on living dangerously,
clearing new ground with a propane mule,
one wrist tied by a stiff rope
to the worn hand-clutch.

CHAPTER 47

MY FATHER'S ILLNESS

Ivan Young

In 1998, my father was diagnosed with schlerosing colingitis, an incurable disease of the liver that causes hardening of the bile ducts. These poems are part of a longer series entitled "My Father's Illness," which was written shortly after his first stay in the hospital. In them I try to come to terms not only with his illness, but also with a father to whom I hadn't been close since my parents' divorce 28 years earlier. Part of the tension for me was the intimacy of dealing with his illness and possible death, while recognizing the huge gap between us—the distance between two people who are related by blood, but who don't really know each other.

1. *The Crossing*

It begins
when the phone rings,
hear tongues
I don't understand
and I drift
away from you.

The car rolls
down a rainy street.
A sign
like a bony hand points
the way. In the mist
Babylon

is a building
on an edge of clouds.
A cross
on the parking lot sign.
I slide away
in the glass doors

as they open.
We are beginning
at the blue line.
All signs
say follow and so
we do.

2. The Stone He Carries

They say your liver is a stone,
use colorful metaphors,
the tree of bile
ducts turned hard so
that nothing escapes you.
Your skin golden
even to the eyes.

Prometheus was chained
to stone,
endured each new day
when birds came
to his chest and made
their sharp incisions.
All for knowledge.

What things do I
see in the rain-
dimmed landscape
as we talk
of the stone
to which he is chained.

What stones
must we throw, full with
sin and no one
to intercede.

3. Betrayals

I could pretend
that we were perfect:
an idyllic photograph
on a postcard, but there
were times when I hated
you. The day you took
my stepbrother's dog,
forgot that you had denied me
the same one year earlier,
how instead of my final play, you chose
a biker's convention.

Sometimes I let slip the burning,
the way you became someone,
something, I couldn't know.
Sometimes I betray to myself
the feeling that you will die
and I will never find you.

4. Stitching

As fathers
and sons do, we have laid

this gap between us, tried
to find our way

across. We speak
as a dark woman threads

tubes into you.
Her white gown is no comfort

nor the delicate
sewing motions she makes

with her hands
as she turns and taps each stopcock.

You are woven
into something larger which clicks

and beeps and suspends
you beside me in a soft wrap of sheets.

There are fates
worse than this, I'm sure. This waiting

for those who will
tell us of the days that lie ahead.

5. How to Read the Story

In the middle
of the day he wakes and reads.
We discuss stories,
but never the same way.

He is fact;
I am metaphor. He talks
of the weapons of Vietnam
and I watch him,

think of Midas and the stone
boy and Gilgamesh. The layers
of story that might insulate
this day. These are my panacea.

6. Reruns

For the third time,
Charles Emerson Winchester III watches
his French horn crushed by a jeep and

for a second
repeat, Ross tells Rachel
they are not
divorced.

For the first time, I don't know
how, I am seeing this
episode of Andy Griffith.
I could stay
all day

and watch the TV lives play out
before me, indulge the instinct
of anticipation, of knowing
what will happen next.

But my father is restless,
he has long since given up
regular shows,
not for their repetition
but for

the interruptions. The strident
voices of ads that break in
just as he reaches a level
of comfort. He longs for
the smooth segue
of cable channels
the hospital doesn't carry.

So we sit each day and watch
those shows we know best,
explore channels so as to bind
the seam between episodes,
those moments of silence
when a nurse comes in
and tests the needle
in his arm.

7. When We Went Camping

I can't help
but think of Pike's Gorge.

The blanket pulled
tight beneath your chin
while you sleep
the last
Percodan off.

Twenty-five years
between you
and my imaginings:
a morning
when I watched you
in your sleeping bag.

You told
me then the Lakota
legend of Coyote,
the prankster
dancing
when he stole the moon.

Tonight
when the full moon
crawls into your window
I will dream a shadow
moves on the sill.
It will take
the night, caper
in the clouds.

8. Forsaken

Where does it begin,
this leaving? When I was 6
my father left, told me
he still loved me, that this pain
was a sacrifice. He had to save
himself from the legacy
of his father, drunken, abusive.

My stepfather stood, crossed
the room, blew his vodka breath
in my face. I held the half
pool cue like a talisman,
hoping it had the power
I didn't feel.

The obvious cliche, "Why
hast thou forsaken me,"
as I look
at the Gideon's Bible
tucked neatly below
the hospital bedstand.
But I am no Christ, what
right do I have to call
to a father I know
will leave me again.

9. Peter

Did you know, when you gave
me this name, that I would leave you
waiting at the baseball field,
forget that you
were ever coming?

Did you foresee the second
time, when I was swimming
and left you standing
at the door, knocking
to a hollow house?

Or the time that I stood
in the bushes and waited,
waited for you to go
because I was angry,
because I had grown used
to watching you leave.

Tonight, as I watch you sleep,
awake occasionally to work
the crushed ice through
your dry mouth, I ask myself
is it too late?
Is it too late to commit
to you?

10. My Father's Illness

In another context
this might be
beautiful. The hard and rugged
rolling of schlerosing, how
colingitis seems to ring
in the ear.

Even *his jaundiced skin*
has some delicate
art. In *this distance*
he is Still Life
with Apricots,
the bowl of which
he touches occasionally

as if in the soft and giving
flesh, he has found some understanding.
I *find myself,*
as we watch TV, writing this
moment that is not yet
written,

His *illness something*
palpable between us I *form*
and shape and push myself away
and push myself
away.

CHAPTER 48

LIFE OF REGRET: A FATHER'S GIFT, A BROTHER'S DEATH

Andrew Collins

In April of 2001, it had been 4 years since I had spoken with either my father or my brother. Regarding my brother, the reason is simple: on April 5, 1997, Christopher Graeme Collins, my older and only brother, died in a car accident at the age of 29. A musician, he was traveling to a gig in Athens, Georgia, bass amp and guitar on the seat beside him, when a commercial truck barreled through a red light and struck his vehicle on the driver's side—killing him, as is often said, "instantly." We take consolation where we can get it.

Only 2 years my senior, Chris and I had always been close. We felt as though we shared a bond similar to that which developed between dough-boys hunkered down in the mud-filled trenches of Europe during the Great War; together, we felt, we had survived something that neither one of us was capable of handling alone. What was that something? In short, it was the period of time in our lives dominated by an emasculated father and an unstable, domineering stepmother. Starting during these years and continuing beyond them, Chris assumed a protective role in our relationship. Since he was often a hideously reckless person himself, I found his almost motherly concern for me both deeply touching and comical, and he never knew (and never will know) that I felt perhaps more concern for him than the other way around.

Regarding my father, the reasons for our complete lack of contact are much more complex and, regrettably, do not represent a significant departure from his and my relationship before the tragedy. Ironically, Chris's death provided my father with one final, desperate, no-holds-barred opportunity to revise (in his own mind, at any rate) his role as father to his lost son. Perhaps this was the perfect opportunity, since the son was not present to object to his own role in this new relationship. Obsessed with this new, posthumous connection, my father neglected to consider his relationship to me, and, predictably, this per-

254

verse exercise in reckless self-delusion only served to permanently snap the nearly insubstantial threads that still connected the two of us.

And what form did this revision take? He sued my mother and me for the rights to Chris's remains. He pictured a good Catholic funeral for Chris in Florida and was determined to realize that vision at all costs—even at the cost of making a connection with the remaining, living son impossible. How hard he fought for this goal was, I believe, in his mind a visible, quantifiable measure of how much he loved his son. He was behaving as he felt a good, caring, outraged parent should. So he fought, and he fought, and he fought.

My mother and I, temporarily living at my step-grandmother's upscale condominium in Atlanta (due to its proximity to Athens), weathered this period steeped in barely-mixed drinks and unusually potent painkillers left on our pillows each night like mints at a fine hotel. My grandmother's husband had died the year before and, consequently, she knew what color pill most effectively granted the oblivion of sleep. The trial lasted for days. Other lawyers, entirely unrelated to our case and almost giddy with curiosity regarding this unprecedented legal battle, sat quietly in the back of the courtroom, day after day.

I previously wrote that it has been more than 4 years since I have spoken with my father. By that I mean, literally, not a single word. In a more general way, though, I don't know if I've ever talked with him. A couple of times, however, we stood on the edge of intimacy, looked into the chasm and, unable to see the bottom or to make sense of the vague shapes below, inched slowly backwards to safety.

Two such occasions stick out in my mind like stilted, amateurish sentences on the otherwise blank page of our lives as father and son—dialogue written by a hack with no ear, the content of which can be summed up in the following dismal equation: life = regret. This sentiment seemed to be the only one he could find words for.

The first of our two conversations happened sometime during my high school career in Andover, Massachusetts. A preface to this conversation will be helpful: my parents divorced in 1979. My brother and I remained in Columbia, South Carolina, in the custody of my father. Every other weekend was spent with my mother, who lived just outside the city. My father, a new divorcé and hopeful frequenter of church-related singles' night events, remarried less than one year later to a woman who not only justifies, but exceeds any and all existing stepmother stereotypes. Nicky—that is her name—was single and Catholic as well. Like my father, she had been previously married. Less than a year before, living somewhere in Michigan, she had fled in the middle of the night from an abusive husband, four young, yawning children in tow. She didn't know where she was going, she said, but she knew she needed to leave. It was that night, she confessed in a low, solemn voice, that God told her where she must go. You must go, He said, to South Carolina. But I've never even *been* to South Carolina, she humbly protested. God insisted. Recovering quickly from her moment of weakness and doubt, she put the car in drive and herself into God's hands, and headed for Interstate 95 South.

But this is not about her. Suffice it to say that my father, who had once been dominant and controlling in his marriage to my mother, relinquished that power to his new wife, Nicky. And she used it. On this particular day I remember her as furious and seething, beyond control, throwing a wine glass full of orange juice at my father. Missing his head just slightly, it shattered against the plaster wall next to the stairs. Sharp pieces of orange-tinted glass remained on the wall for the rest of the time we lived there. To his credit, my father was not always, as my brother used to say, "spineless." What was the offense, then, that warranted such a violent reaction? When ordered to physically punish me for being rude to her, he refused.

When Nicky finally slammed the door to her bedroom and holed up in a defiant silence, my father and I quietly converged by chance on the porch. After a pregnant, interminable silence, I suggested to him, tentatively, as if to a friend I did not know well but for whom I hoped the best, that it might be a good idea for Nicky to seek professional help. I don't remember if he agreed or not. I know, at any rate, that he did not overtly object to the idea. What I remember very well, however, is that he abruptly said to me, "I don't know if I've done anything right since the divorce—anything at all." Eyes wet with tears, he seemed to be asking for my forgiveness.

But the events of the day were soon forgotten. We never talked of them again. Nicky never received treatment, though she needed it more and more. The pieces of glass glued to the wall with dried orange juice, apparently visible only to my brother and me, remained as stubborn reminders of the fragility of that household's already forced equilibrium.

The second of our two conversations occurred a decade ago. As I sat in his office at the publishing company where we both worked (he in some nebulous executive capacity, I in a data-entry position amidst the gray-hued, partitioned, cubicle maze of the floor below us), we chatted no doubt about some small number of things. I forget just what, but the thing I remember, the thing I'm getting to, had to have some kind of context. And here is the philosophical pearl, the heirloom of silence, that was laid so gently at my feet: "Life is what happens to you while you make other plans." A cliché, for God's sake. Perhaps it is the pained, unnamed regret I saw in his eyes as he said this, so reminiscent of that day on the porch, that has gripped my memory by the throat for so long. He did not offer this aphorism as a wry joke or an expression of momentary frustration. He, in his mind, was conveying a universal, unassailable truth. It was a gift.

When the court finally ruled against him and against the good Catholic Florida burial, I approached him in the courtroom. Feeling pity for my father—this man whose desperate attempt at rewriting his own life despite the facts of that life was pathetic enough, not to mention the failure of that attempt—I offered to write a letter to him explaining my role in siding with his enemy, my mother. To which he responded, as if I had asked him if he needed a receipt with his purchase, "That won't be necessary," and immediately turned away toward the exit, bypassing even his crestfallen lawyer.

Apparently, nothing could erase a betrayal such as mine. Or was it the pride of the defeated that prevented him from accepting what I considered to be, under the circumstances, such a magnanimous peace offering? Of all the possible outcomes of my offer, this outright refusal was one I had not even considered. Or perhaps he was disappointed in me. That's it. There can be no other explanation. A real man would have done as my father would have in my position: a real man would have considered writing such a letter, decided not to, and regretted it for a lifetime.

CHAPTER 49

MISSING FATHER: A SINGLE MOM REFLECTS ON MANHOOD

Claudia Smith Brinson

I know all about what a man should be. Of course I do; I'm a woman. Many of us spend at least half our lives critiquing men, the other half reforming them.

But we also bring them up, raise them. So, if we're so all-fired capable, so wise about what makes a good man good, what's our problem with men? It doesn't follow, does it, this everlasting responsibility tied to this everlasting disenchantment?

I think about this a lot because I have a son. A son brought up mostly by me. I love my son with all my heart. But I can say this about my parenting: I am a good mother, but only a so-so father.

If half of all marriages end in divorce, if many of them include children, if half of those children are boys. . . . In my middle-class neighborhood near a university, a neighborhood of bungalows and parks, of azaleas and dogwoods, of schools and libraries within walking distance, there are many boys without fathers. Sometimes the fathers are only a neighborhood away with another wife and other children, but most of the time for these boys the fathers are every-other-weekend fathers, remotely loving fathers, fathers who pay child support on time, a blessing, but fathers who do not fully father, a curse.

If I lined up all the boys on the soccer teams of my son's past, you could not pick out these boys with the sometime fathers. There are no telltale signs; they aren't necessarily the ones with the Mohawk or a nose ring or a cigarette or a bad report card. Boys who miss their fathers don't necessarily turn to drugs or drop out of school or begin a life of petty crime—although they are more likely to do so than boys with their dads still in the home.

But then, I suspect, most men would tell you they grew up boys without fathers.

Years ago I was invited to speak at a weekend seminar by and for marriage and family therapists. I stayed around to watch the outcome of a morning workshop. The men were to talk with each other about issues particular to men, the women with each other about issues particular to women. Then they were to gather, the men to discuss what they had determined while the women listened, then vice versa. The vice versa never happened.

The men sat in a circle facing each other. They were surrounded by a larger circle of the women listening. I do believe at some point most of the women forgot to breathe, they were listening so hard.

The men talked about nothing but their fathers—the nothing of their fathers. Their stories were heartbreaking. One man, trying to learn to be friends with other men, took to standing on his father's grave, listing his grievances, trying to bury them, too. Another man told of his great fear that if he could not love and be loved by his father, he would not, could not properly love and be loved by his son. So he forced himself to visit his father, to bring a gift each visit, to part with a hug. His father did not say thank you for the visits or the gifts, did not return the hugs. But once, as the man was leaving, discouraged, his father said, "Where is my hug?"

The women cried for the men; the men cried for themselves and their fathers and, perhaps, their own sons.

Recently, my son was very sad. He is 22 now, and I offered some advice, and this is what he said: "I don't want to know what you would do. I want to know what my dad would do." And we both knew this was something it would not be easy to discover.

There are things about my son that are a mystery to me because he is my son. My empathy is great, but some of my knowledge is secondhand. I have been a little girl, not a little boy. As the mother of a son and a daughter, I do believe in gender differences. I joke sometimes about how murky this is, how confounding of expectations and yet how inescapable. Once I was mowing the lawn, and my two young children were peering into a hole near the street. Out jumped a toad. My son screamed; my daughter caught it. Of the two, my son is the one who made suggestions about my wardrobe, who wanted to learn to cook, who died his hair pink for one glorious spring month. But my son is also the one who built tents in the house; who figured out how to put together his own Hot Wheels when I couldn't; who takes apart his car; who poured gasoline on a piece of cardboard and lit it, just to see what would happen.

He tells me he is too emotional because of me. I think he means that he learned from his sister and me to feel the way women do, to express feelings the way women do—and pays for it. I thought about this as he was growing up, about how remarkable a son could be without being an outcast. So I was careful. I did stick to a no-toy-guns rule. Mother friends said he would use a stick in war games—and he would play war games. I said I didn't care. They said he would rebel, insist on a cowboy gun, a water pistol; he didn't. They said I would never last, but we did. But I also sent him to basketball camp and soccer camp and science camp and clown camp.

I think it must be very hard for a boy to love someone he does not want to be like: to long for his father, but not want to be like him; to love his mother but want to be not like her, but like a man. What kind of men do such boys grow up to be? All kinds, I suspect. Men who love women; men who resent women; men who understand women; men who hate them.

Children are resilient. Children are strong. Children most likely grow up just fine if somewhere along the way they have one, just one, but hopefully more, adult who loves them wholeheartedly. I would like to ask the women I know, What responsibility do you take? How much of this young man is your work? And how much is the work of absence, of what is missing? I would like the answer to be not about blame but about wishes for the best. But I don't think we're anywhere near that.

And so there are circles and circles of men who miss their fathers. And women who wish they could help but don't quite know how.

CHAPTER 50

DESTROY THIS: A DIVORCE JOURNAL

Ted Kramer (pseudonym)

SPRING 2000

If the salt has lost its savor, wherewith shall it be salted?

I hope the problem is not this bad, for it's hard to imagine such a restoration.

What can I do to protect myself emotionally? Must I attend to the hideous business of divorce, prepare myself mentally for that walk through the Valley of the Shadow? I've checked out books on the subject, started looking into apartment availability. Christ, what desolation.

We've gone from statements about how the marriage is in transition to something darker—a marriage in which one partner's unhappiness is experienced as a terrible hard indifference by the other. How, I ask myself, can she bear to give such pain to someone whose love for her, however flawed, has burned steadily for a decade now? How can she bear to give such pain to someone she loved so long, so deeply? That begs the question, of course: when did it change so catastrophically, the love that expressed itself in iterations of the question "Do you know how much I adore you?" How did it change, the love that she claimed so often to speak of to her friends? When did the response to "Can I do anything for you?" cease being "Only promise to love me forever." When did she stop saying she loved me at morning and eveningtide and on the phone?

How did we fall into this morass? Was this more my selfishness—my stupid behavior about money, my failures to nurture and sustain the nonsexual intimacy she valued? Or was it more her inability to speak up, to say in good time and with sufficient force: please don't do this or that. This or that erodes our relationship. You become less and less lovable when you do this or that.

Of course she did communicate—she was always restive about my financial totalitarianism. My response was always: it's your money too, but I kept signaling my disapprobation. She must have held off until that disapprobation was of no moment to her. At that point, the disapprobation was all hers, and she was hardened against any emotionally coercive gestures on my part. In short, love died, and at that point, who cares what the other party thinks or feels?

That she still feels she cannot be free with money is unfortunate—I swear that, even in large things, her contentment will be my supreme consideration, not some monstrous standard of frugality. But if at times she *does* take my feelings into account, it implies that she cares. For who, heading for divorce, would do such a thing? No, she wants harmony here as I do, so that we can once again be as happy as once we were. All she has to see is that "taking his feelings into account" no longer means anything to do with money—how content I would be if she asked herself only one question about my "feelings": does he know I love him?

Only occasionally did the subject of her taking a more active role in the management of the money come up—and it was always firmly rejected. You are the steward, she said. And generally she accepted the restraints urged by the steward. But inevitably the money decisions came to seem one-sided, a matter of some pathological parent-child dynamic.

Thus, when she went back to work, she was mortified to see that the extra income did not translate to more financial latitude, more little luxuries (I admit that they were little; more importantly, perhaps, I am prepared for them sometimes to be big).

Well, I have sought to reform this. I have abided by a personal resolution, dating from the first blowup, in which my parsimony was denounced in angry, passionate tears. December, I guess this was. The first time in nearly 9 years of marriage that either of us had ever raised our voices. I guess, in retrospect, that this is not something to compliment ourselves on (though the marriage expert says that avoidance of conflict is not necessarily so objectionable).

It is such a bitter irony that at precisely the point at which I am fully engaged in reform of my negative behavior, this elicits only suspicion and disbelief. "You can't change," she says to one who has already changed. And nothing I do pierces the hardness of her heart. She seems beyond melting, beyond feeling the original love.

But God knows, despite the occasional tensions about money and sex, I was the happiest man alive, and often she led me to understand that she, too, was happy at the life we had together, with its many rich experiences, our pride in each other, our beautiful children.

But *was* she ever happy? Did she think that she must accept unhappiness as the price of "rescue?" (How I hate that rescue business—I thought we met as equals, that we rescued each other only from a world full of people unthinkable as spouses, a world—for me at least—of possibly permanent lovelessness.)

* * *

I have come to understand, though, that the real culprit here may have been my failure to nurture intimacy; for example, the daily exchange about her work, her experiences, her news—and of course the "nonsexual touching" she often, plaintively, wished for. That intimacy is, it seems, the fertile soil in which marital longevity flourishes.

I guess I got the wrong idea at the outset. We went to bed together very early on—second date? Third? I had read that relationships should not start that way and actually resisted, for a nanosecond or two, her pulling me toward the bed.

She had told me that sexual relations with her first husband had been miserable—he had allegedly evinced little interest in her that way. That should have been hard to believe, but I believed it, never even reflecting that he was probably just trying to keep the secret that eventually emerged. She had also told me (and I probably have it pretty scrambled in my mind) that she betrayed her husband with someone else. I've never quite understood whether this was to satisfy a need to be desired or just a way to hurt the husband. Was this after the birth of Liza? Naturally, as her anger at me has come to resemble the anger she occasionally still seems to feel toward ***, I have feared that history would repeat itself, that she would inflict on me that supreme cruelty.

What drew us together? Never, I thought, the rescue-fantasy (which she recently spoke of). The wonderful thing seemed to be that we had met just when each had properly healed from a broken marriage. Surely we knew our differences from the first? That I was an introvert, she an extrovert. But each of us loved a child, and I, at least, felt a passionate desire to restore the home I had lost. She seems now to worry that we are too different, but I see the differences as superficial beside the essential things. These include, first, a mutual love and respect—and my respect for her has never faltered. If she values some things I don't particularly value, such as socializing, this is surely just part of two people's differences—as I've told her repeatedly, I was once married to a fellow academic, and in the between-marriages years I had abundant opportunity to canvas my true tastes. I want her as my life partner.

What else is essential? A deep cherishing of the child we made and his siblings (however rocky these relationships), a desire that he not suffer the inevitable damage of a broken home.

I pray that she will not convince herself that Billy's life, without father and mother and home, could be "almost as good" with a proximate noncustodial parent and helpful grandparents. Liza has fared reasonably well, Jessica less so, but neither shows the toll of experiencing divorce as a 7-year-old.

* * *

What do I love about her? First, and with apologies for being a superficial swine, I love her beauty of face and form. My heart soars every time I look at her. Our culture has many ways to inhibit or impair the intellectual growth of beautiful women. Yet for me the ideal was always the beauty *and* the intelligence, the beauty *and* the values. Joanna was all of this. She is not and does not want to be an intellectual, but she has a truly first-rate mind. She's good at math, and I daily congratulate myself for arranging for my son to acquire math genes. She is or has seemed to be quite keen to read widely and to immerse herself in the most enriching part of travel. When we came to Cnidos, her interest in inspecting the ruins was the same as my own. I could have been married to one of those Germans (please, Ilse, come with me to experience three millennia of history).

I feel guilty for being parsimonious about clothes and such when I love for her to look splendid. I truly love her sense of style, and I appreciate more than words can say her transformations in *my* dress and appearance. But maybe I sometimes feel that she dresses for herself or the world—never, really, for me.

What else? I love her liveliness. As an introvert who seldom really enjoys socializing, I have admired and, yes, valued my wife's ability to make friends across a wide spectrum. I was delighted to see her charm that former government minister in the Levant. I was the more welcome in Sweden (even within my own department) because she was so universally accepted and sought out. On the other hand, her lively manner can put people off, for she can seem to be keeping social discourse on too superficial a plane. A friend once remarked, in a candid moment, "That's why we don't do more together as two couples—my wife thinks Joanna, too little interested in serious conversation, her vivacity seems a barrier, she [the wife] would prefer to participate in the husbands' conversation." On the third hand (these situations, as Nabokov says, sprout additional forelimbs all the time), thoughtful professional women like *** and *** (to name only two) seem to find Joanna excellent company.

I love her good sense, her tough-mindedness, her rationalism, her rather scientific turn of mind, her disinclination toward New Age claptrap.

One of the things I have loved seems to have undergone a bit of metamorphosis. I never went looking for a woman who would stay home and be domestic and take care of children and cook, and so forth. I rather thought both parties would have careers and that domestic responsibilities would be shared. But early on, Joanna wanted to stay home, and it was like some powerful drug to have one party who took responsibility for the home front. I was actively discouraged from keeping up my cooking skills. I was ordered to change the work habits of a lifetime and start working at the office ("husbands go to work").

But I've had no difficulty returning to my prior orientation. I have fully accepted her decision to return to work (wives, too, should have careers; wives, too, go to the office). I don't think I harbor any resentment at having to resume cooking and take on more child care responsibilities. Though I like order and predictability and routine, I have sought, since the breakup of my first (17-year) marriage, to cultivate the virtue of flexibility.

I have been intemperate at times in being judgmental about ways of life different from my own. This is easy for anyone who was at an impressionable age when he saw *The Graduate*. One aspires to live authentically, to live the examined life—and never to drift into the world of materialism and superficiality that has ensnared Mrs. Robinson.

An irony. Though Jessica does not make her points in terms of that film, she has become convinced that Joanna and Joanna's parents are denizens of the Mrs. Robinson world. I have argued strenuously that those who aspire to authentic living (or whatever it is) err to despise their neighbors. I have preached a tolerance that came to me first in the good relationship that eventually developed between me and my first mother-in-law—a woman who at one time I had dismissed as a shallow, racist monster. Later I saw the bedrock character there.

But I am still subject to prejudice, and I have been stupid enough to air it in ways that wound Joanna. She rightly says: you despise the category into which I myself fall. Therefore I feel belittled.

I think we sometimes look for ways to seduce our partners into our prejudices. When Joanna would shake her head at the stupidity of someone we both know, I was too ready to assume something broader in her views, some more universal contempt that we might "share."

I was angry at her mother for what struck me as profoundly insulting behavior (this literally in the first days of our marriage). When Joanna became furious at her mother (regarding another matter) and lashed out at her, I sort of joined in, and this was almost a total disaster. I—over 40!—actually failed to understand that what Joanna and her mother were going through was just a slightly larger-than-usual spat. I've spent the years since trying to build bridges with her mother, in hopes of achieving something like the mutual respect and fondness I eventually enjoyed with my first mother-in-law. The occasional shred of approbation that comes to me from her parents means more to me than I have previously been willing to admit.

* * *

I thought she loved in me the very things I most value in myself. I am intelligent, cultured, sensitive, nurturing, stable, responsible, and hard-working (yet chastened by past tendencies to be excessively focused on work). I love my children. My physical beauty is slight, at least beside hers, and at times I worry that she might wish for the physical equivalent of herself, an Adonis to her Venus.

I hope she will think about what she loved in me—and perhaps about what she only thought she loved.

She seems distressed that I know more about art and culture than she does. In the first place, I thought that's what drew her. And this knowledge is essentially professional, all of it linked to my work with literature and language. Now she has her own area of professional expertise, which is vastly more connected to the real business of life than my books and my operas. I love having her school me in the things she knows and cares about. She knows more about dress, manners, and social norms than I do. I realize how important these things are when I see Jessica so in need of them.

I would still like to share some of my aesthetic interests with her, if possible. But having overresponded at times to what may have been mere politeness, I must avoid pedantry and practice more self-censorship. I mean in any event to be sensitive about fostering some kind of pernicious disparity, some perceived hierarchy of knowledge, sophistication, and authority between us. She has alluded to this often recently. It is a natural danger when partners are 14 years apart in age.

We need to undertake constructive exercises to (1) defuse the anger, and (2) restore a little joy in our lives. What might we do to stack the deck in favor of our marriage? The main thing: we must believe in a future together; we must believe that her present "numbness" and confusion stem not from an as yet unfaceable but nonetheless true and absolute and final death of love, but rather are something like a severely pruned rose bush that, come the spring and absent late frosts, will send forth buds.

We should, therefore:

- Continue to think of ways to defuse money tensions. A third checking account with all surplus, to be controlled by her? Take clothing off the budget altogether and quit worrying about spending more or less than the allotted amount?
- Undertake repairs and improvements to the house (itself a metaphor for the relationship). To spend some of our savings need not preclude paying off the house next February.
- Take pains to have meals and other activities as a family (e.g., watching *My Dog Skip* this weekend).
- Plan activities for the two of us—movies, parties, and joint dates with friends.
- Talk often about how things stand (will she be willing?).
- Take the interesting quizzes in that book about why marriages fail or succeed, discussing how we responded.
- Write accounts of our meeting and our early years. My own would be largely rhapsodic. I fear that hers would be what I might never have imagined: negative.
- Write down or verbalize again just what it was that drew us to each other in the first place. I need to let her know how much I admire and respect her—though I cannot understand how she could ever doubt this. She shouldn't construe my different outlook on, say, socializing as a criticism of her. After all, her social confidence was and is among the things I most admire.
- Commit ourselves to the vacation in France, but on different terms than in the past—slower pace, less scrimping (yes, we should have had coffee overlooking the Bosphorus), no expectations about sex. If we cannot imagine a pleasurable trip together 4 or 5 months hence, we are doomed indeed.

SUNDAY, 5 MARCH

Fourteen pages—and all beside the point. The point is only tangentially what might be done to improve the marriage. The real point concerns the state of Joanna's mind. How badly impaired is her love? It's easy to say let time do its work, but one fears that time will only bring fully to consciousness some fundamental revulsion, something that outweighs, in the heart's scale, the hundreds of negatives to divorce.

What can I do to influence the picture that will eventually clarify in her mind? Do I remind her of all the horrors waiting in the wings? The wrangling over money and property, after which all parties are nothing more nor less than poor? Or "dating," kissing frog after frog, every one inferior to the man she discarded—and how many willing to raise other men's children, how many interested in a long-term relationship without the prospect of at least one more child? What of Mary's confusion when the most proximate father (little loved, perhaps, but an element of stability, an often positive influence) goes out of the home she has shared with him as long as she can remember? What of Billy's misery, compounded when he is, one day, faced with the tender mercies of a stepparent or two?

No, no, no, it takes so little to spare oneself and one's children all of this and at the same time to consolidate prospects for an old age blessed with love, companionship, mutual devotion, and the joy of psychologically healthy children who stand some chance of marrying and having children of their own without the most powerful example of marital dysfunction to cast its shadow over their own trip down the aisle.

Oh yes, we have often remarked that we cheerfully accept the pain in our past, including divorce, because it eventually ushered in something good. But did it? And if it did, how many such happy endings is one entitled to? What hope for the twice divorced?

Surely our ability to learn is better than that?

But what can I do? Yes, I'll show every day, every hour, my reform and the true quality of my love. But will she recognize the essential folly of discarding the devotion of a good man? Especially one so amenable to, ah, further training.

When I have spoken of our shared values as important to our marriage, I have at times felt that they are not in fact shared—that she really doesn't care much for home life, that she doesn't see a stable marriage as the sine qua non for raising happy, successful, well-adjusted children, that she sees growing up with lots of books on the walls and parents who read as merely a frill, that a whole family is one of the truly valuable and beautiful things a confused and wretched world will sometimes allow to flourish.

It occurs to me that one problem here, paradoxically, is the strength of the family from which she comes. I have always felt an outsider among the Smiths. She is all the readier to be rid of me because she senses that they would not be so very sorry to have her (and her children, they imagine) all to themselves again. Will she remember how stifling, how emotionally costly, her mother's embrace (however generous or well intentioned) can be?

I must understand that she has been poisonously unhappy for longer than I could have imagined. She must have just thrust that from her mind. She must have thought, first, that I was too set in my ways to respond—that she could only circle around the half-measures that registered discontent without allowing the dangerously violent feelings into the open: the inchoate resistance to one-sided budgetary restraints, the sexual distance, the growing coldness so incapable of communicating constructively. But then she must have felt the rising tide of anger and even of something like hatred, and this she allowed to build and build, to eat away at her love and our domestic tranquillity. The explosion, when it came, was so much more than a release of pent-up feelings. Rather than the catharsis that might allow sober addressing and correction of grievances, this was love itself imploding forever.

And what of the depth charges in my own heart? Now I think only of a particular form of deliverance. But after so much suffering, will I not feel my own disabling and destructive resentment? For my suffering seems in excess of my mistakes.

TUESDAY, 7 MARCH

Another wretched night, awake from 3:30 on. Virtually no touching, Joanna abed and asleep at 8:30 or so (not that dreadful withdrawal, she said, just not feeling well).

I feel as if I am battling a phantom. The phantom is capable of dealing me blow after devastating blow, and I have no arsenal. Such weapons as present themselves—kindness, thoughtfulness, consideration, tenderness, various personal reforms—simply break on the phantom's rough hide. Only patience abides, and the longer one exercises it the more horrible its potential failure.

Why can't I figure out what Joanna wants or loves and strive for that? I don't think the good things she first loved have gone away somewhere. I remain a good family man, a devoted husband and lover, a person of sensitivity, taste, and conspicuous but not overweening intelligence. I'm in good physical condition, not excessively overweight. I am a success in my profession, which affords me many ways to contribute time and energy to my family.

But it's as if she has awakened to a dislike of precisely those parts which are most fundamental to my makeup. She doesn't like it that I live in the world of my reading and my thoughts. She wishes I were more the kind of extroverted, highly social person that she herself grew up as and always surrounded herself with. So was I just the choice of a brief, misguided interest, a temporary wish to absent herself from one way of living and being? And is she now to decide that anything other than a companion on that model will be stifling? Would she not be mollified by my edging closer to what she values? It's probably too late to take up golf or hunting, but I don't have any objection to regular socializing and putting myself out to be reasonably good company. Have I already failed some test among those in her professional circle?

I wish she would think seriously about the contrasts between me and other men she knows. Or does she? Does she look at this or that husband out there who seems ideal? Would she like a ***? a ***? a ***? A version of her father? Someone much richer? Someone intelligent but not "superior?" I am about as prejudiced in this matter as a person could be, but I've known too many men, observed too many marriages, not to know my own value as a husband. I shall study being more like ***. I can't give Joanna the material things *** has, but I can manage more selflessness, more good humor, more of knightly service. How long might Joanna remain happy with a ***?

I tried to draw out *** the other day. Rightly, I suppose, she did not feel that it would be wise to go into her perceptions. But what if she thinks the marriage doomed? What does Joanna say to her or to *** or to her mother or to *** or to *** [her therapist]? What cold comfort if Joanna drives me off, then realizes (as *** did) that she has made an irreparable mistake.

Marriages go through bad periods. They often recover. Don't they?

A LETTER

February 9, 2001

Dear Joanna,

Here on the eve of the actual divorce, I wonder if you ever have second thoughts. My own feelings are considerably more ambivalent than they were a year ago. That is, I find myself liking the single life, and I write now more out of a sense of what's right than from feelings of disappointed love. I do, however, hate being a two-time loser at marriage, and I wonder if, having experienced independence now for some months, you remain certain that you have done the right thing. Eventually I should think you will remarry—but how long will it last next time? Will you still be every man's dream when that one ends? (I admit that I sometimes think it would then be amusing to be your fourth husband.)

I'm under no illusions here. The time since the separation began has afforded me the opportunity to see somewhat more objectively that the marriage had not been healthy for a good while. But it still troubles me that you could see no point in striving to save it. You were unhappy, you ignored or repressed your feelings, you became *really* unhappy, you went to Betty, you left. I, who would have done pretty much anything to make things better, never really had a chance.

I wonder if you would have acted differently if the ideal condo had not been available and affordable at just the right moment.

I know you were convinced that I would never change—but you might have considered that the changes I undertook in, for example, dress and exercise might promise the ability to change in other areas. Nor was abandoning the career-long practice of working at home a small change.

And now, chastened, I anticipate making someone quite happy with my relaxed attitude to money, savings, and retirement. Doesn't mean I would go into debt—just that I wouldn't obsess so. Your successor will get free reign at any hotel minibar, drinks overlooking the Bosphorus, and a maid.

Of course Billy is the most important reason for you to look into your heart. Don't you ever look at his dear face and think how we've failed to give him the most important thing of all? Do you rationalize his growing up between households, thinking that he has easy access to both parents and grandparents? There is no substitute for home and family: mother and father and children all together under one roof.

I would not argue that any and all connubial misery ought to be borne for the sake of the children. The spiritual toll would be too high. I do, however, think that one ought to err on the side of fighting to sustain a marriage—and we really didn't do that.

If you can even conceive of an attempt at reconciliation, you will no doubt reflect that it might be dangerous to raise Billy's hopes. But he is prematurely matured by his experience of the separation, and he would understand if we told him that any such attempt must be highly tentative—all too unlikely to turn out as he might hope.

I do not envision any return to the status quo ante with our property. Even with the sunniest outcome you ought to hang on to the condo as your personal investment (and as a place to retreat to again, as necessary).

I don't imagine you have any vacation coming any time soon, but as part of any marital thaw I would be glad to take all three children on a trip this spring or summer—and you to whatever exotic place you'd like when you were able to go.

I don't know just how we might proceed in the meantime—I imagine we'd simply try to do things as a family from time to time, while you and I went to counseling. We would retire to our respective domiciles at the end of the day, thereby preserving the option of divorce at the beginning of April (speaking of which, though it may seem odd for me to say so in this context, if you're not interested in what is proposed here I would ask that you keep an eye on the calendar so we can at least have timely legal closure).

If what I speak of here is unthinkable (as I can well imagine—it's pretty unthinkable even to me), you need not ever speak of it. But do, please, destroy this letter.

Sincerely,

Ted

VOICES TEN

THE JOURNEY TO WORK

CHAPTER 51

ESCAPING THE CAVE

Ronald L. Applbaum

Things do not change; we change.
    —Henry David Thoreau, *Journal*, 1850

INTO THE LIGHT

The Greek philosopher Plato contended that education was the means of escaping the cave. He believed that through education people would be able to see and comprehend the world around them. Twenty-five hundred years ago, it was the philosopher-teacher who would act as a guide to assist those trapped in the darkness of the cave. Today, it is the teacher, parent, friend, spouse, and even child who opens our eyes and points us toward the light.

We are shaped by what we are taught. Education is the sum of all we dare dream to be as a person, shaping us as a culture and defining us as a people. It was Franklin Delano Roosevelt who said, "You cannot always build the future for our youth, but we can build our youth for the future."

My life has been an educational journey from darkness into the light; an odyssey strewn with a litany of new adventures and challenges; a voyage of discovery that has provided a better understanding of human nature and all its frailties and strengths.

A century ago, Booker T. Washington (1901) said, "Success is to be measured not so much by the position that one has reached in life as by the obstacles which he has overcome while trying to succeed." As I begin the 21st century, my position as a university president is the result of an ongoing education process, which included a series of triumphs and failures over a number of barriers and impediments. Most important, my position is a reflection of the support, guidance, hard work, and patience of my wife, Susan.

THE EYES OF CHILDHOOD

When I reflect upon my childhood the expression that comes immediately to mind is one written by Edgar Allan Poe, "From childhood's hour—I have not been/As others were—I have not seen/As others saw."

I arrived on a cold, dark morning in December 1943. Nine months earlier, my parents had a typical wartime wedding, performed in private by a justice of the peace, uniting two people who knew little of each other and less about their future except that they would soon be separated by war. They had never been married before and would in 48 hours be apart as husband and wife for their first 2 1/2 years of marriage.

My mother, Marion Caplan, took me home from the local hospital to a large two-story brown house owned by my grandmother, Goldie, on Washington Street in Charleroi, Pennsylvania. Goldie was 53 when I was born. She was a remarkable individual—tall, slender, and intense, her hands made hard and calloused from working 30 years as a self-taught tailor to raise and support her five children following the untimely death of her husband in 1919. She was well known and respected in the small town. She was neither ambitious nor temperamental, accepting her lot in life and hoping the best for her children. She was proud of her family and their accomplishments and of being a successful tailor and mother.

Three families were to live in her house for 3 years, including three daughters—Rose, Helen, and Marion, and their sons, Tom, Julian, and Ron. Goldie was in control. Marion, "Babe" as her older sisters always referred to her, was the shortest and youngest in the family. She had a soft, easy voice and a soothing smile and was, in her younger years, irrepressibly friendly. An excellent student and high school graduate, she was forced to discontinue a nursing degree program due to a sudden illness, limited finances, and the outbreak of World War II.

My father, Irwin, was born on November 11, 1918, a day originally known as Armistice Day—the end of World War I. Not surprisingly, he was given the middle name Shalom, the word for peace in Hebrew. The third of four children, he was raised in relative luxury. His father was a successful immigrant from Hungary who had built a thriving grocery business in the small town of Donora, Pennsylvania. In the mid-1930s, the family had traveled to Europe to visit family—the last time they would see their loved ones.

Irwin was "a handsome man" my mother would say, "But he was always moody. There was a sense of sadness, anger, and frustration that would emerge from time to time." He was constantly changing himself, one day charming and affable, the next temperamental and aloof. He could easily become excitable, fiery, headstrong, and impatient. He loved to gamble and talk with the men. He was compulsive, smoking two to three packs of cigarettes a day and drinking coffee cup after cup from morning to night. He was a natty dresser. And he almost had a fetish about cleanliness. Each day he would shave two or three times, splashing on Old Spice after each occasion, washing his hands throughout the day. A high school graduate, he enrolled in a pharmacy program at Duquesne University at the outbreak of the war.

Although I do not remember much as a child, I do remember the first few years as being primarily around women. My grandmother, aunts, and mother were my teachers and guides. Marion kept me busy. She read me stories every night and taught me the basics of reading early in life. We would take long walks to my grandmother's shop, and I would sit in the window playing with the buttons and store cat. But due to the war, there were few men to serve as models in my early formative years. The only children I played with were my cousins.

When Irwin returned at the end of the war in 1945, he had no plans to stay in Goldie's home, but he had to complete his college education before he could support a family. He also had no time for a son, so most of my time as a youngster was spent alone. I would walk to the corner library to read the books and magazines. In the quiet of that one-room building, I would focus not on the world of fiction, but on the real world—science, history, art. I cannot remember a single male friend in those early years. Decades later, my mother would say that I was the perfect child—very quiet, never complaining, never getting into trouble, never making demands on anyone.

In the summer of 1948, following my father's college graduation, we moved to the small town of California, Pennsylvania, where Irwin and his brother, Sydney, opened their first drug store. The only registered pharmacist in the store, he worked 6 or 7 days a week from 9 A.M. to 11 P.M. His life was consumed by his schedule, leaving little time for his wife and even less for a son. Although my sister, Denise, born in 1950, became the apple of his eye, he also had little time to spend with her. At this time, I made my first male friends, two boys who would later become a successful businessman and doctor, respectively. It was a pleasant time. I spent hours enjoying their company, reading books, or listening to the radio alone in the house.

In the summer of 1954, we returned to Charleroi to live and look after Goldie, who had sold her shop. Irwin opened his second and third drug stores during this period of time, each store providing a sufficient income for the family to live comfortably. Once again, I would spend most of my time at the library, reading every book I could find. I had a few male friends with whom I would play basketball and sockie, a version of baseball played with a broomstick and a ball made from old socks tightly bound together, but I never socialized with any of the children living near me. In retrospect, it never really bothered me that I spent so much time alone with books and my own thoughts.

In the summer of 1958, the family moved to a two-story frame house on the top of a hill overlooking the Monogahela River. The house was nestled along a row of identical homes built 30 years earlier, and it was only a 20-minute walk from the center of town and my father's pharmacy. It was a neighborhood of professionals, businessmen, bankers, doctors, and lawyers. Although there were a number of children in the area, none of the boys was my age. And although I was friendly with girls my age, I didn't play with them.

It was at this time I picked up a tennis racquet and taught myself the game. The town had four courts across the tracks in a field that had housed the old glass works. Every summer morning before 10th grade, I would walk to the courts and hit the ball against the backboard and practice serving hundreds of balls. Perhaps it's not surprising that I chose an individual, rather than a team sport. I would play tennis on the high school team and even continue to compete through my first years of college.

As a teenager and young adult, when I lay in bed at night, I did not experience what I believe many young men feel: a sense of comfort, love, or even security. It was clear that my father did not care for me. Throughout my life, he never said he even liked me or was proud of my accomplishments. Our few conversations focused on his expressions of disappointment and resentment regarding my academic performance or choice of school mates. To succeed in any activity was a normal expectation, to be less than the best was unacceptable and a sign of failure.

Perhaps, our final conversation, almost 30 years before his death and after 5 years apart, sums up our relationship. I had been married the previous year and had taken my first job as an assistant professor. I met him outside the apartment complex of his parents, who had retired to Long Beach, California. He said he heard that I had earned a Ph.D. and was teaching at the local university. And then looking away from me as he puffed on a cigarette, he said, "Why did you go and get a Ph.D.? You'll never make any money."

Early in my life, it was my mother who believed in me, who provided what little social support I needed, but it was a lonely road. I had no role models— male or female—and learned the rules of the game as best I could in class and on the job by observing and testing out what was required for success. Perhaps I should have failed, but I wouldn't let myself. I always had faith and believed in my capacity to succeed, never accepting the possibility of failure.

Man Has His Will— But Woman Has Her Way

Almost two centuries ago, Washington Irving observed, "There is in every woman's heart a spark of heavenly fire, which lies dormant in the broad daylight of prosperity; but which kindles up, and beams and blazes in the dark hour of adversity." At the lowest points in my professional life, it has been my wife, Susan, who provided the gentle words of encouragement or screamed to shock me out of self-pity . Without question, I owe my professional success and personal growth to the support and caring provided by my wife over the last 34 years.

It was a mild autumn evening in September of 1966 at a Penn State graduate department orientation dinner when I first met Susan Stone. Years later, reflecting on our first encounter, she should remark honestly that her eyes first focused on my office partner, Deni Berkson, "The most gorgeous man I've ever seen." She flirted through eye contact, asking for a light for her cigarette, turned around, and walked away. Nevertheless, I was immediately struck by her. It would be the beginning of a courtship that would take place over the next 2 years.

Susan Stone was the only child of a well-educated upper-middle-class Jewish family from Queens, New York. Her father was a state labor lawyer—a brilliant and funny man, deeply religious, not afraid to speak his mind and yet open to everyone. Her mother, a homemaker with music degrees from Hunter and Julliard, was extremely proper, cultured, well read, and respected by her friends.

Sue was 21 when she arrived at Penn State to study for a master's degree in speech. A superb student and exceptional writer who really wanted to be in radio-television, she enjoyed talking. She had a sparkle to her soft blue-green eyes and an iridescent personality, cheerful and good humored. She was always in perpetual motion. Everyone liked her.

Assigned together for a teaching internship, we spent hours that first semester developing a friendship. She was straightforward, articulate, and self-assured. Ours was a contrast in styles. In social settings, I was more reserved and quiet, while she was outgoing. I kept my feelings inside, while her feelings seemed immediate and passionate. She preferred being with others, while I sought solitude. However, it was her unthreatening manner that allowed me to express my self-doubts and show my vulnerability.

We fell in love almost immediately and 2 years later were married in a wedding characterized by some of our graduate school colleagues as right out of the movie *Goodbye Columbus*. And, as is often the case, we were too busy to even appreciate the event.

From the beginning, our marriage revolved around education. Our first year was spent in State College, Pennsylvania, as I finished the requirements for my doctoral degree. Prior to graduation, I was offered and accepted a job at my alma mater in California. After graduation in 1969 and on the very day of the Manson murders in Hollywood, we began our lives as Californians.

Once in Long Beach, we quickly located an apartment and Sue found her first job, teaching English and speech in a local high school. The first year was a happy one. It was also a particularly eventful one because, despite our plans to wait 5 years before having a child, Sue became pregnant. Nine months later our son, Lee, was born. An outgoing, dynamic, delightful man, Lee is now my close friend and confidant.

From the very beginning, it became apparent that I wasn't satisfied with my professional career. It simply didn't provide the type of challenge I sought. Although I was performing as expected of a new assistant professor, I wasn't particularly happy, unable to derive personal satisfaction from teaching my classes. Year after year, it became more apparent that I could not spend 40 years as a college instructor, confirmed by my faculty colleague in the next office who burned out and suffered a nervous breakdown after only 15 years.

Discussing a career change, Sue was at first skeptical and dubious. My frustration made her exasperated. And, yet, she never wavered, providing support for any job option or change I expressed—from doctor to lawyer.

When I chose to leave full-time teaching for college administration, it was Susan who was my backbone, who would not bend. She had no reservations regarding my ability to handle the duties and responsibilities. When I expressed self-doubts, she provided the comfort and self-assurances I needed to bolster my psyche.

Being an administrator's wife hasn't been easy. The stresses and strains on Sue have been constant. She reads the criticisms of administrators in the student and local newspapers, hears faculty haranguing about personnel decisions and administrative salaries, is confronted by campus personnel who question her campus involvement, and has had to sacrifice her career for me to ascend the administrative ladder. Recently, we reflected jokingly that each post for me has meant another salary decrease for her. Perhaps the most stressful of all, she has had to continually separate herself from family and friends.

Being a university president's spouse may be the most difficult of all the roles she has played. Life can be lonely, because she can never be completely open with others, particularly people connected with the university. Like a president, everything she says and does is constantly under a microscope. It has been said that the loneliest job is that of the president, but at least the president has the ability to impact directly on decisions that impact on him or her—a spouse rarely controls his or her destiny.

Over our 32 years of marriage, we have faced so many challenges and obstacles. Throughout, we have learned to maintain our optimism and to persevere. We have become truly close friends and colleagues. She has been the one constant in my life, providing the foundation for my resilience under adversity and the catalyst for my ambition. My success is a tribute to her sensitivity, caring, understanding, and love.

LEADERSHIP IS ACTION, NOT A WORD

Twenty-four years ago, as I rode the elevator up seven floors to my faculty office at California State University, Long Beach, I thought only of preparing my lecture notes for the next class, finishing the editing on my fourth book, and getting home in time to play bridge that night with a colleague.

I had no administrative aspirations nor could I have conceived of spending the majority of my professional career as a university administrator. I had no experience or interest in managing an educational enterprise.

The phone rang as I unlocked the door to my office. The school dean wanted to talk about the unexpected resignation of the associate dean of finance. Earlier that morning, a departmental colleague in a passing conversation had suggested my name as a possible replacement. I was familiar with the budgeting process, having served on the faculty budget committee. I did teach the departmental statistics class so I knew something about crunching numbers. Apparently, I was qualified.

Administration succession in a university is an anomaly. Unlike corporations or governmental agencies where leaders are commonly trained for the job, university administrators are amateurs. Few faculty have designs early in their career on senior administrative positions and rarely make such intentions known. Most of us have been educated to become teachers/scholars/service providers. Few of us have had any formal educational training in basic administrative or managerial skills. The academic route does not train or test the breadth of skills needed to be a successful dean, vice president, or president. As a faculty member, I had no firsthand knowledge of the duties or responsibilities of an academic administrator. I'd never read a book or article on the history or philosophy of higher education. Having played only a minor role in campus governance, I had no preconceived notion of how to be an effective or successful college administrator.

Accepting the offer to try my hand at a new position, however, would come as no surprise to people who knew me. I've always sought out change in my professional career. I knew some of the senior administrators at the university. The provost, who would eventually go on to become a successful university president in Illinois, had been present when I defended my master's thesis 10 years earlier. In those days, academic administration was a male preserve. In fact, not a single senior administrator at this large urban university with over 30,000 students, half of whom were women, was female.

There was no orientation program for junior administrators. It was on-the-job-training. Fortunately, I inherited a seasoned secretary who treated me as a professional and watched over me like a mother. She became my teacher. She taught me the value of all campus personnel, but particularly the support staff— the secretaries, maintainers, campus security officers, and groundskeepers.

It has been said that if you don't know where you are going, it doesn't make a difference how you get there. If you don't have a plan, it doesn't matter what you do. If you don't have an objective, who cares if you ever reach it? When I accepted my first administrative post, I had no plan. I didn't view the job as anything more than a new challenge, a higher salary, and new duties and responsibilities. Nevertheless, I had complete confidence that I could do the job. Most importantly, my wife believed I could do it.

Within 18 months, the school was to be restructured and I suddenly found myself at a critical point in my life and career. One road led back to the faculty and, undoubtedly, 30 years as a teacher/scholar. The other road would mean possibly 5 years as an academic dean. I chose a road offered to few and least taken by faculty. I became a dean, the youngest such senior-level academic administrator in the California State University system at the time. My fellow administrators used to jokingly refer to me as the "baby dean."

The ride along the administrative road has not always been smooth, providing its share of potholes and speed bumps. I've been ticketed at times for moving too quickly—a new general education program, higher promotional standards, and merit awards for faculty and staff. While the curves on that road haven't always been predictable, it has been a path of constant forward progress. Each stop along the road as dean, vice president, and president has a story of its own. Each post has been its own learning experience, fraught with a number of successes and, fortunately, few failures. Each job has meant new colleagues, friends, supporters, and detractors. Each move has meant a new geographical stop on the national road map—Long Beach, California; McAllen, Texas; Westfield, Massachusetts; and Union, New Jersey. Each location has meant a new home, neighbors, community customs, and the local service organizations and social clubs.

By 1982 when I made the decision to pursue a vice presidential position, life for Sue, Lee, and for myself would change dramatically. We would become, to borrow a phrase, strangers in a strange land. We would separate ourselves from our own families. We would transport ourselves to a dramatically different culture in southern Texas, a crucial and important experience that would enable me to better understand and become more sensitive to the uniqueness and value of racial, ethnic, and national differences.

For me, it also was to become the first in a series of decisions to accept posts at institutions which had a history of serious internal problems and external image concerns. In recent years, I've jokingly commented that I have become the Red Adair of university administration, putting out major fires and creating stability in unstable conditions.

In my two presidencies, my predecessors had failed, requiring major changes in the campus culture. There was a need to upgrade the academic environment, create a more inclusive and caring community, and institute more effective strategic planning and campus-wide participation. Most importantly, I was required to eliminate, or at least significantly reduce, the hostility, distrust, lack of openness, and professionalism that had developed between administrators and faculty.

Over time, most administrators develop a "credo" or statement of opinions regarding their position. As I reflect over my 24-year career as an administrator, I've been driven by a set of principles I now believe a president must adopt to be an effective leader. Briefly they are as follows:

- As president I *must have courage.*
- As president I *must set the example.*
- As president I *must genuinely value the individual.*
- As president I *am the spokesperson for the institution.*
- As president I *should act as a catalyst for innovation.*
- As president I *must function openly and accessibly.*
- As president I *must earn the respect of others.*

FINAL WORDS

A college president has high public visibility and many social and cultural responsibilities. I find my photo or comments in the newspapers on a regular basis. I'm invited to every political and nonprofit organizational fund-raiser and asked to speak at numerous social and fraternal club meetings.

Over the past decade, the post of university president has become more difficult, providing fewer rewards and subjecting one to more direct pressures than in the past. Presidents face internal conflict, increased external pressures, diminished authority, more special interests, politicization of boards, more perilous financial conditions, and, unfortunately, a tenure that averages only 5 years. Yet, most presidents express satisfaction with the position. Many presidents have a tendency to take an optimistic view of their own situation and sometimes lack a clear picture of reality. The late Senator James William Fulbright, a former president of the University of Arkansas, once said, "There is an inevitable divergence, attributable to the imperfections of the human mind, between the world as it is and the world as man perceives it" (Kerr & Gade, 1989, p. 46).

Charles Handy, the British educator, in his book *The Age of Unreason*, tells us that "The future we predict today is not inevitable. We can influence it, if we know what we want it to be. We can and should be in charge of our own destinies in a time of change." A presidency is a difficult undertaking. It takes perspective, a willingness to accept risk, and an understanding that success is not a guarantee. Robert Maynard Hutchins once said that an "administrator has all of these ways to lose and he has no way to win," and that "almost any decision an administrator makes is a decision against somebody." In today's educational arena, one's successes are short-lived and failings are long-remembered. At best, a president will be remembered as having dedicated him- or herself to making the institution a little better.

In 1912, John Cotton Dana, a librarian at Newark State College, later to become Kean University, was asked one day to find a suitable inscription for placement above the entrance of the institution's new education building. He wrote, "Who dares to teach must never cease to learn."

The last 50 years of my life have been spent in a learning environment—as student, teacher, and administrator. Each morning, as I arise from my bed at 6:45 A.M., preparing to leave for my office at the university, I know that day will provide a new lesson. Each role I've played has been part of a lifelong educational process—as student, father, husband, professor, or president of a university. And because I've continually sought risks and challenge, never content with just one path, life has been fascinating and rewarding.

REFERENCES

Crowley, J. N.(1994). *No equal in the world*. Reno, NV: University of Nevada Press.

Fisher, J. L., & Koch, J. V.(1996). *Presidential leadership making a difference*. Phoenix, AZ: American Council on Education and the Oryx Press.

Kerr, C., & Gade, M. L.(1989). *The many lives of academic presidents: Time, place & character*. Washington, DC: Association of Governing Boards of Universities and Colleges.

Koehane, N.O. (1998, Fall). More power to the president? *The Presidency*, 12–17.

Marchese, T. J., Gamson, Z. F., & Ewell, P. (Eds.).(1998). *America's higher education leaders today & tomorrow*. Change, 30(1).

Shaw, K. A. (1999). *The successful president: "buzzwords" on leadership*. Phoenix, AZ: American Council on Education and the Oryx Press.

CHAPTER 52

FINDING MANY SELVES: IN THE MILITARY, THE CORPORATE, THE LAW, AND ON THE FARM

Fred Gibbs

MOM AND DAD

Basically, I think that growing up during the Depression shaped my earliest experiences. Mom and Dad came without prejudices. They taught me that everybody, no matter who they were, should be respected.

I realized early on that I was not the same as everybody else, that I wasn't better off economically but that my parents were very different. To be truthful, they did have a phobia against Irish Democrats. The police force was Irish. My dad believed that the police were crooks. But besides that, my parents were pretty evenhanded.

My mom was part of the intelligentsia and she often said that we had more responsibility "because we were better off." I would say that politically, my mom was a socialist and looked down on making money. My dad was an agnostic, which was common in the 1930s. Mom was into religion in a mystical way.

My parents struggled to make ends meet. My mom opened and ran the first nursery school in Buffalo, New York. She also ran the Sunday School for various Protestant denominations, so I got a sample of the various sects.

My parents were important influences on me. My dad's parents died after World War I, but my mom's parents remained very much in the picture. And I very much appreciate their impact on me as I grew up to become a man. My grandfather was an attorney. My grandmother was part of a large family and heiress to a large meatpacking fortune. One of my high school teachers introduced me as a boy whose family went from "rags to riches in three generations."

THE BOY

When I was a boy, my family moved around quite a bit. We moved in with my grandparents several times during the Depression. When my father became supervisor of the 22nd Ward, things got better. He was able to provide for us and even buy a home.

My dad had more of an influence on me than my mom. We would fish, hunt, and drink with the good old boys. He smoked cigarettes a lot but told me to stay away from that.

Mom was intellectual in her religion. She believed in a new age of peace and prosperity. And she taught me that I could achieve these things through prayer and belief.

I spent considerable time at my grandfather's farm. Perhaps it was because we had no other place to stay, but I enjoyed the farm and my grandfather. He ran a real working farm and taught me about it all.

I think I had an excellent public school education, which was very possible back in those days. It was an outstanding education. Initially, I had great trouble learning to read, but with my mom's help I became an excellent reader. I read the complete works of Mark Twain. I even had an entire autographed set of his works.

Because we never had much money around, I started to work at a young age. Both of my parents encouraged me to work. I had paper routes, and I went out on the farms with the Italian women who were the "stoop labor," picking crops with them to earn spending money.

I had a nice upbringing. My dad liked to camp a lot. He found and bought a place out on Lake Erie from an eccentric artist who had some fun but rundown cottages. Dad got the best one on a beautiful point of land outside Buffalo. Behind the cottage was a creek that entered the land for 500 yards. We shared it with other families. So there were always people sleeping all over the place, and we would cook suppers for all of them. We spent my summers there until World War II. Then the house fell down. We had to summer in other places.

MY TEEN YEARS

I do remember World War II. Because we had a German side of our family, I would be called Fritz, but that was only until 1942. Then we were at war with Germany and it was out of the question to be called Fritz. It was at that time I changed my name to Freddie.

I have mentioned that I worked at any number of jobs. I was a grocer, a soda counter waiter, and a cashier at a local store. In addition to work, however, I began to play sports. I became the champion breaststroke swimmer in Buffalo. While I might have been bored in school, I excelled in swimming, track and field, and football.

In puberty, I became very aggressive and went through a 5- or 6-year period of regularly fighting other boys. I never belonged to a group or gang. If someone was around who thought he was tough, I would fight him. This kind of behavior didn't win me many friends, so I changed my behavior and had a happier life. I also discovered girls and that calmed me down a bit.

I had a few steady girlfriends in high school but no one on a serious basis. That was the thing in those days. You went steady with one girl one week and another girl the next week. My mother always complained and said that we should go around as a group. Mom and Dad had a problem with my friends. They both wanted to get me away to a private school. I always refused to go.

We lived in a mixed neighborhood with lots of Germans. There were a lot of Waspy (white Anglo-Saxon Protestant) types and a lot of my father's dreaded Irish. And there was a section with African-Americans. That area was a respected one but we didn't socialize with them. I hardly ever ran into any of them.

Mom always had help in the house. One of them was a black woman. Mom had us go out and visit her home. It was very nice and it showed us that black people were just like us.

Most families were working-class. My mom was upset that I didn't have more friends who came from educated families and so she wasn't happy with my friends. It soured me on cliques and groups. I belonged to a fraternity in high school that was completely bigoted. They wouldn't allow Jews; they allowed Catholics but not Italian Catholics. In college, I joined my dad's fraternity and it was just the opposite. It allowed any race, religion, or ethnic group to join and always had a mix of persons. The fraternity also believed in hazing but it was very mild. We were told to clean the house; it was work related. It was the exception to the rule of fraternities.

The other thing is that I was close to my dad and I decided to follow in his footsteps and become an attorney and a politician. Dad wanted to become a judge. He had an outside shot to become a children's court judge in New York. My dad was a candidate and was given a good shot to win. My mom dissuaded him for two reasons: first, he wasn't very good with children, but that doesn't have anything to do with being a child court judge; second, Dad developed a serious drinking problem. He would drink heavily at lunch and then go to a local bar and occasionally never get home at all. On occasion he would become abusive, sometimes drunk, sometimes hung over. He beat me up because I was taunting him. It was one-sided because he was not in the best condition to control himself.

When he planned to run for the court my mom talked him out of it. He made a living as an attorney. He had some big clients of my grandfather's for a while and it looked as if he could support himself. When he lost the clients, he struggled for a while because he was out of politics. He did not have anything to fall back on.

University Days

I was then thinking of going to college. I still wanted to be a politician. My father's dad had been a state senator. My grandfather died early in the Depression. It was a huge blow. He had just gotten married and so the family took a completely different path.

How could I go to college and where would I go? Then came a great surprise. New York State held an examination for college scholarships. Competing for a scholarship was easy and the scholarship was sufficient to pay my tuition. Dad pushed me into his old school, Alfred University.

Mom thought of other New York state schools. The winning of the scholarship would guarantee admission into any school. To everyone's surprise, I won one of those scholarships. I learned that I was a good test taker, which resolved my problem of going to college.

I also had a scholarship to Princeton, part academic and part football. My dad talked me out of Princeton. The only person we knew in Buffalo who had gone to Princeton was Fats Green. He had two promiscuous daughters and so he didn't set a very good example regarding Princeton. If that was the type of person who went to Princeton then I would go to Alfred University and study history and political science. Actually, I am sure that I would have been better off at Princeton, but I did get a good education at Alfred University.

SEEING DIVERSITY

It was an interesting university. Alfred was the second oldest coeducational institution in the country. It had a reasonably good academic reputation. It got the graduates to go on to graduate school. It also accepted Jews. It didn't have a Jewish quota. It had a very large Jewish population by percentage. They were high-quality Jewish students who later went on to be very successful.

My experience with the Jewish students at Alfred was very different from the Jewish people I knew in Buffalo. The Alfred students came from New York City. That was like a foreign country with a very different culture and religion.

I wrote a paper for a leading engineering professor who happened to be Jewish. My paper was on how the Jewish people brought the Holocaust on themselves by calling themselves the Chosen People. I got a long lecture from that professor and then we became particularly good friends. I was not a Nazi. He got me to understand history in a much more accurate way.

LIFE AT ALFRED

Alfred was a rude awakening. Girls were not available. The upperclassmen snatched up the girls. It was an adjustment.

My scholarship covered room and board (about $500 in all). I needed and had earned spending money and I worked all of the time I was in school. I worked at the campus union. It was contracted out to a Greek family and so I worked for them. I was an usher at the campus movie. My job was to keep my fellow students quiet. I was a proctor in the freshman residence. I did yard work. I worked at the local post office on the holidays. Also, I had joined the Marine Corps Reserves in high school but didn't go to Parris Island.

The Korean War came along and I knew that the Marine Corps would call me up so I ended up joining. I was patriotic. I enlisted in the patroon leaders' corps, the officers training group in the marines. And so I was in the marines officer training my first year of college and went to Parris Island during the summer and then worked at the Ford stamping plant. You could get a good job in Buffalo in those days.

The last couple of years that I was in high school, dad was without a car and going through difficult times. He thought he could get a new car from a buddy. I got a ride with friends or by hitchhiking. I hitchhiked a ride back to Alfred. Between the second and third year of college I hitchhiked to Los Angeles. I got a job with North American Aviation for the summer and after that I hitchhiked back. I saw a lot of the country. Weird people.

At Alfred I was quite an athlete. On the wrestling team I lost only one match during my entire collegiate experience. It took me a few years to learn how to win in the regular tournaments.

MY JANICE

I guess I met Janice in my sophomore year. She was in my Spanish class. She was a good Spanish student, very good. We were taking second-year Spanish. Janice was the best looking girl of the undergraduates. Those days, I was very partial to blondes but she was the one I married.

CAREER THINKING

I guess the first plan during college was to either go into government or to follow my father's footsteps and go to the University of Buffalo Law School. One of my political science professors talked me into one semester at the American University. Students from the hinterlands (Midwest) got a chance to see how the federal government worked.

It was a very interesting experience for me. I met a whole different group of young persons from religious colleges who had strange ideas. I found them to be very intolerant regarding other people's beliefs.

I did learn quite a bit about government. I was pretty naive. One poor guy and I were the only Republicans in the room. But, Democrat or Liberal, we all believed that we were overtaxed and that we lost much of our freedom because of it. It was an interesting experience. We met people whose names we had read in the newspapers.

I was recruited by the Central Intelligence Agency (CIA). When they heard that I was already in the marines, they said to wait until later. I would have needed a master's degree in languages. At that time I had only had 2 years of college and that would not cut it. Other branches of the government didn't interest me.

Near graduation, I considered that it was not practical to go to Buffalo Law School. My dad did not have enough law business for himself so his practice didn't seem to offer much opportunity for me. In addition, Dad was out of politics so I wouldn't have a leg up, so I rethought things. Actually, I agonized over it. Mom would be terribly disappointed if I did not become a professional.

While it was not hard to get a job, I found the interviews to be miserable. The best offer I got was from the telephone company. Mom expressed disappointment. Dad was not particularly impressed, but to Mom, I was just going to be a money-grubber and not do good things for people. The telephone company hired me before the marines called me up for service, and so I started out at $100 a week.

Then A Few Good Men

Before long, the marines did call me and I went to serve. I feel that the marines enabled me to truly build up my personal character. The teamwork and leadership experiences, which I had then, were a great help later on in my work career. I think that the best thing I learned from the marine corps was a sense of loyalty and a feeling of being in an elite group of achievers. I believe that they really did an outstanding job, and I carried much of it forward in my life.

I did get a regular commission and I thought of making it a lifelong career. Some of the men I worked with had been in Korea a year or two ahead of me. Vietnam had not started yet. Reluctantly, I left when my tour of duty was over.

Again, I thought about law school. I was married. I had little money, so I went to work for the telephone company. It was no different from the marine corps and not much different than working for the government. It took me a while to figure it out, but they worked on you the same as the marine corps.

All of your friends and associates were telephone people and they worked there for all of their lives. They became Bell Systems people. Fortunately, just like in the marines, I did like it all. But after I had been doing it for 8 or 9 years, I realized that I still had 30 more years to work. It was clear what those 30 years would be. And I didn't see myself as a head of the Bell System.

Then a Corporate Move

The International Telephone and Telegraph Corporation (ITT) was everything that the Bell System and the marine corps were not. It was a professionally managed company. Managers were hired from somewhere else rather than always being promoted from within the corporation. Internationally, there were more foreigners than Americans but the top executives were all Americans. They were not the usual management; they were actually quite different. Certainly, they were not the same type of people as from the telephone company. Often the ITT managers were not as nice as a lot of the Bell people.

ITT had a very different work ethic. The other thing I really liked was that ITT was not as hierarchical as the military. At Bell, you dealt with your boss, and only on rare occasions, the boss's boss.

I remember being at ITT a few weeks and having gone to South America. I got a call from the head of ITT who asked questions about what I should do in the future. I met the executive vice president of ITT who was responsible for both North and South America and we discussed a couple of different management styles. Both in the military and at the phone company your job was described for you with a system designed by them to be run by idiots. There was a policy for everything.

At ITT, I didn't have to do things in a specific way. ITT did not have any policy or job descriptions. I had a vague title and vague responsibilities. An executive was able to make the job any way he chose. It was not complete chaos. An executive was able to figure it all out and decide what would work. You were only limited by yourself. It was very exciting.

I discovered after a year or so at ITT that it was very necessary for managers to speak the local language. It was impossible to attempt to do business all in English. Although it was difficult, I became one of the very few North American executives who could speak more than English. While I was in South America I learned to speak Italian and French, also. This language ability really helped my career.

I went to Brazil in 1977. I was 6,000 miles from headquarters. I ran everything in Portuguese. So I ran the company pretty much as I wanted to. As long as I was successful, that was all that was expected.

CHANGES

That ability to be independent began to change, and my successors down in Brazil got into trouble for not following policies. When I returned, there was a huge staff. Profits went down because of the changes in management style which became strictly money focused; there were controls rather than a strict goals and independent responsibility focus. It became much more of a bureaucracy.

So ITT ended its days as a corporation that capitalized on the innovative strengths of its management and became a traditional monolithic organization. Ultimately, the company was broken into pieces and sold off, so the corporation that I knew in the 1970s no longer exists today.

Yet, I did have a terrific experience at ITT. Success took me out of a common group. I was the chief operating officer of the group and president of the United States Telephone and Telegraph, which had owned a bunch of other companies also.

I was put in charge of the research and development of the digital switching system. I went out of a line operation and into research and development. I stayed there for 3 years. I developed a product line, which was truly revolutionary. I was in charge of it. The engineers in three or four countries developed product lines, which could be used in many countries.

Then the Peter Principle kicked in. Theoretically, some managers reported to me and some did not. They all had mentors. I had the responsibility but not the control. That was the last job I had at ITT.

After being responsible for so long for a huge number of people, I was called back and fired. Management was in a chaotic mess. The division was sold. I was in charge of strengthening the management, either to strengthen or to sell it. When it was sold, that was the end of my career with ITT. I took the responsibility for not pulling it together. The company who bought it made a huge amount of money.

I really had seen that many of my executive vice presidents were getting dismissed or retired so I know that was the new style. And I realized that someone had to take the fall, and I knew that it would be me.

THE FARM AND THE LAW

Because I wanted to have something to fall back on, I went back to the soil and bought a working farm in Pemberton, New Jersey.

I was urged to go out and get another job. I could have gotten another job basically, but they would not have had to pay off the full separation contract.

I started looking for another job. This was before the technological explosion began to roll onto the scene. I returned to thoughts of law school. I took a cram course for the Law School Admission Test (LSAT). I studied hard. I made the top 8% and had no trouble getting into law school. I should have gone to the University of Pennsylvania, but once again I wasn't interested in building a legal career.

At 54, I started at Rutgers University and passed the bar exam at 57. I thought that I would have 10 years to practice at best. So, I went to Rutgers' Camden because it was the closest school.

I commuted from the farm in Pemberton and had a great time at law school. I wasn't as great a student as I thought I would be based on my success on the LSAT. It took me 3 years to write like an attorney. I had my ups and downs in law school. I learned that I could not avoid certain courses and so took advantage of doing the essays and had them corrected by people who knew the law exam. And I got through the bar exam on my first try and a lot of my classmates did not. I am very proud of that. Many of the students could have been my grandchildren and the professors were the age of my children. Some students were my age but they kept in the background.

I was hired by a good law firm in Cherry Hill, New Jersey. I told them to treat me as they would treat any new person. I worked there for 2 years. They wanted me because I looked mature.

By chance, I hung out a shingle on my farmhouse and worked the farm, which I really loved. There was only one other lawyer in Pemberton at the time. He was very bright, but strange, and he turned people off. I got clients doing the same things he did, so his clients came to me.

GIBBS AND GREGORY

I had one major problem in my practice. It was pointless to build it up because I thought that I wouldn't be around much longer. That was until Stan Gregory came to see me.

Stan was an attorney who had just married a lovely woman. As an African-American attorney in Pemberton, he couldn't get a job.

"What do you think?" he started to say. And not knowing if we could make a living, he came on board on a trial basis.

It was great for me to have him, and together we built a thriving law practice. Once he got going, he had lots of support from the whole community. He was picked for the Pemberton Hall of Fame. He was appointed as Pemberton's chief counselor by both Democrats and Republicans. Stan had served a clerkship in family law and had been a public defender. With his background in court as a public defender, he quickly built a terrific reputation in Pemberton.

So Stan and I work very well together and now we employ six additional attorneys and together we have built up a fine practice. Gibbs and Gregory handles workmen's compensation, bankruptcy, real estate, personal injury, and elder care.

And so, my career continues, grows, and flourishes. Am I going to retire? Sure, but not yet.

Chapter 53

When the Sun Shines You Cannot See the Moon

Stephen R. Marrone

I am a single, 43-year-old man, soon to be 44. I have been a registered professional nurse for 22 years. I am an only child of an Italian-American family living in Brooklyn, New York, and was born under the sign of Taurus the Bull—characteristics which I think will become apparent as you read this chapter. Depending on how you look at it I am middle-aged, whatever that means. I remember a nursing professor in my undergraduate program saying that you don't really know when you are "middle-aged" until you die. I don't think that I will be in the mood to write this manuscript then, so the best I can tell you is that I am in my 40s and looking forward to my future. But I realize that I have been living, breathing, learning, making mistakes, learning some more, loving, caring, fighting, and making up, not necessarily in that order, for a long time. In fact, while teaching medical students recently, all of whom were 21 and 22 years old, I remember thinking that I have been "nursing" for as long or longer than they have been breathing! It really makes one think! The word *aging* comes to mind. Ugh! Opportunity or burden? Only I can decide the path. The outcome will be the result of luck, love, strategy, and the will of a higher power.

I am also an avid reader of Dame Agatha Christie, who is my favorite author. I have read all of her novels, plays, and short stories, her autobiography, and even the romance novels she wrote under the pseudonym Mary Westmacott. It was while reading *Death on the Nile* recently for probably the 10th or 11th time that two lines of a paragraph struck me as meaningful, but at the time I didn't know why. The lines in the paragraph read, "It's like the moon when the sun comes out. You don't know it's there anymore." As I continue to explore and redefine my life, I feel in many ways that this sentiment reflects very much how I am feeling at this time. This is a journey of transition. A transition from shining brightly as the sun to gently glowing as the moon. My challenge, however, is not to become invisible.

* * *

I spent much of my early life in the company of my large extended family. Perhaps this explains why, in spite of being an only child, I do not have a problem sharing and I like to feel connected with others and part of a group. I do, however, find that I can be very protective of my "territory" and need, rather than like, my privacy. I think this reflects the fact that I have become accustomed to having my own space and quiet "me" time. In addition to being an only child, I am also the first child, which definitely accounts for my need to be the best that I can be. Having no one else close to my age to compete with, I became very self-competitive, a trait which, at times, I either value or abhor. It works well when it motivates me to become the best that I can be. It sometimes, however, serves as an obstacle for me to enjoy my successes because I am so wrapped up in figuring out how I could do better next time. The word *frustration* comes to mind: the "F" word of my early years.

Much of this frustration came from the messages I received from my parents when I was very young. I always knew that my parents loved me and wanted nothing but the best for me. I am sure my father would have been happy and proud of me as long as I was happy and proud of myself. Unfortunately, I would never describe my father as a great communicator. He was not always comfortable expressing his affection and would often make jokes when he really wanted to say that he was proud of me. I only learned this later in life when I became an adult. I can remember many times when I would bring home good grades from school and my father would say things like "Why only 95, couldn't you get a hundred?" Somehow that was a joke. Hello dad, to a kid this was no joke. What I was hearing was I wasn't good enough and needed to do better.

My mother also instilled in me the need to be the best. I remember my mother saying "I don't care what you decide to do in your life, not even if you choose to clean the streets for a living, just make sure you are the best." Perhaps she forgot to make herself perfectly clear. Years later, after numerous conversations and arguments, my mother told me that she always wanted me to be the best that "I" could be. Somehow she left this little part out. Perhaps if I had been older I would have been able to read between the lines. But young children are not good at reading between the lines. To me it was all the same. Be the best or be my best, I was never satisfied with anything I did. And I never thought that my parents were satisfied with anything I did either. Many years later I learned just how wrong I was.

In spite of the frustration in my early years, I often look back and wonder if this wasn't good for me after all. My parents always did the best that they could. And while I sometimes wish they had done things differently, I know in my heart that they did their best, and I am grateful that they took the time to drive me crazy so that I would become a responsible, if not sometimes overextended, adult.

The expectation to be perfect, for me and oftentimes others, has increased my awareness and sensitivity to being judged. Like most first children, we are expected by our parents to be perfect, to behave, to grow up and get all of the childhood diseases strictly by the book (Dr. Spock, that is—author of several "how to" books for parents). Being a first and only son makes this intensity toward perfection even more profound. After all, I will be expected to carry on the family name. I soon learned during this time that pleasing authority was the safest thing to do. But sometimes this rendered me invisible. Attending Catholic school for 12 years did very little to change my worldview (a word I didn't even know at the time) about this. Fear, punishment, fire and brimstone, and repentance were all a big part of my early school years. All great motivators to learn if you like that sort of thing. Learn or go to hell. I chose to learn. I hate the heat.

* * *

My parents came from poor families and they made it all the way to middle class. I am proud of them, although I don't tell them often enough. My parents, like all parents, wanted me to have more than they had. They worked hard and did everything they could to ensure my safety and success. Nothing was too much and I never heard them complain about their hard work. My mother had a great passion for books, a quality she gained from her father and passed on to me. My mother's father was a longshoreman. He was not well educated and spent long hours in all kinds of weather performing heavy-duty manual labor, yet he loved to read and he loved classical music. So much for judging a book by its cover.

My mother grew up during the Depression. This experience, coupled with her father's influence, shaped her worldview. One outcome of this is my mother's appreciation of learning and the value of money. I was the only kid on the block who at 3 years of age had a complete set of Encyclopedia Britannica reference books. Years later when I asked my mother why she bought the books when I was much too young to read them, she said "Your father and I had the money then so we bought them. I didn't know if we would have the money when you needed them." At the time the word *proactive* was not in my vocabulary, but I think this was my first exposure to the concept of thinking ahead. This quality served me well in my later years. This was also the beginning of my passion for books and for learning. I also remember my mother saying that "books are living things." She made it very clear that one never wrote in books, tore pages out of books, or damaged books in any way. Not bad advice. To this day I have difficulty using a highlighter when reading a text or journal article. Thanks Mom!

From reading so much though I have to wear eyeglasses. Not a bad outcome when you think how much you gain from having a passion for reading. I have worn eyeglasses since I was 12 years old and have just recently graduated to wearing bifocals. Just another privilege of middle age, I suppose.

I think that my family life was, in part, responsible for my choosing nursing as a career. Since my parents did not instill in me any gender-specific notions about roles, I was not hampered by stereotypical views of what careers men could or should choose. I know that my parents were the driving force behind many of my later personal and professional successes. My parents always get angry when I say thank you because they feel that whatever they did they did with love, and that family shouldn't speak to each other like strangers. Nevertheless, to my mother and father who always put me first I do say thank you. I could not have done it without you.

In spite of my Italian-American heritage, my family did not embrace the stereotypical male and female role identities and role relationships, that is, both men and women were equal partners. My father, Anthony, was an only child from the age of 5 (his brother and sister died when they were children). My mother, Patricia, was one of eight children, seven girls and one boy. Perhaps this contributed to the lack of strictly defined male and female roles. I don't mean that my parents were ambiguous about role relationships. They, each through their respective life experiences, were in my mind ahead of the times regarding the age-old issue of men versus women. In my home there was no such thing.

My mother worked part-time and my father worked full-time and often worked a second job. Until I was old enough to help out around the house my parents shared the housework. My father usually did the heavier cleaning like vacuuming and washing the windows since my mother suffers from chronic lung disease. At first I thought this sharing of the housework was unique to my family and largely because of my mother's poor health. After all, this wasn't what I saw on *Leave It To Beaver*! My mother never wore a frilly white apron, pearls, and pumps at 7 o'clock in the morning, and my father never came to the dinner table wearing a suit. Laugh about it if you like, but for a couple of years I thought, "How did I get stuck with such slobs as parents? We don't even have a dining room!" Little did I know at the time that I was living in the real world of simple, loving, and caring parents. Thank you God for that privilege.

This sharing of responsibilities in my family continues today. Now that my father is retired, Friday night is his night to cook dinner. My mother considers this the best night of the week since she doesn't have to figure out what to make for dinner. I wouldn't have thought that this was such a big deal, yet I find myself at a loss for suggestions when my mother asks, "What do you feel like having for dinner tonight?" Is that your final answer? Oh, by the way, I don't live with my parents anymore and haven't for years, but I'm not sure they have accepted that fact yet. My mother still asks me what I want for dinner. That's her way of asking, "Are you eating well? Do you need anything?" If I tell her what I'm in the mood for she spends the day cooking it, and my father dutifully brings it over and leaves it on my kitchen counter. Thanks Dad! At least I don't have to give him a tip. Perhaps this is why I so highly value effective communication. My parents often talked in code. Love comes in many ways.

While my mother worked I would spend the mornings with her oldest sister, my Aunt Mary, who lived around the corner. Aunt Mary had a passion for daytime soap operas, most of which took place exclusively or in part in a hospital. I was probably the only 5-year-old boy in my neighborhood who knew the story lines for *General Hospital* and *As the World Turns*. The outcome of this immersion in the soaps was a fascination for hospitals, and for some unknown reason I identified with the nurses. So enters Nurse Stephen Marrone. I remember sterilizing wooden toothpicks in boiling water on the stove. My aunt would of course oversee this project and protect me from getting hurt. I would remove the sterilized wooden "needles" with a pair of forceps, also known to mere mortals as eyebrow tweezers, and then attach red thread from my aunt's sewing kit to the "sterilized" toothpick. I would secure the toothpick on my aunt's arm with a Band-Aid and tie the other end to the pole lamp in the living room. While having her transfusion my aunt would enjoy her soaps. I firmly believe that my Aunt Mary lived as long as she did because of all those transfusions and adherence to strict aseptic technique.

* * *

To complement my family life, school played an important part in shaping me as a person. My values and beliefs are largely grounded in Catholic doctrine, in spite of the jokes I occasionally make about my 12 years of Catholic school. You might say that I spent the first third of my life trying to fit in and mold myself into whatever seemed to be what people around me expected. Although I received an excellent grammar school education, my motivation to learn was driven by fear and punishment from both my teachers and my parents. Not easy considering that everyone had different expectations and sometimes these external expectations were different from the expectations I had of myself. I sometimes think that I became a nurse educator just so that I would never fear teachers again. Infiltrate the enemy. Or maybe it was just the red pen. But no one told me that teachers had to do their homework too. What a bummer.

I don't think I was savvy enough at the time to know that I was in conflict. I just thought, "This is confusing." The idea of having expectations of others was also slowly emerging. This experience served as a new beginning for me and continued to develop in high school.

My high school years were probably some of the most confusing in my life. I attended an all-male Catholic high school which was considered the best Catholic high school in Brooklyn. It still is. I remember being so proud that I was accepted because only a small percentage of academically gifted boys were admitted each year. I always received good grades in school (remember, I had to please everyone and fear is a powerful motivator). It wasn't until high school, however, that I began trying to do well for myself. The curriculum was more flexible than in grammar school and much more in touch with the real world. Remember you can learn from bad examples and bad experiences too!

The passion for learning which my mother, and indirectly my maternal grandfather, instilled in me earlier in my life continued to blossom in high school. I continued to worry about getting good grades, but I began to lose the fear of teachers that I had in grammar school. The faculty seemed more caring and approachable. I wonder if they seemed more approachable because most of them were young men who were also Xaverian Brothers. No, not an all-male family singing group, but a religious order of men. Perhaps I perceived them, without realizing it at the time, as role models who represented possibilities for me in my future. I wonder if this wasn't one reason why high school became a positive turning point in my student career. In my later years of high school my fear of teachers, and authority as a whole, was transformed into a true respect for the teachers' skill, compassion (something I didn't see much of before), and ability to open up a world of new and exciting opportunities.

High school was also the time when I developed my sense of humor. It may sound strange but it was a conscious decision on my part to do so. Humor is the one quality I possess that I truly feel has kept me going when times get rough. This may sound arrogant, but I do feel that I am an incredibly funny person. I even crack myself up!

My humor, however, is very situational. I don't think I would be as funny if I rehearsed my lines beforehand. You need a lot of humor to make heads or tails out of life. Especially today when we are living on the edge of chaos. The real reason I developed a sense of humor was that I found if you made people laugh they more easily accepted you. In high school I needed to be accepted because I was the smart but "plump" guy with glasses. I wasn't a jock and I wasn't so smart that everyone wanted my homework. So I needed a gimmick. As the characters Miss Mazeppa, Miss Electra, and Miss Tessie Tura sang in the production of *Gypsy* . . . "Get yourself a gimmick and you too could be a star."

Humor was my gimmick and I had most everyone eating out of my hand. Perhaps it was about control. Perhaps it was about acceptance. Perhaps it was fear of being vulnerable. Most likely all three. As long as I kept them laughing, it worked like a charm. Whatever works. And it continues to work today.

* * *

It has been a while since I gave my aunt blood transfusions in her living room, but my desire to become a nurse continued to grow. In spite of what I have already said about my family's lack of rigid stereotypical views of male and female roles, I was embarrassed to tell my parents, particularly my father, that I wanted to become a nurse. I would say that I was thinking of becoming a pathologist or a pharmacist. At least I would get them thinking of health care. To this point in my life I didn't know of any male role models in nursing. I also wanted to learn more about nursing as an option for men. All of the nurses in the soaps were women. I knew no men in nursing and wasn't even sure this career choice was possible. I needed to get a close-up view of hospitals and how nurses worked. So, in my junior year of high school I applied and was accepted as a volunteer at a local community hospital. I was fortunate to be assigned to a newly opened intensive care unit where I learned from nurses what nursing was and was proud, and relieved, to learn that men were valued members of the profession.

I also had a bird's-eye view of what nurses did. And I liked what I saw. I observed that while other health care providers came and went, it was the nurse who spent time with the patients. Quality time it seemed to me. I would see the patients' faces light up when the nurse came to their bedside to provide care. There appeared to be inherent trust in the nurse-patient relationship. Perhaps this is why the American public continues to identify nursing as the most trusted profession. I also noticed that nursing was not medications, procedures, bedpans, and backrubs, but human caring. It was the nurse who truly touched the lives of patients and families. And I was amazed to learn how patients touched the lives of nurses. To this day, I can remember so many of the patients I helped care for while in high school and throughout my career. They taught me just as much as my nursing faculty did.

I was amazed at the support I received to become a nurse from the men and women who had already taken that path. With my passion for becoming a nurse thus fueled, I proudly announced my desire to become a nurse to my parents, gladly filled out the thousands of papers required of applicants to university nursing programs, and announced to my high school counselor that I wanted to study nursing in college.

Surprise! My parents thought it was great, although my father had to get used to saying "my son the nurse." I think my father's reaction was essentially a conditioned response. He is a highly decorated World War II veteran and it was probably hard for him to think of me as a "ministering angel." Now, after 22 years in the profession, my father proudly tells anyone who is willing to stand still long enough to listen about his son the nurse. With time comes acceptance and hopefully growth and enlightenment. With time, and with God's grace, also comes maturity and wisdom, and for me, forgiveness. At least that's what I tell myself.

Over 90% of my graduating high school class were awarded Regent's scholarships to attend college. I remember anxiously awaiting the day when all of our names would be announced alphabetically over the school loudspeaker. When the M's had come and gone, my name was never announced. Sadly I returned home to look again at the Regent's scholarship award that I had received in the mail earlier in the week. I'm sure it said that I was a winner. Well, guess what? I won a Regent's "Nursing" Scholarship and my high school, being an all-boys school, never even requested this list. This is probably the only scar that high school left on me.

Essentially the response at my high school to my decision to study nursing in college was silence, or comments such as "nursing is not a profession for men" and "someone as smart as you should become a doctor." Sad but true, I continue to hear these comments today. The message was clear—boys don't become nurses. Well guess again, this boy did! There is still a stigma to overcome. But now I say to people who tell me that I should have become a doctor . . . "Yes, you are absolutely right. And in five years I will be a doctor . . . a Doctor of Education in Nursing!" Funny how most people don't know that you can earn a doctorate in nursing. And what really freaks people out is that now they don't even know what to call you. How can you be a doctor nurse? Well I won't earn my doctorate for another 5 years, so they have time to figure it out.

Until my graduation from high school I would frequently be quoted as saying "I hate school." And it was true. I never really liked school and always felt pressured to do well, but mostly for all of the wrong reasons. College was quite different. For the first time in my career as a student I was studying subjects that I enjoyed and which had meaning for my future. I was becoming a nurse. I guess it was those adult learning principles coming through. I loved my undergraduate nursing program, difficult as it was. My graduate program in nursing was also a stressful but rewarding experience. And now, as I write, I am awaiting to begin my doctorate in nursing. So much for hating school. Do you think this is payback time? "I'll get you my pretty, and your little dog too!" Wicked Witch. Oz. You know the rest.

* * *

By now you are probably wondering, where does this sun and moon thing come in?

Am I right? Well the concept of the shining star, the sun, first began in college.

After years of trying to do well in school, developing the art of humor and finally studying to become a nurse all came together like a mosaic. Many of my nursing written assignments were copied and used as examples of how to write a nursing care plan (yuk!!!) for future classes, and my instructors often encouraged me to publish some of my term paper assignments. My confidence to share my work beyond my immediate world was not yet developed, but the seed was planted. I think that my value of the written word and respect for books also made the idea of publishing my work in a journal or text seem too overwhelming for me. What could I possibly say that should be printed on these hallowed pages of learning?

Upon graduation I received one of the five nursing departmental awards for outstanding academic achievement in nursing. I also received a fellowship to attend graduate school. I was beginning to see some external and tangible recognition for my hard work. Negative external factors, fear and punishment, had for many years been the driving force behind most of my successes. What a privilege, and a sense of freedom, it was to transform my thinking to a point where I am internally driven to achieve outcomes that are meaningful for myself and contribute to the health and well-being of others. Although external factors are no longer my principle driving force, they certainly helped with my ego enhancement. My professional biography has been included in *Who's Who in American Nursing*, *Who's Who in Medicine and Healthcare*, and *Who's Who in America*. Not bad for a kid from Brooklyn!

Success did not only come in nursing. One of the assignments in my undergraduate speech class was to do a commercial. Well, being a big fan of the *I Love Lucy* show I did the "Vitameatavegamin" commercial so well known from that series. It was a hit. I had graduated from using humor one-to-one and in small groups in high school, mostly as a way to keep from getting beaten up, to working a whole room. Watch out *Saturday Night Live*! Now isn't that special!

My nursing career has been enriched with many "shining" moments. In spite of being discouraged by some in my quest to become a nurse, I found that men often excel in the profession. We frequently choose specialty areas that are highly technical in nature, settings such as the intensive care unit, operating room, and emergency room. Are these natural for us because of our assertive, no-nonsense styles? Perhaps. Do we have to prove ourselves? Could be. Are we given more opportunities to grow? Maybe. Are men natural born leaders? Who is to say? If this were true I don't think that I would have gotten very far in the profession as the vast majority of my mentors have been exceptional women. One reason I think men do well in nursing by and large is that male physicians can't play those doctor-nurse games with us. These games, of course, are nothing more than male-female games where the rules are stacked in the favor of men. And no, just for the record, if you think that I am a "male nurse" you are mistaken. I am a nurse who is male. Big difference.

* * *

My first nursing position was as a staff nurse in the Cardiothoracic Surgical Intensive Care Unit at the Mount Sinai Hospital in New York City. What a thrill to be a cardiothoracic critical care nurse immediately after graduation. I can remember reading the *Physicians' Desk Reference* (PDR), a Bible of sorts of drug information, on the subway each morning on my way to work. God forbid I didn't know all of the drips and other medications my patient was on. As I whisked through underground tunnels toward work, I would have flashbacks of earlier days where fear drove my learning. Interestingly enough I didn't find these high practice expectations overwhelming. I was inspired to excel and wanted to rise to the occasion. I worked hard, had wonderful educators, preceptors (we didn't use the word *mentor* much then), and managers helping me along the way, and I soon became successful in my chosen profession. I owe many of my successes to the rich learning and practice environment at the Mount, as many of the staff affectionately call the hospital. I quickly moved up the ranks from staff nurse to education specialist, caring for cardiac surgical patients and their families in the critical care and perioperative settings.

And then I left. After working at the Mount Sinai Hospital for 10 years I began to wonder if I would be able to practice effectively in any other environment. Was I really any good? Or was it a case of "been there, done that?" If taken out of my usual surroundings would I be a fish out of water or would I simply find a new pond? So I went out on my own for a few years and consulted in a variety of management and education roles. Guess what . . . I could do it! So far I mastered the science of nursing. Now I was beginning to understand the art of nursing. This shining star, the sun, was taking his act on the road.

This road eventually led me to the Kingdom of Saudi Arabia, affectionately called the Magic Kingdom by expatriates, where I lived and worked for 7 years. If you want to learn about yourself, who you really are, why you think this way or that, what's right, what's wrong, or what is just different, then live in another culture. This experience by far was the best education I have ever received. Until then I was not a strong believer in the school of life. I used to think that people who said they were graduates of the school of life were really deadbeats with passable vocabularies. In the Kingdom my life was enriched and changed forever. I had the privilege of experiencing a culture that is still essentially closed to the outside world. Where customs and traditions, some fascinating and some frightening, are centuries old. And where the strength of the family unit is still highly valued.

This experience also afforded me the opportunity to live and work with people from all over the world and enabled me to develop, and over time refine, my global perspective. It is like taking a trip around the world without leaving your living room. Tremendous personal growth took place during these 7 years. I will never be the same again. Just in case you are wondering, this is a good thing.

* * *

My nursing career in Saudi Arabia continued to evolve, mature, and grow. I was fortunate to live and work in an environment that was ripe for cross-cultural research. Thus inspired, I had the privilege and opportunity to champion the design of the first competency-based nursing practice model in a multicultural setting. Saudi graduate students of nursing have adapted parts of this model for their master's theses in pursuit of the development of nursing practice standards for the Kingdom. Words cannot express the honor I felt for having contributed in some way to a model of education and practice which has been recognized as meaningful to the health and care of the people of Saudi Arabia and the profession of nursing in the global arena.

As a result of this accomplishment, I have published a number of articles related to competency-based practice (CBP), traveled throughout the Kingdom and the Middle East to present the model, and conducted workshops for hospitals to adapt the model to the needs of their organizations. In Saudi Arabia my nickname was CBP Steve! Yes, not-so-little Stephen Marrone from Brooklyn, New York, has made a global impact. This may sound like arrogance but I am still in awe of this accomplishment and am humbled by the work of others who have inspired and taught me to think globally.

Did it help to be a man in Saudi Arabia? Yes, I think it did. The Saudi culture is patriarchal and men have certain definite advantages in the corporate decision-making arena. In the Middle East nursing is a profession with a much higher percentage of men than in the West. Therefore being a male was helpful in trying to develop a nursing model, and furthermore trying to expand the application of the model to other organizations throughout the Kingdom. So be it. For the record, many of my mentors were women.

Because the interior of Saudi Arabia is essentially flat desert, you can simultaneously witness the sunset in the west and the rising of the moon in the east. This is one of the most spectacular sights that I have ever seen—and a sight that inspired me to think of my life as it continues to unfold. Hence the title of this chapter. See how that sun and moon thing fits in? And now, don't be shy. I know you want to ask me the question everyone asks: "Is it hot in Saudi Arabia?" Yes it is. And it is the biggest beach without water in the world.

* * *

I am back at the Mount Sinai Hospital and feeling at home. And my career continues to skyrocket. The sun does shine brightly, but with such glare. On a personal and professional level this glare is being felt with dramatic results. I now find myself shining so brightly that I am getting burned. Too much of a good thing perhaps? Looking for love in all the wrong places? I do, however, recognize the need to revisit and reevaluate other aspects of my life. Personal development has for too long been linked with professional development. I am always a nurse. But I am a person, a son, a cousin, a nephew, a godfather, a godson, a lover, and a friend too. No wonder I am so tired. I am working hard to strike a balance in my life. Yes it is like a juggling act and sometimes I drop a few balls. Before I would dwell on the fact that I wasn't perfect. Well surprise, no one is. And who would want to be around someone who is perfect anyway?

How irritating that would be. Now I just pick up those dropped balls, dust them off, bang out a few dents, say I'm sorry, and move on. Oh yeah, I try to learn from the experience too!

I am not afraid anymore. Fear, of people, of failure, no longer drives my personal and professional decisions. And I have finally gained the insight to distinguish the difference between being selfish and taking care of myself. I am more content with myself and with my priorities. I have a track record of success and know how to continue being successful. But I can't continue saying yes to everything. I am now more comfortable saying no. Thank you Nancy Reagan!

My priorities have also changed. Family and friends are more important now. Perhaps they always were but I don't think I realized it. Until now I don't remember when and how they fit into the equation. When I was younger I didn't think about my demise or the demise of others, and I took things, and people, for granted. While in Saudi Arabia I lost one half of my family, and three of my friends moved to the West Coast. I left behind parents whom I never thought of as old and came home to find an old man and old woman. Sometimes I feel saddened, and even angry, not to have been more a part of my parents' last years. Our memories are of telephone conversations and bad connections from 7,000 miles away. Memories of flowers sent electronically rather than hugs and kisses with real lips on real cheeks. I now have a greater appreciation of the word *good-bye*. For all we know it may be our last good-bye. Also, don't go to bed mad at anyone. Didn't your mother ever tell you that? Now I never do.

My love of travel—I have visited over 50 countries—has encouraged me to develop adaptive skills which help me to appreciate different or even bizarre surroundings. Sometimes bizarre can be fun! But nothing in my travel experiences could have prepared me for the challenge of repatriating to the United States. There are even courses on reentry. Can you believe it? They have courses on how to go home! There are some who say you can never go home again. But that's another chapter.

* * *

Repatriation was a harder transition for me than I could ever have imagined. It was much more difficult than adapting to the culture and societal norms of Saudi Arabia, a culture very different from my own. When you enter another culture you expect to feel a little off balance for a while. But seriously, who thinks that returning "home" would be difficult? Home is home. After living in Saudi Arabia for 7 years, however, I was not really returning to the home I left. Home had changed. Time did not stand still in New York City while I was continuing to live my life in Saudi Arabia. I came home changed also. It seems so obvious but you just don't think of it. Reverse culture shock can be, and is, overwhelming. And it makes me angry to feel like an outsider in my own city and culture. I sometimes feel lonely too. People can't relate to the stories that I tell about my time and experiences in Saudi Arabia or other travels to parts unknown.

During the first 2 years of my repatriation, I was filled with a profound sense of loss. Loss of family. Loss of friends. And the loss of a health care system that I knew. These losses had a most significant impact on my life—an impact that thrust me into personal and professional turmoil. I believe this is the reason I was so moved by the lines that Agatha Christie wrote about the sun and the moon. Moved to the point of recognizing my need to reflect on my life. My need to rethink the direction my life was taking versus the direction I wanted my life to take. My need to explore opportunities—and the paths to achieve them—that were open to me. Or paths, in some cases, which I needed to create for myself. In essence, I needed "me" time. I am slowly able to say truthfully that I am glad to be home. Click heels three times . . . "There's no place like home." Dorothy. Glinda. That Oz thing again.

Luckily I still have my parents and have vowed that I will always be with them, especially for holidays and other special occasions, until the good Lord decides it is time for us to part. I also value and cherish my long-term friends and the more recent friendships I made with the people I met in Saudi Arabia. My friends live in all four corners of the world. So far I have been faithful in keeping in touch. There's really no excuse not to these days with e-mail and such. What peace! Internal rewards have won out over external. Too bad I didn't learn this earlier. But I am glad that I learned this now. Some people never do.

Throughout my life, classical music and the ballet have played important roles in releasing my mind from the day-to-day trials and tribulations that clutter my thinking when trying to make important and oftentimes difficult decisions. This passion for music was instilled in me at an early age by my mother who, in turn, was exposed to beautiful music by her father. Music in general helps me to transcend the boundaries of the physical world and to imagine endless possibilities. When watching the ballet I am also moved by the dancer's ability to blend movement and music into one seamless artistic feast. I think of ballet as an orgy for the soul and secretly envy the dancers their ability to create exquisite beauty with their bodies. A timeless beauty which touches the lives and souls of strangers. As you might expect, I have been listening to a lot of classical music lately. I have also been a frequent visitor to Lincoln Center to see the ballet. There is nothing quite like watching a live ballet performance. Thousands of hearts beating at the same time, each being transformed by the music into swans, sylphs, princesses, princes, lovers, and sometimes thieves and other evil villains. I have always felt art was a form of therapy. At least music and ballet have always been therapeutic for me.

* * *

When I wrote my personal statement as part of my undergraduate application for nursing, I remember ending by saying that I wanted people in the highest places in nursing to know that Stephen Marrone came their way. I think I have done that. Recently when writing my personal statement as part of my doctoral application, I concluded with the remark that I wanted to make a difference. I think I have done that as well. A friend wrote in my high school yearbook, "May the happiest days of your past be the saddest days of your future." I feel certain that I have lived up to this sentiment, draining as it may be to do so. And I feel confident that I will continue to touch the lives of others and look forward to the ways in which others' lives will continue to touch mine. I guess you could say that I got what I asked for.

While this is certainly not an original statement, I find myself saying it over and over again: "Be careful what you ask for, you may get it!" I used to say this with pessimism. Now I have reframed my thinking and have shifted my conceptual paradigm. (Ooh nice . . . got that paradigm word in there!) And not a moment too soon. It is now more about the journey, not the destination. The growth that comes with transition can be more than the transition itself. And remember the moon is also a star.

So as I gently navigate through the remainder of my life for however long that may be, I look forward to my journey toward peace, contentment, and satisfaction with my life and my contributions—to the ways I touch the lives of others and the ways others have touched and become part of my life. My journey of transition from sun to moon is unfolding. There is something subtle, peaceful, and calming about the moon, her soft rays gently caressing the night sky, keeping company with the stars. So as the years go by other "sons" will shine brightly. I hope that I will be content to be the moon, still shining brightly but perhaps with less glare, not invisible yet still in the company of stars. Amen.

CHAPTER 54

AN ARTIST'S BEING

Dee McFarland

Seldom is the life of an artist a smooth journey. Seldom is the life of an artist without detours. I am just glad I now feel, after many detours, as though I am an artist. This is a story about how I came to be one.

WHEN I WAS A CHILD ARTIST

My love of art goes back to early childhood. I spent hours at my grandparents' house listening to the radio and drawing. Their small house seemed large to me as a child. It sat on a sloping lot near the top of a steep hill where a number of similar houses perched precariously within a few feet of a tortuous one-lane gravel road. The dining room resided in the walkout basement adjacent to the kitchen. It measured 9 by 12 feet or less, just large enough to accommodate the oak table, six chairs, a sideboard that held the radio, and a small curved glass-front cabinet. There was barely enough room to walk around the table. A small gas stove stood guard at the doorway.

This was the pretelevision era when radio broadcast a number of kids programs, complete with advertisements often disguised as special offers. All I had to do was send in 25 cents and four box tops from the hero's favorite cereal. "Be the first on your block to have your own Lone Ranger Pedometer," the announcer said in his deep, gravelly voice. I wondered if the Lone Ranger actually had worn such a gadget, but sent for one anyway. While listening, I drew, from my imagination, what I liked best about cowboys and horses.

Each Friday night Dad would take my brother and me to one of the theaters that had it all for 16 cents: a newsreel, previews of coming attractions, a cartoon, a short feature (my favorite being *The Three Stooges*), a thrilling serial that ran for about 10 weeks, and finally, the feature B western. I yearned to be a cowboy and seek out evil wherever it lurked.

By the time I was 12 years old, I tried painting with oils on small canvas boards purchased at the downtown bookstore that sold a few art supplies. The dream of becoming a cowboy hero had faded. My subjects now were landscapes. I tried to copy rural scenes from a calendar and to finish each painting in a single afternoon. Oh, to be that fast now! One of the paintings won a ribbon at the county fair. Fifty years later it hangs at Mom's house in the hall next to her bedroom.

Living in a small town, which was a rural county seat, meant my early exposure was to traditional art. The impact of 20th-century art had not yet reached me in the Ohio River town of Marietta. I'm sure some contemporary art existed here, but it escaped my attention. My main interest had now shifted to science. Later in high school I discovered abstract expressionism. This may have been through record covers and other contemporary art used in advertising, or learning from the beatniks who hung out at the college coffeehouse. My drawing style became more abstract. During my senior year the yearbook staff chose my graphic designs as section dividers—my first published work! What a thrill!

OTHER PULLS

As much as I relished the process of drawing and painting, the mystique and logic of math and the sciences now captured my attention. By the time I finished high school, I had decided to become a scientist, specifically a chemist. The son-in-law of our next-door neighbor was a chemist, and my dad said that he made a lot of money. That statement stuck with me. When I entered Marietta College, I declared my major as chemistry. Perhaps I had heard that most artists were very poor!

Yet through high school, and even before, I maintained a great desire to play music, another art form. Since we did not have a piano and I did not seriously consider taking band, knowing we could not afford a band instrument, I started by picking my grandfather's five-string banjo. Mom gave me a plastic ukulele and showed me some chords. Later I bought my first guitar for $10 at Montgomery Ward. My earliest music influences included country, bluegrass, and the polka music from Wheeling, West Virginia, my grandmother listened to on Sundays. Each Saturday night I listened to the Grand Ole Opry. My grandfather played the fiddle, and I vaguely remember him playing for me when I was young. Mom preferred the popular and swing styles of the 1940s.

By the mid-1950s, antennas began sprouting from rooftops. Dad bought our first television set. Across the river, 12 miles away in Parkersburg, West Virginia, the fledgling WTAP became one of the few stations we could receive with any clarity. To fill air time they often showed old silent cartoons, such as *Felix the Cat*, *Farmer Alfalfa*, and *Mickey Mouse*. As background they played recordings of the Sal Salvador quartet. This was my introduction to jazz, and I loved it.

TEENAGE MUSICIAN

I played guitar briefly in the high school dance band even though I could not read music. Fortunately, the guitar chart consisted only of the names of the chords (C7, Gdim, etc.) and featured no solos. I played the designated chords or ones closest to those I knew. It did not really matter, as my guitar had no amplification and could scarcely be heard at all. But I relished being part of something.

As part of the rhythm section, I sat near the drummer. Immediately I knew this was my instrument. At home I practiced using pencils as drumsticks, the banjo head as a snare, and coat hangers as cymbals. Then I acquired an inexpensive secondhand set of drums. By observing and listening I learned to play well enough to join a band. My intuition also came in handy.

FROM ART TO SCIENCE AND MARRIAGE

Other than the music, the first 2 years of college were a depressing time for me, emotionally and academically. Art was not on my mind at all. The art department had only one faculty member, a jaunty fellow who drove a red 1947 Lincoln Continental. My choice of a major (chemistry) was a mistake. My grades fell to such a level that I was placed on academic probation. I wanted to quit.

Exactly how it happened I'm not sure, but the dean of men and the college president convinced me to stay and even gave me financial aid. This was overwhelming and a turning point for me, just to think they had faith in me and gave me another chance! For the last 2 years my grades improved dramatically.

But my course in life was far from set. I ended up with a major in biology, the only major for which I could satisfy the course requirements in time for graduation. Few opportunities existed for biology majors, so I ended up without a job and apprehensive about what the future would hold.

Sometimes life just happens, yet turns out better than if it had been planned. After 2 months of scooping ice cream and flipping hamburgers for less than minimum wage, I crammed my drums and other belongings into a 10-year-old Plymouth and moved to Cleveland. The only job I could find was at the Cleveland State Hospital as a lab technician. A dark gray and castle-like structure, the state hospital was nicknamed "Turney Tech" by those living in the Turney Road area. The bleak walls seemed to exude the mental anguish and torment of its patients. I had no background in medical technology, but the pathologist took a chance and trained me on the job—another turning point.

Late one night, a surgery resident offered to let me observe emergency surgery for an abdominal obstruction. I washed, and put on surgical scrubs, gown, and mask. For a moment I thought of the Lone Ranger masked, but on the side of good, seeking out the evil in this poor patient's abdomen. The attending physician thought I was a medical student. From this experience and the encouragement of my boss, a kind-hearted and straightforward woman pathologist, I became convinced that I should go to medical school.

For the first time, I was truly excited about the future. But, in order to meet admission requirements and attempt to raise the marginal academic record from my first 2 years in college, I went back to my alma mater, Marietta College, and took the required pre-med courses. A year later, I was accepted to Bowman Gray School of Medicine. On the first day there, I met Kay, became engaged on our second date, and married 11 months later. So much for my theory that I was destined to be eternally single.

Thoughts of art hardly surfaced as gross anatomy, pathology, pharmacology, and physiology usurped my time during the first 2 years, and clinical rotations excluded most other activities during the last 2 years and internship. From Winston-Salem we moved to Cleveland, where I started a pathology residency and later subspecialized in neuropathology at Case Western University and University Hospital.

The hippie era brought pop art into vogue. My art and cultural education came by watching *Sesame Street* with our first child. Bert and Ernie were in tune with the times.

In stark contrast the Vietnam conflict erupted and the medical community got caught up in current events. Student unrest and riots at nearby Kent State produced a ripple effect. Soon protests occurred all over the country and medical students at Case Western Reserve University began protesting the war as well as contesting teaching methods and format.

Faculty members dressed more mod, some even wearing necklaces and sporting long hair, whether bald on top or not. I grew a moustache, longer hair, and joined the fashion wave, with patterned shirts, flowered ties, and plaid trousers. I became different like everyone else and thus the same.

THE ARTIST STIRS AGAIN

In our duplex basement my inner artist began to stir. At night I began to paint rural Ohio scenes with oil on canvas while listening to Mose Allison. Other creative ventures, squeezed in between work, studying, and family activities, consisted of drawing homemade greeting cards and banners for parties. When we recently visited Emmy, the dear Slovenian woman who took care of our girls, we saw a rustic house and pasture scene, which I had painted in the 1960s, still adorning her living room wall.

After residency, we moved to Georgia where our son was born. During the 7 years we lived in Augusta, I served on the Medical College of Georgia faculty, joined a pathology group at University Hospital, and later took further residency training in clinical pathology. We bought our first house, a small brick ranch with a single carport, where I learned much about home maintenance and repair. Acrylic latex on walls replaced oils on canvas.

More years passed and we had a larger house built. I graduated from repair jobs to home improvement ventures, including bricklaying. Someone asked our son what I did for a living. He replied, "My dad works with hammers and saws." I designed a 90-foot serpentine brick patio wall and then hand-mixed cement for the concrete footer and mortar for the bricks. My hospital job, family activities, a side cytology business, and bricklaying filled most evenings and weekends during the next 2 years. Little time remained for other creative efforts like drawing and painting.

FROM STIRRINGS TO DRAWINGS

Cartoons became the inspiration for my renewed interest in art. Even if I didn't look at the rest of the paper, I always read the comic pages. Kay wrote a patient-oriented booklet on hypertension and she asked me to illustrate it in a humorous style. Suddenly my childhood affection for cartoons resurfaced. This proved a good style for the time, because I could complete a cartoon in less time than a formal drawing or painting.

In 1977, we moved to Columbia, South Carolina, where I became a member of the pathology group at the county hospital. I joined a group interested in cartooning and learned how to submit cartoons freelance and unsolicited to magazines. Soon I discovered pink slips came in many colors. But I did have some of my work published and also used cartoons to illustrate a hospital employee manual. When you are inwardly an artist, small accomplishments lend themselves to "being" an artist.

Our first house in Columbia was not convenient to downtown and our work, so we chose to move closer to the city. Armed with a T square, drawing board, previous house plans as samples, and a few architectural templates, I produced a set of working plans for our new home, based on our ideas. This required more precision than I was used to, but processing the black-and-white plans as blueprints gave them an aura of credibility. As I look back, this was probably satisfying my artistic and creative "me."

ACTUALLY BECOMING AN ART STUDENT

As home improvement projects diminished, I began drawing and painting again. I enrolled in several university art courses, taking one or two at a time, and I found these encouraging and stimulating. I knew that I wanted to pursue this further even though none of the advanced courses were offered at nights or on weekends. The 30-credit-hour maximum came at about the same time I ran out of night and weekend course offerings.

I tried to fit in a daytime higher level course, but could not work it out with my medical practice schedule. Although pathology had become an integral part of my life, I began to realize how important art and music had become. After much thought and support from my wife, I retired from pathology practice and applied to the graduate studio art program at the University of South Carolina. This brought varying responses. My colleagues said they were envious. The laboratory staff thought I was crazy to give up a good job. However, the spirit of art was calling to me, deep within my very being. I listened and moved forward.

In the fall of 1988, I went from medical specialist and teacher to an entry-level art student. Now I had two identification cards—one student and one faculty. Though I wondered initially how I might adapt to this quantum shift in status, the transition proved surprisingly easy and pleasant. The oldest of our four children had already graduated from USC. Our second daughter, a pre-med student at Carolina, occasionally came over to the art building to check on me. I guess she was making sure that I was actually doing what I said I was.

The liberal arts building, the less than optimum art department hub, had character with its high windows and open halls. Exposure to a wide range of styles, techniques, and philosophies did not require elegant surroundings. Since drawing was my favorite means of expression, and I liked traditional and craft-related techniques, I concentrated on printmaking. I loved working the 100-year-old etching press, and the carving involved producing woodcuts. My master's thesis combined art and science. With my background in neuropathology, I examined evidence for the biologic basis of graphic ability.

DEEMED AN ARTIST BY A UNIVERSITY

In late spring of 1990, the University of South Carolina, by the way of a master's degree, deemed me an artist. It had been a long journey but I knew now, not just because I had an official degree, that this was the road I was going to travel on for now. But I asked, how? Though motivated, I lacked the desire and need to promote and sell myself as an artist. My career as a pathologist had provided sufficient financial security. So my varied interests took over again. I played the guitar and drums, and also delved into woodworking with hand tools and model railroading. All of these varied art forms are reflected in my drawings and paintings.

Most subjects hold some appeal for me; my interests are wide and varied. I look for unusual or seemingly contradictory elements of nature and culture, especially those that I see as humorous or ironic. Unexpected arrangements of man-made objects and shapes of nature are all around. I view the elements of language in a similar manner. Signs, written directions, and legal documents often communicate misleading or ambiguous information, a continual reminder that perfection is elusive.

I work with various media in more than one style, alternating between realism and abstraction. Pointillist pen-and-ink and colored pencil drawings intrigue me most, forming images that appear real from numerous small abstract shapes, just as perceived reality consists of an infinite combination of basic elements.

ANOTHER SOURCE OF MATERIAL: MOODS

Moods and feelings of those close to me tend to influence my mood. I can sense how others feel. Sometimes this is an advantage, if the feelings are positive. If the feeling or mood is stressed or negative in any way, then I am likewise affected. Even when I play music in a group or band, the nature of the music and the mood of the other players affect my performance. For the last couple of years I have begun showing my work publicly. At the same time, my desire to play music has continued and I have joined an eclectic group of musicians as the drummer. Sometimes I wonder how it would have been if I had started out as an artist or musician. Certainly my priorities would have been different. Some sort of daytime job probably would have been necessary for survival. For me, the way it evolved proved ideal. Perhaps, after all is said and done, pathology was my daytime job.

I think that artistic creativity significantly influences our culture as a whole. Recently I participated in Columbia's answer to the Chicago and New York Cows and the Cincinnati Pigs. Instead of cows and pigs, Columbia created a Palmetto Tree Collection. The city planted the 80 plus artists' imaginatively different versions of these trees all around the city and then auctioned them on eBay or locally. Bidding has become high tech, showing that art has moved commercially with the times.

I created a child-oriented image of a fictitious, friendly animal that conformed to the tree's shape. The 9-foot-tall structure consisted of half a dozen steel shapes bolted together. With the aid of a few basic physics principles, I managed to load and transport these heavy weights in our minivan. The garage became my temporary studio.

After the auction, I learned that "my" Palmetto would reside at Irmo Elementary School. At the dedication ceremony I gave a short talk, following which the children asked question after question, including, is it a girl or boy? I hadn't thought of that one. Their enthusiastic reception once again showed me how art can create wonder and stimulate curiosity and creativity. To be part of this was truly a gift.

SERENDIPITY, ART, AND BECOMING

Youthful minds are wide open, ready to learn and explore. The spell and grammar checks of our culture have yet to be inserted into the edit files of their brains. They can explore and create with a freedom that tends to diminish over time. As an artist I try to carry that freedom the best as I can throughout my life and to encourage others to do the same. Every child is an artist. The problem is how to remain an artist when one is growing up and is discouraged, while encouraged to follow more secure pursuits.

Significant events have guided me in directions that I would not have anticipated. My desire to draw and paint began at an early age and dwindled in early adulthood when my interest in the sciences prevailed. The faith others had in me encouraged me to finish college and later apply to medical school, and most recently promote my art. During my years as a hospital pathologist, the creative urge resurfaced and led me back to pursue art.

I do not believe that my creative urge ever died. It lay dormant and took up residence in other ways. It pulsed through me with hammer and nails. Designing my own home, working with bricks and mortar, were all artistic expressions. I hope I practiced medicine as an art form. My day job was a privilege and enabled me to give to others. I think an empathic perspective arose from artistic sensibility. Lurking in the background, though, was the idea of being a "real" artist, my overarching life dream: the being of an artist.

CHAPTER 55

DOORS OPENED, DOORS CLOSED, OPENING DOORS

Larry Purnell

Talking about oneself in terms of work accomplishments in a professional setting is easy. Offering personal information and discussing feelings with friends is easy. However, writing personal stuff about oneself is difficult. I received an electronic mail from my guru mentor colleague Connie Vance, suggesting that I make a contribution to this book. Actually, subtle begging was more like it. I reluctantly agreed to write "something." Later that week, I decided I could not do it; I just did not have the time to write an article on such short notice. However, this did not work; Dr. Connie agreed to interview me and help write the article.

Now I am writing the article myself. To get started, I asked myself the following questions: Who was I? Who am I? and Who will I become? To answer these questions, I also asked trusted friends, colleagues, and former students to respond to the following question: How would you describe Larry Purnell to someone else? Their comments will follow later. An important thing to remember is that my successes are not all my own. Although I have not had one person whom I identify as a mentor over time, I have had several who have guided me in decreasing my personality weaknesses and in helping me develop my intellectual capabilities. This article is not about marriage and children; nor is it a dossier to submit to a university promotion and tenure committee. This article is about a road out of poverty and a repressive childhood and into an educated person. It is about the events and people who either closed or opened doors for me. What I am now is a product of my multicultural background. Now, I am in a better position to open (or heaven forbid, close) doors for other people.

IN THE BEGINNING

I was a poor, skinny, stubborn, sarcastic, Appalachian child who had difficulty constructively directing his anger and impulses, but excelled in elementary and secondary school. At the time of graduation from high school, I weighed

92 pounds, wore a size 13 man's shoe and a size 13 ring, and had elephantine ears. Because of my physical appearance, and because I attended school without shoes and wore hand-me-down pants with holes and/or patches (this was not in vogue in the 1950s), other students made fun of me. Out of self-defense, I became the school bully in high school.

I liked nature and wildlife, and at the age of 5 years I "talked to the animals." I wandered for hours in the Appalachian hills and sometimes didn't even come home at night. I slept in a cave or under a tree rather than go home to a repressive environment. To prevent my wandering away, I was placed in a chest harness and tied to the fence. However, as soon as I was untied and sometimes sent to bed without dinner because of my bad behavior, I climbed out the window and returned to the woods, returning home the next day when I could no longer stand the hunger.

By the time I actually entered college, I had lived with families of diverse cultural, religious, educational, occupational, and socioeconomic back-grounds. Cultural backgrounds included German, English, Irish, Spanish, and Appalachian. I lived with grocers, dairy and subsistence farmers, teachers, an ambassador, and an artist. Religious backgrounds included Methodists, Pres-byterians, Baptists, and snake handlers. Some families were very poor and un-educated, whereas others were financially comfortable and well educated. This latter combination I noticed early in my life and knew that I wanted to become educated so I would not have to live in poverty.

During my college years, I gravitated to students from other ethnic and religious backgrounds. I found things that I liked and disliked in each religion and culture. Accordingly, to me, one culture or religion was not better or worse than another culture or religion; they were just different. I found good and bad people in each one.

AN EVOLVING JOURNEY

Currently, I am a multicultural, bilingual white male, farmer, animal lover, author, university professor, carpenter, and self-determined risk-taker. At times, I am still stubborn and sarcastic, have to control road rage, and continue directing my anger in constructive ways, although I too frequently turn it inward. I have rafted and canoed the rivers in several states in the United States and Canada, the headwaters of the Amazon River, and rivers in Africa. I wrote the majority of my doctoral dissertation (the research having been done previously) while hiking and camping in the Alaskan wilderness. I have built my own stable, garage, and house, including furniture and cabinetry. I am a university professor and have authored four books, multiple textbook chapters, and a host of articles. I am bilingual and teach in Spanish, and sometimes *Spanglish*, in two universities in Panama. I am comfortable with and enjoy interacting with people from diverse ethnocultural backgrounds.

I am equally comfortable wearing my Australian outback hat, jungle boots, and frayed farm pants as I am wearing a three-piece suit or tuxedo. I still love to travel, and I have had the opportunity to present papers in multiple states in the United States, England, Scotland, Spain, Belize, Panama, Australia, China, and Hong Kong. I still like animals: they seem to accept me for just being me. The horses and cats eagerly greet me whenever I come home. Having a home with glass doors and windows and surrounded by woods allows me to see the deer, foxes, snakes, rabbits, skunks, and possums. This is my spirituality. I love spending time by myself because solitude allows me time to think and evolve.

WHAT OTHER PEOPLE SAY

I asked several friends, two colleagues, and a former student to answer this question: "How would you describe Larry Purnell to someone else?" Their responses follow. "You are tireless, and hard working; you do not believe in standing still; you believe in growth and thriving; and you are caring and concerned and are rational and helpful to others without being too emotional" (Virgil Volpe, manager of a nursery and friend of 18 years). "You are dedicated, engaging, embracing, and a workaholic. You're extremely intelligent, and make other people feel comfortable around you; and we are glad to know you" (Don and Mary Galloway, my Indiana parents; their attorney son Doug, who is my best friend; and their daughter Cindy, who is director of a geriatric community center). My colleague, friend, and dean for 12 years wrote " . . . is a highly motivated and goal-directed self-starter. His commitment to tasks and exceptional organizational skills allow him to get the job done ahead of the deadline. Personally, he is a dedicated friend and colleague" (Betty Paulanka, EdD, RN).

I am a little embarrassed to include the next quote, but feel I must include it in its entirety because I asked for it. To not include it would be a disservice to her because she took the time to really think about a quote.

> Knowing Larry as both a colleague and friend is a gift. The intermingling of these makes our relationship fun and productive—a great combination. Whether our conversations are related to work or personal matters, Larry brings intuition, sensitivity, and his acute intelligence to the situation. Besides, he has a wicked sense of humor, and his playfulness keeps things in perspective. It is great to have a male friend who brings a different perspective and who is honest and unafraid to share his "truth" or "take" on things. This makes me feel free to share difficult situations and to seek his opinion, which he is always willing to give. I like his kindness and generosity. When I'm with Larry, I always learn something—does he know he is always teaching? Is this his way of being? Bravo for men like my friend and colleague—they are scarce treasures. (Connie Vance, EdD, RN, FAAN)

The next quote comes from a former graduate student in the nursing administration program, which I head at the University of Delaware. Actually, her quote is rather appropriate, because one of the things that I do with graduate students is frequently disagree with them, regardless of what they say. If they take one side of an issue, I take the other side of the issue. Many do not immediately catch on to this teaching tactic.

> Being a late bloomer, everything I needed to learn in life occurred during graduate school, and Dr. Purnell was my guide. Knowing you have talent and believing it are two very different perspectives. Putting that talent to good use is perhaps the greatest leap of faith. That's where Larry comes in. On and off for three years, this man lectured, while I listened. Then he made me lecture him. Unrelenting in his goal, he required that I write; then he asked me to re-write again and again *ad infinitum*. He even cranked it up a notch when we began to argue intensely over policy and theory, even when I was obviously right! "To what end?" I would often ask myself.

> About six months after completing my graduate education, I figured it out. A business friend and I started a training and education company for the healthcare industry. Our business plan was written and we were ready to go; the only thing I forgot to do was tell the world we were here and waiting for their business. So I did what I had become expert in doing. I lectured myself, I argued with myself, I re-wrote my plans, and I went out and got the business. Today, the business is thriving and I practice what my guide taught me, reduce the complicated into the simplest of terms. Larry has given me the greatest gift any teacher can give a student; believe in your abilities and make your own luck. (Kate Salvato, MSN, RN, Vice-President, Corexcel)

These people, friends, colleagues, and students are good for my self-esteem because I know they will always be there for me and I appreciate that. Other people by name or title will be mentioned in this article because they have either closed doors or they have opened doors for me.

FROM THERE TO HERE

My elementary education in Appalachia was in a four-room schoolhouse with two grades per teacher. When I was age 7 years, the school got a fifth teacher whose job it was to teach the slower learners and students with behavior problems. I had a behavior problem; thus, Mrs. Chandler inherited me. Actually, I was mischievous because I was bored with the slow pace of the classroom. Because of a repressive home environment, I hid from the family with whom I lived and read my school books and other textbooks; accordingly, I became bored in the classroom because I already knew the material. Initially, Mrs. Chandler tried to punish me for my mischievous behavior by making me copy extended passages from my textbooks, an activity I liked because I was learning. Next she made me write 500 copies of the same line, such as "I will sit still in class and not bother other children." This activity I initially hated; accordingly, I learned to be creative and tape five pencils together allowing me to write five sentences simultaneously. I creatively finished my punishment quickly, ensuring that I would get into more trouble. Being the smart teacher she was, she soon caught onto my problem of boredom and gave me extra assignments such as running errands, distributing class materials, cleaning the chalkboard, helping the slower learners, and giving me books that were not part of the regular curriculum as extra homework. Mrs. Chandler introduced me to being an independent learner and gave me recognition for gaining knowledge. Mrs. Chandler opened a door for me.

Because I was no longer a behavior problem after 2 years, I was allowed to progress to the regular fifth and sixth grade class where I again became a behavior problem. Fortunately for me, that teacher resigned and Mrs. Chandler was moved from the "special education/problems" class to the regular fifth and sixth grade class. She continued her previously effective strategies and my behavior problem quickly came under control again.

When I moved into the regular seventh and eighth grade class, Mr. Wyatt, the teacher and principal, ensured that my mind was kept busy—most of the time anyway. When I finished my seventh grade class work, he let me sit in on the eighth grade class work. Thus, by the eighth grade, he gave me more advanced work and encouraged me to participate in the regional spelling bee. When the family with whom I lived could not or were unwilling to take me to the regional spelling bee, he and his wife took me. Mr. Wyatt opened the door for me and let me continue to gain recognition for intellectual achievement. I think I placed third or fourth in the National Spelling Bee that year, but I cannot remember for sure.

High school was another era. Several small elementary schools merged into one larger school where there were more than 100 students per grade. This larger size student body divided students by their abilities and I was immediately placed into the "accelerated classes." However, outside the classroom, my physical appearance and dress meant that other students teased and taunted me. This I would not tolerate and defended myself with my fists, just as my poor Appalachian background had taught me to do. Even though I was the smallest student in my class, I was able to use leverage and speed and became the school bully. I had more than the lion's share of fights, many ending in blackened eyes and bruises. However, this was really not that much different from home life.

I remember coming to school with a bruised face from an abusive home beating. I was instructed to tell the teachers and other students that I fell out of the hayloft. I could not participate in sports because I frequently had marks on my back and legs from the "switchings" I received for minor infractions at home. Fortunately, a kindly family threatened to report my guardians to the legal authorities if this physically abusive behavior continued. At that time I promised myself that nobody would ever physically abuse me again, and that if I ever suspected or saw anyone abusing someone else I would take action against them. This family opened a door that told me that abuse was not to be tolerated. Thus, I dispel the myth that if one comes from an abusive home life, the person goes on to being abusive as an adult.

WHAT I LEARNED FROM DIVERSE CULTURAL BACKGROUNDS

Only in the last few years have I fully appreciated what I learned from my early years of living with diverse families in the Appalachian culture. Of course, some of the values of the Appalachian culture I have discarded because to me they were either wrong or they held me back from evolving. Home to me is a connection to the land, not a physical structure. I also inherited from the Appalachian culture the deep-seated work ethic, pride in being independent and doing for oneself, honesty, resourcefulness, and the ethic of neutrality. This ethic wherein one (a) avoids aggressiveness and assertiveness, (b) does not interfere with other peoples' lives, (c) avoids dominance over others, and (d) avoids arguments and seeks agreement continues to shape my life today. I continue to idealize self-reliant behavior and individualism in others, outwardly continue to deny anger, and I do not trust easily because my loyalty to others has been turned against me in more than one instance over the years.

Many of my communication patterns from the Appalachian culture continue. At times, I still use the plural *we* instead of the singular I when referring to myself. Others might refer to this as the "royal we," but in Appalachia the concept is one of the importance of family, a concept which extends far from just blood relations. I still have trouble using adjectives and adverbs in expository writing because these are subjective terms and Appalachians do not judge. To this day, I am more likely to describe something in rather concrete terms; for example, "The house is white and is on top of a hill" rather than "the beautiful big house" because *big* and *beautiful* are subjective words. When I am tired or verbally expressing my dislike about something, I easily fall into the Appalachian pronunciation pattern and will say such things as "Am goin to warsh the care" (I'm going to wash the car).

To many Appalachians, having adequate food is a sign of wealth. During part of my childhood, I was far too frequently hungry. As I have become more financially comfortable, one of the things that I do is to make sure there is always plenty of food in my house, and one of the ways that I express generosity is to treat people to a meal. Being able to do this means that I am wealthy! As a child, I was given teaspoons of bacon fat to make me healthy. To this day, I could still eat teaspoons of grease, but instead I eat rare bacon. Of course, the German families with whom I lived always had a high-fat diet and even fried their hamburgers in lard. I have reformed my eating habits somewhat.

Two things I rejected from my Appalachian background were the culture of "being" and the fatalistic approach to the environment. I have difficulty just "being"; I must be "doing." Besides, doing has been responsible for my coming out of poverty and becoming educated. I also do not adhere to the Appalachian concept of relaxed time, probably because one of the German families with whom I lived was very time conscious. The cows were to be milked promptly at 6:00 A.M., not 6:01! A slight delay could mean physical punishment and hours of verbal berating. To this day, my anxiety increases if I think I am going to be late even one minute for a social engagement. I would rather arrive early and wait than be late.

I also did not acculturate to the Appalachian value of being "present oriented" and acting spontaneously. I am future oriented. I plan every day (including any leisure time), make lists of things to do, and prepare for the future financially. I adopted this futuristic orientation in high school. I was very unhappy with and felt I had little control over my home life. My art teacher, Max Hendershott, was handicapped and on crutches. He taught me that it was up to the individual to make the best for oneself. At times, one had to exist in the present and live for the future. I did just that until I could really be on my own.

THE COLLEGE YEARS

After high school, I wanted to become a physician because the father of one of my high school friends was a dentist. These people accepted me for what I was, encouraged me to continue learning, and allowed me to stop at their home for breakfast on my way to school. However, my high school guidance counselor discouraged my becoming a physician because I did not have the financial means to get through medical school, even though I would probably be able to get scholastic scholarships. The door was closed, no encouragement.

I was still determined to go to college. My friend and his parents took me to visit colleges and helped me to decide on a state-supported university where tuition and living costs were affordable, and where I could work my way through college. My high school Spanish teacher encouraged this, as did my Latin teacher. If I could not become a physician, then perhaps I could study languages, which I found easy. In fact, both of these teachers took me into their homes for short periods of time, accepted me, treated me with kindness, and opened the door to what caring really meant, although they were not demonstrative.

In the summer of 1965, I entered the Honors Program at Ohio University where I received a tuition scholarship and worked as a janitor at the local high school. While on the job that first summer, I slipped in the soapy water and fell on my face while using an electric floor scrubber. I knocked out all of my front teeth and cut off my lower lip. The hospital did an admirable job with my facial repair, and I gave the credit to the nurses as much as to the surgeon. When I asked the nurses about their training, they told me that nursing was a woman's profession and that if I was interested in medicine, I should consider being a doctor. Thus, nursing was still not an option. I did not even know that men could be nurses, at least not in Appalachia at that time. The accident reinforced that I wanted to be a physician. The door to nursing was closed—but only temporarily.

After successfully completing 2 years of college, I moved to Cleveland, Ohio, for the summer and lived with my best friend's parents, who were Jewish. To them, I had successfully completed 2 years of college, why not change to pre-med? I had made it 2 years, why not 3 or 4 years? The Silvers opened the door and I became a pre-med, zoology major. Soon after this door opened, it closed. I had an automobile accident and was left in a body cast for several months. Those nurses were wonderful and told me about the Alexian Brothers School of Nursing. Two months after I was discharged from the hospital, I visited the Alexian Brother's Hospital to apply for admission. The school was closing, and they recommended that I apply at St. John's baccalaureate program in nursing. I sent in my application and quickly received a letter telling me that the school only took females; thus, the door was closed temporarily. I went to work at Mount Sinai Hospital in Cleveland, Ohio, where I was trained to be a technician in the Intensive Care Unit. I drew blood gases, maintained ventilators, and assisted physicians and nurses with procedures. I liked the job. However, I found it interesting that I could do some things that the nurses could not do such as draw blood gases, and the nurses could do things that I was not permitted to do such as give injections.

At that time, the Cuyahoga Community Associate Degree Nursing program began and I was accepted into their first class. Because of the experiences I had in ICU, they allowed me to credit by exam the first two semesters of nursing courses. The door was opened. I graduated and immediately enrolled in Kent State University's first baccalaureate nursing program, and they allowed me to take several courses as credit by examination. Another door was opened.

After 5 years at Mount Sinai Hospital in staff, assistant head nurse, and head nurse positions, I moved to Chicago to attend graduate school. I had met Luther Christman, the dean of nursing at Rush University and the Rush Presbyterian St. Lukes Medical Center at the Michigan Male Nurses Convention. He offered me a position in the department of quality assurance as the education coordinator for surgical intensive therapy. Luther Christman opened the door and I enrolled in Rush University's first master's program to become a cardiovascular clinical nurse specialist.

After graduation, I worked as a supervisor/educator and as a clinical specialist for the intensive care units in Chicago before moving to Athens, Ohio, to become the chief nursing officer for the community teaching hospital for Ohio University College of Medicine. This hospital, although it was a new building, was the same hospital where I had my facial surgery when I was a janitor at Athens High School. I continued my education and got my doctorate in health services administration, and then moved to Washington, D.C., to become the clinical director for critical care and shock trauma services for Region V of Maryland. What a wonderful, challenging position. I could combine my administrative and clinical education into one position.

After a while, I took a month's vacation and did an African safari with four other men. Upon return, I was fired because I was "becoming too powerful" in the organization—a door closed. I looked for a job for 6 months. Every place I interviewed I was told that they had no position for which my qualifications were appropriate. They did not need a nurse with a doctorate. I was turned down for one chief nursing officer position because the doctors did not think the "girls" (female nurses) would want a male as head of the nursing department. Gender bias closed this door.

I started my own construction and remodeling company because no hospital wanted to hire a nurse with a Ph.D. I had not yet considered a teaching position. A doctorate was not needed in acute care hospitals. Within 2 years, I felt the need to return to nursing. Construction was just not fulfilling so I got a part-time job as a staff nurse in a trauma emergency department. The chief nursing officer did not care that I had been fired; she knew the person who fired me. She opened the door. I dissolved my construction business after a few years, and returned to nursing full-time in hospital inservice and teaching part-time in a community college in the Washington, D.C. area.

My free time was spent camping and hiking in the Shenandoah Mountains and rafting and canoeing the local rivers. I had loved my African safari and decided to see another part of the wilderness and took a month to raft and canoe the headwaters of the Amazon and went to the Galapagos Islands. Upon return, I knew I really wanted to live in a rural area instead of the city. I bought land on the eastern shore of Maryland, built my own house with the help of some friends, and have been there ever since.

ACADEMIA

While my house was under construction, I called the University of Delaware for a teaching position. They offered me a one-semester position on soft money with no guarantee that the contract would be renewed. Ten weeks later they offered me a permanent position. A week or so later, an engrained faculty member informed me that if I planned on staying at the university and getting tenured I should rethink the idea. She would do everything she could to see that I did not get tenure. Clearly, she felt men should not be in nursing. She tried to close the door, but by this time, I was not letting someone close the door. My self-confidence was good and my stubborn streak said that I would prove her wrong because I decided that I wanted to remain in teaching. She had power, but not enough to close the door. I am still there and have been thriving personally and professionally ever since. After 10 years, I am a full professor, am very active in professional organizations, and thoroughly enjoy teaching and writing.

Although I have authored numerous publications, writing still does not come easy for me. I do many drafts before I have a final product. Up to the time I came to the university, my writing was technical with reports, directives, policies, and procedures. Just the facts and steps were no problem. With expository writing, I had to use adjectives and adverbs and write such things as *essential, important,* or *crucial.* One of my first publications was on "Assessing the Comatose Patient in the Emergency Department" for the *Journal of Emergency Nursing.* I drafted the article, which was grammatically correct, well organized, and conceptually accurate. However, I asked my dean, Dr. Betty Paulanka, to look at it before I sent it to the journal. She returned it with comments written between the typed lines, along the margins, and on the backside of the page. The grammar and organization were fine she said, and she added no content. She "massaged" the article and filled in adjectives, adverbs, and other words I felt were superfluous to the content. The article was longer by 30% than when I had given it to her. The article was accepted. The next 20 or so articles I published went to her for advice and "editing" before I sent them to a journal. She mentored me through scholastic, expository writing. Years later, she told the story about the most boring, cryptic, terse, awful article she had ever read! Of course, she was referring to that first article I wrote and we both laugh about it to this day. Now, I help other people with their writing. Dr. Paulanka opened the door to writing as well as the door to academia. I still refer to her as "a nudge."

One of the most wonderful things about reaching the full professor position is that I can now help open doors for other people, especially in helping them publish by directing authorship opportunities to them, helping review and critique manuscripts, and helping and encouraging my students get their theses, scholarly papers, and dissertations accepted for publication or presentation. I also enjoy my work with professional nursing organizations such as Sigma Theta Tau, American Nurses Association, Global Society for Nursing and Health, Transcultural Nursing Society, and Partners of the Americas.

To me, my most important accomplishment is the creation of the Purnell Model for Cultural Competence and its Organizing Framework and the book that applies the model to 29 ethnocultural groups. Shortly after it was published, it won the Brandon Hill Book Award. Now, the model has been translated into Spanish, French, and Flemish. By creating this model, I feel that I have made a positive contribution and impact on nursing and health care around the world. Other accomplishments of which I am proud are (a) teaching Belizeans to make crutches, canes, and walkers out of PVC pipe and (b) designing a portable, collapsible stretcher that is used for jungle rescue missions. When assembled, the stretcher—which is again made from PVC pipe—is attached to buoys and floated on the river. Used car seat belts hold the patient in place on the stretcher. A nurse or paramedic sits with his or her back to the spraying water to protect the patient's head. The floating stretcher is then towed behind a powerboat to a local airstrip for evacuation from the jungle.

WHERE TO GO

I am becoming better at directing my anger in constructive ways. I am still sarcastic, but less so than earlier in my career. For the future, I plan to take a sabbatical, semi-retire, and then continue writing, teaching, building, mentoring, traveling, and farming. I am confident other doors will open soon. What might they be? In closing, my best friend tells me that the following is my motto: "Why delay until tomorrow what I could have done yesterday." Perhaps he is correct for once. Darn, I must get control of that sarcasm.

CHAPTER 56

RIGHT CHOICES, ODD REASONS*

Michael Shawn Stinson

I firmly believe that we often make career choices for odd reasons. I majored in psychology in college because of *The Bob Newhart Show*—the early show when he played a clinical psychologist by the name of Bob Hartley. Having no family members in the medical fields, I'm still not quite sure why I went into medicine. Sure, I wanted to make a difference in people's lives and help in a personal way, but there are other means for doing this. Looking back, I've never regretted making this decision.

I'd like to tell you a few things that made tremendous impacts on me during medical school and after. And I'd like to share four rules I've learned about making decisions.

Although my performance during the basic science year of medical school was less than stellar, I did well during the clinical years. I can only hope that you enjoy the wards as much as I did during my first year of clinical medicine. I found one thing very frustrating, though. I could not decide on what career path I would choose. I could envision entering every field I encountered. Surgery was fascinating—the chance to cure; medicine enticed me—the challenge of disease management; Ob-Gyn—where you get both medicine and surgery; pediatrics—making a difference in young lives; family medicine—the ability to address essentially anything that walks in; psychiatry—simply fascinating in itself; radiology, and so on. I was sure that I would never decide. Rather than looking for reasons to enter a field, I began to look for reasons *not* to follow a particular direction. And so the process began.

Surgery was my second rotation. The chief of surgery was (and still is) a very imposing figure; he "ruled" his department and housestaff with an iron fist. But he was one of the best teachers and most friendly individuals in the institution when it came to his dealings with the medical students. He had an "open door" policy; outside of the operating room he would stop whatever he was doing if a

---

*From an address given to a graduating class.

student wanted to talk to him. He learned each of our names and used them frequently when passing in the hallway, when lecturing, or in the OR. I was in my usual mindset of "I can see myself doing this for life," yet I was very concerned that what I saw as the "surgical lifestyle" might not be consistent with my vision of my future life. Already married, I wanted nothing that would interfere with family plans. My exposure to surgery was limited to housestaff on call *every other night* for at least 5 of the 7 or more years of training, or that of to hard-driving academic surgeons with busy research labs and OR schedules. So, one night I dropped by the chair's office—he was still at his desk long after dark (my first clue).

"Mr. Stinson, what brings you by?" he asked (I was so proud he knew my name I could hardly speak). I explained that I enjoyed surgery but was concerned that the demands of this career and my desire for a strong family life might not be compatible. His face fell and his eyes rolled. The words that followed have stayed with me since and immediately ended any thought of going into his field, "Mr. Stinson, your family does not **want** you around for everything." He continued, "You will be there for the important events: your child's sixteenth birthday, graduation day . . ." He listed a few others, but I'm not sure I heard them all. My exposure to the surgical housestaff training and this one interaction with someone who had never practiced surgery outside of academia had such an influence on me that I would never again think of this career possibility. **Rule number one: Don't make your choices based on the lifestyle of trainees or trainers.** Residency training and academic practice may have little resemblance to your professional life afterwards.

My choice to enter internal medicine was anything but easy. When it finally came down to it, I saw it as a way of delaying a real decision about a career choice. Surely I would pursue subspecialty training and medicine was the field with the largest number of fellowships. Simple. I went into medicine.

When the time came for my next decision, I looked to role models. The best teachers that I had been exposed to in both medical school and residency were cardiologists. I liked them. They were enthusiastic, enjoyed taking care of patients, had superb bedside diagnostic skills, and worked with neat equipment. **Rule number two: Just because you like someone does not mean that you have to follow in their footsteps.**

I interviewed around for a position, not only in cardiology, but in an electrophysiology track—very subspecialized. I saw this as a way that I could surely secure a job in an ivory tower, teach, see patients, and do research. I matched in a program where cardiology had an outstanding tradition of education, patient care, and research. Finally, I had chosen a career that seemed to match my goals. What could be better?

The October before I was to start the fellowship program, my wife and I discovered that we were going to have triplets. From a financial standpoint with mounting student loans, there was simply no way to consider a fellowship in the foreseeable future. I didn't sleep for 2 weeks. My career in cardiology was over before it had even started. All of my fellow residents, it seemed, were about to pursue fellowship training. I started looking for a private practice job as an internist. A future in education seemed gone. **Rule number three: Just when you think you've gotten your life figured out, the unexpected will probably happen and change everything.**

That was about 5 years ago—just about the time that academic centers began to build their clinical general internal medicine divisions for increased primary care capacity and teaching. I was asked to come aboard. Work was great and I became very active in teaching, patient care, some research, and even hospital administration. I began to set long-term goals. Early last year, I talked with my department chairman during a yearly evaluation. When asked about my 10-year goal(s), I told him that I would like to be a residency program director in a small to medium-sized program in the Southeast. A few months later, on returning home from work one evening, my wife handed me a slip of paper with the following scribbled on it:

Charles Bryan, M.D.
Univ. of S.C.
(803) 540-1000

I started work here July of 1996. **Rule number four: Be careful of what you want; you just might get it.**

I'm amazed at the defining events in my life, at how the oddest occurrences have influenced me. I can't imagine that I am different in this respect than many of you. Earlier, when I told you that I could only hope for you to enjoy the wards as much as I, I wasn't completely right. If I had just one hope for you, it would be that your choices work out for you as well as they have for me to date. Life's not perfect, but there are few days when I don't look forward to coming in to work in the morning. The balance seems right; my family has me around even though, as I was told, they may not want me there.

If you had asked me during my college years when I was a Bob Hartley wannabe, "Where do you see yourself in 15 years?", I would never have thought of this place and this job. Today, I can't imagine myself anywhere else.

VOICES ELEVEN

HEALTH IN SOCIAL CONTEXTS

Chapter 57

Vigil

Jack Brannon

I write often about the importance of my father and our relationship in my life. Like many young men, I found in my father a model and companion, a source of inspiration and frustration. "I was a little boy standing before a giant, a chip balanced on either shoulder, struggling to begin." I count among my chief blessings the experience with my father of unconditional love, a feeling recalled in this poem.

> This is what my father did for me.
> When I lingered for days with an illness
> stricken by a blinding throb in my head
> he came from the city, from the sickbed
> where he would die in 2 years,
> a doctor with a failing heart, a
> wounded healer. When the pills
> did not help, when the steam did not
> help, when I faced another night in
> pain and dread, my father took ice
> and a towel from the kitchen
> and sculpted a cap around my head.
>
> He held it in place with his great
> brown surgeon's hands, held his
> caring hands to my head while the hours passed,
> 2 o'clock, 3, 4, until he had frozen
> the ache away, had willed the pain
> gone, until he had given me rest.
> Then he slept on my floor until dawn.
>
> This is what one man can do for another
> out of an extraordinary love, can hold
> another's head in his hands so the strongest
> feelings pass between the skin and blood.
> A man can hold another man in his pain
> through the night until he is healed.

CHAPTER 58

TO HAVE AND TO HOLD

Jack Brannon

Love poems come in all shapes and sizes, but perhaps not so often do they begin in the hospital emergency room. Health disruptions can challenge both individuals and relationships in unique ways. If the relationship is one that does not fit neatly into official forms, there may be additional challenges. This poem describes a harrowing night's journey through pain and surgery, and the remarkable impact of a partner who is there when it matters most.

> *Our trip to the emergency room*
> *was strictly a precaution. You insisted*
> *on driving though I had mended all day.*
> *Then just as I began, calmly enough,*
> *to tell a nurse of last night's misery,*
> *my right side erupted in a flush of exploding fire.*
> *Searing white heat poured like storm troops*
> *across my lower frontier,*
> *what little residue remained in my stricken belly*
> *flooding up like wild-eyed refugees*
> *while I fell down against gray floor tiles*
> *searching for an escape route of my own.*
>
> *I did not know pain like this existed,*
> *a demon, its entire purpose*
> *to push me from my body,*
> *the pain a place I could not stay.*
> *The nurse would say only, "I'm sorry,*
> *you can have nothing for it.*
> *Your doctor is on the way."*
> *So that's how I fell down here,*
> *cubicle two—circle seven, the damned*
> *and forgotten. There is nothing in this place*

except unbearable hurting and you.
We are two men stranded among gurneys
and the paraphernalia of misery.

I lean against your chest, clear only
that this is my world, its limits
your knit black shirt,
ridges of your sturdy pectorals,
twin anchors of your nipples.
I lean against you, hard,
cry out all the agony I cannot evade,
know this connection requires no explanation,
next of kin, life partner,
was there a line on the admission form
for my world, my rock?
Five years mated,
mates in no state but our own,
we rock with the tides of my vaulting
storm waves and you hold.

I ask for what no one can give me now,
watch instead how you rub my feet,
survivor struggling in a caustic surf,
messenger of comfort that says
even this night is not forever.
When the doctor arrives you become
my translator, retrieving
realities I have fled beyond, a portion of pain
traded for the edge of drugged oblivion.
We embark on a torturous journey
through a night in which I remember:
tiled heavens filled with hosts of fluorescence,
porcelain body tubes of broken scanners
that cast only a blind eye for techno-seers
who in turn deny me sleep,
gods in blue scrubs pronouncing their alarm,
huddled faces of angels bearing knives,
the hurt I never quite lose track of—and you.

You, when I return whimpering
from the rack of X-ray,
you, when I wake in the cemetery-hush
of Recovery, where a face on a TV screen
says a princess is dead,
you, here, in the furthest reaches of night.
The last sight my eyes see in this odyssey

you, stretched on a cot beside my bed
fine brown hair still wet
from the rip tide, your body
firmly deployed between me and the deep.

CHAPTER 59

TOM'S STORY OF DEPRESSION

As told to Carolyn Brown

Tom hovers in his early 60s. He's a nice guy who will do just about anything for a friend or family member. He goes out of his way to be helpful, expecting nothing in return. When he feels good, he approaches life with a twinkle in his eye, a devilish sense of humor reminiscent of the little boy who still lives inside him. Like many men, Tom hates to write, so I volunteered to try to tell his story. He will read it, and make sure that I am not going too far afield. Who am I? I am his wife, long-time companion and friend, lover, co-parent, and so on. I live with him and love him, sharing his space, often intruding, and swinging between being what he needs to feel better and being a reason he feels bad. We muddle along together, learning how to make a life when one partner is chronically ill, in this case with depression and other autoimmune diseases.

A LITTLE BIT OF HISTORY

Tom grew up in an austere, poverty-stricken southern community. Home was a small wooden structure, at first in the country, and then later in town (a very small town) by the railroad track. The family's central purpose was work, as it was in most poverty-driven homes. He remembers doing laundry, ironing his sister's pinafores, scrubbing, tending the garden, helping put up vegetables, weeding, cutting, mowing, picking, watching his little sister, and later, working at the hardware store. His little sister was adored by all. His older brother was very well behaved, a good student who was never in trouble. Tom's role in the family, on the other hand, was to be in trouble. He worked hard, tried hard, but nothing he did measured up to expectation, so rarely did he hear words of praise for what he accomplished. He grew up feeling he was a "screw-up." He dropped out of high school and ran with a wild crowd. Eventually, because he wanted to join the military, he went back to high school at night while he worked during the day. As soon as he could, he signed on with the military and left the community where he was born and raised. There is a lot more history, but let's skip to his going to Vietnam, where he saw more atrocities than anyone should have to experience. He came home to an ungrateful nation, having learned how to survive under incredibly harsh realities—knowing that anyone who was Vietnamese could be either friend or foe, and could switch roles just that fast; your life depended on your figuring out who was who, and doing it fast. He came home, cringing and jumping for cover at every loud sharp noise, and dreaming of violence that never ended. He still has nightmares about that experience nearly 40 years later.

DEPRESSION—WHAT IT FEELS LIKE

Depression, as experienced by someone else, cannot be adequately described by an outsider, even a very close outsider. Even when you live with them every day, you can't crawl inside their skin and know what they feel. You can surmise, based on your own human experience, but that is the extent of it. Even therapists, unless they suffer depression themselves, cannot know that individual's experience. That person's experience is closed to us, unless he or she chooses to share it, and then the words are not adequate to tell the story. Tom feels so much more than this chapter will ever tell. I can tell you what he tells me. I can also tell you what I see. If you have never been depressed, I know that what you find here will not be enough to tell the whole story, to help you to understand what he experiences, but I will try.

At the time he tried to describe how he experiences being depressed, he was in the middle of a fairly severe depressive episode. Bear in mind he tried to tell his experience devoid of the usual sugar coating. What he told of experiencing is not the face he shows to the world. To the work world, and to most friends and acquaintances, he is a competent, compassionate, highly professional person, usually demonstrating a sense of humor. His clients benefit by his presence. He is sought after by many who value his competence. His story belies his appearance. Tricia Munhall (1995) has written about part of Tom's existence in "The Pretending I." I know both sides of his experience. This is part of how he speaks of experiencing depression:

> *T:* Right now I feel miserable. I'm fuzzy-headed, sleepy, got a headache. I don't want to do anything, I don't want to have to think. . . . I was getting comfortable out there on the couch, then I tried to lie down. I just wasn't comfortable, then I got up and moved around a little bit. I go through these ups and downs, feeling a little more lively and then like I can't wiggle. I can't turn the crank in there, it's all rusted up and it won't go. And that happens to me at work. I need to sit down at the desk and do some writing, some paperwork, and I don't do it. I sit down and I start getting muddle-headed and I start falling asleep and I have to get up and walk around to wake up. I have a variety of feelings that go with depression. I'm sure, at one time or the other, I touch all on of the various

textbook signs and symptoms for depression. It's not consistent. It's not constant. I have trouble focusing, concentrating; that's pretty broad and widespread with anything I do. Reading the newspaper is easier than some things. Sometimes I read it and I don't know what I've read. In TV, I generally get into the show. I try to lose myself by paying attention to what is going on. There are times, though, when it just agitates me, irritates me, but for the most part it's a kind of escape. A way to get out of and not focus on what's going on with me. By paying attention to that, I can leave it a little bit. Then there are times that trying to get into something else is very unbearable. I try to make myself focus on it. Then I get agitated because I can't do it. I have trouble with that a lot at work. There I can't choose and pick when things happen or what I'm expected to do. And sometimes when things happen, and I should be doing things, that's the last thing I feel I should be doing. It's really painful to try to do it. I mean, it HURTS!

In explanation, a lot of Tom's work is crisis work. He has no control over when he will be needed. Speaking personally, in any crisis or emergency, I would choose him first as someone who would keep a level head and respond appropriately. When he was in Vietnam, he did crisis work with the hill people and as a field medic, doing first aid in battle situations. In his later military career, he worked in areas of child, sexual, and other forms of abuse, mental health crisis work, and drug and alcohol crisis work. I believe we do not look at the cost to those who serve in crisis, whether military action or other crises. People who serve well in these areas see the very worst of human conditions, and other than the usual employment compensations, are given no assistance to deal with emotional and physical scarring. Even policemen are given counseling when they have found it necessary to kill. Our military are not afforded this luxury. If they look good, present through the "Pretending I," a competent exterior, they go their way, with the effects likely to turn up later.

THE PAIN OF DEPRESSION

In the paragraph above, Tom spoke of the pain he experiences with depression. This pain is equivalent to any physical pain; in fact, it shows itself as physical pain. To understand how someone experiences depression, you must understand that the experience is so much more than a simple sad or low mood. It is as severe as any physical illness one might experience. Sometimes even more so.

T: In a way the pain is kind of equivalent to a physical pain, but it isn't a physical pain. Although I do have physical pain, that's associated with depression . . . I am sure of that. Some of those pains I think come out of the physiological state of my body when I'm

depressed, and some of it's an interaction of the medication, a reaction to or a side effect of the medication I'm taking. Like the last
couple of days, I'd get out of bed and I just couldn't . . ., I'd stagger
down the hall, not really in control. It would be painful to move my
body, my head. I just want to close my eyes. That somehow eases
the intrusion of anything on my body just a little bit. When I'm in
that state, any intrusion of any external stimulus can be just pure
misery. Just having to get out of bed, get showered, eat breakfast,
get dressed, and go somewhere . . . and then when I get there of
course I may come face to face with people who are going to do
something that seemed insurmountable for me to deal with. I don't
know . . . I guess it's the fact that I do have windows of feeling more
human, normal, feeling like doing things, windows when it doesn't
hurt and it's not painful, that I feel like I can do it. That's what keeps
me getting through these other times; thinking it will get back to
more of when I can, but when I have long periods when it's more
negative, and I'm not feeling good, it gets rather discouraging . . . It's
just like right then [he shook his head, not even vigorously] I shook
my head, and it hurt. I don't know if it's because of the chemical stuff
in my head [the actions of neurotransmitters], or it's the medication
reaction, or what. At times it's just like you're taking on a grinding
machine and coming out raw hamburger, . . . there are times it's kind
of like that. It creates a pain in my head, it hurts . . .

He described the pain as being all over his head, a rawness. He went on to
say, "It's like sometimes you take a breath and it's like the next one is not going to come. When I sigh around here, you ask me what's going on. . . . Man, I
don't know!! I just feel like I'm not going to make it to the next breath. It's difficult. Miserable. Awful."

WINDOWS OF FEELING NORMAL

Windows of feeling more normal, as he described in the paragraph above, give
hope that things might be better, although when Tom is in the middle of feeling depressed, he always fears it might not get better. So far, it always has.

T: I go through these cycles. I know I go through these periods that
things are different. I'm better, but during depressed times I just
want to pull back.

T: It's those longer spans, a couple days, weeks, a few months . . . it's
realizing that it might happen again, that keeps me going, I hope
for that, I go for that, otherwise I would just want to go lie down and
close my eyes and not open them. . . . Just get rid of it, just get out
of it. It gets so miserable and discouraging that you don't want to
be any more . . .

FEELING LIKE NOT GOING ON

We talked pretty openly about Tom's thoughts of suicide. This was very difficult to talk about, yet given the depth of his feelings of despair and pain during depression, I think I can understand it. As I write this, I feel tears at the
back of my eyes. It is so difficult to even think about, yet so much a part of him,
that I must write about it for him.

C: When you say you don't want to be, are you talking suicide?
T: I'm talking dying, being dead . . .
C: . . . either that it would happen naturally, or you would make
       it happen?
T: There have been times I would lie down and close my eyes and
       wish that I would just fade off and be gone . . . misery . . .

As I write this, I realize that it might be better if it were not his wife trying to
tell his story. It is very painful for me. I didn't think this would happen, because
I share the day-to-day ups and downs of chronic depression with him. In any
case, I changed the subject because I couldn't bear to go on with talking about
him wanting to die. I cannot imagine living life without him, nor how I would feel
if he ever did kill himself. I didn't want to imagine it, so I changed the subject. If
I were with someone other than Tom trying to tell his story, a story so intertwined
with my own, I know I could listen better. I have done so with a myriad of clients.

At another time, he talked more openly about times he felt suicidal, about
how discouraged he was with the uncertainty of depression. This conversation
followed our talking about what we, as a couple, missed because of depression.

T: Sometimes I'd like to toss myself out the window, get lost, just stay
       away. I don't know what that means. Get on a boat and just sail off
       to sea, and never come back. Just go into oblivion . . .
C: You're talking suicide.
T: Sometimes that seems the better part of valor. Sometimes it just
       gets so damn overwhelming.
C: When it's overwhelming you don't even have the hope of the
       window . . .?
T: Sometimes I don't feel like it's ever coming back. You'd like to flip
       the switch, or turn the page, or whatever, and make it different, but
       you can't do that . . . I don't know . . .

BEING WITH OTHERS

We spent a fair amount of time discussing what it was like for him to relate to
others, to me as his wife, to his son and his fiancée, to friends, to his family.
His feelings are poignant, so different from what these many folk see when
Tom is with them. Again, we see the "Pretending I."

T: I know a lot of times it can't be pleasant to be with or around me.
      I feel bad about that, in a way I feel guilty, like I should be able to
      do something about that. But, in reality, I don't know what I can do
      about it. It makes me feel flawed, inferior, inadequate, just not up
      to par. It's terrible. There's the feeling bad that comes with where
      you are at the time, the misery, the inability to do things, the lack
      of concentration, the discomfort, the grating or the grinding.
      You're miserable with that . . . and then there's the interaction with
      the world around you, people. I'm terribly sensitive to that at
      times. It feels like I'm not fulfilling my spot in the world; I'm not
      able to do that . . . and I feel bad about that. I feel that somehow,
      in spite of it all, I should be able to do that . . . [pause] . . . it's a
      miserable bullshit feeling . . .

T: It's just like on days I get up when I don't feel like going to work, I
      feel like I couldn't face it . . . and if I don't go I feel guilty. I feel like,
      my God, I should be doing that. I feel guilty. I should be able to do
      that, why can't I do that. . . . It's like there's a fight going on . . . all the
      time . . . there's a pull and a push. I know if I could back off, lay down
      and relax, and not worry about anything, not have to deal with any-
      thing, I could be more peaceful within myself. Somehow I can't al-
      low that to happen. I feel guilty for not persisting, not trying to hang
      on . . . and if you ask me to do something around the house, I tell
      you I don't feel like it now, I don't want to do it now, then I think,
      "Damn it, I should be able to do that!" It just creates more push pull.
      I feel like I need to meet those expectations, it's horrible, it's part of
      participating in the world and being part of it and so forth and it's
      the old bad feeling that I can't do that and it's uncomfortable . . .

T: Sometimes I am lifted out of it, and better, and sometimes I just
      don't want to try. It's just too miserable. I just want to get out of
      there. It's not worth the effort to be a human being, to be with
      somebody. I don't feel good about being unpleasant to be around,
      making a fool of myself, I'd rather pull back than try to be OK. I
      don't know [sounds really down at this point].

We are talking about how he feels now, when he is depressed. After the last
statement above, I ask about times he might feel more hopeful. "Have you
seen any light? Windows?"

T: I guess I'd have to say no to that. I'm (lets out a big breath) . . . [long
      silence.] I don't have any answers, overwhelming insights or under-
      standing. . . . I guess I'm very tired, worn out, it's hard to keep fight-
      ing, and every day I have to go to work and do these things I don't
      want to do.

C: And there's no part of work that's pleasurable?

T: It may be part of me, but nevertheless that's the way it is . . .

C: Is it worse when you interact with depressed people?

I am trying desperately to understand. I have moods that are depressed. They come and they go, but work, interaction with people is something I en-joy. I love so much of what I do, and what I continue to learn even when rela-tionships are difficult. I know I have trouble understanding how deep depression can strip life of any joy, anything that feels meaningful and energy producing, even though I have worked in psychiatry/mental health, as Tom does currently. Here I am in no way trying to be therapeutic, but rather, am a wife trying to understand.

> T: I find when I am fairly depressed myself, and I try to interact with people who are delusional, I don't have the patience to cope with that. A lot of my clients are delusional. Some of them are very sick, very fragile people. Two have died in the last couple of weeks, so you never know if this will be the last time you see some of them. You see them and, *bang*, they're gone. My reserves, I don't have any, I am running on empty, on an uphill treadmill constantly, and . . . I guess recently, the really good times are few and far between, when I feel energetic, feel OK, those times seem to be fairly rare anymore.
>
> C: Looking at us, what do you gain from our relationship . . . ?
>
> T: It's not that easy to answer. . . . Sometimes I just want to be left alone, given a little space, not messed with [pause]. But then, I do feel the need for the warmth and the support, that's helpful, and you are very often able to do that . . . I don't know. . . . While it helps, makes it easier, it doesn't change the situation, just makes it more tolerable . . .

When people have expectations during times he is depressed, Tom feels like he should meet those expectations, yet every fiber of his being says "No, I can't do that now." He said he would feel better if he could just pull back, and let himself just be, but that is not the way the world works. There are always expectations.

TRYING TO HOLD IT ALL TOGETHER

> C: When you are depressed, it feels to me like you are very tight wrapped, meaning that you're holding yourself in and trying to keep it all together.
>
> T: Well, sometimes that's true. That's a very accurate description of how I feel. Other times it's not that I'm tight wrapped. I'm very loose; it's like I'm jelly. That's a very good description of when I'm kind of wound tight, and it's hard and you try to do that . . . and there are other times. . . . There's one thing I can say about depression, it's not consistent, it's hard for me to be consistent at anything; you're not consistently on the bottom, on the top, or in the middle.

At another point in our conversation, we were talking about the effect of depression on how Tom is with other people. I know Tom to be a very compassionate and warm person, someone who has a wealth of understanding about how it is to experience life's difficulties. He listens very well. In response, he shared, "Well, there are times, when I'm a little bit depressed and it's OK, but there are times that I'm too busy trying to keep it together to feel much of anything. It's a struggle just to be. If you don't know what that feels like, it's difficult to verbalize it."

IT NEVER REALLY GETS BETTER

We talked about the long-term effects of depression, how it never goes away. Tom does not have episodic depression. His is present all of the time, in a chronic way, such that it is a constant struggle to keep on top of it and to meet life's demands. Even when he feels better, there are some effects he struggles with. For example, "I don't feel terribly depressed today. I don't know if it's aftermath, or whether it's medication, or whether it's something totally unrelated. I just don't have the impetus to move, I have a headache. I went out in the garage, and I puttered around and in a way it felt good, but in another way I started feeling shaky and bad and I just had to quit. It's very frustrating to me . . . I don't understand what's going on with me exactly. All I know is, it's unpleasant. I just get so damn disgusted."

WHO AM I?

We were talking about how it is to live with depression and I said I realized that he was not his depression, that he was so much more. He answered,

T: Sometimes I kind of lose sight of that. I *am* my depression. That's who and what I am.

C: I don't see you that way, but that doesn't mean you don't feel that way. You mean you become your depression? I don't understand.

T: I feel that way, that's what I am. The depression and all that encompasses, what I create.

At another point in our conversations, he talked about how he felt about himself as a human being. I had asked if, as a man, it affected him differently. Looking back, it was a dumb question. How can someone see something other than through the eyes of who he is? Tom is a man, and he sees through a man's eyes. So he answered as a human being because he believes how he experiences depression has little to do with his being a man.

T: I don't know that it [being a man who is depressed] has any impact. More so, as for being a person, it does. I just feel terribly inadequate, hopeless. It bothers me that I don't function any better than I do, that I feel so rotten all the time.

We continued to talk about how he has so many difficulties that are au-toimmune related, all of which interact to create his feeling crummy most of the time. If one condition gets better, another flares up, so that it is very dif-ficult to find a balance. He never knows how he will feel from day to day.

IS THE TREATMENT WORSE THAN THE DISEASE?

When talking about depression and medications, Tom acknowledged that medications didn't always have a positive effect, and that after taking medications for a while, they would stop being effective. He described, "There have been periods of when I've done well with relatively few side effects and even doing the same things, that changes." We went on to talk about the things everyone says are good for you to stave off depression: exercise, relaxation, meditation, and so on. After a huge sigh and long si-lence, he said, "I get so tired of fighting and doing things that are uncom-fortable and then when I don't feel like it, to push on through and exercise anyway, it's . . . not worth it if there is no result on the other end. Struggle, struggle, struggle."

One ray of hope for alleviating the pain of depression was a medication he hadn't tried. . . . "Well there's one new one that I haven't taken. I don't know the name. It's the same action as Prozac, but has fewer side effects. It depends on whether I can get it. On any health care plan, you don't always have a choice of what medications you try unless you have a lot of money, because they're expensive. . . . Insurance doesn't want to pay for them. I didn't realize that Prozac is about three dollars a pill, so. . . ."

He did try the medication, Celexa, in combination with Welbutrin, and had about a month of feeling more normal, with a higher level of energy. Then the side effects began to rear their ugly heads, and he went off the Celexa. The Welbutrin worked a little less well, but the side effects were more manageable.

A huge part of Tom's struggle is how to walk the tightrope of treatment that keeps depression at bay. He must monitor how he feels daily and de-cide whether to take a medication at all and risk the specter of depression but be less affected by side effects, or to take a reduced dose and hope it is enough to stave off depression *and* side effects, or take the full dose and know the side effects will get worse. Medications are a constant balancing act, and each new psychiatrist who does medication management tries to fit him into the normative box. What works for the majority of people under the normal curve does not necessarily work for Tom. His body chemistry puts him in the outer area of the normal curve for medication management. His biochemistry is extremely sensitive to any variation, no matter how small. We joke about his being a "brittle depressive." Those who know about diabetes know that *brittle diabetic* is the term used to describe some-one whose biochemistry fluctuates wildly.

HOME: A PLACE TO LET GO OF THE "PRETENDING I"

I know Tom sees home as a haven, a place he needs to pretend less that he feels well. Yet, even when he is home, he meets situations where he feels the need to pretend, to be "up." At other times he feels more normal, that he is not pretending when he acts more normal.

> C: I think the world very rarely sees what I see with you . . . The world doesn't see you feeling deeply depressed. Most people just see the aftermath, like one day you said you tried to get words out and they just didn't come. But they don't see the full depth of depression. You put on a happy face . . .
>
> T: I try, but sometimes I'm not very successful. Other times I can do quite well.
>
> C: Sometimes do you do that with me too?
>
> T: Sometimes I'm fine.
>
> C: I never know for sure what's happening. Sometimes I ask you how you feel. It's probably irritating sometimes, but I don't know how to plot my life with you. It's just never knowing how you are feeling.
>
> T: I really strain to push myself to go to work, and do things out there. Then I feel like I need to be able to come home and pull back and not have to respond positively . . . but that's what makes it tough for you . . .

We go on to acknowledge that it is tough for both of us, that there is guilt and sadness on both sides because we are not able to fulfill one another's expectations. Yet we do love and care about one another, and recognize we try to find ways to meet our own needs when the other is not able. So far, there have always been windows of Tom's feeling good to keep us going. Our greatest difficulties come when both of us have high needs for support at the same time. I suppose that isn't any different from other marriages, except that with depression, the chances are greater that the depressed person will be in a state of higher need.

AN ENDING?

Most stories and chapters come to some sort of conclusion. Maybe someone else could write a conclusion to this story. Tom and I continue to live it. It is often discouraging and wearying. We pray for the windows when he feels better, and take full advantage of them by laughing (Tom has a wonderful sense of humor) and doing a lot of things we don't do when he is deeply depressed. Right now he feels somewhat better, although that varies widely from day to day. That is the way it is when you have a sensitive biochemistry, have a "brittle depression." Truly, love is what keeps us going. Love and faith, and long experience that says there will be windows.

REFERENCE

This is not academic writing. It is purely one man's experience. So, there is only one reference, included because it speaks to the heart.

Munhall, P. L. (1995). The pretending "I": Women's secrets and silences. In P. L. Munhall(Ed.), *In women's experience* (Vol. II, pp. 185–209). New York: NLN, Pub. No. 14-2687.

CHAPTER 60

TRANSFORMATION OF ANGER BY MEN

Patricia L. Munhall

As I write this, I realize last Saturday was the second anniversary of the Columbine High School massacre. Actually that is what it is called—a "massacre." A massacre is defined as an act or an instance of killing a large number of human beings indiscriminately and cruelly. It was April 21, 1999. Twelve students and one teacher were killed and 24 students severely injured. I would predict that innumerable students and parents have been severely psychologically traumatized not only at that high school, but at others as well.

About a month ago another high school killing spree took place at Santana High School near San Diego. Because two people were killed, I guess it is not enough to be called a massacre. I forgot to mention that in the Columbine massacre, the two teenage boys who were designated the killers turned their own guns on themselves and did away with their own lives. The young 15-year-old boy from Santana High School was captured, and in a courtroom proceeding looked like a very scared child. The court was attempting to decide whether he should be tried as an adult or a child. This is just one of many decisions by courts that I do not understand. He is 15 years old, so why is this a question?

Today vendors prepare T-shirts for Timothy McVeigh's execution.* Most will recall the horror of the 1995 bombing of the Oklahoma City Federal Building where 168 people died.

In the first volume of this *Emergence* series, the one on women, I wrote that blood was being splattered on the earth of Bosnia and that the human atrocities were unimaginable. Four years later, in the second volume of this series, the one on family, I wrote that blood was being splattered on the earth of Kosovo, and there the atrocities were, of course, once again unimaginable unless you were suffering through them. In this volume I suppose I should mention that this inevitable blood is being splattered and the atrocities continue. Headlines point to the never-ending conflict between Israel and Palestine.

---

*Timothy McVeigh's actual execution took place on June 11, 2001.

Blood is being spilled in Africa, East Timor, and other countries. Blood spurts out of arteries and veins in wars, police work, and gang wars. According to the news reports, which consider blood to be big news, the country and the world are awash in violence.

A Cancer of Violence

Another war zone: the home where blood and guts emotionally ooze, often in silence. Until there is another murder . . . I have called this the cancer of violence. Most of the time, but not all, men are the perpetrators. There are many talking heads, living and dead, who speak or have spoken to the inevitability of this within our species. They certainly seem correct to me. *On target.* Our language is warlike.

I want you to know that this chapter is not necessarily about violence; it is about anger in its less violent forms. Yet, my difficulty is this: Is there really anger in less violent forms? Or is there violence in less angry forms? I know we can quantify our questions by doing body counts, murder rates, and domestic violence and child abuse statistics. Wearing a McVeigh T-shirt, surely, is less violent than the crime, but is there not some violence to the spirit when "entrepreneurs" are hoping to cash in on this tragedy? The T-shirt is emblazoned with a large syringe, symbolizing the lethal execution scheduled for McVeigh on May 16, this year. So, I find it difficult not to talk about violence within the context of anger.

The execution, another form of violence, is extolled by capital punishment proponents and is expected to bring healing to the victims' families. Some of the members of the victim families will be allowed in the execution suite. Others, because of space reasons, will watch it in rooms with closed-circuit televisions. Yet, others voice the senselessness in this killing. They say it won't bring back their loved ones.

How can I write about anger in men or how men experience anger, when what first comes to my mind is the extreme? Perhaps I am writing on a continuum. Starting with the worst-case scenario. But then I am right back to the home. The doors are shut, the windows are closed, a woman is being physically attacked or emotionally murdered, the child is being hit with a blunt instrument until he bleeds, or perhaps a child is being sexually molested. Is this still the extreme?

This is not the case with most men and how they manage their anger. And who am I to say that all men even experience anger? And are women any different? Perhaps I do not know how to differentiate between anger and violence from the perspective of a cancer of violence. Cancer comes when least expected. It is unpredictable and it comes in the dark, unannounced except by a lump, a symptom. Perhaps the lump or the symptom of violence is a display of anger. But we know, just as with cancer, one can skip the symptom phase and still be a victim.

Some would say that some victims of violence or those who repress anger turn their symptoms inward. Some might even develop cancer. So it seems whether repressed anger or victims of anger, people affected often do develop other conditions. Freud called this "conversion hysteria."* We seldom speak like that today. The term used is psychosomatic disorders, which many individuals believe are then not "real." Not "real" illness. Something in the head. I am not sure what difference that makes. Perhaps a heart attack is psychosomatic, the mind manifesting a phenomenon physically. Perhaps most illness is a combination of the mind, body, and spirit. Western medicine and public thinking still perpetuate dualism, the separateness of mind and body. Many will not even discuss the spirit. In a chapter on anger, it seems, they must all be considered interconnected.

IN CONTRAST TO "VIOLENCE"

I reviewed a chapter I wrote entitled "The Transformation of Anger by Women into Pathology" (Munhall, 1995). Many men read that chapter and reported to me that in their experience, they expressed or did not express anger in much the same way. Working as a therapist bears that out. However, the men who come into therapy are much fewer than women, yet the main problem does seem to be the same dynamic as with women. So readers of that chapter and patients have told me that anger is unacceptable to them, and they have found other ways to keep it under wraps or repressed. Their anger, as with women, seems then to be transformed into physical, social, or psychological conditions. Sometimes I interpret this as violence against the self.

I would like to emphasize somewhere here in the beginning of this chapter that my research on men and anger bears out the similarities for most men who agreed to participate. However, in neither study did I talk to men and women who crossed the line and got caught or did not get caught. I did not visit a prison, where the anger was transformed into socially unacceptable behavior. Those incidences of anger, I mostly read about them in the paper or they were related to me by women or children who live with abusive men. Men who strike in the middle of the night. I need to emphasize the contrast, where anger was interpreted to be transformed into socially acceptable behavior or conditions. Like it is OK to have a coronary. No one can hold that against you.

This transformation has a bit of irony or perhaps tragedy as a part of this dynamic. The socially acceptable places where anger can become transformed, because this is a chapter on men and anger, are massive heart attacks, coronary problems, gastrointestinal problems, substance abuse, and obesity, as anger resides in and through the body and mind and spirit. This kind of anger

---

*A conversion of psychological trauma into physiological symptoms.

then is manifested through physical ailments. Anger seeps up within the body eventually and, if not diffused, will erupt. Now, I am a person deeply suspicious of statistical inferences and will use them cautiously to demonstrate a point. So it is with utmost caution I cite a study that looked at 118 lawyers and found that of those who scored in the top quarter for hostility, one in five was dead by age 50 (Dolnick, 1995).

Hostility is often believed to be anger seething, not often manifested, but left smoldering in rage. This anger is held in, like the precancerous cells, waiting to erupt.

MORE ON TRANSFORMATION

If Anger Ruins Your Day, It Can Shrink Your Life

During anger, the sympathetic nervous system raises blood pressure and heart rate. In the chronically hostile, the parasympathetic system fails to restore hormones to normal. Stiffened arteries, a weakened heart and other problems can result.

(*Health*, 1990)

Actually anger and its physical manifestations are like body language. The body expresses the rage by increasing the blood pressure, stiffening the arteries as though the person is paralyzed to act, clogging blood vessels with stuffed anger, and eventually exploding as in a "stroke" or "heart attack." Recently there was a picture of former Vice President Al Gore in the paper. Four months had passed since he won the popular vote and lost the electoral college. I think Mr. Gore has a lot to be angry about, though he casts himself in the role of the good patriot of his country. In the article it spoke to the observation that he has gained 30 to 40 pounds. Is Mr. Gore transforming his anger and storing it in his body?

WHEN MEN TRANSFORM ANGER INTO PSYCHOLOGICAL CONDITIONS

I don't believe there are men who want to be depressed or to have low self-esteem, self-doubt, feelings of emptiness and powerlessness, or, worse, self-hatred. Yet these are the psychological ways that men can repress their anger. These are ways to stay out of jail. These conditions in men are not as socially acceptable as they are in women. Men, it is noted, do not talk out loud about these conditions to friends. Many believe such psychological conditions will make them appear weak. So another irony appears, which is different from women. The anger is repressed into these psychological conditions, and then the psychological conditions are also repressed as actually not being socially acceptable. Men are at a disadvantage here, for sure.

Pity the poor fellow who has turned his anger against himself—which is better, I suppose, than against another but not as good as getting therapy—and who spends his days in self-loathing. Many men on the margins of our society are caught in this bind. I am reminded of conversations I have had with gay men and listening to their stories before they "came out." The suffering, self-hatred, and anger are palpable in their past or present stories.

Anger in men that is repressed also manifests itself in social interactions and relationships. Here again we see a difference between men and women. Women can screw up friendships and relationships as well as any man, but they usually have a larger support system. They often have many more friends than men. So men often have the unpleasant experience of repressed anger interfering with relationships.

So if the above is true, is that why so many men sit in front of televisions watching competitive sports where, whatever good things take place, there is enough anger to be watched and vicariously lived through?

Better that than a sick expression of anger in the home war zone.

So, I am not finished with violence.

There is the real world, never ending, senseless killing and torturing of other humans. One becomes numb to it all. How can we take it all in? It is so irrational and after all, man (woman) prides himself on the illusion of rationality.

"Go ahead, make my day," a provocation that has entered our lexicon, a provocation to violence. "Hasta la vista, baby" as the terminator showers death with his huge gun. And these are the good guys!!!! So we come to another irony. Good guys can kill as well. In fact, they protect us from the bad guys. The bad guys on the streets, the bad guys on the other side of the war game, but (and this is a big but) not so much as the bad guys in the home.

If you are looking for a point, I need to say I am attempting to make many points, because space is short and the killing continues. And so much must go unsaid because of the scope of this chapter. The overall point, though, is to stimulate critical reflection about anger among men and its many manifestations, as well as about what it leaves in its wake.

Now it is time to return to the second anniversary of Columbine. A friend is visiting me and watching this report on television. I begin to jot down notes as to what is being said. The report is about high school killings. A mother of one of the children who was killed is talking about how the killers were bullied by others in the high school. The child from Santana High School claims, and his friends validate, that he was incessantly bullied. According to news reports, others ostracized all three of these children. Made fun of. Did not belong. These kids walked on the margins, were felt to be marginal.

So on come the talking heads about the nature of bullying. First the statistics. Two thirds of children who commit violent acts have been bullied. What is a bully? A person who is habitually cruel, aggressive, and threatening, especially to weaker people.

Now what happens is that in these cases, the weaker children become angrier and angrier till they can no longer bear it. Dad just happens to own a gun or two, which is locked, and then all hell breaks loose. The talking heads are talking seriously about parents being more involved with their children and knowing who their children's friends are and having their children's friends to their homes. Have they forgotten so soon the nature of being a teenager?

I am not saying these are not good ideas and perhaps parents can strive toward more connection with their teenage sons, but I remember from Psychology 101 that the peer group becomes the most important group in the necessary process of separating and differentiating oneself into an adult.

Now, if I were one of the talking heads, I would ask when will fathers remove guns from their homes if they have children? How many children have to die in their own homes or in high schools before some law is enacted to prevent having firearms in a home where children live? Yes, I know all about the Second Amendment. And the powerful NRA, whose spokesperson has been the actor Charleton Heston. Another actor, one who became president, Ronald Reagan, used the "make my day" line in a speech. Just provoke me and see what happens. We can see that a law to keep guns locked does not work. Once again I ask, how many deaths will it take? Reagan was shot at outside the White House. An assassination attempt. He was hospitalized and recovered. His press secretary, James Brady, was not so fortunate. A bullet knifed through his brain and he is paralyzed to this day from the waist down and his speech is still impaired. Just what will it take?

Sometimes I feel like I am losing my bearings. Most of the time I do not understand not only the above but politics that allow the killing of children to continue. And for that matter the killing of women by men, who are most often their "partners," with a gun. The killer could have had the gun locked, but of course he does have the key. He also has the rage.

Keep the bloody guns in a hunting lodge, if you must kill animals. (Is this me becoming angry?)

Now we come upon another tragic kind of irony. Sons usually learn how to manage and express their anger by watching and imitating their fathers. The repetition of abuse of a child into an abusive parent has been perhaps overly documented. I say overly, because there are many children from abusive, angry homes who vow and accomplish not to perpetuate the anger, ever again. However, when they are children and witness abuse or are victims themselves, many become enraged and so angry they become "bullies."

Bullying is not a socially acceptable way of expressing anger or rage. Ending this cycle begins with ending the wars in the home and ending the at-home torture of a child.

But Anger Is So Easily Accessed

For all the complexities that result from anger, apparently anger is easily arousable in others by others. Sometimes the perceptions are real, and other times they are imagined. That seldom makes a difference.

Most of the time anger is directed toward friends and intimates. This, of course, makes sense because we care about these people. What typically gives rise to anger is a perceived misdeed. A man becomes angry when he believes he has been provoked. The source could be a statement or act, which the man believes was unjustified. In other words, it was not fair, right, or was harmful, and the person responds with an expression of anger.

Some people understand anger on an aforementioned continuum from mild irritation to rage and fury. Yet results of being angry are so unpredictable that what mildly irritates one person might infuriate another, and their responses may be the same in intensity.

As suggested above, the anger response may be transformed into chest pain, a headache, anxiety, withdrawal from others, or some kind of substance abuse. Substance abuse, especially alcohol, is an easy way to transform anger. It seems that because it is more socially acceptable in men to visit bars or taverns alone, many angry men take up a second home in them. This is very scary. First, the alcohol may calm a man down, but invariably if it is abused, the anger is very much escalated. I see in my mind a drunken man who is angry, coming back to his first home, out of control and now violent.

Rent the film *Affliction* for a powerful portrayal of the course of anger and alcohol. It is about an abusive father who drinks and what happens to his two sons when they are adults. Almost everything said thus far is in this film. The film is stark. During it and afterwards, I cried for all the pain and suffering that I knew was out there beyond the theater, in similar homes, around the world. Perhaps it was too close to homes I know about. Perhaps I cried for all of us.

AND NOW EATING DISORDERS, TOO?

A short chapter on anger cannot be but a small snapshot of an enormously complex and far-reaching emotion. However, I do want to mention the growing evidence of men, not only women, developing serious eating disorders. Though arguments about causes and precursors are controversial, the need to exercise control is often mentioned as one of the dynamics. Whatever else may be going on in a man's life, he can "control" his weight. Wishing to "control" others is also thought to be a manifestation of anger and, like alcohol, backfires. Once a man becomes aware of his impotence to control others, he becomes more enraged.

Now, if these enraged men could "control" others, they could prevent others from doing the things that make them angry. So it is postulated that this is also an underlying dynamic in domestic violence and child abuse. When a man abuses his wife, partner, or child, it is when he perceives he is losing control of them. Similarly when a man who might be a manager or supervisor of people at work believes he is losing control, he may become outright abusive to his employees. He becomes enraged that he is losing control.

Now, say a man works for such a man. He wishes to keep his job, so he is now rendered powerless. This is a common source of anger for men. The feeling of powerlessness is so "powerful" that it often becomes explosive. The need to control others and be powerful can be seen as one and the same. Such a man who is feeling powerless would wish to control his boss' behavior, but he can't if he wishes to stay employed. So where can his rage go?

MEN GOING "POSTAL" AT WORK

The anger and rage may be directed at the target(s), and the angry person may kill the perceived person or people who have caused this person to become so enraged. Office killings are becoming more and more prevalent. Someone is aggrieved. He gets a gun. He returns to the workplace and begins to kill. Not just the person who slighted him but usually others in his path. Just this past year in Atlanta and in Boston, terror reigned and lives were shot away when no one expected it. Violence does not knock on the office door: the armed man enraged at being rendered powerless arrives with the blast of a shotgun.

It seems to me that this is the same narrative as Columbine and Santana. Far be it from me to take on the infamous question that academics love to ask: Does art imitate life or does life imitate art? If you have seen the film *Falling Down* with Michael Douglas (and if you have not, I would suggest obtaining this film, as well), you watched a man who is so overcome by the things he cannot control—people and the environment, the environment being downtown Los Angeles—that he takes on every provocation or provocateur with a rather large rifle.

Yes, this is a film, but what a nerve it struck when it was in the theaters. There is a man "not taking it anymore," acting out our darkest impulses. So the audience cheered him on his day of bloody revenge. This response is different than one of the most popular films this year, *Hannibal*. Most of us cannot identify with Hannibal Lector, the psychokiller, who is somewhat made into a hero because he is so clever, cunning, and intellectual. Yes, very intellectual. Perhaps I am wrong. Maybe there is some identification or wish to be clever, cunning, and intellectual, but the way Lector's talents are put to use repulses most of us, and we cringe in the darkened theater and turn our heads away.

But in *Falling Down*, we have the everyman, the man on the street, the average "Joe" who works for his family. I think he is an engineer of some type and commutes in heavy traffic on Los Angeles freeways. He encounters all the frustrations of modern life that we can identify with, from the mildly irritating to the ones which enrage us. This then becomes a man we can cheer on to do our dirty work. If films like this make us feel better because we can live for a few hours vicariously through the character, this may be a good outlet for some diffusion of anger. Also, we know our darkest impulses are shared. The differentiating factor is that most men do not act out these impulses. Enough do, though, to make the world a scary place.

Stephen King, John Grisham, and Robin Cook, popular novelists, allow men to also live in the suspended state of imagination of our dark impulses, our shadow self. These writers are best-selling novelists, not because they are great writers (I admit, that is a personal evaluation) but because they serve to the reader gory, nightmarish acts of terror and murder either for retaliation or revenge. We cheer on the protagonists, whatever it takes to even things out. Quentin Tarantino, the screenwriter of the film *Pulp Fiction* and others of that genre, introduces violence in its goriest depictions, acted out by fellows you kind of get to like. Well, killing is a job and some licensed killers are guys we like. However, often these licensed killers go too far. They cross a line and we begin discussing police or prison guards' brutality. And it must be emphasized—because the police departments emphasize this— that these cases are the exception. Tell that to the mother of Amadou Diallo. Tell that to the mother of the "exception" who was killed.

It seems to me with the number of "exceptions" that we know about and thinking that there must be many we do not know about—there should be no room for exceptions. Exceptions are killing and brutalizing people.

Evening Things Out or Getting Even

"Evening things out"—is that not what Columbine was about? On a grander scale, is that not what the Oklahoma City bombing was about? Is that not what fuels the Mideast situation?

"An eye for an eye" is the essence of many religions and cultures. "Turning the other cheek" is often seen as an act of weakness, not courage. Young boys are often taught to stand up for themselves, not take anything from anyone, and fight back. Some fathers call their sons sissies for not doing so. Some fathers say, "You act like a little girl" if they don't go deliver a blow to someone. The father invites shame on the boy—a shame tied to gender identity.

I could say it certainly would serve a better outcome if these men and boys transformed their anger. However, transforming anger into pathology, whether physical, psychological, or social, while still better than violence toward others, is nonetheless violence against oneself. It is almost idiomatic to hear mental health professionals say that depression is anger turned against the self, turned inward. Another widely held belief among these same professionals is that most suicides are examples of this dynamic. Instead of killing the person who has enraged the man, made him feel powerless, or humiliated him, the man kills himself.

I wonder sometimes, is this all inevitable? I read about testosterone, markers on a male chromosome, the biology-versus-environment debate, and read one conflicting report after another. For the purposes here, I acknowledge the literature on testosterone suggests that the hormone makes men more aggressive and therefore better competitive athletes. But we now have some contrast situations. We have enormously competitive women athletes who seem to be just as aggressive. We have men in prisons and we have women in prisons. So is the testosterone aggression link, while a link, the whole story, or should we consider the social construction of roles?

In spite of the women's movement and the idealistic version of bringing up both boys and girls with equal opportunities, the old social construction of what boys do and what girls do in childhood remains mostly grounded in the old customs or traditions before they enter a school setting. Girls are still protected from danger or adventure. Boys, on the other hand, are expected to be adventurous, play in dirt, get into fistfights, and not take anything from anyone. The expectation is that the boy won't take guff from anyone.

IN THE LITTLE LEAGUES AND THE BIG LEAGUE

Admittedly this is a generalization. Yet, the press has chosen to call our attention to the violent acts of fathers at sports events, where they perceive the coach or referee has done an injustice to their sons. The father's anger actually results in physical threats or actions, and the son is all riled up and becomes one with his father. His own father is telling him that another adult, the coach, is to be dealt with in an angry fashion. The boy watches and learns. He is learning about sports. He is learning about sportsmanlike behavior. He is learning he does not have to take anything, even from his coach. As one might expect, coaches and referees for young boys' sports are leaving the game. Why should they become the target of rage, on a volunteer basis no less?

Last fall, during the World Series between the New York Yankees and the New York Mets, I was shocked, and I am not usually shocked at things I see in men's so-called athletic games. Roger Clemens, the pitcher, had thrown a pitch to a so-called enemy of his from the opposing team who was up at bat. Mike Piazza hit the ball. The bat broke upon impact with the ball, and Clemens grabbed the part of the broken bat which was shaped liked a missile, and surely looked like a weapon that could kill. In front of all in the stadium and the men and boys glued to the television, Clemens picked up the missile and threw it directly at Piazza. The missile barely missed Piazza. If it had hit him, I believe it could have easily killed him and most assuredly would have caused tremendous injury. Piazza would have been either out of the game of life or baseball.

Perhaps you can understand why I was shocked. But I was more shocked, in fact appalled, that Clemens was allowed to continue to play in this "game." Is "play" the correct word here? What kind of "game" is this? Where are the rules? The umpires decided to keep him in the game. The game went on, the Yankees won the Series, and Clemens was fined a negligible sum. After all, it is well known Clemens has a temper.

So that is OK. That explains it. He has a temper. How did men react to this outright act of what could have been murder? Piazza, if hit, could have been seriously injured, if not killed. As this is going on, so is the social construction of roles for boys, all at once, simultaneously. They are learning what men do. They are learning about anger. But that is not all they learn.

This encounter evolved into anger and fights among men and boys as to who was right and who was wrong. The Yankees team—and that is an important concept to men, "team," so they speak in one voice—said he did not mean any harm. They said he lost his temper and maintained that Clemens knew it would not hit Piazza. On the other side of the field, the Mets team was out for blood. I thought I was going to witness a blood bath. The coaches for the Mets were holding them down, holding them back, and preventing the players from attacking the other team. The Mets manager finally calmed them down, but the people in the stadium did not want the Mets calmed down. They wanted them out there fighting. "Fight, fight, fight," echoed throughout the stadium.

If you were wondering who won the Series last year, I would say no one. I would say no one because Clemens should have been removed from the game. Boys at home needed to see that a hero does not throw missiles at another player. That night they learned another sad lesson in sportsmanship, or lack of such. They learned they could get away with attempted assault.

The Yankees won, but did they really? What if Clemens had been removed from the Series? What if attempted assault was reason enough to remove people from baseball games, offices, and homes?

THE HOME FRONT

Back in some home war zone, boys and girls unfortunately are exposed to their fathers throwing things and exploding in anger. They are afraid of where it will be directed. Lessons from the foregoing example give permission for their fathers to throw missiles. Fathers who inflict violence in the home often have learned it from their own fathers. Some men who inflict violence in the home have little control anywhere in their lives so they must control the home situation, and in particular the wife or "lover."

Domestic violence is a major public health problem. Every 15 seconds in this country a woman is battered. It is so epidemic that one in five women experience battering incidents each year. The most dangerous place for women is the home, the war zone. Violence is the leading cause of injury for all women. Not automobile accidents, muggings, not sports, but violence. Anger inflicted by the physically stronger person. I continue to be incredulous that over 4,000 women are killed each year in this country by their partner or lover. Domestic violence among homosexuals is now becoming more acknowledged as a serious health problem as well.

And I am not talking here about stereotypes—drunks who come home to a trailer and beat their poor wives to a pulp. I am not speaking about the "redneck" who pushes his partner around to teach her a lesson about leaving the house without his permission. While violence may happen in those kinds of situations, I am talking about men who work as attorneys, professors, engineers, managers, pilots, and ministers who live next door to you, the reader. It happens in middle and upper economic brackets, as well as the lower income, undereducated class.

There is no doubt that women can be verbally abusive, emotionally abusive, and physically abusive. That being said, this chapter is about men's transformation of anger. In this case the man can transform his anger into emotional or verbal abuse toward his partner or children. By now, we know this can be as damaging or worse than physical abuse. I once had a patient who said his father literally "foamed" at the mouth with rage at him. He never could do anything right. Never. He lived in fear of these explosive unpredictable rages. He would not bring friends home. He hid in his room. That did not work. When his father fumed, he came to find the son in order to roar. Think, little boy, of the big man who is the father.

This little boy, now a man, told me he actually wished his father had hit him and left marks on him. He would have preferred that to the emotional assaults that left damage no one could see. By the age of 45 this patient had already had two heart attacks. I would postulate that his repressed rage at his father was transformed into illness.

So What to Do

So what is a man to do with his anger? Thus far we see he can act on it, to hurt and perhaps kill people. He can emotionally scar his children for life. He can get licensed to kill.

He can transform his anger into some socially acceptable condition, some pathology, whether physical, psychological, or social. This is when he has repressed his anger and rage. Of course, this is very sad. When the anger is underground, concealed, it manifests itself in a way that people might even have sympathy for the poor man. And he is a poor man in the sense that I believe there must be a better way than either killing yourself or killing others around you. Whatever form it takes, whether it is emotional killing or sexual and physical abuse of children and women, there must be better ways. Those forms of killing murder the spirit. In my practice I have seen the scars of the victims who are alive and yet dead. Victims themselves of their own repressed rage, or victims of another man's rage.

The angry or threatening man, or the man who commits murder—say he kills his wife—produces a trickle down effect. A message is then sent to all women. Men who are angry, not sexually in search of a sexual experience, rape women. Another message is sent to women. Sometimes I wonder if men are aware of how they use these instances of violence to control the women and daughters in their lives. If women are scared, they are prey to control for protection. If O.J. Simpson is innocent, women need to be scared.

Bringing up Simpson, I wonder what is going on down in Miami. How many times does Simpson have to be arrested for his outbursts of anger toward other citizens before he goes to jail? Recently he jumped out of his car and, in a fit of rage, lunged at a driver who pissed him off. Has Simpson become lo-cal color? Please help me understand this lunacy. Think back to the days when Nicole Simpson was alive. Was she not a tramp? Did she not provoke him to murder? This is what many men silently think. Political correctness prevents this from being said aloud. But as is said, he walked.

Another lesson for women. You better be good, meaning you better not act like a man, you must be subservient to a man, you must remain the virgin, while men like Simpson search for whores. Did the man with Nicole have to be murdered also? Of course, the rage extended to another the killer could not control.

Perhaps you think I am dealing too much with the extreme. Remember though, this extreme that we read about is only the visible part of what is also occurring in our homes. Which brings me to family values and one in particular. The one I want to address that is related to home anger, aggression, or violence, is *loyalty*.

QUESTION LOYALTY AS A FAMILY VALUE

Much of what occurs in the home—the children's broken arms, the wife's con-tinual inability to leave the home or go to the emergency room—is never talked about because of "loyalty." I know it is also fear, but for this essay I would like to discuss loyalty. Children and wives can be brainwashed to be-lieve that anything that happens in the home must remain in the home. Loy-alty to the family comes first. After all, Daddy did not mean to hit Mommy or his darling little girl. He certainly meant no harm, touching her in places where he said is their little secret and threatening her if she should tell anyone. Be-lieve me, this all has to do with anger.

I would like to say in defense of these men, but not their actions, that most have suffered from similar abuse or have been the victim of someone close to them, often their own father's rage. So the anger, temper, aggression, and vio-lence must be placed in the context of their past lives and how being a man was socially constructed or demonstrated to them.

As I mentioned earlier in this piece, those men, once again because of the social construction of what a "real" man is like, often will not seek therapeutic help. Unfortunately, they will be in an emergency room with tightness of the chest, a bleeding ulcer, or a stroke. Medical help is acceptable. Psychological help for most men is still considered a sign of weakness. Some men, though, are unaware of what is morally reprehensible and inhumane. However, many women will tell these men, or a coworker, that they need help.

Did anyone tell Ted Kaczynski that he needed help? The Unabomber iso-lated himself and was terribly misguided. Ironically, he was for the oppressed in society, but he also was diagnosably psychotic. Many people need mental help. That is one part of the solution. But we need to be willing to take the risk of suggesting to a friend or partner that he or she needs help. I am aware this may sound naïve in some ways, but patients I have had were actually unaware of many of the dynamics of their own lives. Unfortunately, the help is sought after an illness or an arrest, or is court mandated. I still believe it is better to take the risk than to do nothing but watch an angry man transform his anger.

WHY IS IT SLOW GOING?

As long as men are angry or violent, women and children will need men. How is that? Because of fear. Fear of the cancer of violence. Who can protect women? The usual protector is a man, one with the similar body strength as other men. So what is perpetuated is the need for man as protector.

And there are many good men who play that role. However, that role would not be necessary if there were ways to prevent acting out of anger. So many men actually understand at some level that the angry man affords them power of their own, the power of the protector. So the nonangry man in some way benefits from the acting out of angry men. So men may be slow to become activists against what inherently gives them power. There are few male activists fighting against domestic violence, for example.

If you are a good man, there is more to do than just protection. You need to be as vigilant as women and children. Men need to reflect deeply on their attitudes toward what occurs in our society and how they themselves handle anger. I asked many men in the course of this research how they handle anger. I was met with more blank stares than I could believe. It was like they never thought about it. Some men did respond with phrases indicating that they were angry, some very angry about "something." Asking if I could talk to them about it resulted in more broken interview appointments. Men need to talk. Perhaps there would be fewer illnesses and broken spirits.

Men also need to help each other beyond the socially constructed boundaries of men "not being that way." When a man sees an angry man or suspects violence, the subject needs to be broached in the most gingerly way. I am not sure anger management courses work. Their statistics say they do, but I've already suggested how I feel about statistics. However, I would rather see a man try an anger management course than have a disease and die. There are as many prescriptions on how to deal with anger as there are types of anger. And therein lies the rub.

Anger is multivaried and multistoried. It is not just one response. It does not show itself in ways that are readily discernible. Yes, there sometimes are similarities in the demonstration of anger, but the backdrop will often be different. As with so many other complex phenomena, there is no one way to handle, diffuse, or transform anger into some healthy manifestation of behavior.

The other day I was reading just the kind of article a person might pick up who is aware that he has a problem with anger. I read it with utter disbelief. The article disregards all other approaches. It states that we are on the wrong path dealing with anger and that what a person should do before he blows up is to distract himself. He is to stop and think about whether this is worth getting angry about, make a decision that it is not, and then find something else to think about or do instead.

All right, perhaps that might work for some people, so let us not completely disregard this suggestion.

Actually, it is not all that different from those suggestions to take up a physical activity and work off the anger. I know a lot of angry runners who say that running clears their heads. This is also a good suggestion. I am trying to imagine some men I know who abuse their wives taking up running for a cure, but for some it might work.

The crux here is to individually find out what is best for the angry man who transforms his anger into illness or perpetuates it onto some innocent victim. The idea of one-size-fits-all has not led us to solving the problem. Anger, like love, is so multidimensional that the sheer complexity of it demands individual problem-solving strategies.

Since I am a therapist and a psychoanalytic one at that, the reader will guess what I believe to be the most helpful aid. And I will not deny that the right therapist, who can encourage expressions of anger from the client without fear, offers probably the most effective way of resolving anger, even if it is anger at work. Talking angry feelings out, with affect, to a safe person has amazing therapeutic effects. One of the best outcomes of therapy is the letting go of "the illusion of control." What a difficult lesson, in particular, with men: to come to accept there is so much beyond their control. Nor is it desirable to hold on to "control" of others.

Now for many men who are not aware that they have an anger problem, seeking counseling is not going to happen. What else then? "Experts" have urged more physical exercise, a better diet, stress-reducing techniques, talking with your partner, work, or love—in other words, "working it out between the two of you." I am skeptical of the last one. There was a theory once to let it "all hang out," tell whomever you're angry with the whole story, why you are angry and when you are angry, and tell the other person in the moment.

That approach kind of lost appeal when such action seemed to escalate arguments and anger. I will tell you two approaches I have found helpful both in my own life and in listening to patients and friends. One is not as simple as it sounds, takes practice, and is not meant for Hannibal Lector or Ted Kaczynski. That is to lower your expectations. The other is to remove yourself from the situation.

LOWERING EXPECTATIONS

You might recall in the beginning of this chapter that I said that anger is often stimulated by the perception that someone has done a misdeed or an injustice toward you. That is legitimate, and I must emphasize that anger is a healthy symptom to be reflected on. However, so much of our anger and disappointment, regardless of gender, comes from our expectations not being met. We become infuriated. We become hurt, the flip side of anger. Sometimes we become enraged.

Yet the expectations are there. Man or woman, we all have needs. The most dangerous one for a close partner is that the partner can meet all our needs. If you have that expectation, it will never be fulfilled, and you might ultimately become furious. It is an unreasonable expectation. If a man's need to control is constantly frustrated, as previously mentioned, he will indeed become infuriated. The need is impossible to fulfill.

Lowering expectations could also be translated to having your expectations met in different ways through different activities with different people. When I personally came to realize that as a woman I was expecting too much from one man, I cut him a lot of slack. I came to terms with the fact that I will never have what I really want, whatever that might be, and that if provided it might not really be what I want after all. I became increasingly aware of such illusionary thinking. I have found many men have similar ways of thinking. Thinking illusions and expecting their fruition. Quite simply, wishful thinking.

Being angry because someone, boss or partner, does not meet our expectations is a doomed position. Internalizing that this is a doomed proposition takes much work and reflection. Not internalizing this leads to constant frustration, anger toward another, and perhaps violence. Regardless of all one's anger, frustration and violence will not change things. Most people will one day or another disappoint us; it is inevitable. Most people will not meet our expectations, especially if we set them so high as to be unreasonable. We will be once again doomed and leave ourselves open to frustration, anger, and rage.

ANOTHER WAY OUT

One last way out I have found effective with clients—and I wish Nicole Simpson and many others who are now dead had employed it—is to remove yourself from angry people and from situations of continual anger. Move, change jobs, do not stay put. Excuses to this idea are usually resistance, wanting to stay for the highs and lows of angry situations. Remember, anger itself can become an addiction. The dramas, the roller coaster, and the makeups are all quite seductive. One needs to ask, "Have I become an anger addict or lover because it generates excitement?" Some men feel alive when in an angry state and look for opportunities for that adrenaline rush. That is why when the line is crossed, the next cot in the prison is filled.

Domestic violence is an example of this roller coaster. Violence, makeup, promises, and then repeat violence. It is too dangerous a game . . . wait, it is not a game, it is too dangerous a dynamic to continue. Someone is really going to get hurt.

Children also come to mind. They cannot lower their expectations, nor can they remove themselves from the source of anger. Here I can only say, perhaps plead, if you know a child, even your own, who is mixed up in this mess, please seek help. If you know another man whose story this is, please help him for the sake of the child. If not, the cycle continues. The cancer of violence continues. Too many children are being left, if alive, to foster care or to breakups, even from siblings and from love. What can one expect from these children when they become adults? This is the cycle I speak of: the victims become the perpetrators.

This is not the ending. This chapter is an attempt at consciousness raising for men. A similar chapter for women as mentioned is already in print. There can be no ending because we will always get angry. There will always be a perceived injustice or misdeed done to us. Every day, each of us gets angry, to varying degrees, the difference being what we do with that anger.

I am angry that teenagers are dead from high school shootings or massacres. I am angry at the strength of the National Rifle Association. I would like to know what would have happened in those situations and others where men have gone postal, whether at work or at home, if guns had not been available. So that gets me angry. I have lowered my expectations about gun control, but will raise my voice for it, when I can.

The question each individual must ask, because of the continuum of anger, is: How much is it eating at you? Before you are in an emergency room or divorced, ask this question and ponder it fully. Think about other ways of living through this experience. Do not hurt yourself. Do not hurt others.

For those who do not have such problems, reach out to those you know who do.

HOW MANY ROADS MUST A MAN WALK DOWN?

How many Columbines will it take? Rodney Kings? Nicole Simpson and the other 4,000 dead women? Hate crimes? Matthew Shepard, James Byrd, Oklahoma City, the World Trade Center. Just plain wars, where guns are placed in young boys' hands. Legs are shot off. Bombs burst in air. Planes shot down. Children orphaned. Humans dead.

How much blood needs to be shed? How much blood and guts must be blown away for control, for power? How much brutality must be visited upon the preyed upon? How much violence to the spirit of man must there be from those more powerful? How many children must cry themselves to sleep at night for the war zones they live in, whether in Chechnya or their own homes?

* * *

As I come to the close of this incomplete narrative, yet enough for me to deal with in this moment, there is an ironic feeling. I feel a sense of frustration, powerlessness, and even anger. Hate crimes particularly enrage me. The murder of children and women enrages me. I wish I could control some of these tragedies. Stop them. Stop men on the road to destruction.

Some people say all this is inevitable. From the beginning of time, violence, anger, power, and control have motivated men's lives. So I conclude this chapter feeling the very emotion I sat down to write about. In fact, in the course of writing this, I was often aware of my anger at different points.

I think I was less angry when I was writing about men transforming the anger into physical, psychological, and social conditions. I suppose if a man has a choice, hurting himself might be preferable to hurting others. Now I think of how many people are hurt when a father, a wonderful uncle, or a favorite friend takes this path. This is not the way to go either.

If enough people would get angry and use the anger productively as an outlet, as energy to address these problems (and many, many people are), I feel there may be hope for some. What angers you most you can "fight" against. Use the Web to find the groups who are demonstrating, lobbying, and implementing strategies to stop the carnage, whether physical or psychological.

On October 14, 1999, the same year as Columbine, Senate Majority Leader Trent Lott helped the Republican Party to "kill" a hate crimes bill, saying it was offensive. I hope that action makes many readers angry. Perhaps one of the best transformations of anger is into some type of activity that will help us move toward a more peaceful way of relating to one another.

Perhaps the next chapter I will write will be entitled "The Transformation of Anger by Men into Political Activism." Remember, the woman being hit with a bat could be your mother or your sister. Remember, the man who represses his anger and dies from it could be your father or your brother. Remember the child in the school yard who is killed could be yours.

REFERENCES

Dolnick, Edward. (1995). Hotheads and heart attacks. *Health*: July/August.

Munhall, P. (1995). The transformation of anger into pathology. In Munhall, P. *In Women's Experience: Volume I*, National League of Nursing. New York.

Health. (1990). If anger ruins your day, it can ruin your life. *New York Times*, December 13.

CHAPTER 61

STIGMA AND HEALTH IN GAY MEN

Kenneth D. Phillips
Richard L. Sowell

Each of us experiences the phenomena of being stigmatized and of stigmatizing others to varying degrees and for diverse reasons. The term *stigma* connotes a mark. In the Bible, the mark of Cain signified an act so shameful as to warrant divine wrath. Returned runaway Greek slaves were branded with marks of shame. Goffman (1963) referred to stigma as a mark of shame that spoils a person's identity. Jones et al. (1984) conceptualized stigma as a dilemma of being different that alters relationships between individuals. On one hand, the uniqueness of the individual is highly prized; on the other hand, a unique characteristic may be the basis of stigmatization.

The antecedents of stigmatization may be inalterable attributes of an individual (gender, sexual identity, race or ethnicity, the color of one's skin, or even the tone or hue of one's skin) or attributes that are changeable or perceived as changeable (obesity, sexual identity). The consequences of stigma may result in physiological, psychological, or sociological changes to a person's health. The purpose of this chapter is to explore the health consequences of stigma in gay men.

THE STIGMA OF GAY SEXUAL IDENTITY

Two terms have been used to describe the stigma of gay sexual identity, *heterosexism* and *homophobia*. Heterosexism, which refers to discrimination based on sexual orientation, is the term that the American Psychological Association prefers (Committee on Lesbian and Gay Concerns, 1991). Weinberg (1972) coined the term homophobia. Simply stated, homophobia means a fear of homosexuality. Nungesser (1983) defined homophobia as "the personal dynamic of irrational fear on the part of heterosexuals of being in close proximity, in general to people they believe to be homosexual" (p. 138). Levine (1979) concluded that on the social level, homophobia arises from (1) religious belief that homosexuality is immoral, (2) scientific theory that considers homosexuality to be a medical sickness or a societal deviance, and/or (3) societal belief that homosexuality causes the downfall of civilization. In the western world, homophobia is not the exception; it is the norm.

Homophobia leads to serious consequences, for those who are gay and for society (Blumefeld, 1992). For society, it limits the full use of individual talents and undermines the value of diversity and the full scope of the human condition. This takes on greater significance when it was estimated in 1995 that 6.2% (5.6 million) of all adult males in the United States reported engaging in sex with another man during the previous 5 years. Additionally, 20.8% (18.9 million) of all adult males report having been sexually attracted to another man during that same period (Sells, Wells, & Wypij, 1995). For homosexuals, homophobia leads to discriminatory practices in housing, employment, entitlements, healthcare provision, and other basic civil rights. Such discrimination can be overt, such as persons losing their job or housing when it is learned that they are gay, or it can be subtle, such as not being included in groups or considered for job advancement solely based on sexual orientation.

> In a recent conversation, a colleague reported that a supportive coworker had commented to him that it was a shame that he [the colleague] would not be considered for a promotion since he was the most qualified person in the organization for the promotion. The reason that was given for his not being considered for promotion was that he was too open about his gay lifestyle. The supportive coworker further shared that it was acceptable in the organization for an employee to be gay, because that demonstrated the organization's openness to diversity, but in a leadership position, a homosexual would not be acceptable to the "good ole boys" who ultimately made decisions about promotions.

Many gay men and women must endure rejection by family members, friends, and peers. Homophobia can also result in violence against gay men and women (Dean, Wu, & Martin, 1992). In two high-profile cases in recent years, Matthew Shepard and Billy Jack Gaither were killed because they were gay. Matthew Shepard, a young college student, was beaten and left tied to a fence to die in a remote area of Wyoming. Similarly, in Alabama, Billy Jack Gaither was beaten and then his body burned. The motivation for both of these heinous crimes was homophobia.

INTERNALIZED HOMOPHOBIA

Internalized homophobia is defined as fear or hatred toward homosexuality that has been internalized, has become a significant part of the homosexual's self-concept, and has resulted in varying degrees of self-hatred (Nungesser,

1983). That homophobia can be and is internalized by gay individuals is of even greater concern than societal homophobia. Internalized homophobia appears to be an additional source of emotional distress for gay men with HIV infection not found in other groups. For example, Moulton, Sweet, Temoshok, and Mandel (1987) found higher levels of acute emotional distress among gay men with AIDS than that found in a comparison group of hemophiliacs with AIDS. As an individual moves through the stages of coming out, it is likely that there will be a decrease in the internalization of homophobia. However, internalized homophobia may be experienced to some degree in all stages of self-acceptance of one's sexual identity (Herek & Glunt, 1995; McDonald, 1982; Nungesser, 1983; Wolcott et al., 1986). For instance, Dean and Meyer (1995) reported that two thirds of the gay men in a study of the impact of HIV disease reported some level of internalized homophobia. Gonsoriek (1993) has pointed out that internalized homophobia can range from feelings of self-doubt to feelings of self-hatred. Internalized homophobia is exemplified by the following situation.

> Bob is a 27-year-old male who grew up in rural Georgia. Clearly, his family and friends were traditional in their views of family and sexuality. Bob played football in high school and worked to maintain his "jock" image during college. Even though he suspected that he was probably gay in high school, a suspicion he later confirmed in college, he maintained a facade of being heterosexual. After college, Bob moved to Atlanta to work. Although Bob had gay friends, they were usually guys who were interested in sports and outdoor activities. Bob did not want his coworkers to know he was gay and usually took a female friend to company functions. Although Bob was uncomfortable around many gay men, he did frequent the bars and participate in community events. However, Bob was very critical and sometimes even verbally abusive of more flamboyant gay men who fit what he felt was a stereotypical gay image. When asked by a friend if he thought he had a prejudice against many members of the gay community, he responded he certainly enjoyed having sex with men, but he just did not want to be seen as one of those "queers." He just hated "those people" for giving all gay men a bad name.

A person's self-concept consists of all the beliefs and feelings that he or she has formed about him- or herself. The self-concept is formed both from internal perceptions and from the perceptions of others. From one's self-concept, a sexual identity is formed. A person's sexual identity is broadly categorized as being heterosexual, bisexual, homosexual, or transgendered. Each of these groups experiences its own stigma. This stigmatization becomes evident in the slang terms that are used by members of one group when referring to the sexual identity of another group (i.e., breeders and queers).*

Coming out refers to the psychological processes by which an individual comes to realize that one is romantically and sexually attracted to persons of

---

*This comparison should not suggest that forms of stigmatization are equivalent. Stigma is tied to larger social structures of power, prejudice, and discrimination.

one's own gender that leads to an integrated sense of self and identity. Cass (1979) proposed a model of the coming-out process that proceeds in stages of psychological changes. In the first stage, **identity confusion,** the individual questions and wonders whether he or she is gay. In **identity comparison,** the individual begins to think he or she might be gay but continues to present to others as straight. In **identity tolerance,** the individual demonstrates greater commitment to gay identity but attempts to pass as straight. As the person moves into the stage of **identity acceptance,** he or she accepts being gay as normal. In the stage of **identity pride,** the gay individual becomes less concerned with heterosexuals' opinions about homosexuality and becomes more open about sexual identity. In the stage of **identity synthesis,** with greater acceptance of the proposition that "this is who I am," there is less inconsistency between the individual's self-perception and other perceptions. When family, friends, and societal institutions do not support young gay men through these stages of coming out, they struggle through this developmental process in isolation and often fail to develop an integrated sense of self and identity.

THE STIGMA OF HIV/AIDS

Persons living with AIDS (PLWA) may suffer more stigmatization than any other group in the United States today (McCain & Gramling, 1992). The experience of stigmatization by HIV-infected individuals may be a near universal response (Morin, Charles, & Malyon, 1984; Siegel & Krauss, 1991). In fact, AIDS has been called an epidemic of stigma (Herek & Capitanio, 1993; Herek & Glunt, 1988). AIDS-related stigma is "stigma directed at persons perceived to be infected with HIV, regardless of whether they are actually infected and of whether they manifest symptoms of AIDS" (Herek & Glunt, 1988, p. 886). Stigmatization may emanate from family, friends, lovers, employers, physicians, nurses, religious organizations, or governmental agencies. Stigma may create a variety of problems for the PLWA. Not only must they contend with the diagnosis of a life-threatening illness, multiple symptoms, and losses beyond comprehension, but they must also deal with the reactions of others to the disease and to them. Among many other losses, stigma-related losses experienced by a PLWA may include the loss of relationships, employment, income, and medical benefits. Stigma may create barriers to receiving health care (Gee, 1988). Factors that help to account for the stigmatization associated with AIDS are presented below (Conrad, 1986; Kayal, 1992; Kelly, St. Lawrence, Smith, Hood, & Cook, 1987; Sontag, 1988; Strommen, 1989; Yedidia, Barr, & Berry, 1993):

- AIDS is incurable.
- AIDS is progressive.
- AIDS is transmissible by sexual intercourse.
- Persons with AIDS are blamed for having acquired the disease.
- The symptoms of AIDS may be visible and disfiguring.
- AIDS confronts all members of society with their own mortality.
- AIDS often afflicts groups of individuals who are already stigmatized.

Although it has been two decades since the advent of AIDS, the stigmatization of people with AIDS continues today. In 1993, Herek and Capitanio conducted a random telephone survey. In that survey, many of the respondents reported being angry (27%), disgusted (28%), and afraid (36%). Many respondents (36%) believed that persons with AIDS should be separated from the rest of society. Twenty-one percent felt that people with AIDS "got what they deserved." Persons with AIDS were stigmatized in some way by more than three fourths of the telephone sample.

The stigma of AIDS has been compared to that of leprosy (Volinn, 1989). In the early days of the AIDS epidemic, one of the news journals recorded the following scenario.

> In Arcadia, Florida, three brothers tested positive for the human immunodeficiency virus (HIV). After word spread of their infection, their barber refused to cut the boys' hair, and the family's minister suggested that they stay away from Sunday church services. Eventually, the family's house was burned down.

In addition to the stigma incurred as a result of having a contagious life-threatening illness (Worden, 1991), many PLWA are already stigmatized for being members of groups seen as aberrant or deviant (Bishop, Alva, Cantu, & Rittiman, 1991; Caldwell, 1991; Crandall, 1991; Grossman, 1991; Siminoff, Erlen, & Lidz, 1991). A recount of the experience of Corey, a young man known to one of these authors, tells of the horror of the stigma associated with AIDS.

> At the age of 22, Corey decided to be tested for HIV. He went to see the physician whom he trusted and who had provided medical care for him for a number of years. The physician performed a perfunctory physical examination and asked his office assistant to draw blood from Corey to perform an ELISA test. The physician instructed Corey to return in two weeks for his results. Unfortunately, when he returned to the physician for the results of his ELISA test, he learned that he was HIV positive. The physician said, "You are HIV positive. I don't believe in your lifestyle. You will have to find another doctor." Later that year Corey committed suicide.

Conditions that are seen as preventable produce greater stigma, whereas conditions that are unavoidable produce lesser stigma. Weiner, Perry, and Magnusson (1988) demonstrated that individuals who were labeled as responsible for a condition such as obesity, AIDS, or drug addiction were not liked as much and evoked less pity from the participants in their study. Likewise, American and German students who participated in a study by Murphy-Berman and Berman (1991) felt more anger and less pity toward AIDS patients if they had failed to take precautions against becoming HIV-infected. McBride (1998) presented vignettes to 181 undergraduate psychology students that described the mode of HIV transmission and the sexual preference of an HIV-positive male. McBride showed that bisexuals were judged as more responsible than heterosexuals for becoming HIV-infected. People who contracted HIV disease through homosexual intercourse or IV drug use are stigmatized more than those who were infected through a transfusion (Lewis & Range, 1992).

Likewise, conditions that are reversible produce lesser stigma than those that are irreversible. Most individuals in society view AIDS as both preventable and irreversible, thereby generating increased levels of stigma.

Stigma has enormous potential to impact negatively on the quality of health care that is delivered. A qualitative study by Cavalaris (1987) supported two types of stigma associated with AIDS: the stigma associated with the disease itself and the stigma associated with lifestyles. In her study a hemophiliac patient who was refused needed surgery as a result of his HIV status said:

> I came into the hospital, was factored up and ready to go, you know, all set for the next morning. The surgeon walked in that evening after I'd spent the whole day there and said, "I see on your chart that you're HIV positive. I'm sorry. I can't do it." I had no option. He flatly refused. (Cavalaris, 1987, p. 42)

INTERNALIZATION OF THE STIGMA OF AIDS

Internalized stigma of AIDS is a state of ineffective adaptation manifested through the self-concept in which the PLWA sees himself or herself as guilty, shameful, victimized, marked, dangerous, immoral, evil, or inferior to others in society (Phillips, 1994).

> Kevin had been married and had two daughters. He had lived in an open relationship with a male partner for six years. In the early days of the epidemic, Kevin was convinced that he was HIV-infected. Fearing the outcome, he decided against having the AIDS test. He blamed his lifestyle for having HIV/AIDS. He was very afraid of transmitting the virus to his daughters by cooking for them. He felt dirty and washed his hands numerous times while cooking the meal. Finally, he decided to be tested for HIV infection. Upon confirming his fears that he was HIV-infected, he no longer cooked for his family and was reluctant to hold his grandchildren.

HEALTH CONSEQUENCES OF STIGMA IN GAY MEN

Historically in the Western tradition, health has been viewed as the absence of disease. In 1974, the World Health Organization defined health as a state of complete physical, mental, or social well-being and not merely the absence of disease or infirmity. Health is considered from this holistic perspective in this study of the associations between stigma and health in gay men.

Stigma and Health in Gay Men

Mental Health. Gay men who internalize negative societal attitudes about their sexuality are more likely to experience a variety of mental health problems (Gonsoriek, 1988; Isay, 1989; Malyon, 1982; Marmor, 1980a; Marmor, 1980b; McHenry & Johnson, 1993; Stein & Cohen, 1984; Weinberg, 1972). Men with greater internalized homophobia have a lower self-esteem (Nicholson & Long, 1990), and they experience more frequent mood disturbances, especially depression (Meyer, 1995; Nicholson & Long, 1990; Shidlo, 1994; Wolcott, Namir, Fawzy, Gottlieb, & Mitsuyasu, 1986). Attempted suicides are more frequent in gay men with greater internalized homophobia (Rofes, 1983). They are more likely to use avoidant coping rather than active coping, often a more effective way of coping (Nicholson & Long, 1990).

Substance Abuse. Alcoholism is more common in gay men with greater internalized homophobia (Finnegan & Cook, 1984). The same is true of other types of substance abuse (Glaus, 1988). In fact, internalized homophobia and substance abuse share many common traits.

Intimate Relationships. Men who internalize homophobia have greater difficulty in forming and maintaining emotionally intimate relationships. In a study of HIV-infected and HIV-negative gay men, the participants were asked to rate the quality of their intimate relationships with the person whom they considered to be the most emotionally intimate person in their life. Statistically significant inverse relationships between internalized homophobia and emotional intimacy were observed. This finding suggests that gay men who have internalized homophobia to a greater degree may have greater difficulty in forming emotionally intimate relationships. Lack of emotional intimacy may lead to disruptions of all aspects of gay relationships.

Safer Sexual Behavior. Herek and Glunt (1995) found an indirect relationship between self-acceptance and sexual risk-taking behavior. Individuals with greater homophobia reported less self-efficacy for safer sex and more barriers to practicing safe sex. Men who reported lower self-efficacy for safer sexual behavior and more barriers to practicing safer sex were more likely to participate in risk-taking behavior. Meyer (1995) found that gay or bisexual men who were the very highest level of sexual risk takers (unprotected receptive anal intercourse with multiple partners) were more likely to have mental health problems, to abuse substances, and to have higher levels of internalized homophobia.

Stigma and Health in HIV-Infected Gay Men

From the perspective of eudaemonistic health (Fryback, 1993), HIV-infected individuals can achieve a high level of health. Fryback conducted a naturalistic study to examine how people with terminal diseases describe health. Factors they identified as contributing to their health were hope, love, control, belief in a higher power, recognition of their mortality, self-actualization, feeling good, health-promoting activities, and a relationship with their physician. Their disease was seen as part of their health. Many terminally ill individuals in that study believed that they became healthier because of their diagnoses. It is from that perspective that the relationship between stigma and health is explored.

Homophobia and the AIDS Epidemic.   Ames (1996) suggests that heterosexism has "had an enormous impact on the way a disease, AIDS, has been socially understood, scientifically researched, and medically treated" (p. 239). In the early days of the AIDS epidemic, AIDS was referred to as GRID (gay-related immune disorder) and the "gay plague." Viewing AIDS as a gay disease allowed society to ignore the spreading epidemic in heterosexual populations. Because AIDS was perceived to afflict only marginalized, disenfranchised members of society, development of public health policies was delayed.

Because specific homosexual behaviors, such as anal intercourse, were viewed as abnormal, there was hesitancy to address these behaviors in prevention programs. Ames, Atchinson, and Rose (1995) reported from their research in a small city that many gay men do not even like anal intercourse. Ames (1996) points out that gay men, like heterosexuals, participate in a number of sexual behaviors, some that are associated with great risk for the transmission of HIV and some that are associated with little or no risk. Public health programs have often failed to address this diversity. Failing to address this diversity sounds a great deal like saying that all members of a race look alike. Public health programs often focus on specific sexual behaviors and fail to address love and commitment.

When AIDS began appearing in hemophiliacs, transfusion recipients, and babies in the early days of the epidemic, they were referred to as the "innocent victims" of AIDS. Labels of innocence and guilt exemplify the stigma associated with HIV/AIDS.

Stigma and Illness.   According to Conrad (1986), stigmatizing illnesses are associated with deviant behavior either by producing deviant behavior (i.e., epilepsy or mental illness) or by resulting from deviant behavior (i.e., AIDS or genital herpes). Individuals who are afflicted by a stigmatizing illness are apt to be devalued, shunned, or to have fewer opportunities than others.

Stigma and Health Status.   Nicholson and Long (1990) found an association between the level of internalized homophobia and subjective health status reported by gay and bisexual men with AIDS. Explanations for this relationship are not presently available.

Access to Health Care.   Persons with HIV disease frequently encounter barriers that prevent them from receiving the level of health care that they deserve. Stigma is one such barrier. A number of studies have suggested that discrimination against people with AIDS is more related to homophobia than to fear of AIDS (Jackson & Hunter, 1992). The fear of being stigmatized may actually prevent many individuals from being tested for HIV (Herek & Glunt, 1988).

In 1990, a nationwide survey of physicians was conducted. A large majority of the respondents reported a belief that physicians have a responsibility to treat persons with HIV disease, but half of them responded that, given the choice, they would prefer not to do so (Gerbert et al., 1990).

Most, but not all, nurses agree that they have an ethical responsibility to provide nursing care to anyone in need of nursing care. Corley and Goren (1998) refer to the "dark side of nursing." Dark side nursing behaviors do not contribute to the well-being of patients. Dark side nursing behaviors include those that marginalize, label, stereotype, or stigmatize patients (i.e., hostile, angry, or distancing behaviors, minimizing or avoiding contact with patients, failing to provide needed care, or providing more care than is necessary). Swanson, Chenitz, Zalar, and Stoll (1990) found that AIDS patients actually received less care than other patients.

Although legal protections have been enacted to protect persons with HIV from discriminatory health care (i.e., Americans with Disabilities Act), discriminatory acts continue, but have become more covert (Rubenstein, Eisenberg, & Gostin, 1996). Although such legal protections were necessary, it is a sad commentary that laws were needed to ensure that persons who are ill and in need of health care would be treated humanely in health care institutions by health care providers.

Mental Health.   Stigmatized individuals are predisposed to a number of negative emotions that include loneliness, anxiety, depression, guilt, hostility, and anger. Meyer (1995) studied psychological distress in a cohort of HIV-infected men and found significant relationships between internalized homophobia and demoralization, internalized homophobia and guilt feelings, and internalized homophobia and suicidal ideation and behavior.

A number of researchers have found evidence to suggest that the incidence of suicide, attempted suicide, and thoughts of suicide are increasing among HIV-infected individuals (Belkin, Fleishman, Stein, Piette, & Mor, 1992; Demi, Bakeman, Sowell, Moneyham, & Seals, 1998). Stigma has been identified as a major stressor for people with HIV disease (Gilmore & Somerville, 1994). Demi et al. (1998) demonstrated that perceived stigma, HIV-related symptoms, and depressive mood were higher in women with AIDS who had suicidal thoughts than in those who did not.

Sexual Health.   HIV-infected men with high levels of internalized homophobia were found to be four times more likely to experience some form of sexual dysfunction (inhibited sexual desire, inhibited excitement, inhibited orgasm) during the year prior to their interview in the Longitudinal AIDS Impact Project (Dean & Meyer, 1995).

Intimate Relationships.   Bennett (1990) reported stigmatizing behaviors that people with AIDS experience, which included people shying away from them, refusing to touch them or shake their hands, staring at visible symptoms, and expressing revulsion, disgust, or fear. People with AIDS often report being avoided by friends, family members, neighbors, and coworkers (Herek & Capitanio, 1993). People with AIDS report feeling alienated from others (Bennett, 1990; Zich & Temoshok, 1990). Fearing rejection, an HIV-infected person may disengage from his or her relationships, leading to greater social isolation (Barrett, 1995; Bennett, 1990; Crandall & Coleman, 1992; Longo, Sprose, & Locke, 1990). As stated before, some HIV-infected individuals internalize the stigma of AIDS to a greater degree. Phillips (1994), in a study of 24 HIV-infected gay males, found a significant inverse relationship between internalized stigma of AIDS and emotional intimacy ($r = -.45$, $p = .03$).

Dean and Meyer (1995) examined the stability of relationships of coupled men who were HIV-infected. They found significant associations between internalized homophobia and the length of relationship ($r = -.16$, $p < .05$), cohabitation ($\chi2 = 5.5$, $p < .05$), and relationship discord ($r = .11$, $p < .05$). Individuals experiencing higher internalized homophobia had considered ending the relationship with their partners more often ($r = .11$, $p < .05$).

CONSIDERATIONS

The literature reviewed in this chapter indicates that stigma may lead to serious consequences related to the health status and well-being of gay men. Two of the most prevalent types of stigma for gay men are homophobia and the stigma associated with HIV infection. While such society-based stigma has the potential for extremely negative consequences for gay men on a number of levels, internalized homophobia and AIDS stigma can be even more devastating to the well-being of gay men. Individuals who have internalized homophobia and the stigma of HIV infection most often are not aware that these negative feelings have entered their self-concepts. It may be important for both the health care provider and the gay individual to recognize the potential negative influences of internalized homophobia and AIDS stigma. An individual's becoming aware of and dealing with the negative thoughts that he holds about himself may prove quite beneficial in improving his self-concept. This may have enormous impact on his health and well-being. Consistently, self-concept or self-esteem has been shown to be an important factor in being able to take the necessary actions to promote health and quality of life.

Health care providers must acknowledge the level of stigma they assign to homosexuality and to HIV-infected individuals. It is important for health care providers to realistically assess how such beliefs or negative views play out in their professional life. Is the quality of care provided to homosexuals of less importance? What is the basis of negative attitudes and actions that a health care provider takes toward homosexuals? Often we hear, "T*hose people* just make me uncomfortable." Such remarks beg the question—what makes you uncomfortable? In the patient-provider relationship there is very little chance of the health care provider being placed in moral or physical jeopardy. Such a relationship may be troubling for health care providers who have strong religious beliefs concerning homosexuality or who have unresolved issues related to same-sex intimacy. If that stigma arises from a religious perspective, they might ask themselves if their religion condones hate and not having compassion for others. Health care providers must be cognizant that internalized homophobia and internalized stigma of AIDS are not behaviors that are readily identified simply by observing a patient. Health care providers should be aware that HIV-infected individuals may feel, although erroneously, that they are dangerous or undesirable to others. Likewise, internalized homophobia may be the source of psychological distress (i.e., depression, anxiety, or substance use). As healers, health care providers are charged with positively addressing issues that potentially affect the health of those for whom they provide care and treatment. Certainly, there is a mandate to *do no harm*.

REFERENCES

Ames, L. J. (1996). Homo-phobia, homo-ignorance, homo-hate: Heterosexism and AIDS. In E. D. Rothblum & L. A. Bond (Eds.), *Preventing heterosexism and homophobia* (pp. 239–252). Thousand Oaks, CA: Sage.

Ames, L. J., Atchinson, A. B., & Rose, D. T. (1995). Love, lust, and fear: Sexual decision-making among gay men. *Journal of Homosexuality*, 30(1), 53–73.

Barrett, R. K. (1995). Elephant people: The phenomena of social withdrawal and self-imposed isolation of dying people with AIDS. AIDS *Patient Care*, 9, 240–244.

Belkin, G. S., Fleishman, J. A., Stein, M. D., Piette, J., & Mor, V. (1992). Physical symptoms and depressive symptoms among individuals with HIV infection. *Psychosomatics*, 33(4), 416–427.

Bennett, M. J. (1990). Stigmatization: Experiences of persons with acquired immune deficiency syndrome. *Issues in Mental Health Nursing*, 11(2), 141–154.

Bishop, G. D., Alva, A. L., Cantu, L., & Rittiman, T. K. (1991). Responses to persons with AIDS: Fear of contagion or stigma? *Journal of Applied Psychology*, 21(23), 1877–1888.

Blumefeld, W. J. (Ed.). (1992). *Homophobia: How we all pay the price*. Boston: Beacon Press.

Caldwell, S. (1991). Twice removed: The stigma suffered by gay men with AIDS. *Smith College Studies in Social Work*, 61(3), 236–246.

Cass, V. C. (1979). Homosexual identity formation: A theoretical model. *Journal of Homosexuality*, 4, 219–235.

Cavalaris, D. (1987). *Perceptions of persons with either a positive HIV antibody test or AIDS toward their health care providers*. Unpublished master's thesis. Knoxville, TN: University of Tennessee.

Committee on Lesbian and Gay Concerns. (1991). Avoiding heterosexual bias in language. *American Psychologist*, 46, 973–974.

Conrad, P. (1986). The social meaning of AIDS. *Social Policy*, 17, 51.

Corley, M. C., & Goren, S. (1998). The dark side of nursing: Impact of stigmatizing responses on patients. *Scholarly Inquiry for Nursing Practice*, 12(2), 99–118.

Crandall, C. S. (1991). Multiple stigma and AIDS: Illness stigma and attitudes toward homosexuals and IV drug users in AIDS-related stigmatization. *Journal of Community and Applied Social Psychology*, 1(2), 165–172.

Crandall, C. S., & Coleman, R. (1992). AIDS-related stigmatization and the disruption of social relationships. *Journal of Social and Personal Relationships*, 9, 163–177.

Dean, L., & Meyer, I. H. (1995). HIV prevalence and sexual behavior in a cohort of young New York City gay men (aged 18–24). *Journal of Acquired Immune Deficiency Syndromes*, 8, 208–211.

Dean, L., Wu, S., & Martin, J. L. (1992). Trends in violence and discrimination against gay men in New York City: 1984–1990. In G. M. Herek & K. T. Berrill (Eds.), *Hate crimes: Confronting violence against lesbian and gay men* (pp. 46–64). Newberry Park, CA: Sage.

Demi, A., Bakeman, R., Sowell, R., Moneyham, L., & Seals, B. (1998). Suicidal thoughts of women with HIV infection. Effect of stressors and moderating effects of family cohesion. *Journal of Family Psychology*, 12(3), 344–353.

Finnegan, D. G., & Cook, D. (1984). Special issues affecting the treatment of male and lesbian alcoholics. *Alcoholism Treatment Quarterly*, 1, 85–98.

Fryback, P. B. (1993). Health for people with a terminal diagnosis. *Nursing Science Quarterly*, 6(3), 147–149.

Gee, G. (1988). Individual psychosocial responses to HIV infection. In G. Gee & T. A. Moran (Eds.), *AIDS: Concepts in nursing practice* (pp. 361–378). Baltimore: Williams & Wilkins.

Gerbert, B., Maguire, B. T., Bleecker, T., Coates, T. J., & McPhee, S. J. (1990). Primary care physicians and AIDS: Attitudinal and structural barriers to care. *Journal of the American Medical Association*, 266(20), 2837–2842.

Gilmore, N., & Somerville, M. A. (1994). Stigmatization, scapegoating and discrimination in sexually transmitted diseases: Overcoming "them and us." *Social Science and Medicine*, 39(9), 1339–1358.

Glaus, O. K. (1988). Alcoholism, chemical dependency, and the lesbian client. *Women and Therapy*, 8, 131–144.

Goffman, E. (1963). *Stigma: Notes on the management of spoiled identity*. Englewood Cliffs, NJ: Prentice Hall.

Gonsoriek, J. C. (1988). Mental health issues of gay and lesbian adolescents. *Journal of Adolescent Health Care*, 9(2), 114–122.

Gonsoriek, J. C. (1993). Mental health issues of gay and lesbian adolescents. In L. D. Garnets & D. C. Kimmel (Eds.), *Homosexuality: Research implications for public policy* (pp. 115–136). Newberry Park, CA: Sage.

Grossman, A. H. (1991). Gay men and HIV/AIDS: Understanding the double stigma. *Journal of the Association of Nurses in AIDS Care*, 2, 28–32.

Herek, G. M., & Capitanio, J. P. (1993). Public reactions to AIDS in the United States: A second decade of stigma. *American Journal of Public Health*, 83, 574–577.

Herek, G. M., & Glunt, E. K. (1988). An epidemic of stigma. Public reactions to AIDS. *American Psychologist*, 43(11), 886–891.

Herek, G. M., & Glunt, E. K. (1995). Identity and community among gay and bisexual men in the AIDS era. In G. M. Herek & B. Greene (Eds.), *AIDS, identity, and community: The HIV epidemic and lesbians and gay men* (pp. 55–84). Thousand Oaks, CA: Sage.

Isay, R. A. (1989). *Being homosexual: Gay men and their development*. New York: Ferrar, Straus, & Giroux.

Jackson, M. H., & Hunter, N. D. (1992). "The very fabric of health care": The duty of health care providers to treat people infected by HIV. In N. Hunter & W. Rubenstein (Eds.), AIDS *agenda: Emerging issues in civil rights* (pp. 123–146). New York: New Press.

Jones, E. E., Farina, A., Hastorf, A. H., Markus, H., Miller, D. T., & Scott, R. A. (1984). *Social stigma: The psychology of marked relationships.* New York: W. H. Freeman and Company.

Kayal, P. M. (1992). Healing homophobia: Volunteerism and "sacredness" in AIDS. *Journal of Religion and Health,* 31, 113.

Kelly, J. A., St. Lawrence, J. S., Smith, S., Hood, H. V., & Cook, D. J. (1987). Stigmatization of AIDS patients by physicians. *American Journal of Public Health,* 77, 789.

Levine, M. P. (1979). *Gay men: The sociology of male homosexuality.* New York: Harper & Row.

Lewis, L. S., & Range, L. M. (1992). Do means of transmission, risk knowledge, and gender affect AIDS stigma and social interactions? *Journal of Social Behavior and Personality,* 7, 211–216.

Longo, M. B., Sprose, J. A., & Locke, A. M. (1990). Identifying major concerns of persons with acquired immunodeficiency syndrome: A replication. *Clinical Nurse Specialist,* 4, 21–26.

Malyon, A. (1982). Psychotherapeutic implications of internalized homophobia in gay men. *Journal of Homosexuality,* 7(2–3), 59–69.

Marmor, J. (Ed.). (1980a). Epilogue: Homosexuality and the issue of mental illness. In J. Marmor (Ed.), *Homosexual behavior: A modern reappraisal* (pp. 391–401). New York: Basic Books.

Marmor, J. (Ed.). (1980b). *Homosexual behavior: A modern reappraisal* (pp. 391–401). New York: Basic Books.

McBride, C. A. (1998). The discounting principle and attitudes toward victims of HIV infection. *Journal of Applied Social Psychology,* 28(7), 595–608.

McCain, N. L., & Gramling, L. F. (1992). Living with dying: Coping with HIV disease. *Mental Health Nursing,* 13, 271–284.

McDonald, D. J. (1982). Individual differences in the coming out process for gay men: Implications for theoretical models. *Journal of Homosexuality,* 8(1), 47–60.

McHenry, S., & Johnson, J. (1993). Homophobia in the therapist and gay or lesbian client: Conscious and unconscious collisions in self-hate. *Psychotherapy,* 30, 141–151.

Meyer, I. H. (1995). Minority stress and mental health in gay men. *Journal of Health and Social Behavior,* 36, 38–56.

Morin, S. F., Charles, K., & Malyon, A. K. (1984). Psychosocial impact of AIDS on gay men. *American Psychologist,* 39, 1288–1293.

Moulton, J. M., Sweet, D. M., Temoshok, L., & Mandel, J. S. (1987). Attributions of blame and responsibility in relation to distress and health behavior change in people with AIDS and AIDS-related complex. *Journal of Applied Social Psychology,* 17(5), 493–506.

Murphy-Berman, V. A., & Berman, J. J. (1991). Perceptions of justice and attitudes towards people with AIDS: German-U.S. comparisons. *Social Behavior and Personality,* 19, 29–38.

Nicholson, W. D., & Long, B. C. (1990). Self-esteem, social support, internalized homophobia, and coping strategies of HIV+ gay men. *Journal of Consulting and Clinical Psychology,* 58(6), 873–876.

Nungesser, L. G. (1983). *Homosexual acts, actors, and identities.* New York: Praeger.

Phillips, K. D. (1994). *Testing biobehavioral adaptation in persons living with AIDS using Roy's Theory of the Person as an Adaptive System.* Unpublished dissertation, University of Tennessee, Knoxville.

Rofes, E. E. (1983). *I thought people like that killed themselves: Lesbians, gay men, and suicide.* San Francisco: Grey Fox.

Rubenstein, W. B., Eisenberg, R., & Gostin, L. O. (1996). *The rights of people who are HIV positive.* Carbondale, IL: Southern Illinois University Press.

Sells, R. L., Wells, J. A., & Wypij, D. (1995). The prevalence of homosexual behavior and attraction in the United States, the United Kingdom, and France: Results of national-based samples. *Archives of Sexual Behavior, 24,* 235–248.

Shidlo, A. (1994). Internalized homophobia: Conceptual and empirical issues in measurement. In B. Greene & G. M. Herek (Eds.), *Lesbian and gay psychology: Theory, research, and clinical applications* (pp. 176–205). Thousand Oaks, CA: Sage.

Siegel, K., & Krauss, B. J. (1991). Living with HIV infection: Adaptive tasks of seropositive gay men. *Journal of Health and Social Behavior, 32,* 17–32.

Siminoff, L. A., Erlen, J. A., & Lidz, C. W. (1991). Stigma, AIDS and quality of nursing care. *Journal of Advanced Nursing, 16,* 262–269.

Sontag, S. (1988). *AIDS and its metaphors.* New York: Farrar, Straus, and Giroux.

Stein, T. S., & Cohen, C. J. (1984). Psychotherapy with gay men and lesbians: An examination of homophobia, coming out, and identity. In E. S. Hetrick & T. A. Stein (Eds.), *Innovations in psychotherapy with homosexuals* (pp. 59–73). Washington, DC: American Psychiatric Association Press.

Strommen, E. F. (1989). Hidden branches and growing pains: Homosexuality and the family tree. *Marriage and Family Review, 14,* 9.

Swanson, J. M., Chenitz, C., Zalar, M., & Stoll, P. (1990). A critical review of human immunodeficiency virus infection—and acquired immunodeficiency syndrome-related research: The knowledge, attitudes, and practice of nurses. *Journal of Professional Nursing, 6*(6), 341–355.

Volinn, I. J. (1989). Issues of definitions and their implications. AIDS and leprosy. *Social Science and Medicine, 20*(10), 1157–1162.

Weinberg, G. (1972). *Society and the healthy homosexual.* New York: St. Martin's Press.

Weiner, B., Perry, R. P., & Magnusson, J. (1988). An attributional analysis of reactions to stigmas. *Journal of Personality and Social Psychology, 55*(5), 73–74.

Wolcott, D. L., Namir, S., Fawzy, F. I., Gottlieb, M. S., & Mitsuyasu, R. T. (1986). Illness concerns, attitudes towards homosexuality, and social support in gay men with AIDS. *General Hospital Psychiatry, 8,* 395–403.

Worden, J. W. (1991). Grieving a loss from AIDS. *Hospital Journal, 7*(1–2), 143–150.

Yedidia, M. J., Barr, J. K., & Berry, C. A. (1993). Physician's attitudes toward AIDS at different career stages: A comparison of internists and surgeons. *Journal of Health and Social Behavior, 34,* 272.

Zich, J., & Temoshok, L. (1990). Perceptions of social support, distress, and hopelessness in men with AIDS and ARC: Clinical implications. In L. Temoshok & A. Baum (Eds.), *Psychosocial perspectives on AIDS: Etiology, prevention, and treatment* (pp. 201–224). Hillsdale, NJ: Lawrence Erlbaum.

CHAPTER 62

ONE MAN'S PATH TO VEGETARIANISM: OHIO, ETHIOPIA, NEW JERSEY

Timothy D. Riegle

Usually the first thing people ask when they hear about the vegetarian diet is, "What's wrong with eating meat?" They might add, "Several billion people have been doing it for several million years. Why should I stop?" Those of us who follow any of the many diet preferences collectively referred to as vegetarianism have heard all of the usual comments: "How can you live on rabbit food?" "I don't feel full and satisfied unless I have meat at a meal." "Eggs without bacon?" "I hate tofu!" "Would you like me to make you a grass sandwich?" "God put all things here for our benefit." And so on.

My decision to become a vegetarian has its roots in one of the central male experiences for many men of the last century: military service. It was my experiences in the armed services during the Vietnam era that set the foundation for the decisions which have led to my spending more than half of my life as a vegetarian—especially my experiences overseas, where I saw the poverty and hunger of the Third World. It was also those overseas experiences that set the foundation for a second and not unrelated political and lifestyle concern for environmental issues and environmental activism. Vegetarianism isn't simply a healthy alternative or lifestyle choice; choosing to live as a vegetarian may be a political choice as well.

WHAT'S IN A NAME

The term *vegetarianism* means many different things to many different people. To some it means an aging "hippie" from the 1960s with a new cause. To others it means a person who loves animals and hates people who wear fur. To still others it means an unhealthy diet of cereal and pasta.

There are actually many different diet practitioners who refer to themselves as vegetarians. Some vegetarians eat seafood, while others eat fish and chicken. Some, commonly referred to as "lacto-ovo," will eat dairy and egg-based products, but no meat or meat by-products of any kind. Finally there are "vegans" (vegetables, nuts, and fruits only) and fruitarians (which is self-explanatory), who have no meat or meat by-products whatsoever.

OHIOAN ROOTS

As a youth growing up in a small farm town in southwestern Ohio, I don't even know if I was familiar with the term *vegetarian* and certainly knew nothing of the range of diets that fall under that category. My Italian mother was a post–World War II transplant from Brooklyn. She and my father met on a blind date when his ship came into New York Harbor upon his return from duty in the North Atlantic. My father's parents were dairy farmers, with the associated feed crops, cash crops, and various other livestock. My mother's first visit to Ohio, after my father's separation from the service, almost ended in disaster when she asked about the bathroom facilities, and my grandmother moved the dining room curtain aside and pointed to the outhouse at the back of the raspberry and rhubarb patch. It was actually a nicely wallpapered, quite roomy two-seater. She recovered from the shock, and the engagement and marriage back in New York proceeded as planned.

Growing up, my brother and I spent many days, nights, and weekends at my grandparents' farm. We couldn't wait to get up for the 4 A.M. milking. We would help with the livestock (cattle, hogs, chickens), and help to feed, groom, and of course ride the horses. We would also hike the woods and fields to hunt whatever game was in season, or look for wild mushrooms with my grandfather. He knew which were the good ones and which were the poisonous ones. He also seemed to know exactly when and where they would be "popping up." Years later my father told us that he was able to do that because he would bury the remains of animals (such as a groundhog shot to keep from doing damage to the valuable soybean crops) and carving wastes, which contributed to the fungus formation. It was in my later years that I realized the weekends at the farm for my younger brother and myself (our youngest brother and sister were separated from the two of us by 9 and 16 years) were as much for my parents as they were for us. These weekends allowed for parents in their mid-20s, with two young boys, to have a relatively healthy social life, for at least one or two weekends a month.

SOME EARLY STEPS TO MY VEGETARIANISM

Helping with the livestock also meant working in the slaughterhouse and the smokehouse. It was probably due to those experiences that the killing of animals has never been part of my personal philosophy in support of a vegetarian diet. Twisting off the head of a freshly shot rabbit before it went into the game bag, or cutting off the head of a live chicken and watching the headless animal run around the barnyard just seemed like a normal part of life. My East Coast and university friends are always a little shocked to hear some of those stories—to realize, for example, that the saying "running around like a chicken with its head cut off" comes directly from reality.

Needless to say, given these situations, we grew up with the freshest and best possible meat and produce on our table at mealtime. Contributing further to this realization was my Old World, East Coast mother, who always peppered the traditional meat-and-potatoes Midwest diet with a healthy dose of great Italian dishes. I didn't realize until years later just how much I had learned about cooking from time spent with my mother and grandmother in the kitchen. Thinking back on those times, I did enjoy cooking and baking, and was actually quite good at it, but it wasn't a cool thing for a guy to be into. For the past 25 years in my own family, I have always done all the food shopping and probably 90% of the cooking. Recently I took family leave from the university and moved back to Ohio to help my mother take care of my father, who was dying of advanced bone cancer. My parents and I shared more than one chuckle when I received frantic calls from my wife about how to set the oven to timed bake, how to defrost things in the microwave, or where that damn colander was.

My early away-from-home and off-the-farm dining experiences were almost always less than satisfying. I was very disappointed when I first tasted bacon from the grocery. It was nothing like the thick juicy slices of "fresh smoked side" I was used to. There was no such thing as a fast-food restaurant in my hometown during the mid-1960s to early 1970s. My first experience of a Mc-Donald's hamburger was not worth the 2-hour round-trip drive to Dayton. I failed to see all the excitement over a dry, pressed sheet of ground meat and wilted lettuce on a compressed, soggy bun. There were many other similar experiences that eventually led me to realize that the food I was growing up with was not the "normal" diet of the time.

I remember begging a grade-school friend to invite me to stay for dinner because I wanted to eat the fresh-out-of-the-can Spaghetti-O's his mother was serving. What a revolting experience! The first mouthful made me think of white glue with ketchup. It was probably my upbringing—and the fear of what my father would do to me if I spat the first taste into my napkin and ran out of the house—that made me stay and finish that meal. From that time on, when there were invitations to eat over at a friend's house, I usually passed, or said I had already eaten.

COLLEGE

My first long-term, away-from-home eating experience was going away to college. I found the dorm food in the late 1960s to be just a step or two above my Spaghetti-O's experience, and the only way I could describe the meat there would be as overcooked, gray shoe leather. The housing policy was that all freshmen, except for commuting students, were required to live on campus.

My roommate was a good friend and classmate from my high school with twin older brothers who were preveterinary medicine upperclassmen living off campus. Within 2 months, I had bargained with them for a place to stay in the basement in exchange for doing the cooking.

The off-campus living, as well as my fraternity membership, were both great for my social life at a university with 45,000 students, where being more than just a number was difficult, but it probably was not the best environment for a preengineering student trying to master calculus and organic chemistry. After four less-than-successful semesters, the last two of which I spent on academic probation, my father said he had enough of throwing his money away, and I was on my own.

IN THE ARMY

Choosing to drop out over getting student loans and paying for college myself, I quickly found the Selective Service changing my status from a 2-S student deferment to 1-A, and giving a date to report for my physical. It was the typical sequence of events for the nonmarried, nonfarm worker, nonstudent male of that time period, whose family was not politically connected. It was not too many months after I passed the physical exam when the letter of congratulations arrived in my mailbox with the unwelcome reality of my reporting date.

Well, that was it. The next years of my life, perhaps the last years of my life, had been made for me. There was some initial contemplation of possibly heading north to Canada. Surprisingly, my father said if that was to be my decision, I could take the 1965 Volkswagen Beetle with me. Even though he was an active member of the Veterans of Foreign Wars (VFW), he had some questions about our involvement in what was becoming an ever more unpopular war. At that time, going to Canada meant going there for life, and I ultimately decided against it.

During the Vietnam era, the short-term options for fulfilling one's military obligation were limited. There were extensive waiting lists for the National Guard, the Reserves, and most of the desirable job titles in all branches of the service. Those desirable titles were generally of two types: those which had the potential to lead to a lucrative civilian career, and those that led to a safe assignment. If I were to enlist in something prior to the date I was to report for induction, among my limited enlistment options were the following: the Marine Corps, the Army's infantry and artillery divisions, and the Army Security Agency.

The availability of the first two should need no explanation, since they involved a minimum of basic and advanced training and practically a guarantee of being in-country in Southeast Asia within 6 months or so. The last was a group I neither knew anything about nor knew why there would be immediate openings. I hope that recent changes regarding what I can legally talk about publicly, as a result of the Freedom of Information Act, mean that I am not in violation of federal regulations by revealing some of the following points of discussion.

The Army Security Agency (ASA) was a division whose chain of command left the military at a certain level and proceeded up through civilian channels of the National Security Agency. There were several reasons for there being immediate placements available. The first reason was that the enlistment period was for 4 years when most other enlisted positions in the army were 3 years and the period for draftees was 2 years. This was due to the extensive advanced training necessary before being available for overseas placement. There were also requirements of having completed some college and passing a rigorous battery of intelligence and psychological tests. Finally, there was the requirement of qualifying for a top-secret, crypto-access security clearance.

I looked into the job training possibilities and decided to take the qualifying tests. The ASA was the best of the alternatives, not only because of the possibilities of training on advanced computer systems, but also because of the fact that the overseas assignments within the ASA were in places where I was not likely to get shot at or be asked to shoot at someone else. I passed, and was told that the next step would be a complete background investigation by the FBI and a lie detector interview. My problem was that the looming date to report for my draft induction did not allow enough time for the background investigation. The only option, which I took, was to enlist for the 4 years in the ASA, and wait for the results of the security clearance investigation to be completed sometime during my initial 8 weeks of basic training. The only catch was that if I did not pass the background investigation, I would not qualify for the required top-secret, crypto-access clearance. However, I would have to serve the full 4-year enlistment in whatever job title the military chose to place me.

I took the chance—not too many options left—and ultimately qualified for service in the ASA. The year and a half after basic training was spent in communications and computer programming classes at bases in Massachusetts and Florida, and at the National Security Agency offices in Maryland. Near the end of my advanced individual training assignments, I received orders for Ethiopia for an 18-month assignment involving non-Morse satellite communication intercept.

TO ETHIOPIA VIA ATHENS

It was in the small towns and villages of Ethiopia that I actually experienced firsthand what real poverty looked like. I also began to understand the interrelationships of food production, food distribution, poverty, world hunger, and environmental degradation, as well as how the philosophies of some vegetarians were driven by these interrelationships. However, the journey itself to Ethiopia was not without some unforeseen twists and turns.

After completing the final training and getting all the shots I needed to enter that part of Africa, I went back to Ohio for the traditional several days of leave that the army usually grants prior to shipping someone to an overseas assignment. I also went to Washington, D.C., to get my diplomatic passport. The policy of the agency was that servicemen in my position would always travel in civilian clothes and be issued a red diplomatic passport, the theory being that we would be less identifiable as ASA personnel. There would be less chance of being kidnapped by a foreign power and tortured for our secret information. That was certainly reassuring, like there was anything I knew that would be of any interest to anyone. After my short leave back home, I flew to JFK Airport in New York to get my flight to Athens via Hamburg, where I would make a connection to Addis Ababa, Ethiopia.

At JFK I found that the military assistance office there not only didn't have my tickets, but they had no record of who I was or my destination. My first trip out of the good old U.S. of A. was not beginning as expected. I even sensed some animosity from the sergeant in charge at the desk as to why I was dressed in civilian clothes and was traveling on a diplomatic passport containing a picture of me, again, dressed in "civies." After several hours we made no progress toward a solution for my situation. Since it was Friday, I was asked to spend the weekend at Fort Hamilton and come back on Monday to work on a resolution. Rather than spend that weekend at an unfamiliar military base, I spent it with an aunt and uncle in New Jersey (part of my transplanted mother's Brooklyn family). I ended up spending 3 weeks in New Jersey, sitting tight and waiting for further instructions.

After 3 weeks of sleeping on a cot in my aunt and uncle's basement, and almost daily phone calls to and from agencies up and down the East Coast, things were finally straightened out, and I was on my way to Athens. Even leaving Athens, however, was somewhat of a problem. The shot record I needed to enter Ethiopia was incomplete, and I was directed to an Air Force base in Athens to get the required inoculations—one of which required a 21-day incubation period, a period I spent in an Athens hotel, courtesy of Uncle Sam. After another 3 weeks of seeing the sights in Athens, I was off to Addis Ababa and then on to Asmara, Ethiopia.

ASMARA

As a specialist third class, taking home about $140 a month, I didn't realize I would be among the richest people in Asmara. Military personnel choosing to live off base could get a great local apartment, with a housekeeper, for less than $50 a month. I was told that, at that time in Ethiopia, the average yearly income for a family was less than $20.

I saw plenty of "houses" that were little more than a piece of corrugated sheet metal held up with sticks and maybe a partition or two. The occupants often included three or more generations and whatever livestock they could afford to keep and wished to protect. I was also told that some of the richest locals were the "house boys" (how *not* PC is that!), who worked for those of us who lived in the barracks, and the local ladies of the evening.

The "house boy" in my building was a great local Ethiopian with the not-so-local name of Elvis. Each of the approximately 40 of us in the building paid him $2 a month to make our beds, shine our shoes, clean the living spaces and the latrines, and keep the outside of the building policed. A few others in our building and I got to be very good friends with Elvis. We would buy him things at the military P.X. (Post Exchange) that either were not available or cost a fortune locally, and he would take us to local tradespeople, who would barter their goods for American cigarettes. A carton at that time was about $2 and could be traded for a custom-tailored shirt, a pair of handmade sandals, or beautiful local crafts and carvings.

Elvis also turned us onto which local restaurants took the most care with their water used and food preparation. As it turned out, some members of Miscellanea's troops stayed around after Ethiopia was liberated by the Allied forces and started local businesses. It was quite astounding to find great Italian food on top of this mountain in the middle of an African desert. I also had many meals at Elvis' house. It wasn't surprising to find that he owned a very modest but nice house, and his kids went to private school.

Asmara was in Eritrea, which was an independent state prior to occupation during World War II. After liberation, the returning emperor of Ethiopia took Eritrea as part of his empire, resulting in the formation of a local resistance group called the Eritrea Liberation Front (ELF). This loosely organized group was not on the friendliest of terms with the United States, and often took pot shots at military personnel traveling far from the base, especially when traveling down the mountain to Massawa, a resort port on the Red Sea.

One of the best Elvis experiences was when he invited two of us to his sister's wedding. The location was out in the bush about 2 hours from the base with most of the latter half of the trip off the road four-wheeling. Given this remote location, we were a little reluctant to go bushwhacking out into what could be ELF-controlled territories.

Elvis arranged for a cousin to travel with us to see that we didn't get lost and to vouch for us as "friendlies" should we encounter any local freedom fighters. As we were soon to find out, Elvis' cousin was the perfect escort for a couple of naive Yankees out in the bush, as he was also a weapon-packing and bullet-belt-carrying member of the ELF.

At the wedding site, a collection of tents in the middle of nowhere, we found that the ceremony was over, but the celebration was just getting started. We had a great time dancing, drumming, and eating. That was some of the best-tasting and spiciest food that I had ever had. It turned out that more than a few of the guests were active and armed members of the ELF, but there couldn't have been a more open and friendly atmosphere. As it got dark and the fires were lit, we were invited to camp out with Elvis' family and continue the celebrating the next day. We reluctantly declined and were given a safe escort home by another relative.

There were two other groups with whom I became acquainted during my tour there that were to greatly influence many of my future life decisions. One group was local lay missionaries who were there to spread the Word, and the other was the local contingent of Peace Corps workers. Among other things that members of both groups had in common, some in each group were following a vegetarian diet. Both groups were also involved, though somewhat covertly, in educating servicemen about their individual rights related to action by the military, providing nonviolent resistance and antiwar literature, in addition to information about conscientious objector status.

Their reasons for choosing a vegetarian diet were directly related to the world hunger situation, some of the worst of which they were personally observing. Not eating grain-fed animals meant that more grain could be made available for direct consumption or to be processed into grain-based food products. Since the green revolution of the 1950s (irrigation, artificial fertilizers, pesticides and herbicides, hybrid seeds), the planet has grown more than enough to feed everyone. Unfortunately, a large part of that goes to the production of animal feed. It seems that the typical domesticated livestock animal is extremely poor at converting vegetable protein into animal protein.

Spending those early years on my grandparents' farm, I thought it was perfectly normal to feed cattle, swine, and poultry the corn, oats, and other grains grown on the farm. I never really thought much about how the animal converts those grains into flesh on its bones. What I was to learn from my new friends in Ethiopia, and from the world hunger literature they provided, was that it is very wasteful to cycle food products through an animal to "put the meat on the table."

The conversion rate for cattle is some dismal 12–16 pounds of vegetable protein that is consumed to add 1 pound of meat protein to its skeletal frame. That number is 5–7 to one for swine and 2–3 to one for poultry. It is fairly simple to see from these figures that if that grain were to go directly into food products for human consumption, the food that we as a planet grow would go much farther in meeting the basic nutritional needs of all people.

If the lower number for each ratio were used, and if the distribution of production were equal across the three groups, it would come out to more than six times more people that could be fed with a given amount of grain. It is also easily understandable to see why it is only the richest of societies that can afford this wasteful diet. Globally, approximately 60% of food crops are fed to livestock that go to feed about 10% of the population. That means that those 10% of us in the developed world use 60% of the yearly amount of global food production while the remaining 90% of the population must sustain themselves on the 40% that is left.

Of course my decision to be a vegetarian is only my personal position, but this reasoning is why I am not opposed to the hunting and consumption of nonendangered wildlife (white-tail deer in the United States, for instance) or livestock raised by grazing on pasture land, as are most of those in the Third World. In both cases the animal is using a non–human-digestible food source in the form of cellulose to put meat on its frame that can be a human protein source. I feel the same about non–farm-raised fish. Fish farming (confined environment and grain fed) has about the same negative protein return as poultry. In their natural environment fish are using aquatic sources of non–human-consumable nourishment and turning it into something that can be a reliable protein source. Of course, the global fish catch can only be up to a maximum level that allows for a remaining and sustainable healthy adult population, so reproduction can replace the approximately 100 million tons per year of non–farm-raised fish caught.

I also learned that there were many other reasons to justify a non–meat-based diet. At this point in our evolutionary development, there are a number of physiological factors that indicate that we humans are vegetarian animals. On many levels of comparison, we are much more closely associated with the leaf/grass/fruit eaters of the planet than we are with the carnivores. Among those factors are the following: intestinal tract length to body length ratio (3:1 for meat eaters, 12:1 for us); strength of stomach acids (hydrochloric acid 20 times stronger in meat eaters); presence of skin pores for perspiration (we have them, they don't); teeth structure (they have sharp, pointed fanglike teeth, we have flat back molars for grinding); size of salivary glands (theirs are quite small, ours are well developed); and predigestive properties of the saliva's ptyalin enzymes (alkaline with high levels of ptyalin for us, acid with no ptyalin for them).

There is also the issue of food distribution. Population centers are not necessarily next door to the world's grain belts. Often food is used to achieve political ends. An example of this kind of situation could have been seen recently in Somalia. Foreign aid agencies had gotten more than enough basic foods and grains into the country. Those foods came under the control of, and were used as a means of coercion by, competing tribal warlords, with distribution based not on need but on action taken on behalf of the powers that be.

In addition to the hunger argument and the physiological factors to justify vegetarianism, there are many other components that would lead one to follow the path of a non–meat-based diet. Among the environmental arguments are the topsoil loss, deforestation, fossil fuel consumption, and extinctions related to habitat destruction associated with a meat-centered diet. There are also issues related to the consumption of natural resources. More than half of all the water used in the United States is consumed in the process of livestock production. The production of 1 pound of meat takes 100 times more fresh water than does the production of 1 pound of wheat. The food energy return for the amount of fossil fuels used is 10 times greater for direct food production as opposed to meat production.

It was this kind of information that led to my developing an awareness of the breadth of causes and effects of a meat-centered diet. I also began to note the place of meat in society and cultures. I became more aware of the use of terms like "brings home the bacon" or "puts the meat on the table." Why not bring home the rice and beans or put the vegetable casserole on the table? Society says that a breadwinner (now there is a nonmeat term) is more "successful" if he or she provides a "meat and potatoes" dinner, than if the meal is made up of salad, bread, rice, and beans. I also became aware of the relationship of a healthy planet, environmentally speaking, and its ability to feed the world. Things like ecosystem degradation, landfills, industrial wastes, and air and water pollution were inhibiting the natural ability of the earth's systems to provide for the needs of all of its plant and animal inhabitants.

BIRTH OF AN ACTIVIST

Those early experiences in Ethiopia not only led to lifelong dietary changes but also were the foundation for becoming an outspoken, card-carrying, environmental activist. This goes back to the mid-1970s when a number of us started an organization to show our municipality that recycling glass, metals, and newspapers was not only good for the environment but it was also profitable. By scheduling and advertising drop-off locations and selling the materials to a reprocessor, we had two trucks and $1,000 in the bank within a year.

We also attended town council meetings to show them our books and to lobby for mandatory residential recycling. After several unsuccessful attempts at getting the mayor and council to consider legislation, the group disbanded, sold the vehicles, and donated the monies to some needy local nonprofits. The feeling of the powers that be at the time was that individuals would not participate. My family and others involved in the effort continued to recycle privately. I am proud to say that I have not added a newspaper, nor a piece of glass or metal, to the waste stream in the past 25 years.

As time passed, it was personally vindicating to see the advent of statewide mandatory recycling, here in New Jersey and elsewhere, and for recycles to become officially listed on the commodities markets.

KNOWING MORE

I also became cognizant of using foods that have complementary amino acids at the same meal to get complete protein from nonmeat sources. Not only does this provide complete protein, but it also does it at a lower financial cost to the consumer. Additional benefits to using complementary amino acids include no cholesterol (found only in the animal kingdom), fewer fats, fewer pesticide residues, a broader range of vitamins and minerals, and more fiber.

There is also the issue of variety. There are several hundred types of vegetables and grains consumed by different cultures around the world while the animals used for food are a mere handful. Another important aspect of this type of diet is that a greater part of caloric intake is in the form of carbohydrates as opposed to fats and proteins. It is carbohydrates that our bodies burn most efficiently for energy. Marathon runners bulk up the day before a race with pasta and candy bars, not steaks and cheeseburgers.

As the years have gone by since I first became aware of the direct relationship between world hunger and vegetarian diets, and made what at the time was fundamentally an ethical and moral decision, there have been many other things that have further supported that decision. While I'm not necessarily an animal rights activist, I have learned that slaughterhouse and feedlot practices are nauseating. Also, although it is much more of a human welfare issue, the occupation in the United States with the highest turnover rate and the highest on-the-job injury rate is that of a slaughterhouse worker. In addition, over the past almost 30 years there have been mountains of reports and studies that demonstrate how a non–meat-based, low-fat, high-fiber diet has positive effects on many types of cancer, heart disease, strokes, and many other aspects of physical and mental health.

The Problem and a Solution

Approximately 60 million people die of starvation per year. The number of children among them is such that a child dies every 2 seconds. The average African consumes only 85% of the minimum daily caloric intake. In other words, the average African is slowly starving to death. If Americans were to reduce their meat consumption by only 10%, the amount of grain saved could feed an additional 60 million people. What a numerical coincidence; a 10% reduction by U.S. meat eaters could feed those 60 million people who starve to death each year. That is only making menu changes in perhaps two meals a week. To me, that doesn't seem like too much to ask to save 60 million lives a year.

So, the next time you are at the market doing your weekly grocery shopping, pick up some tofu and the makings for a "veggie" casserole. You will be doing your part to save the world.

VOICES TWELVE

MAN'S SEARCH FOR MEANING

CHAPTER 63

LESSONS FROM JEFF AND JAMES*

Michael Shawn Stinson

I'd like to tell you a sad story, the ending of which has not yet been written. Last summer, my family and I spent time with my wife's cousin and his family during a weekend at the beach. Jeff was 38 years old. He had two young kids and a charming wife. He and his wife had promising careers—she, a former FBI agent then working as a parole officer; he, an IRS agent. Jeff was tall, handsome, very fit, and fun to be around.

Last fall, Jeff experienced some memory loss. At first he simply ignored it, likely chalking it up to stress. As the symptoms progressed and new symptoms (including double vision) were added, he sought medical help. An MRI demonstrated a brain tumor. Surgery was performed and a grade 3 astrocytoma discovered. He was referred to a major medical center in a neighboring state where further surgery was performed and chemotherapy begun. His prognosis was poor, yet he returned home and even went back to work . . . knowing what was likely to come and hoping that it wouldn't.

One of my favorite modern-day philosophers is the singer/songwriter James Taylor. Though apparently much of his early work was composed in a drug-induced haze, his simple stories had some very powerful messages. Probably my favorite is *"The Secret of Life"* in which he begins with the verse, "The secret of life is enjoying the passage of time."

I've been thinking a lot about Jeff and about this song lately. Although I have enjoyed my brief sojourn on this planet immensely so far, I have spent most of it hoping about and working for what is to come. I suspect that most of you have as well. The high school years were spent preparing for college. The college years were spent with the fear that a poor performance on the next test could wipe out your career plans. Next came preparing for the MCAT, and then medical school. How many of you are enjoying this passage of time? I hope all of you are, but I can imagine that the first and second year students can't wait for the clinical years. The third years look to the fourth year as the last great

---

*Adapted from a short speech to graduating medical students, applicable to all graduating students.

hoorah. The fourth years are now starting to worry that they are really not as prepared as they should be for residency . . . and so on.

You'd think that by entering the job market one might begin to long less for the future and enjoy the present more. What I've found from my experience and that of my friends, colleagues, neighbors, and patients is that this concern for tomorrow probably only intensifies for most of us. There are always deadlines at work, a bigger house, a nicer car, having kids, waiting for them to walk, wishing that they were old enough for school, sending them there, planning the next vacation, lusting for a boat or a place at the lake, a promotion at work, moving to a warmer climate, retirement—it just doesn't end.

It often isn't until a major (and sometimes irreversible) life event occurs that we pause to reflect on what is happening today and notice what might be passing us by. I'm really struggling with Jeff's illness. We're the same age; our kids are roughly the same age; we're in the same phase of our careers. He won't likely see his youngest start school, and I'm so damn worried about tomorrow that I'm frequently oblivious to the joys of today. All he's got is today and a few tomorrows. You know, I bet he enjoys each day more than I do—and probably more than you do as well. I bet that he asks his wife about her day and then listens to her answer better than I do. I bet he enjoys helping his oldest son with his homework more than I do. I bet he looks at things around him with clarity of vision that I can't imagine.

Well, it's time to change. The problem is that I don't know how. I'd like for each of you to spend some time thinking about this. Call me with the answer, I'm serious. Don't get me wrong, I still want as much or even more than ever to set goals and work hard to achieve them. That's what Jeff is doing; I mean, for heaven's sake, he continues to work! What I need help with, though, is learning how to take full advantage of today. How do we dream, plan, and work for tomorrow, without robbing ourselves of today?

One of my concerns is that I'll approach this the same way I approach most everything else—I'll worry so much about enjoying today that I miss out on the actual enjoyment of it. Maybe it's not so hard after all. It's possible that with just a bit of attention and appreciation of our experiences we really can enjoy the passage of time. Think of it . . . shouldn't the excitement of learning all we can be enjoyable? Shouldn't taking care of those who need it, even paying $10,000 a year and at 3 A.M., be exciting? Why not approach internship with its every fourth night call as one of the great experiences of our lives? Maybe we just have to *allow* ourselves to become immersed and take advantage of what the day has to offer and stop worrying so much for tomorrow. Perhaps James Taylor is right, and we should follow his advice when he closes his song with, "Try not to try too hard, it's such a lovely ride."

CHAPTER 64

CHRISTIANITY AND BLACK MASCULINITY

Brian Johnson

According to recent U.S. health statistics, roughly 60% of all new HIV infections are among black men. These same statistics suggest that either homicide or acquired immune deficiency syndrome (AIDS) is the leading cause of death among black men between the ages of 18–35. Furthermore, while blacks in America comprise nearly 13% of the total population, black men are incarcerated at a rate many times higher than males from other races. Such statistics are familiar enough, but the question remains, how has the black community responded in the last 20 years to such harrowing figures about the status of black males in America?

The work of the Nation of Islam under Louis Farrakhan has been well documented. Under the direction of Farrakhan, the Million Man March of 1996 rallied together, I dare say, the largest gathering of black men ever assembled on American soil for a united social purpose. Historically, the Nation of Islam has been a haven and a place of regeneration for black men who have been incarcerated. Other responses, which are arguably in the tradition of Marcus Garvey, have sought to combat the ills within the black male community by offering an African-centered paradigm for resolving these issues. Nevertheless, I find it odd that in the midst of such a maelstrom of alarm, the black community has not relied upon its strongest, most enduring, and, arguably, most reliable vehicle for facilitating societal change: Christianity.

The most infamous literary characterization in all of American literary history, the black Christian Uncle Tom, provided a fictional agency that assisted Harriet Beecher Stowe 's *Uncle Tom's Cabin* in stimulating the moral impetus for civil war. And while the depiction of Uncle Tom is largely imaginary, idealistic, and sentimental, its usefulness in embodying the tenets of Christianity in the middle of hostile social forces is understandable. Uncle Tom, who when introduced in the novel is leading prayers and hymns, represented the highest measure of black humanity in a period during which the moral status of the Christian preacher or laity was virtually the only position in society that black men could enter into with relative ease.

The engagement by black males with Christianity in overcoming unique problems encountering the black community can be born out in a larger historical framework than that of any other black tradition, including that of the Nation of Islam and much of the newfangled ideology of Afrocentricism. From autobiographical slave narratives best represented by Josiah Henson and Frederick Douglass, which narrate the efficacy of Christian morality in overcoming slavery, to the turbulent 1960s when a man named Martin Luther King invoked the phrase "turn the other cheek" and nonviolent protest as a means for dismantling Jim Crow and ushering in civil rights legislation, Christianity has been the most profitable stalwart against the immorality facing contemporary black males.

The autobiographies of Henson and Douglass offer intimate portraits of inward renewals through their engagements with Christianity, which produced the moral vigor to surpass the social impositions of race in such a difficult period. Further, King's plan of action, which adopts much of the Christian ideology, persuaded much of the black community to combat the outward enemy of racism by training themselves internally through nonviolent resistance.

For black men today, questions of ethics, morality, and values are unavoidable when dealing with promiscuity, incarceration, urban hip-hop, and education. These issues are common elements discussed in relation to the cultural status of black males. Still, when black "think tanks" and educators discuss these pressing issues, they rarely speak in terms of immorality. Their answers usually resemble retorts, which are plausible, but, often, fairly inadequate. To the question of black males and promiscuity, the response is that its roots lie in African polygamy and slave breeding. To the question of incarceration, the retort suggests that there are discriminatory practices in the judicial system. To the question of misogynistic and violent lyrics in urban hip-hop, polemicists reply that rock music does the same and free speech and creativity should be encouraged. To the question of education, the retort follows many lines of thought—all of which revolve around historical practices of discrimination in the public schools. What links these retorts is a shifting of focus to outside societal pressures and forces, which can never precipitate large-scale change upon any level.

Change comes from within, I would argue, and a Christian paradigm offers the most comprehensive viewpoint for the preservation of black males because it redirects all energies from an outward gaze to an inward one. Black males need (1) temperance or self-control to combat promiscuity; (2) moral fortitude or wisdom, if you will, to distinguish between right and wrong in order to combat incarceration; (3) a deep and abiding love for people and of self to combat much of the immorality found in urban hip-hop; and (4) industry and perseverance to combat problems in the field of education. These tenets lie at the heart of the values and belief systems found in biblical Christianity. And, in truth, this utility extends far beyond that of black masculinity.

Much of the spirituality that has been ascribed to the black community is based upon the Christian feats of black persons of a time past. Their names and achievements are far beyond the scope of this essay. Much of that spirituality is not based upon any new accomplishments, but on a tradition that has passed away. While the phrase "Am I my brother's keeper?" is a popular saying largely used in the black community as a call to unity, its meaning—derived from the biblical incident of Cain and his brother, Abel—often loses its thrust because current usage does not draw on the original context. Cain offers this response to God's inquiry about Abel after Cain has already killed his brother in the fields. However, two verses earlier, God provides Cain with the solution to the bitter jealousy that enflamed his rage. God says, "Why are you angry? And why do you look sad and depressed and dejected? If you do well, will you not be accepted? If you do not do well, sin crouches at your door; its desire is for you, but *you must master it.*"

Similar to Cain, black males have it well within their ability to "master it," and they *must master* the moral perversions that threaten to annihilate their existence. When speaking about young black people (including black males), Dr. Cornel West of Harvard University, a Christian humanist, suggests that they "represent the very best and brightest of a very grand and glorious tradition." A very grand and glorious one, indeed—one that is entrenched in the values of Christianity.

My recognition of the very profound sense of a black masculine engagement with Christianity occurred in the fall of 1994, just after hearing Dr. West make this powerful statement. During that fall, I was a member of the Student Government Association at Johnson C. Smith University. My friends and I were the principal instigators in year-long series of rallies and activities concerning many of the policies at the University. On the surface, the rallies appeared to be focused on enhancing the rigor of academic environment. Yet, what really was at the core of our concerns was the lack of attention paid by campus administrators and professors to the moral and ethical dimensions of the campus environment.

What I discovered then and I am still coming to terms with now is that moral and ethical leadership, similar to academics, cannot be taught by those who do not possess them. In fact, teaching morals and ethics does not involve the espousal of creeds but must be seen in praxis. As a result, I stood at a crossroads. As a 21-year-old, first-generation college student with wanton morals and hailing from a single-parent home in an impoverished inner-city environment, I was determined to discover morality and ethics for myself. I chose Christianity.

And, ever since, in my endeavors to become a scholar and teacher of youth, I have sought to follow the advice of Charles W. Chesnutt. In a speech to the Normal Literary Society in Fayetteville, NC in 1883, he gave his idea of a teacher. He wrote:

> I have a very high ideal of those qualities, which apart from his literary
> attainments and skill in teaching, should make up the character of an
> instructor of youth; and my ideal of a teacher can be tersely but clearly
> expressed in two words—a Christian Gentleman. By the word Christian,
> I mean not merely a church-member or outward professor of religion;
> but one who is imbued with the true spirit of Christ; one who goes out,
> as did He, the Great Teacher, to instruct the world in the ways of truth.

These are the words I try to follow.

CHAPTER 65

A MAN OF THE CLOTH: MEANING AND SPIRITUALITY FOR A CATHOLIC PRIEST

Rev. Gerald F. Greaves

Reverend Gerald Greaves, a Roman Catholic priest for 26 years, is in active ministry as a pastor in a suburban New Jersey upper-middle-class parish. He holds degrees as a master of divinity and a master in pastoral counseling. As he reflects on his life now at middle age, he begins:

One of the things that has dawned on me is the aging factor. I don't think the same way as I did even last year or in previous years. This is not a negative thing, but I have become more respectful of that aging process. And now I do see that I have gained a greater intimacy with God, and with the reality of meeting God and facing God.

But more than seeing myself at the age that I am, I have the realization of seeing people who are younger, the same age as I am, and older than I am. I have come to be more sensitive to the understanding that this life is temporary. But I also realize that in many ways in our society, in our personal relationships and in the ways we think and act, it is as if this life is forever. And this life is not forever.

GOD—SURPRISE AND ENCOUNTER

Now there is a realization within me that each and every one of us has his or her own reality, and there is a part of it that can be called sinfulness, and that is within all of us. But I have asked God to take this sinfulness away. I now believe that it is in our weakness that we encounter God and that it is through Him that we move toward goodness.

I am and have been surprised by the way God is the God of surprises for us. At the moment that I think that God has been found, and this can be so satisfying, it is precisely at this point God surprises me in revealing Himself in a totally different and new way. However, at the same time, I would have to say that the time-proven ways that God offers us His very self still remain a dramatic and special encounter, as through the recitation of the psalms—found in the breviary (a book of daily prayers said by all religious in the Catholic Church). These prayers include the entire sacred scriptures and the encounter with Christ in the Eucharist.

And, of course, the most challenging thing for each of us to do with our lives is to encounter God within one another. I believe that the challenge is for each of us to come to that point like a Mother Teresa of Calcutta. She actually not only said, but also believed and did cherish and held tenderly the Christ who is found in the other. We can also say, believe, and hold tenderly and cherish the God who is found in the other.

Of course, the most dramatic of all is to open our hearts to see the Christ in everyone, especially the poor, the stranger, the alienated, and the migrant. We can see Him in anyone who is new to us and new to our frame of reference. We can seek to identify Christ's presence.

There is so much that we have to let go of that we don't realize that our own lives have been conditioned in so many ways that are filled with prejudice ways that separate us from each other.

Pain and Spiritual Insight

I guess growing up is not only about letting go, but is a relearning of how to be with one another as God has intended us to be. It is only when we take the opportunity to pray, to reflect, and to share our lives with a faith community of people that we can dispose ourselves to the realities of God and God's thoughts for us.

What is most present in my mind is that experience that I am living this past year, grieving the loss of relationships in a previous parish and grieving the way of life with those people, and grieving the loss by death of a very close friend. And during that year—and even now I am still going through it, I still feel the pain of that separation and wonder, why?

The pain was so deep this past year that I was unable to hear the comfort and consolation of God and others. However, because of God's grace I was able to continue to function and perform the responsibilities and obligations entrusted to me.

Now being a person of faith, I was also beating myself up so much that I was not able to grieve appropriately or to trust or to hope in God who remained with me. I wasn't able to do so until recently, after reading one of my favorite authors, Henry Nouwen. In his book *And with Burning Hearts*, while describing the two disciples on their walk to Amais, Nouven recalled the beatitude, "Blessed are they who mourn, for they shall be comforted." And it struck me so deeply that I didn't have to do anything but grieve and God was blessing me.

My Priesthood

This connection gave me comfort and consolation. So this experience places me in an awkward way to enter into this millennium. I have this baggage to carry but not alone. My strongest conviction this year, as in any year, would be that as long as we are faithful to God, God continues to reveal His will for us.

It is difficult for me and yet I know that it is a challenge. The way I experienced pastoring in other places will be different for me in this place. And although I bring a wealth of experience, the way to do things here is not necessarily the same as I did them in the past. For that reason, I know that I have to be patient and open to what God is asking of me at this time of my life in this place and with the people of God entrusted to me. I think as a priest in this new millennium and as a Church, we want to be open to what God is saying to us about leadership and about priesthood.

The ways that go along with others who have been priests to the community are rapidly changing and probably for the good. I think that the priest should be asked to become much more of a celebrant, not only of sacraments but also in broader contexts of celebrating with others in sharing faith. It needs to be negotiated with each community/church. Administrative responsibilities consume much more time than we would like to admit.

I am drawn as a man and as a priest to the Eucharist. I realize the privilege of presiding at the liturgy of the Eucharist. I take that responsibility seriously and am humbled each and every day at the moments and times of that celebration. Christ's presence is so real for me in the Eucharist so that it is not only in the celebrating with the community but also in the quiet moments of adoration, prayer, and praise that I am nourished by Christ, my God who is my friend.

It is amazing that I can take the presence of Christ from the Eucharist and be reminded of His presence throughout the day. I am tempted in so many ways to fill my life with the noise of radio or the company of others and at the same time have come to appreciate the silence in my room, in the car, and in my office, or at those moments when there is no one else around. It is in those times of silence that it is like being with an old friend. I am grateful that I am not afraid to be alone with the Lord or to be alone with the silence. I have come to realize my companion in the silence.

Another challenge for me is my personality type. I took the Meyers-Briggs test and it identified me as always wanting to seek a new experience. Looking for God has been that experience. I believe that God has shown me another way and tempered the anxiety that comes with looking for God in the other experience. Again I am grateful.

I appreciate God's presence in the ordinariness of life. I used to wonder whether or not God would be calling me to other lands or a missionary life, and I have come to realize that God comes to me right where I am and not somewhere else. If God wanted me to be somewhere else, He would have provided those opportunities.

I enjoy the hands-on experience of serving the Lord and the poor. I appreciate the fact that it is not due to the poor's need that we do the things for them, but it is our need. It is an opportunity to be humble and to share the gifts that God has given me with others.

Recently, my parish group went into the Bronx one evening to distribute clothing and food. I have no fear of those encounters. My biggest question is, "How much is God asking of me to share my life with others in this way?" That experience has prompted our community to desire to go once a month and to bring our young people and to do the same as we did that evening. And that is where I wonder, "Does God call me to facilitate others in this sharing?" It is a question that I ask myself, I guess.

JOY AND ANXIETY

I think that some of the simple joys of this life are the children. Maybe that is a joy that is given to me because I don't have my own children. But this has brought me understanding as a pastor and a father to men. It just gladdens my heart and puts a smile on my face to see those whom I baptize, the young children and their innocence. This does not exclude teenagers. I enjoy teenagers when they feel more comfortable to be with me, now that they call me an old man.

It is strange but I look upon them with understanding. To be a teenager, as I recall, was filled with a lot of anxiety and insecurity. I felt terror and fear about growing up, having relationships, and about who I was going to become. This seems so evident on the teenagers' faces today and yet once they feel comfortable, which takes a long time, a smile usually breaks through or a softness of their disposition which allows a relationship or dialogue.

Of course, it is always easier to be with people who like you and appreciate you; to be along with the people who want to grow in faith with you. I feel that I have grown to respect the movement of God in other people's lives, again if I open myself to listen to people with that third ear.

It is always a surprise to see how God is blessing other people, and from one another we can learn so much about God's ways. Some of the hard moments of life I think are when we have to make decisions about ourselves and about the lives of others and the direction that we want to go in as a leader. That's an area of life I continue to struggle with in this way. The best decisions I have ever made have always been when I have given it over to the Lord and waited on the Lord to respond through an inspiration or sign. God always honors our requests when we bring them before Him. Most of the time it is not in our timing but in God's timing. I know that if I jumpstart that timing, I wind up in a disastrous situation.

Such a significant time in my life happened a couple of years ago and for whatever reason, God was encouraging me to let go of my possessions in the sense of my attitudes of what I possessed. St. Francis of Assisi heard the words, "Build my church." He started to build the church, and I started to give things away—not that I had a lot of possessions. I found a new freedom that I had not experienced before, and it translated into the stewardship of the miniscule salary that I get as a priest. Once again when I did this, I no longer became anxious or worried about money. To this day, I realize that God has provided me with everything that I need. Like everyone else, my wants are greater than my needs, but my needs are satisfied, and for that I am grateful to God.

STEWARDSHIP

Stewardship as a way of life has really had a profound impact on my life as an individual and as a priest. I always thought that I am giving my time, talents, and life to God through the Church and the ministry of the priesthood. However, I have come to realize that I have time of my own and talents that God has given me, and I am responsible to the Lord for how I use my talents and how I use my time.

SPIRITUAL DIRECTION

I am fortunate in my life to have a spiritual director. When we think of spiritual direction, we might be put off by having someone else telling us how to be, but this is far from the truth.

A spiritual director listens and just offers me the opportunity to reflect upon where God is in the turmoil and the joys of my life. I am grateful to my spiritual director, who is a lay woman and mother. She brings all of the sensitivity and nurturing to spiritual direction that I have never experienced before this. There is never any judgment. There is always the question, "Where can God be found in all of this?"

AND SO

Although I speak understandingly of not being alone, and that is true, there is, at certain times, a loneliness that prevails over my life. I don't believe that I am afraid of that loneliness any more.

When I was younger, I was afraid of that darkness, that emptiness that can be a part of loneliness. And there is a temptation in that loneliness to fill it with either things or people or events. Sometimes that loneliness can try to trick us into believing that it can be satisfied. But it really can't be satisfied in the ways that we may try to fill it.

I have found the loneliness livable—to just be with the loneliness and to acknowledge it within myself and with God. I don't think that a miracle would have to happen in order to have God flood me with satisfaction. I still attain an understanding of a companion bigger than all of us who is with me in that loneliness. Perhaps it is another way of saying I have a friend in the darkness.

REFERENCES

Nouwen, H. J. (2000). *With burning hearts: A meditation on the eucharistic life*. Maryknoll, NY: Orbis Books.

CHAPTER 66

MEMORY, RELIGION, AND VISION: A FATHER, AN UNCLE, AND THE INHERITANCE OF A WORLD AT WAR*

Kevin Lewis

My sister, my mother, my grandparents, a dog—all inhabit my earliest memories. But my father is not there.

To me, my earliest childhood memories seem like fleeting glimpses of a mythic past, an original and static time before our own chronological time began. We strain with dreamlike scraps of earliest memory to grasp the world of that primal past, a golden age, which our selective, fragmentary recall provides so tantalizing and yet so inadequate a means of knowing. A child falls into the conflicts and ambiguities of history from a once-upon-a-time world, a sort of dream time. And those first memories, in contrast to the stories told of that time by parents and grandparents, hold the crux of our origins as conscious beings. They seem the truer link, somehow, to the first grounding of the self, to the persons we travel the subsequent years to become—in my case, son, brother, husband, and father.

My father did subsequently enter my life. Memories of him as a vital pillar of the family, as a hard-working professional, as a bookish, map-loving intellectual and community servant, are clear and strong. Indeed, from my early years he marked me in some ways that have been easy to trace and in others that I am still working to understand. In my youth the shape of his undoubted love for me, like mine for him, was elusive. That reciprocal love was strong, but neither well scripted nor spontaneous. Undemonstrative as we were together, our love was difficult to express and, thus, to clarify and cherish. Like other sons, I am occupied in later life by a need to fathom and to honor that love.

*Originally published as "Innocence and Experience" in *Born Into A World at War*, Manchester: St. Jerome Publishing, 2000. Reprinted with permission.

What is the connection, if there is one, between the absence of my father from my earliest memories and the quality of our relationship in the later years of my youth and young manhood? I have been worrying about this question for half my lifetime in my father's absence. He has been dead for 34 years. Soon after I graduated from college, my father died in a hospital bed, at the age of 54, from system shock at the amputation of a foot, necessitated by the diabetes he developed as an adult. It was an illness that perhaps, or so I believe the doctors said, he might have fought more conscientiously than he did over many years, preoccupied as he was by the pastoral work into which he threw himself with gusto as a Presbyterian minister with a progressive vision of social change.

Father sailed for France in May, 1945, when I was 22 months old. He returned after a stint of service with a French Protestant refugee relief organization in June 1946, in time for my third birthday that July, or so I am told. My older sister's fifth birthday would come later that summer. My younger sister was 6 months old. Soon after his return my father left for another year, to raise money around the country for the World Council of Churches fund to rebuild churches in Europe destroyed during the war. I have no retrievable memory of my father until after I turned 4.

As often as we revisit our earliest memories, they are never sufficient. Always we are haunted by the thought of what more we might see if our own gaze into the dream time would clear. We want to know what else happened then and what mattered that matters still. Retrieve what it will and refuse what it won't, selective memory holds clues to the people we became and are becoming. I borrow this belief from the psychologists. And we work the collective family memory and the historical record over against the mystery of personal memory, back and forth, to sound the waters of the self. In my case, I work to recover a father who was not there at first and whose work consumed him when he was.

In 1945 Father resigned from a church pastorate in Glendale, a suburb of Cincinnati, in order to put into practice on an international scale the social gospel he had learned earlier at McCormick Seminary in Chicago. As a clergyman deferred from the draft, he had not served in the armed forces. But he felt an obligation to his generation. And, as later when he passed it on to his children, he was prompted by his own family's interest in global affairs—at Princeton he had thought he was headed for a career as a diplomat. With my mother's concurrence, he had decided he was called to a France in crisis after the war. He was 32 years old. He left my 30-year-old mother, pregnant with her third child, to find shelter with myself and my older sister in the home of my welcoming maternal grandparents in Asheville, North Carolina.

Father, for whom French was a second language, together with a Belgian-born minister-colleague, were the first two representatives of the Presbyterian Church (U.S.A.) to be sent to Europe to work with CIMADE (*Comité Inter-Mouvements auprès des Evacués*, or the Inter-Movement Committee Serving Evacuees). This was a Protestant interdenominational organization founded in

1939, in conscious memory of the courageous Huguenot resistance to tyranny and persecution. Its purpose at first was to save Nazi victims during the war and then later, following the cease-fire, to provide humanitarian aid to victims and refugees in France. Its religious purpose was to aid in the reconstruction of the morale necessary to rebuild civic culture and to restore sociopolitical order amid the wreckage in Europe.

At 2 and 3 years old, I was passively aware that I had no father to go with my mother—"passively," meaning I had no way of knowing someone was missing. Though I am certain I was told where he was—indeed I was probably reminded constantly—I have no memory of knowing who or where he was at the age when consciousness establishes the fixed members of the immediate family circle.

I have long since passed the age of 32, at which he left the family briefly, and have even passed 54, his age when he died. At his death I was 24, too young to respond sufficiently to him and his experience, to have crossed that divide of reticence between father and son. What makes this particularly poignant is to come upon the postcards he addressed to me from France in 1945–1946. My mother saved them, along with his letters to her, his postcards to my sister, and his photos of coworkers, bombed-out towns, and CIMADE chalet retreat houses, as well as newspaper and church magazine articles describing the organization's initiatives.

I do not remember seeing this material my mother saved until 5 years ago when, deciding it was time to pass it on to her children, she made copies of everything for each of us. "Dear little boy" or "dear little son," he addresses me, some of the cards typed, some written in a consistent, decisive hand. "When I can't see you, it gives me great joy to write to you." On the back of a *carte postale* featuring a sepia photo of an interior of a country dwelling, labeled *chambre de paysans*, he writes, "This is where a little boy lives in this part of the world. It is quite different from what you have at Grandmother's and Grandfather's, isn't it? And do you know, they heat their rooms with a stove that stands right in the middle of this room! Every day now I see little boys helping their fathers gather wood on the mountain side for the long cold winter, which they will burn in their stoves."

Father's home base was St. Dié, a market town on the river Meurthe in Lorraine. The Nazis had devastated it in 1944. The letters he wrote my mother tell of doing anything and everything relief workers could do to help bring hope and the most basic of services back to that city. He preached in French at services of worship. He counseled, he married, he baptized. Through an interpreter he conducted occasional services for German prisoners of war quartered in French army barracks outside St. Dié. And everywhere he found, as he put it, "the sickness of Europe, the corrosion of the moral fibre." In March, 1946, he saw it "everywhere like a great suffocating wave." More damaging than the earlier bombs and fires and loss of lives was the numbed spirit of the inhabitants. It was this demoralization in a landscape following war that he was most driven to fight against by his American idealism and his Christian belief, and his strong physical constitution made the fight possible.

His work took him temporarily to Le Chambon sur Lignon, the old Huguenot village in the highlands south of Lyons, where Calvin's Protestants had withstood the royalist persecutions of the 17th century, where the Camisards had fought for religious liberty in the nearby Cevennes. During the war the entire village of Le Chambon had shared the risk of giving sanctuary to Jews and others fleeing the Nazis. (This unique place was the subject of Bill Moyers's film, *Weapons of the Spirit*.) Father was asked to aid the resettlement of the older, more fragile refugees still remaining in the village.

Coincidentally, Albert Camus, a year younger than my father, had spent several months during the winter of 1942–1943 in seclusion at Panelier, near Le Chambon. Fighting the tuberculosis which would recur a decade later, Camus was writing for the Resistance paper *Combat* and working out the plan of his allegory of war, *The Plague*, a novel I teach regularly to my undergraduates. In the spring before my father arrived at Le Chambon, Camus glanced at the "sickness of Europe" and commented in his notebooks: "Utter disgust for all society. Temptation to flee and to accept the decadence of one's era. . . . But disgust, nauseating disgust for such dispersion in others. . . ." He writes, "Meaning of my work: So many men are deprived of grace. How can one live without grace? One has to try and do what Christianity never did: be concerned with the damned."

These and other entries in those notebooks connect me to my father who—unknown to me at the time, bound as I was in the chrysalis of dawning self-consciousness—was working to be an example, confronting the paralyzing corruptions and compromises of Europe's defeated spirit, Camus' "decadence." As he understood it, my father was going about the business of restoring once more the hope of living with grace, by concerning himself daily with the "damned" of Europe.

But Father found French colleagues who were not to be counted among the damned. Again and again his letters recount working side by side with men and women who, though they had suffered during the Occupation, had behaved not only well but with extreme courage. These were a rare few who, when civic values had collapsed on all sides, had proved and were proving capable of what Father termed "sacrificial witness" and of acts of heroism born of a special "purity and intensity of spirituality." Father writes of finding these "saints of the earth" wherever CIMADE assigned him: Paris, Le Chambon, Boulogne, Calais, Dunkirk, and St. Dié.

He attended a meeting of the city fathers to hear Le Corbusier present a plan for rebuilding the rubble of St. Dié into "the first completely modern city in the world." Noting, realistically, that "the French peasant and small landholder" found it difficult to envision this, Father added, "You can see how deeply I am interested in the result from the fact that we are trying to bring the Gospel to bear in the architectural as in other areas of reconstruction." His was a hopeful, liberal religious vision of collaborative transformation in all the connected parts of the ailing body of Europe. A consistent note, deeply religious, deeply humane, is sounded in each of the letters from that year, all retyped by my mother. This record makes me more proud of him with each rereading. He voluntarily suffered privations, he adapted to awful conditions, and he worked side by side with local city governments, churches, and various other aid organizations without tiring and without losing his idealism. And he voiced his special interest and hope in "the youth of France, and I suppose it is general all over Europe, [who] are alone going to save it."

My father, Burt, had a younger brother. Uncle Archie was to come gradually into my life years later, outliving my father by 23 years and serving as a father figure to me after my father's death. Following service during the war as a first lieutenant and captain in intelligence assigned to an artillery unit from 1942 to 1946, my uncle held appointments as a medieval historian at the University of South Carolina (where I have taught for over 25 years), at the University of Texas at Austin, and then at the University of Massachusetts at Amherst. By temperament a peacemaker, he chaired the history departments at both the latter universities. His career as an academic seemed as exuberant as it was peripatetic. As children we relished occasional visits from this vibrant, jolly man who told stories of frequent travel to archives in exotic European and Japanese cities. He, the younger brother, was neither as solemn nor as religious as my father.

After Father's death, as my own academic career was slowly getting off the ground, Uncle Archie took a welcome fatherly interest. His touch was always light. His advice—publish soon and often, don't worry about getting it perfect—was helpful. His example inspired me. He was one of the first Fulbrighters in Egypt, and, by his encouragement, partly responsible for my taking a Fulbright in Poland 13 years ago. And he was affected by the war.

In 1989, a year before he died, my uncle published a memoir, written in the 1940s, of his experiences trekking with the American First Army from Omaha Beach through St. Lô in pursuit of the retreating Germans, through the same northern French landscape Father was to travel a year later in 1945. Uncle Archie took part in the bitter campaign in the Hurtgen Forest of the Ardennes in the fall of 1944, as 12 American divisions struggled to take the Roer Dams and then to cross the Rhine at Remagen. His memoir takes him on the dash across Germany to Leipzig and then to Pilsen and the celebrated meeting with the Red Army. But what he does not include—I had to discover this by asking him directly—is an account of his participation in the liberation of Buchenwald.

The absence of that portion of his wartime experiences from the record he kept is as striking and as important to me as the detailed, wry, and avowedly pessimistic descriptions of the people and places he encountered elsewhere during his wartime service. In his introduction to the memoir, written in 1989, my uncle remembers everywhere noting evidence of the "brooding evil of Nazi occupation," as he witnessed the endgame of the war in Europe playing itself out around him. When, near the end of his life, I asked him finally what he had done and what he had seen at Buchenwald, he replied that he could not tell me. But—and this is the only religious statement I can remember him ever making, either before or after—he said with uncharacteristic gravity that what he had seen made him believe in Calvin's doctrine of original sin.

How did the war affect my family? For me the question shades invariably into the personal question of identity. Raising the one leads to addressing the other. My older sister and I were born into a world at war, just before the baby boom. On the day in July 1943 when I came into the world, the 200 Jews of Michniów, Póland, reportedly departed it, massacred by an E*insatzgruppen* unit, a "special duty group" clearing the "eastern territories" for settlement by Aryan stock. (Michniów appears only on the most detailed maps of present-day Poland, a few kilometers south of Skarzysko-Kamiena, north of Kielce, on rolling, forested farmland. It sits on the edge of the Sieradowicki national park preserve, named for the nearby Monastery of the Holy Cross.) My younger sister joined the family in a world straining to recover from war and its considerable effects. Ours became a close and happy family, as families go, and lucky. I have never wished things other than they were.

Only later, much later, did growth of mind compel attempts to imagine and to grasp as well as I could the condition of Europe under Nazi terror. Only later, as an academic, did my evolving mix of personal and professional concerns begin to include fascination with the same grim reality that my father had struggled briefly to heal before returning to the responsibilities of marriage and fatherhood, as well as fascination with the most awful feature of that same reality, the death camps, of which my uncle chose not to speak. And only later, in middle age, have I begun to see how deeply influenced I have been all along by the interests and values that set in motion those two brothers, Burt and Archie. Their personalities and career choices differed. But they are linked by the common encounter with the effects of that disorienting terror that fell over Europe, and by their respective efforts to record and to interpret.

Of course it is not as simple as this: personal identity described through some sort of triangulation between influence of father and uncle, respectively. Obviously I have left out the influence of my mother, who was far more affected by the war than my sisters or I. Her strength in mothering under adversity, like her profound devotion to her husband in life and in death, remains a living inspiration for her children, whom she continues in her 80s to nurture. I have left out my grandfather, my sisters, and my younger brother, who was born in the early 1950s. I have left out teachers, not the least of whom was the existentialist Paul Tillich during my first 2 years at Harvard, followed by the Anglican churchman Stephen Sykes and the philosopher of religion John Hick, when I spent 2 years at the University of Cambridge. I have left out a failed marriage followed by the miraculous emotional and intellectual support of Becky, my wife of 24 years. It was she who leaped at the opportunity in the 1980s to spend a year with me in Durham, England, and then a more challenging year in Krakow, Poland—where the physical and political effects of war had lingered on for 40 years. It was in Poland in 1988–1989 that I came closest to the "sickness of Europe" that my father had left the family in 1945 to challenge.

In Poland I certainly came closer to the Holocaust. By 1988 I had been teaching about it for 15 years in South Carolina. I had read the accounts of deportations and concentration camps. I had seen the films. I had taught Miklos Nyiszli's A *Doctor's Eyewitness Account* and Tadeusz Borowski's *This Way for the Gas, Ladies and Gentlemen* again and again. I had screened Alain Resnais' *Night and Fog* in so many classes I knew it by heart, frame by frame. In Krakow we were 35 miles from Auschwitz-Birkenau, and I visited it on five separate occasions that year, wanting to see deeper into the riddle of its evil, deeper into the source of Primo Levi's recurring dream after "liberation" (see Levi's *If This Is a Man* and *The Truce*). From teaching American literature and culture that year to young Poles, most of whom seemed to want only enough facility in spoken and written English to make it in the West, I returned a more knowing interpreter. I wrote a piece on Auschwitz for the liberal Protestant weekly *The Christian Century*, then found in the republished autobiographical memoirs of Rudolf Hoss (*Death Dealer*, 1992)—he was the camp commandant of Auschwitz—tantalizing insight into the formation of his particular Nazi heart of darkness.

I have been immersed in Holocaust materials all this while, I realize, with the enabling support of a particular religious heritage. I am not sure I understand it fully. In one hand I carry my father's intellectual, liberal Calvinism. He loved Calvin, and I recall his occasional mentoring conversations with me about the great reformer's attempts as an intellectual system-builder to balance human freedom with the absolute sovereignty of God. Camus, in a notebook entry, hoping against long odds to reconcile liberty and justice, seems driven to a similar, perhaps the same, pass. In the other hand I carry the immensely liberating precept borrowed from the Roman playwright Terence by Montaigne: *Homo sum, humani nihil alienum a me puto* ("I am a man, and nothing human can be alien to me"). Why did this refusal of all parochialisms, this permission granted by traditional humanism to search any and every dark corner of experience for the truth it will yield, fall upon such fertile soil in me? I do not know, unless it was somehow because of my father's passionate contextualizing of his Calvinist conviction of original sin. It was he who must have initially prepared me to look steadily into the gas chambers for a fuller understanding of the human heart. When much later I read in Simone Weil the assertion that it does not matter what path toward a truth one takes, for all paths lead eventually to the Truth, I recognized myself instantly.

When I read Borowski's much anthologized work of short fiction, "Silence," I see my uncle in the idealistic American officer who arrives at the door of the newly liberated camp barracks to urge the inmates to forgive their tormentors and look to a better future. I see him in that officer who then leaves, hoping for the best, whereupon the freed prisoners proceed to trample their kapo to death in revenge. But I see in my father, carrying his reasoned, prophetic Calvinism into the world, a toughness of spirit and a worldly survivor realism. The pastoral social vision I have grown to admire in him seems better armed and provisioned than alternative visions of progressive social change upon which we are asked to pin our hopes. A flexible toughness of spirit sustained him in France and returned home with him when he resumed his short career in the Presbyterian ministry. A firmly grounded visionary fervor shored up his native idealism, enabling him to face down the cycle of revenge which perpetuates evil. Father was not "deprived of grace."

Seeping down to me from the remembered war experiences of the previous generation, through my father and uncle in particular, seems to have come permission to embrace a self-critical doubleness of mind. Wartime response to cumulative trauma teaches it as a practical survivor strategy. Other evils in life bestow it, also, enabling some to discover great evil, maintain belief in good, and go on productively, as the religious would say, in grace. But then of course some experience it pathologically. We treat darker forms of this doubleness as a disability, for instance, in Vietnam veterans of my generation. Josef Mengele, at the work of "selection" on the arrival platform at Auschwitz, thrived notoriously between conflicting value systems. Robert Jay Lifton, in *The Nazi Doctors* (1986) has aptly described in Mengele a functional "doubling" of personalities. Some learn doubleness for good, others for dysfunction or evil.

Twenty years ago, writing initially on doubleness and dualism, as I did, as an untried philosopher of religion trying to make sense of enduring personal religious belief, I gave no thought to the influence of family intellectual or spiritual inheritance. But the strategic doubleness I then proposed—"metaphysical schizophrenia" seemed an appropriate label—has continued to prove for me a life-giving instrument for the balancing of useful but irreconcilable claims upon the modern mind. I see it now as a gift, this experience-driven, critical affirmation that the wished-for unity of one's mind can helpfully be understood as a balancing of more minds than one. It was my father primarily but also my uncle who, by precept and example in their different respective ways, prepared me thus to negotiate the pervading cognitive dissonance and ambiguity of our era. Without their intending it—double-mindedness would disconcert my theological father—nevertheless their works, their values, their passions absorbed in me have gradually drawn me to the Emersonian adage: "A foolish consistency is the hobgoblin of little minds." Only the innocent will discard this pragmatic old saw as frivolous. But it can only *be* true by *coming* true through the long blood, sweat, and tears of undeflected experience and responding reflection.

REFERENCES

Borowski, T. (1976). *This Way for the Gas, Ladies and Gentlemen.* (Tr. Barbara Vedder). New York: Penguin.

Eliade, M. (1959). *Cosmos and History: The Myth of the Eternal Return.* (Tr. Willard R. Trask). New York: Harper, 1959.

Levi, P. (1987). *If This Is a Man and The Truce.* (Tr. Stuart Woolf). London: Abacus.

Lewis, A. R. (1989). A *War in the West*. Worcester, MA: Heffernan Press.

Lewis, K. (1981). "Anybody Who Isn't Schizophrenic These Days Just Isn't Thinking Clearly." In C. Edward Kaylor (Ed.), *The Humanities: Philosophical Designs and Practical Visions*. Charleston: Medical School Press of MUSC, (pp. 26–31).

_____(1991). The Clash of Memories at Auschwitz. *The Christian Century*, 108 (January 23) 75–77.

Lifton, R. J. (1986). *The Nazi Doctors: Medical Killing and the Psychology of Genocide*. New York: Basic Books.

Nyiszli, M. (1960). *Auschwitz: A Doctor's Eyewitness Account*. (Tr. Tibere Kremer and Richard Seaver). Forword by Bruno Bettelheim. New York: F. Fell.

Weil, S. (1951). *Waiting for God*. (Tr. Emma Cruafurd). Introduction by Leslie Fiedler. New York: Putnam.

CHAPTER 67

PHILOSOPHICAL PONDERINGS ON OUR FUTURE

Robert Sitelman and Florence Sitelman

In all victory is defeat. A battle begun approximately 250 years ago, starting with the onset of the Enlightenment, is these days rapidly drawing to a conclusion. Surly offspring of a brooding Protestantism, nourished by a buoyant secularism, and abetted by the emergence of mathematical logic and the new sciences, the success of modern liberalism and, with it, the birth of what we may refer to as sovereign individualism, have together given shape to a new cultural reality. The all-pervasive dominance of this modern condition has become so impressed into our ethos as to barely make its historical and highly particular character discernible were it not for the tensions it bears and the conflicts it creates. Any serious discussion of the state of contemporary man, like that of contemporary woman, must proceed in the light of that new state of consciousness which our current cultural realities dictate, that very particular social reality which we can now name and, therefore, distance ourselves from and speak to, that historical condition that has taken hold, called "modernism" or "secular liberalism."

Like all cultural realities, contemporary modernism is packed with its own myths, its own largely unrecognized metaphors, its own poetics literally perceived—or should we say, "misperceived"?—its own reifications and idiosyncratic distinctions. And it comes to us decorated in the cloth of emancipation, a new freedom that would seem to liberate us from those restraints and bonds that were the excretions of an older mindset, an alien political and social order, a rigid and stultifying hierarchy now perceived as riddled with superstition, arbitrary premise, and false conjunction—in contrast, of course, to the liberated mindset that bespeaks our own age! But while that emancipation would seem to engender its own constraints and articulate its own discomfiture, propose new hazards, and generate new dangers, there is no going back, and, indeed, the effort to retain or restore what was best in the old, what was comforting in the past, feeds the contentions of our age, even while failing to address what now needs to be addressed—namely, where do we go from here?

We propose to discuss some of the central myths and reifications that mark our modern temperament, something of the history that led us here, what the gains are and what the losses may be. And, in discussing some of the dangers and difficulties that mark our times, set the groundwork for a consideration of where men are to go from here.

CONTEMPORARY MYTH AND REIFICATION

What are some of the central myths and reifications? We have already suggested that modernism, or what we may choose to characterize as democratic, secular liberalism, finds its roots in Protestantism, a movement whose rejection of hierarchy and of structured authority presumed the existence of a good equally available to all men inclined to perceive it. The subsequent democratization of value and the substitution of many goods (what once might have been understood as false idols or paganism) for one catholic good (that straight and narrow path that leads to God) was but the natural consequence of the denial of the special rights of a privileged reason, a gift of the select, to dictate the terms of discourse. The notion of what we once called "wisdom" fell into disuse, and aristocratic reason became slave to what was in common to us all, to that which, then, required no rational justification but which, on the contrary, provided the foundation for rational justification, which answered to nothing and was subject only to itself and its own interests, namely, the passions, desires, or cravings. Desires and passions were depicted as foundational givens whose expression and realization was understood to lie in the very arbitrariness and unanswerable whimsicality by which they articulated themselves.

It was a bumpy ride, because the programmatic obliteration of authority that led to a humiliation of reason and to what we may refer to as "privileged discernment," that special precinct of the gifted few, was, of course, countered historically in the 18th century by a continuing upheaval of legitimated hierarchy precisely in the name of universal reason. But not only had the terms changed their meaning (reason, for example, no longer meaning what it had meant in the classical and medieval past, or even what it meant in the 16th century, when it could still exhibit proper ends and purposes), but the project also, insofar as it would locate morals if not values in reason, quickly collapsed as reason became something else once again. Meanwhile, the ancient connection, as exhibited by reason, between the world as is and what men ought do was irredeemably, it would seem, broken.

The consequence was a disjunct between reason and choice: what was nonrational was recognized to be not irrational. It was in the divide between the rational and the irrational, in that third rotation, that freedom was deposited. And somewhere from within that gap, that third dimension, emerged what we may term, "the individual," the "modern self," the "man" referred to in expressions like "all men are created equal" or "men have rights to life, liberty and the pursuit of happiness [or 'property']," etc. Now, this new being, the individual, a commonness shared by all men everywhere, had to be defined in terms that are not distinctive of any particular man and was, consequently, depicted in negative language, a neither this nor that, except as constituted by its free choices. Constituted by, but equally distinct from, its choices.

Men are not equal in shape, color, face, or design, let alone profession, intellect, ambition, character, or virtue—not in matters of taste, inclination, or aspiration, not in matters genetic or cultural or even, as it turns out, sexual. So, in what respect are we equal? We are equal, despite all the differences, because, it is said, we are individual human beings. Two things happen: as individual human beings we are not defined by our differences, and, therefore, not by social status, cultural or historical place, not by physiognomy, behavior, or psychology, not by birth or financial condition. The individual eludes and transcends all that, and becomes, therefore, an isolated negativity distinct from its articulations—articulations that distinguish and particularize us. It is that isolated negativity, mysterious in its emptiness and its untethered nonrationality, capricious, nonlawful, and unfixed, which is both the individual I am and, as such, constitutes the commonness I share with all other men. It is this being which is also an emptiness to which rights are ascribed and who is said to be free.

The notion of freedom in modernity as we speak of it here, these days, is not the same as what it was in the past or even today in much of the world, where it was and is understood as liberation (from alien and hostile powers), and, therefore, as the ability to be one's self and become what one would become—as an acorn, properly served, would be an oak. Instead, the idea of freedom, connected as it is to the concept of the individual understood as an isolated negativity, is conceived as a kind of unbound nothingness which shakes off all definition, a being whose actions issue from nothing. In short, we have given birth to the individual and conceived it as nothing.

The other thing that has happened is the following: the particulars which once but no longer constitute us in our entirety become, as suggested above, articulations of a transcendent negativity, that emptiness which is my individuality and my freedom. And, as such, they do not bind or define but only express my freedom, a freedom that is not exhausted by its choices, nor issues from the conditions in which it finds itself, but which hovers aloof from its choices—even, we might add, its commitments, obligations, and duties. In this context, choice becomes the scourge of authority, the enemy of order, even the restless nemesis of reason—or what may be referred to, conservatively, as good sense. In such a realm, creativity and spontaneity hold dominion, cleverness and new sensation is all, commonness and repetitiveness is the enemy, boredom is the foe.

But the allusion to a condition in which all commitment becomes constraint and all constraint, by definition, is antithetical to freedom and, hence, to our individuality, is to us at once both alluring and repugnant and, therefore, constitutes the current argument of our culture.

Positively, the idea that the individual is a freedom that transcends the particulars of his or her situation and is not one with them has broad ramifications for our notions of collective responsibility and the correlated concepts of racism, bigotry, and anti-Semitism, the assault upon which is to the profit of individual justice. Human beings are to be judged, praised, or blamed in terms of their individual decisions, and, in some situations, in cases of blame (e.g., it is specific pieces of behavior and not even the individuals who engage in them which are the deposits of our judgments).

This phenomenon, justice understood in individual terms, has provided important ammunition to the pacifist's arsenal of arguments: Modern warfare entails massive actions that will capture the innocent in its fire. But modern justice demands that the innocent be spared the unwarranted punishment that physical conflict produces. Since the latter is impossible in the context of the former, pacifism remains the only moral alternative. Yet this argument has force only within a sphere of discourse that rejects collective responsibility in favor of an individualism that does not equate the person with his or her citizenship, culture, or race. Today, we are plotting to isolate and punish national leaders even as we ship food and medical supplies to the very people those leaders claim to represent, those whom we will deem innocent, we say, until they are proven guilty.

Today, too, we believe in the redemptive powers of individuals in the face of behavior that in the past would have surely condemned them—permanently. Just punishment is distinguished from revenge and rationalized as deterrence or rehabilitation, and is, therefore, limited by its purpose. Positively, caste, breeding, and privileged aristocracy have been exchanged for social fluidity and opportunity. The static has given way to the dynamic, as the democratic way has unleashed new and previously unacknowledged potential and untapped energies. It can now be said, with some truth and plenty of proviso, that any American citizen (so far, only white, Christian males, but that too we recognize is only a matter of time) can become President of the United States, and that the economic and social elite is determined by a shifting and unstable population, that we live in a time when millions of dollars, if not to say billions, may be made overnight, and that educational opportunities have become universalized even in the face of favoritism, lingering cronyism, entrenched advantage, privilege, and inevitable social bias. This much and more, all to the good, the general good, and the good of the individual. Even the entrenched elites are beneficiaries of the new talent and enriched energies given play by the modern spirit.

Our culture bespeaks the new condition. Recent movies relate tales of individuals without a past, without a history that delimits and circumscribes present behavior or future status, reaching up toward the very pinnacles of a social order that is theirs neither by birth, breeding, or even natural gifts. Sometimes they achieve their ends by hook or by crook, occasionally by dint of wit, energy, or personal charm. Like films, television daily legitimizes homosexuality and transsexualism. It gives allowance to mothers who have sex with their children's friends, as well as to men and women who have operations to radically transform their appearance, give youth to age, even change gender and exchange sexual roles—to people who go to salons, spas, and retreats of various sorts to cash in for something better, a better look, personality, or style of living. And each of these stories gives voice to a common theme, that such-and-such and so-and-so are doable, even for ourselves if only vicariously, that these things are acceptable, even if outrageous, that such experiences are perfectly human, even as they violate norms and challenge values. The ads and commercials encourage us to wear clothes, drive cars, put on makeup, or cultivate an image not of our time, place, or circumstance, unreflective of our professions, of where and how we live. We daily eat foods that cross ethnic lines and mingle cultures. In our dramas, we flit with the flick of a button across the centuries from far distant galaxies to ancient civilizations. More important, we rotate heroes and villains as we might circulate crops, moving from gentle intellectuals to strong-willed gladiators to refined aesthetes to cold-hearted killers to brilliant academics, from ambitious salesmen with unlimited charm to slender warriors who can even defy the laws of gravity, to tender and vulnerable lovers, each holding up to us a model by which to measure our own self-actualization. What a crowded field of idols we see looking back at us as we peer into the glass and ask ourselves who and what we are or will be.

Nor do our new technologies curtail our imaginative reach. The new sciences promise us infinity, both spatial and temporal. Each discovery is only the basis for new discovery, and each movement would seem to secure further advance. Our new physics allows us to move with a smooth, mathematical flourish from the infinitesimal to the infinite, from the utmost subparticle to the outermost reaches of the cosmos, with poise and brash assurance. Our new biotechnologies offer us the promise of unending life, of organ replacements and perpetual, self-regenerating tissue. We hover at the cusp of all things and challenge eternity—it would seem. And with such prospects comes the opportunity to live not one, elongated, infinitely extended life, but an infinite variety of finite lives, to wander an existence in which all decisions and all incidents are impermanent, transitory, and reversible at will, thereby reinforcing the whimsical and capricious, nonserious character of choice.

There was a time when choice was circumscribed by duty and obligation (failure to do one's duty was generally regarded as error or weakness of will), and a later time when duty and obligation became a matter of choice, but a choice of momentous dimensions. However, when duty and obligation are regarded as subject to choice, as the issuance of consent, then as choice goes, so will go duty and obligation. And if meaning is the progeny of finitude—if we were infinite or limitless (e.g., if we lived forever), the philosopher Martin

Heidegger once argued, our thoughts and actions would be meaningless—as limitation goes, so goes meaning, meaningful action, meaningful thought, purpose or desire, meaningful decision, judgment, choice, meaningful duty, or obligation.

FREEDOM, MEANING, AND PLEASURE

Today, we still grow old, and we still die. We continue to suffer the limits of time and place, of history, the constraints of economic and social condition. Our choices and commitments remain, to us, at least, of some significance, and duty and obligation retain, if only in fractured form, a grip on our behavior. But if, within our imagination, we perceive promise, then our vision is but an elaborated extension of our present condition—the condition which extends the promise our imagination elaborates. So the individual, to the extent that he or she becomes or is understood to be an isolated negativity of unbound freedom, all the particulars, all the defining and distinguishing features of his or her life, comes under question; they assume the character of role-playing and charade, behind which looms a large, unsatisfied emptiness, and each chore and purpose becomes the plaything of an insubstantial whimsy for whom all is arbitrary happenstance and nothing is rationally sustained. And as we distance ourselves from all that we are, as we set ourselves adrift, and as our commitments and obligations shrivel—to tradition and convention, to family, to parents, lovers, and children, let alone career or profession—meaningfulness in our lives is itself demeaned. In such a context, freedom becomes the enemy of meaning.

But where freedom becomes the contrary of commitment, and choice, therefore, becomes play, time is splintered and immediacy takes the place of long-range projects. Pleasure fills the void created by lost passion or meaning, and means become, if not ends, then the wherewithal to immediate gratification. Life is then reduced to immediate pleasure and the pursuit of wherewithal and power understood as a means to gratification of desire. Here technology is crown prince. And, indeed, the age of technology is upon us.

Our current art gives expression to our situation, dedicated in great measure to style and cleverness; its appeal is all too often intentionally momentary and fleeting, given to virtual realities and appearance, devoted to mind games and illusion, consecrated to form with little or no concern for content. Current art mostly seeks to be neither serious nor responsible, and would answer only to itself, free and autonomous play. However, though a free-floating style unwed to content provides no ground upon which art can be judged, transcending norms, it often does presume to judge us and the society around us. Its adopted stance is frequently mockery, and in mockery, anger, and in this particular anger, despair, for it testifies to no adequate alternative and suffers no real solution, so that its mockery, in the end, is also self-mockery. Lacking standards upon which to judge, it cannot be serious, but only quirky. Such expression serves little more than a simple need to fill up space, to take up time, to distract, to communicate without having anything to say, to preoccupy the spectator with . . . with nothing, really. What once was serious, iconic, the residence of gods, an arena for conflict and resolution of clashing values, a home for heroes, now becomes the stuff of distraction, the chaff of entertainment. The slight prevails over the serious.

Leisure, then, is upon us, and to be preoccupied without being serious is our signal project. The ascent of pleasure as an ultimate value is complement to the decline of meaning. But the pursuit of pleasure unconstrained by a sense of obligation, duty, or meaning is a dangerous thing, growing ever more potentially destructive as it flitters forward. First, pleasure would exhaust its object and then dismiss it. Pleasure is not love. Love, of course, knows pleasure, but a pleasure that would preserve its object in its very elusive fullness, even as it would occupy that object. Love invites occupation even as it occupies. Love wants time. Pleasure pure and simple is not like that. Pleasure untrammeled would tear its object to pieces and demolish its integrity, if it did not tire of it first. Pleasure either annihilates or abandons what it at first seeks out. It despises tedium, and tedium is its object once attained. Unharnessed, it rapidly becomes nihilistic and contemptuous of its object. It either destroys or discards. Disenchantment is not only its future but its purpose. Between individuals, pleasure unconditioned by something more would command the other's autonomy, denigrate the other's freedom, and put the other at one's disposal. The test of its success is the level of submission it can induce—where submission invites contempt, and contempt invites ever greater submission.

The pleasure principle is embodied by certain actors of our times, film stars who would seem to express our age. They are cold, self-contained, and dispassionate, characterized by a sneering if not snarling temperament, finicky and curiously asexual, or, rather, their sexuality is a mystery. They propose themselves, paradoxically, as sexual objects for others, heavy-lidded and intelligent, witty but bored, cynical and devoid of higher purpose, dilettantes untouched by questions of ethics, justice, or social reform. Self-absorbed and expecting others to be absorbed in them, they intend themselves as the objects of our fascination and our passions, contemptuous all the while of those they would have love them. Not enthusiastic themselves, they would induce enthusiasm in others, an enthusiasm they can only despise as they despise all enthusiasms.

But tedium uncheckered must ultimately become tedious to itself, and contempt complete must ultimately become contempt for itself. So, in the end, the art of mockery must ultimately mock art itself and, therefore, become self-mockery. And so, in the end, the pleasure seeker must become bored with himself, and, therefore, his own worst foe. What pleasure, after all, is there in the conquest of those for whom one only has contempt? Love, for such individuals, is not a possibility, for what loves them cannot complement them and is diminished by their love. The individual as an isolated negativity looking at itself finally finds nothing to admire and nothing in others from whom it would draw succor. And unable, ultimately, to nourish itself, it becomes either despairing or desperate or both.

OBLIGATION, PURPOSE, AND SATISFACTION

We know what would satisfy us insofar as we are wage earners, parents, children, Christians or Jews, citizens of this or that country, home owners, and lovers—what rituals to perform, what taxes to pay, what salaries to earn. We know what would satisfy us insofar as we are homemakers, carpenters, farmers, car mechanics, or clock-makers. And we have recognizable and acknowledged standards by which to assess our efforts and declare success. But what would satisfy us as individuals independent from our roles as wage earner, family member, Christian, Jew, or citizen? What will satisfy an isolated negativity, a transcending not-ness lacking location or definition?

The term "satisfy" has at least two distinct if interrelated meanings. I can be satisfied in the sense that I have successfully completed my purpose or mission, that condition entailing that I have fulfilled my duties and met my obligations. I can be satisfied in the sense that I am happy, content, or fully gratified. And the two meanings at a certain superficial level are not the same, for, at that level, we can, presumably, have one without the other. That is, I might be content or gratified without achieving a purpose or accomplishing a mission: I might accomplish my mission or purpose and not feel gratified. But at another level, the two meanings become intertwined, and, therefore, are truthfully or revealingly conveyed by the same word. For at that deeper level, happiness, contentment, or full gratification is only possible with purpose realized and mission fulfilled, where happiness or contentment cannot coexist with a sense that one's mission is incomplete, that one's purposes remain unrealized. And, conversely, one cannot feel that one's mission is complete, one's purpose realized, if one feels ungratified, discontent, or unhappy. In this understanding of the matter, fulfillment and happiness are fused, and that entails all duties and obligations met!

But while I recognize my duties and obligations as an employee, as a father, son, citizen, and, perhaps, even as a lover, what are my duties and obligations as an individual distinct from all that? What are the duties and obligations to others distinct from the particular roles I play? What are my duties and obligations to myself distinct from the particular roles I play? But with regard to myself, as an isolated negativity, there are no obligations or duties, for as an individual distinct from my roles, I can discern no mission or purpose, since all my missions and purposes are embedded in the roles I perform. What are duties and obligations, what would they even be like, unattached to missions and purposes?

It might be noted here that one of the world's greatest and most refined moral philosophers, that very embodiment of Enlightenment thinking, Immanuel Kant, attempted just such an enterprise, to give voice to a moral autonomy, a pure, practical reason that could discriminate duties and obligations free of missions and purposes, that could dictate how we ought to behave and what in form, at least, we should and should not do. Needless to say, he failed. That great, heroic experiment failed. And if he failed, it was not for lack of genius. And if the whole project failed, it was not for lack of someone else to say it better. Perhaps Kant failed, the project failed, because he attempted the impossible, that is, to collar the individual, freedom itself, distinct from its particular roles where purposes and missions are embedded. But if his effort failed because it entailed a contradiction—the bound negativity—it did succeed in giving expression to a great poignancy, for it argued profoundly and successfully that insofar as they applied to the individual as such, the free, independent person, the Enlightened man, duties and obligations cannot be and are not functions of missions and purposes—which are, in fact, to be discovered in the various roles we play. What a situation to be in, then! Surely there are duties and obligations and things we ought and ought not do independent of and transcendent to our particular roles, things we owe to each other and to ourselves as individuals, but there are not, and how could there be, duties and obligations that are ours by virtue of our being free individuals! We recall that the Age of Reason gave birth to the Age of Romanticism, and the French Revolution to the rebirth of autocracy, to Metternich and the forces of religious conservatism, to an assault on the forces and excesses of pure reason.

The reification of the individual as free and independent came with the dedication of certain rights—life, liberty, the pursuit of happiness, and so on. And with those rights the ascription of certain minimal obligations—the obligation to give recognition of those rights to others, in myself qua individual and, therefore, as an act of reason, in others, qua individuals. But those obligations we may characterize as negative obligations, just as those rights are negative rights—appropriate to a being understood as an isolated negativity. The right to life simply means no one has a right to take my life, such as it is, from me, and hence operates in negative terms. By law, no individual has an obligation to save my life, but every individual has an obligation not to take it. Liberty in this context is also a negative concept, meaning nothing more than lack of restraint (except insofar as the exercise of my liberty would inhibit the liberty of others). Notice, all this only insofar as I consider myself as an individual, for as father, son, and wage earner, there are duties, obligations, constraints, and restrictions. Likewise, the right to pursue happiness is a negative right because happiness is an empty concept, and the so-called right to pursue it simply comes down to the right to be left alone, that is, the right of privacy. Our obligations and duties as individuals are only negative obligations and duties, and as such cannot promote or support mission or purposes—nor realization, fulfillment, or satisfaction in both senses considered above.

THE CONTRADICTION OF MODERN, LIBERAL POLITICS

The birth of the individual is coincident with the emergence of a politic with which it is, in fact, one—that is, the politic of modern, secular liberalism. Political authority, like all other authority, derives its legitimacy by virtue of its service to the benefit of those over whom it would exercise influence. A doctor, lawyer, or bureaucratic figure is given authority by us because that person is ostensibly serving our interests. Nor should expertise in itself generate authority over our actions except insofar as that expertise is put to our service. In this respect, even those who may be said to have been given their authority by God are deemed legitimate because they would guide us for our good. What benefits us or is to our good is what is conducive to our well-being and happiness, and, therefore, legitimate political authority must be conducive to our well-being and happiness. But to give concrete expression to well-being and happiness and, therefore, to benefit, as legitimate political authority must do, is to give definition and, therefore, to delimit what authority would serve.

Happiness, like well-being, is an abstract and highly variable concept whose content is generally in flux, tending to vary from individual to individual and, within an individual, changing from moment to moment. Thus, any attempt to give concrete definition to happiness must in some respect or other curtail and offend it.

Moreover, the modern individual, understood as an isolated negativity, will only support a negative notion of benefit. For such an individual, what benefits is what adduces to freedom, what neutralizes that which would put constraints on freedom—ill health, a lack of education, poverty, and so on. For the modern individual, however, what gives definition and, therefore, establishes limitation to our freedom will not be understood as a benefit to our freedom or conducive to the individual's happiness. Thus, political authority, as the term was traditionally understood, becomes a contradictory notion in the modern state and, therefore, undergoes a shift in meaning which tends to weaken its connection to the concept of legitimacy. Political authority, because it would set a social agenda and channel behavior, its connection to legitimacy loosened, expresses itself as raw power and becomes the pursuit of power for its own sake. So perceived, we will seek to delimit and circumscribe it. We become suspicious of it even as we would yield to it, and it becomes suspicious of us even as it would serve us. Power delegitimized is shifting, vulnerable power. It will be weak and subject to rapid change or it will seek to entrench itself, in which case it may slide into dogma and tyranny. So, in our modern condition, political authority fragments and is ephemeralized as it is drained of legitimacy and becomes ever weaker, assumes a thousand faces and sprouts chaotically from, sometimes, the most untested quarters. It becomes at once haphazard, whimsical, and subject to fad. And the fad itself is whimsy. Style and manner are associated with challenge, and what is sexy is what is defiant and unorthodox.

But whimsical power is dangerous. Brooding in the background is the urging that will not relent, the power that must counterpose itself against our freedom as now understood, the would-be authority that is threatened by an isolated negativity which keeps itself in reserve from all that would delimit and, therefore, constrain it, the free and independent individual jealous of his or her rights. And in such a confrontation between potential tyranny (itself, in a certain sense, whimsical and arbitrary, lacking rational mooring or moral constraint) and whimsy (as expressed by the disassociated freedom of an isolated negativity), whimsy (realized as detached arbitrariness) may protect itself—as a matter of whimsy—and, at other times, as a matter of whimsy, it will not. And then, tyranny will prevail. But so will political authority, so all authority.

LOOKING TO THE FUTURE

The near future, as has always been the case, will be constituted by a reaction to, as well as an extension of, what came before. That future will emerge from the tensions generated by the contradictions that define our own age, and will, no doubt, articulate its own tensions. And, like our own age and the ages that have come before us, it will produce its own ideologies, its own myths and reifications. Ideology and myth articulate the human condition, give voice to standards, ideals, history, goals, and purposes, the machinery that helps to define our very humanness, that provides ends and guides means, that secures the basis for human action—and with it, a foundation for the realization of human freedom. Indeed, it would not go too far to claim that without ideology and myth, there is no humanness. Our current ideology sharply distinguishes fact from value, regards the former as a given, the proper subject matter of science, and depicts the latter as the stuff of personal choice, the floating, arbitrary precipitates of freedom. The notion of an isolatable field of value-neutral facts is, of course, as much the stuff of contemporary myth as is the individual infused with natural rights generating values out of an arbitrary, desire-punctuated nothingness that constitutes human freedom.

The recent explosion of scientific knowledge, perhaps best exemplified by the current work in mathematical physics, and the newly fashioned progress in technology and electronics will, of course, change the material conditions of our lives in ways others can anticipate better than we, in some ways that none of us can anticipate. And these advances will, no doubt, affect how we think of ourselves. But we want to suggest here that as what is now often referred to as "pure" science (mistakenly, because there is no such thing, all things in this world being relative) and what we specify these days as "practical" science (that is, technology) more and more converge, the ideology which would separate fact from value will become ever more untenable, and the effort to derive values from facts will force a redefinition of the facts, one in which facts are inextricable from values and bear consequences for behavior.

Efforts to advance technology are often characterized by some writers as the pursuit of value-free know-how for its own sake, power dedicated and responsible to no purpose or ideal beyond itself, subject to no higher ends, the latter to be imposed from without, a science of manipulation aimed at the creation of instruments whose use remains to be determined. In this respect, technology is often depicted as an "instrumental" science whose purpose is the generation of useful tools, but a value-neutral endeavor not given to the question of ultimate purpose. Machinery, it is sometimes argued, can be used to kill or to save lives, but on such questions the machinery itself is silent. In fact, however, technology as a generation of means bespeaks ends that are implicit in its products. And how could it be otherwise? How can we even isolate means, use instrumentation, without reference to ends, values, and purposes? Modern technology is, in fact, a testament to our values, a bible of norms and purposes and ideal states. The computer, it is argued, increases our power to communicate, but does not dictate what we shall communicate, forgetting that the desirability of communication is itself the expression of a value. The kitchen utensil expresses a value. So does the pencil. Of course, there are instruments created for deadly purposes, although even these are often produced for defensive reasons, and, of course, machinery may be misused in order to kill or maim or to force others to one's will—as can many natural things. But technology overwhelmingly is developed and employed in order to enhance our lives, serve our desires and aspirations, satisfy, not kill us. And as technology advances, its values will become ever more explicit. In fact, it shall become ever more the truism that technology is a science of values.

At the same time, the growing amalgam between "pure" science and technology will empower technology even as it implants and illuminates value in science. What we call "pure" science will be ever more bent to purpose, ever more reflective of human need and drive, ever more expressive of human instrumentalities dedicated to human ends. Our "truth," in short, will articulate our values in ever increasing fashion, as our values become ever more responsible to our truth. But what does all that mean with respect to how we are and what we shall become?

The free individual, currently understood, we have argued earlier, as an isolated negativity, bears the dangers and prospects already alluded to above. Man can free himself from the shackles of convention as he never could in the past. There are no more authorities beyond question, and all roles, including that of being a man or a woman, are open for reconsideration and redefinition. Values and social norms no longer bind but provide opportunity, as free choice absorbs all aspects of our lives. More and more, members of the male gender, like members of the female gender, can address in their free behavior, in their free choices, and in their free lifestyles, this question: what does it mean to be a human being, a man or a woman?

Conversely, as we have also suggested earlier, men and women, individuals understood as isolated negativities, are ever less privy to what it would take to answer such questions in a rational, nonarbitrary, or noncapricious fashion.

There is such a thing felt as too much freedom, as a dangerous nonrationality afloat in a purposeless space, disassociated from a tradition, history, or custom, as that cynical hedonism which acknowledges no meaning, norm, or value beyond its own pleasure, as that pointless drift untouched by others, neither enthralled by others nor in their grip, neither subject to the claims of others nor their needs, an unbound but hungry emptiness which ultimately becomes destructive, either to others or to itself, potentially murderous, suicidal, or both.

Politically, If history always unfolds as a series of reactions to what comes before, then what is perceived as excessive, irrational freedom, sometimes described as chaos or anarchy, suffers the prospect of becoming the parent of tyranny, of an irrationality become supreme. A capriciousness that is total risks the danger of becoming capricious even about its own survival. An unbound freedom that would know itself will ultimately seek to know itself bound. A nonrationality that would make all institutions and norms irrational may, indeed, bear the full fruits of its own labor.

What, then, is needed? Values, norms, and purposes are the constructs of human beings embedded within communities. Individuals do not exhibit a power to generate values, norms, and purposes from out of themselves in isolation. Nor can a person understood as an isolated negativity produce a definition of him- or herself, or, indeed, in any way get a grip on him- or herself, neither know, understand, nor even perceive him- or herself, find in him- or herself any basis for action, locate any grounds upon which to make a decision.

A social order, however, produces social facts. And these social facts are truths in which what we currently distinguish as facts and separate out as values merge, so that from these social truths values may be drawn. It is only within the context of a community that a human being can become a person, emerge as an individual. That community (humanity) already exists, but, as we suggested earlier, only as an abstraction, the reification of an ideology that is yet to be grounded. The consequence is the abstract individual in danger of losing him- or herself.

The individual is now with us. Nor, as we suggested earlier, is there any going back, although there are many, as is to be expected, who would do so. But this individual, resisting definition, must find a content for him- or herself, must gather and evolve new levels of association appropriate to its newly forged freedom, forms of engagement that will entail a community shaped by a common history and culture necessary to the articulation of that fixed sense of purpose and meaning, that web of goals, values, and norms by which one can be realized and measured, by which character is anchored and identity established. In the process, no doubt, freedom will be redefined, and the individual will once again merge with his or her roles, however those roles are redefined. Those roles will be integrated with one's character, and form, once again, the bases for duty, obligation, discipline, and commitment. They will, no doubt, establish new grounds for honesty and promise keeping, as the practical and the ethical once more become derivative of each other, the factual and the moral become expressive of one another and provide guiding norms and tests for each other.

But all this is within that sphere of given purposes that is the product of human community. What kind of community will it be, composed of free and equal but bound individuals, whose associations express freedom but are steeped in commitment, whose authority is defined not by power but by mutuality, whose connection demonstrates dependence but is not based on weakness or inequality, whose need is the expression of strength and self-possession not inadequacy, whose unity provides the basis for respect for individuality, whose conjunction would preserve even as it would possess, care for and cherish even as it would absorb, be honest to even as it would integrate within itself? In short, it will be a community as a form of free association that supports the dignity and integrity of the person, even as that person submits him- or herself—a community that bestows respect on the individual who enters into it, honor by virtue of his or her participation in it. We want to suggest that this kind of nonreductive relationship is rare but not completely unknown to us even today; that it falls upon us so infrequently as to appear to be a gift, so that when we dream or speak of it, we tend to think of ourselves as romantic or sentimental; that when it does appear, it tends to be limited to private, personal associations to the exclusion of other persons; that most of us are not as yet capable of it even in limited form, though most of us crave it without really knowing exactly what it is, often confusing it with something else or foolishly trading it in for something different—sometimes out of despair or misperception, often out of suspicion and fear. We want to suggest that its presence makes one stalwart, and fills one with virtue, with wisdom, courage, generosity, self-discipline, internal harmony, and high-spiritedness, that it produces justice in the soul, and that those few who have known it are the true Nietzschean ubermenschen. They are our future.

ADDITIONAL READINGS

MacIntyre, A. (1981). *After virtue.* South Bend, IN: University of Notre Dame Press.

Putnam, R. (2000). *Bowling alone.* New York: Simon and Schuster.

Rich, F. (1999, December 12). American pseudo. *The New York Times Magazine*, 80–114.

Rosen, J. (2001, February 4). In lieu of manners. *The New York Times Magazine*, 46–51.

Chapter 68

A Noble and Famous Man

Betty Forbes

A Daughter Speaks for Her Father

My name is Elmer Woodburn Forbes and I was born August 26, 1905. My life expectancy is 48.7 years; however, I was 95 years old when I died on December 12, 2000. I fought the good fight to the end; I ran the race to the finish, and kept the faith. At the funeral the minister said my name Elmer means noble and famous. I never knew the origin of my name; however, from all that I did and accomplished in my lifetime, I think I lived a full, noble, and famous life. I always worked hard, holding varied positions since my 12th birthday. During my lifetime I witnessed the most advanced medical technology, the extinction of some life-threatening diseases such as polio, and the current discovery of life—the decoding of the "human genome." I lived through many achievements and catastrophes of the 20th century, and saw the millennium celebration and beginning of the 21st century. I can remember the flu epidemic of 1918, the establishment of the League of Nations that was to end all wars, the first transatlantic crossing by an airplane in 1919, and women voting in 1920. In addition, I observed the stock market collapse in 1929, the Depression, Prohibition, the first moving picture academy (Oscars) awards, the invention of radio and television, the tragedies of the *Titanic* and *Hindenburg*, the growth of the nation to 50 states, the administrations of 17 presidents, and the Gore-Bush fiasco for the election of the 18th president. I lived through and supported five major wars not to mention all the cold wars. I have a grown daughter and son. There are four grandchildren, all girls, and three great-grandchildren, two boys and a girl. I was the caregiver of my wife for 8 years because she had a stroke, and I am the patriarchal center for the Forbes and our extended family.

The Early Years

I was the second son of seven children, four of whom (three boys and one girl) died when they were babies or toddlers. It was very common at the turn of the century to have large families because of the high infant mortality rate. This left me the middle child with a brother 18 months older and a sister, the baby of the family, 13 years younger. Before they died I used to babysit my younger brothers and would pull them around in a wagon. My other siblings died from meningitis and diphtheria because antibiotics had not yet been discovered. When I was growing up in South Philadelphia, my family rented and lived in three different row houses (town houses today) on the same block. No one owned their own homes at that time, though later my father did purchase the last house we lived in. My maternal grandparents, Aunt Sarah, and Uncle Robbie lived across the street. This extended family also molded my personality. My grandfather would mend my shoes by nailing a half sole of leather on them. For this assistance, my grandfather would give me 10 cents to go to the corner bar to get half a pint of whiskey in the special bucket given to me. In the bar the whiskey was kept in barrels called rats. The whiskey had no name and I didn't know where it came from. A young child 8 or 10 years old could go into any bar with his bucket and buy whiskey or beer to take home. I wouldn't dream of trying to drink any of this whiskey myself.

Every time I came into the living room of my grandparents, I had to bow to a large portrait over the fireplace of King William of Orange on a big white horse with a sword.* For following this ritual, I received from my grandmother 2 cents, a lot of money to spend on candy treats. My grandparents came to America in 1865 from Ireland by ship, third-class steerage, the lowest class where the food was thrown down a chute for the passengers to eat, and they were allowed on deck for a short time once a day. They had all their belongings in one trunk that later housed their potatoes. It took 28 days for them to arrive in America. When they got off the ship, all the buildings were draped in black bunting because this country was mourning the assassination of President Lincoln.

I was not a scholar and disliked school and would throw the books away that my parents purchased. I was always one step ahead of the truant officers. When I was in school the only kids attending school on a regular basis were those whose parents came from a foreign country. They highly valued the free public education. I was more interested in working and earning money.

Automobiles were not around and transportation was by horse and carriage. When I was 11 years old I worked on the weekends cleaning the horse stables, rubbing down and grooming the horses. A veterinarian who took care of the horses offered me a job at the slaughterhouse where they prepared the cattle

---

*King William of Orange is the historical figure who conquered Ireland and set into place the English occupation of Ireland. This occupation is the genesis of the long history of political and religious conflict in Ireland. Tribute to or disdain for King William marks the distinction between those Irish who are loyalists to Britain and those Irish who still seek a united, free and independent Republic of Ireland.

and pigs for market. Despite my youth I had enough brains to know what I was doing, and if there were any questions about my safety the horse doctor would protect me and take care of me. It was hard work. One thousand pigs were slaughtered in a day. It took an additional 2 days to cut them up and stamp them with the government seal. The procedure I followed for my job consisted of standing on a stool with a government stamp in each hand. The conveyer belt would swing by, and I would stamp the different parts of the pig. Developing the manual dexterity to use both hands rapidly to correctly stamp the hog was an art that as a 12-year-old I soon learned. Bacon could be purchased with or without the skin. A machine with a 5-pound mallet would roll around and hook the hog and take the skin off the back of the hog for skinless bacon. Another aspect of the job was washing the floors down and sweeping up the 10 to 12 hogs that were gutted up and thrown away on the floor from the conveyer belt. I had to wear special thick wooden shoes on the wet floor. One minute I was cold from being in the ice box and the next minute I was sweating. At night I would help to load the meat on the horse-drawn wagons. I had to pat the meat up and shape it like it was fresh to be sent to the butcher shops.

For all this hard work I was paid 18 cents an hour, $1.44 a day, or $7.20 a week. I was proud of these earnings because some grown men didn't make this much money. To put my salary in perspective, bread only cost 3 cents a loaf. A lot of my teachers warned me that if I didn't finish my education I would be doing hard labor work all my life. But it is different when you are young, you do not necessarily listen. You know the system is crooked and that there are a lot of smart people out there who hire kids and take advantage of them. There were no child labor laws or fines on any of the companies, so they did whatever they wanted to their young workers. I would bring my salary home every Friday to my mother, who was waiting in the kitchen with her apron spread open to collect the money. She in turn would give me whatever she wanted. It was usually very little spending money in return for my week of hard work. Turning your salary over to your parents was a common occurrence in Irish families. This procedure was followed until my 21st birthday when I told my mother that I would now give her an amount of money I could afford.

My family spent the summers out of the city at the family bungalow. My father and his two brothers had built a one-story, three-bedroom house in Blackwood, New Jersey. My two uncles also owned houses close by in the woods. The family would travel via a horse and wagon on the ferry boat for the trip to Jersey. The house was far off the road up a dirt hill, where you could see the porch and a second house owned by an uncle. The summer house had no plumbing, running water, or electricity. There was a pump that had to be primed and pumped for an extended period until the cold brown water coming out turned clear. The water was hard with lots of minerals and took a long time to boil for coffee on the coal oil stove.

Food was kept in an icebox constructed of porcelain tile and lined with opal glass. There was a door to the department where the ice was kept and the box was constructed for perfect circulation of pure cold air and to remain absolutely dry. The melting ice would drip into the drip pan and the ice was replaced every few days, depending on how large a piece of ice was purchased, and how many times the ice box doors were opened. When I was big enough, it became my job to buy and carry the ice in my wagon and place it in the ice box. Another chore was to travel through the woods to the gas station and get the coal oil can filled. Upon returning home I would fill the oil lamps for light and the stove for my mother to cook the meals. Sometimes, more than one trip to the gas station was needed to fill all the lamps and stove.

The bathroom was an outhouse with two holes, a large one for an adult and a small one for a child. During the night a commode was placed in one of the bedrooms to be used if needed, or you could walk through the woods with a flashlight to the outhouse. Each bedroom had a marble-top table with a beautiful pitcher and basin on it to be used for washing in cold pump water. Of course the water could be heated on the stove if you had time to wait. Large galvanized tubs were filled in the morning and placed in the sun to warm up so the children could take a bath. These same tubs were used with a scrubbing board to wash the clothes. The family would go swimming almost every day at Sunset Beach, or Chicken Beach, Almonesin, New Jersey. The family would take a bar of soap with them and get washed at the lake. I was an excellent swimmer and diver as were my siblings. We also learned to ride horses and as city children we loved this sport. Uncle Steve (my father's brother) lived close by and we fed his chickens, collected the eggs for breakfast, and cleaned the chicken coop.

The Middle Years and Beyond

It cost my father 50 cents to vote in the elections. If you didn't have the money, the politicians would give you the money and you voted how they told you. There were no curtains at the voting booth, and the politician accompanied you into the voting area. When my father bought a car, a driver's license automatically came with it and the car dealer showed you how to drive the car. Upon my father's death, this driver's license was passed on to my older brother, my father's namesake. However, I wasn't so lucky and had to take a driver's test to get my license. When the Social Security Act was passed in 1935, I did not contribute to the program; however, my older brother followed the law. Social Security was in effect for several years before I finally joined the program. I think I got away with this because I was paid with cash; they did not use paychecks.

As a boxing fan, I loved the fights, and enjoyed watching them on TV. I saw Jack Dempsey and Joe Louis fight. I also enjoyed the theater and took my wife to see the show *Rosemarie* with Jannette McDonald and Nelson Eddie with real horses on stage. I was too young to participate in World War I and was disappointed I was not drafted for World War II because I was 36 years old and had two children. However, I did contribute to the war effort through defense work and was A1 next in line to be drafted.

I started working for the Atlantic Refining Company (later the name changed to ARCO) when I was 16 years old. My first job was driving a horse-drawn wagon delivering coal oil to the wealthy homes in Philadelphia. The maids would say, "Here comes that dirty oil man" and make me go to the back door and wipe my feet. I had to arrive at the stable early before my work day started in order to feed and get the horses harnessed to the wagon. If it was raining the rain gear had to be put on the horses. At the end of the day, the job included rubbing the horses down and feeding them. I was not paid for all this extra time and the company took better care of the horses than the men. Men were easy to replace but it was harder to replace and find a trained horse. I graduated from this job to driving a truck to deliver mail to the executives in the Atlantic Building. I had to dress appropriately in a white shirt and tie. I later had the responsibility of driving the payroll truck with all the money. This consisted of gold coins of all denominations because everyone was paid in gold before paper money. When gold was recalled by the banks, I kept a small sample of the gold coins from my salary, which my daughter will inherit.

I got married in 1931 when I was 26 years old. I bought my first row house in Philadelphia in 1934 for $1,500. It had a porch, living room, dining room, kitchen, three bedrooms, bath, basement, and garage. I lived there for 22 years raising my daughter and son in the city. I moved the family to the Delaware County suburbs, outside of Philadelphia in 1956, into a single, three-bedroom, family room home. I steadily moved upward at ARCO to driving a large truck that delivered gas. When World War II broke out, I moved into the garage doing defense work and later, through a series of different positions, ended my career as a first-class mechanic. I was very patriotic and had money taken out of my pay to purchase bonds, which I finally cashed in after 50 years. I always had a job, even during the Depression. It was during the Depression when I worked in center city that I literally saw men jump out of office windows over money. This influenced my philosophy that money is evil, and anytime you have to kill yourself to make a buck, it is time to look for another job and quit. I learned the value of a dollar from the Depression because my hours were cut down. However, I was able to keep working.

The employees at ARCO finally got a company union. My fellow workers liked me and I was elected as a union representative for 1,000 men. This is where I got all my brains and learned about the workings of large companies, business, management, personnel, and employee rights. I started walking to work during the war because I loaned my car to my brother, who needed it for transportation to his work place, which was 12 miles away. In all kinds of weather—rain, snow, cold, and heat—I walked the 6 miles to work. This daily exercise and the demands of my physical job probably contributed to my longevity. I had to retire in 1970 at age 65 because it was ARCO's company policy. I never could understand why the common worker has to retire, while doctors, congressmen, and senators can continue working well into their 90s. At long last, society is finally recognizing that people are productive after 65. I outlived all the money I put into my pension plan and started collecting ARCO's money for my pension checks.

I was one of the original founders and a member of the Atlantic Credit Union. This was started by an employee to whom the men gave money each week to save for them. When the men needed money to buy something, he loaned them the money. He kept track of all the money taken in and out with accurate records in a copy book. When word got around in the company, these transactions rapidly grew and in 1936 a bank was started: the Atlantic Credit Union for employees and their families.

I never went to a doctor. I just had my yearly physicals by the company doctor. We also had four industrial nurses at the company who would make hospital and home visits to the employees out sick. Unfortunately, I smoked cigarettes, starting as a kid, until I got pneumonia and was told I had the beginnings of emphysema and that I needed to stop smoking, which I did "cold turkey" in 1970. I had a silent heart attack that was detected on an electrocardiogram in 1978. My second heart attack sent me to the hospital in 1986 after 7 years of caring for my wife with a stroke. My doctor recently asked me what I do to look so good for my age. I told him I don't worry, I don't cry over spilled milk, and I have a cocktail hour of orange juice and vodka every day. I have enjoyed beer and whiskey all my life and had to buy the distilling equipment to start making my own liquor and beer during Prohibition, not only for my own use but for my family and friends.

Coming to the End of My Years

The last 6 months of my life I had to use a nebulizer because of my emphysema. However, I continued to collect my coupons and was driven to the supermarkets by my daughter. I did all the food shopping and cooking for my daughter who lived with me. I was diagnosed with congestive heart failure in October, 2000. I visited my pulmonologist on November 8, 2000, and he was pleased to find my breathing tests were the best they had ever been, and there were no signs of congestive heart failure. I told him I thought I had a slight stroke the month before because I had a few days of difficulty walking and had to use a cane. On Tuesday, November 28, I had a good day and was walking up and down the steps without any help and ate a good dinner. I went to bed at my usually early 7 P.M. but had difficulty breathing and had to take a couple of nebulizer treatments and nitroglycerin tablets during the night. I even tried to sleep in the lounge chair downstairs. During a wakeful, difficult night my daughter asked me if I wanted to go to the hospital.

So early in the morning, on Wednesday, November 29, 2000, my daughter drove me to the hospital at 4:00 A.M. because I was having difficulty breathing. They gave me an emergency treatment of oxygen, steroids, and antibiotics and admitted me with a diagnosis of acute respiratory failure and aspiration pneumonia. When asked about my advanced directives, or code status, I elected no heroic measures and no code. I walked into the hospital, but after the first day in bed I was so weak it affected my ambulating ability. Physical therapists gave me exercises to do and instructions in using a walker. Speech therapists assessed my swallowing ability and placed me on a soft diet with honey consistency liquids. This meant I couldn't drink any water, and my milk, juice, soup, and desserts were all thick like honey. I thought I would be going home in a couple of days after my breathing was straightened out. I was assessed as a high risk for a fall by the nurses and the high-risk care plan/pathway intervention was to be followed.

On December 2, 2000, at 5 A.M., I tried to get out of bed to use the urinal and fell and fractured my left hip. They couldn't operate right away because of my medical status. I was confined to bed for 5 days before the operation and was in pain every time I was moved. Tylenol was my only pain medicine. The surgeon thought I should have an opportunity to have my hip repaired since I was an alert, active adult who walked into the hospital, but he needed medical clearance to operate. Plan B was to do nothing and let the hip heal itself, and I would probably be chairbound the rest of my life. While in the hospital, I experienced ageism from the nurses, a negative attitude toward me because of my age, and no code status which affected my level of nursing care. In fact, one young nurse said to my daughter, "Do you expect him to live forever? After all, he is 95." I was appalled that three of my doctors agreed that a no code status does not affect the nursing care a patient receives.

I was operated on Thursday, December 7, 2000, at 3:30 P.M. The surgeon told my daughter that everyone in the operating room could not believe how great my muscles were for my age. The surgeon told them that anyone who lived this long would have to be in good shape. He said he had such a hard time trying to get through my bones with the drill and that I had "bones of steel." I did not need a blood transfusion because I lost very little blood and tolerated the operation well. The anesthesiologist suctioned my lungs and I was breathing well with oxygen. The plan was for me to spend the night in intensive care and be transferred to the orthopedic unit the next day and be out of bed and walking the second day with physical therapy's help. However, there were medical complications, and I had no urinary output the first 24 hours.

I never did get out of intensive care. My kidneys started working the second day and were just holding their own. My potassium, blood urea nitrogen (BUN), and creatinine were high. I received all kinds of medicines intravenously to decrease my blood chemistry counts and respiratory therapy for my pneumonia. Each day I was being lifted out of bed into a chair, and I had no appetite. My daughter was at my bed side constantly. My son, daughter-in-law, and granddaughters visited me. I wanted to go home and on Monday night, December 11, I told my daughter to take me home that night. She said she had made all the arrangements to take me home on hospice care the next day. I told her tomorrow would be too late. On Tuesday, my daughter was with me all morning and afternoon waiting for the ambulance to arrive at 3 P.M. I was having a hard time breathing, the ambulance was late, and my daughter went out to the desk to complain. She returned and continued talking to me, and I took a couple of deep breaths, slipping away, dying peacefully at 3:43 P.M.

Two nurses came rushing in because the monitors went off. They checked the time and pronounced me dead and tried to comfort my daughter and give her some water. One nurse wanted to know if anyone else was coming in to see me and how soon they could get the body to the morgue because they needed the bed. This last statement shocked my daughter into reality, and the insensitivity of the nurse is something she will always remember.

My Funeral

My family arranged a beautiful funeral for me in a very short time. I even had a program with three colored pictures of me on the front with my great-grandchildren, which my granddaughter Michele had printed. The service was held at the funeral home because I had not been inside a Protestant church in years, but I did have a minister who conducted the services. The service had a song of dedication where I was honored by Ella Fitzgerald singing *Elmer's Tune*, a 1930s song. The minister spoke about my life and all of the things I had witnessed in the 20th century. There were five speakers who eulogized me and a singer who sang "On Eagle's Wings." My family and friends attended the service and funeral. It was a fitting closure and tribute to my life. I had no idea I was held in such high esteem and a role model for my granddaughters. My family got through the first Christmas and holidays without me. Each year it will be easier.

INDEX